ORIGIN OF WHY?

The Proven Purpose and Meaning of Life

VITO GRIGOROV

Copyright © Vito Grigorov 2015
Published by Prosperist Publishing
Paperback ISBN-13: 978-0-6483314-0-7
Digital ISBN-13: 978-0-6483314-1-4

Contact and permission requests can be made via www.orginofwhy.com or by email vitojgrigorov@gmail.com

The author would like to thank all copyright holders for granting permission to reproduce content in this publication

To my mum and family.
I learned not only from what you did,
but also from what you did not do.

To the 5% who take action after reading,
the world belongs to you.

Table of Contents

Preface

"The meaning of life is the most urgent of questions."
Albert Camus[1]

Have you ever wondered why you're here?

You either have or will do it at some point. But why? Because we will die. Yes, technology will improve, and maybe one day we won't face death. Perhaps life will seem like an endless sci-fi movie. But that day is not yet tomorrow. The clock is ticking. Today our short time demands that we ask and answer... *what are we here for?*

Many have asked this question before. Nobel Prize novelist Albert Camus was one of them. Trapped in Paris in June 1940, as Nazi forces were closing in, he started work on his book, *The Myth of Sisyphus.* It begins with a simple thought: "Judging whether life is or is not worth living amounts to answering the fundamental question of philosophy. All the rest... comes afterwards."[2] Sisyphus was his answer – a Greek king forced by Zeus to forever roll a rock up a hill. No matter how many times he tried, the rock would always roll back down. Each day was the same as the one before. His life seemed to be a big joke. Can you see the same in your life? Camus thought that unless we found meaning in what we did every day, life would be that absurd.

Many books keep to the safety of retelling the same facts in different ways. *I hope this is not one of them.* Instead, we're going to dig into the dirt to try to find some new truths.

As you read, you may think I have complete confidence in what's written here. I haven't. Many who devote their lives to something end up thinking it's the key to everything, but the idea that the first version of a work is perfect, is likely wrong. No human creation stays the same *forever.* It eventually changes in some way. It may take an hour or a thousand years. If what's written here is good enough, it will be further improved by others in the future. If you feel any hesitation when you're reading, know that I also have felt it.

This book tries to leave something more lasting than the latest trends. It's not about imposing my own views masked as magical truths on those who need to believe in something.

The question of the meaning of life is at the root of our existence. It's likely the most important question we can ask. It's time to try to answer it, and get others thinking about its impact on every part of life. But it's also an awkward question. We see this when we realize that few answers have been given that are based on reason. Perhaps you believe there is no one single answer, or that the answer is different for each person. Such a bottomless approach doesn't suit the world we live in. We cannot treat the millions of *possible answers as equals*. If people lived in caves fearing the sun's light would melt them, we would never have come to know the world as we do today.

Truth is not bottomless. Truth is about the facts, and facts can be confirmed. The best way to do that is with healthy doubt that seeks to prove itself wrong. This is the scientific method. So, let me say sorry right now. There are no tooth-fairy mysteries here. People the world over speak and think differently yet it's the language of science (quick definition… What must the world be like to give us what our senses observe?) that unites most. With it, our understanding of the world continues to evolve. With it, we will continue to discover and make new tools and skills that in the long run will leave us better off.

It took a telescope to show that the earth is not the center of the universe. It proved that for centuries most people were wrong. If we still believed that shadows are ghosts, or that fire happens when the gods are angry, we wouldn't have advanced to where we are today. Are there twenty-four hours in a day? Yes. Should killing an innocent person for the fun of it be punished? Yes. Most new truths are often laughed at, but those same truths are the ones that eventually gain respect and help us prosper, yet it takes time for new truths to be accepted, even once they have been proven to be true. Adding a few lemons to prevent sailor deaths from lack of vitamin C took centuries. No area of human knowledge is free from doubt. What's in this book won't be either.

My goal here is to explore with you a simple, scientific answer to the question, "What is the meaning of life?" The answer I will share touches all the everyday workings of the world. The result of accepting this answer will impact your every action.

Others have long known this. Religions have owned the idea of "life after death." If you don't want pitchforks in hell but to enter heaven, then do as those reading from the holy books tell you. In some parts of the world it's best to pretend to believe these teachings, as it may be the only way to avoid jail or death.

Such ancient answers seem like an escape from the question. Given that they're so old, *they fail to explain and learn* from the long journey we've taken as we evolved. Once, we were apes struggling to find food. Now, we build skyscrapers and fly to the moon. You and I are lucky to benefit from all those leaps. Many today think we have the chance to change the world, but we first need to know *what is best to change* in the short time we're on this planet.

Buildings of Lost Dreams

1. YOU HAVE 5 YEARS OF TIME LEFT BEFORE YOU DIE
To fully live, you need control of your time, you need free time

As time is short, what's most worthwhile and unique for us humans to do?

2. THE UNIQUE HUMAN FUNCTION IS TO INNOVATE
Improve upon what we have

When done for many people, you fulfil…

3. THE MEANING OF LIFE
To seek the greatest good for the greatest number

But how?

4. THE PURPOSE OF LIFE
What you do to seek the meaning

Which is a result of your...

5. ACTIONS
Movements that you can control

Which add mixed values to society...

6. VALUE
Four Value factors form your Actions:
Time, Money, Health, Intelligence
Leading to either
Value-creative actions / Value-destructive actions

Your actions affect how well you live as seen through...

7. PRODUCTIVITY
When you do more with less Action

Which leads over time in a change in...

8. LIFE EXPECTANCY
The average age of death in society

But how is this done?

9. INNOVATIONS
Everything humans make fit into three groups:
Productive, Unproductive, Counterproductive

But who seeks to make innovations the most?

10. ENTREPRENEUR
They experiment to find productivity others have missed

Which results in…

11. INNOVATION COMBINATION
Mixing innovations sparks new ones, creating the world around us

This happens because innovations must go through…

12. HISTORICAL SELECTION
Society selects which innovations live or die.
Leading to 6 turning points in history.

…With future turning points to come.

13. THE 7ᵗʰ TURNING POINT
Automation replaces most jobs, entrepreneurship becomes one of the last paths left.

Each comic strip above shows up inside the book at the part it represents.

Introduction

"We do not have knowledge of a thing until we have grasped its why, that is to say, its cause."[1]
Aristotle

"The two most important days in your life, are the day you are born and the day you find out why."
Anonymous

How many years do you have left to live?

There's a scary question. Why even ask it? Because the answer will help you see why this book is important, especially as the answer is close to...

1826 days (5 years)

Yes. Five years. Worse than you thought? When we think of our lives, it's easy to pick out people who are 80, 90, or 100 years old. We see them and wonder, "Gee, they've lived for a long time!" It makes life seem almost endless, especially when we're younger, but we're only fooling ourselves.

What does it really mean to "live?" It all starts *with being free*. There's not much to life if you're trapped in a cave, or forced to do things you don't want to do. It's why most nations' worst punishment (other than execution), is locking people up in prison. Free time is at the root of that magical word "happiness," which we will soon explore. As children at school, we dreamed of the holidays. Working adults do the same. We need time that we control to reach our goals in life, without distractions. We call this free time. On our deathbeds, we want to know that we tried our best to make our life *worth something*. Indeed, the greatest regret of those dying is that they lived the way others wanted them to.[2]

Free time is needed, if we want to make anything. Rome was not built in a day goes the saying and it takes time for things to change. Yet most of us run our lives on autopilot. In a plane that *someone else* is flying. The fuel tank is getting close to empty, and when it does the plane will fall. You know this is true for you when you find it hard to answer the question,

"What have I done in all the years I've lived?" Life is time, and it's ticking right now until we're gone.

So, how much of your time is free? You might think it's the same as the life expectancy of the nation you live in. Say it's 77 years for your country. Do you think you have 77 years of free time?

To find out, let's look at 24 hours of the daily life of Jen, our city office worker. She…

- Sleeps the recommended 8 hours = 33% of daily time

- Works a boring job over 8 hours = 33% of daily time

- Dresses, prepares, and travels in 1 hour 40 min = 7% of daily time

---

Pt. 1 BUILDINGS OF LOST DREAMS

YOU HAVE 5 YEARS OF TIME LEFT BEFORE YOU DIE
To fully live, you need control of your time, you need free time

73% of her time is *Not Free*. Let's not forget though, if she was to add a life partner to the mix and later raise a family, the 27% of her time that was free would shrink smaller. Add to that the rest of life's activities, like shopping for food, exercise, visiting friends and family, browsing the internet and TV, and our Jen may have close to 0% free time.

Unsurprisingly, if we didn't need money, most people like Jen would not be working. At the end of this book we offer our tips for how you may take such a path. Surprisingly, it was Karl Marx, the 19th century socialist writer of *Capital* and *The Communist Manifesto,* who wrote that a worker does "not count the labor itself as a part of his life; it is rather a sacrifice of his life. It is a commodity that he has auctioned off to another." As much as 87% of employees today live this reality with Gallup polling showing large drops in worker engagement for every decade polls were done since the 1950s.[3]

Recently, the Families and Work Institute found that over 50% of women surveyed had 90 minutes of free time per day, 29% had fewer than 45 minutes free, while 4% had no free time at all.[4]

What happens when we use this data as an average for Jen's life? The graph below breaks it all down.

Let's give her 1 hour of free time for each workday in the year.
Add 4 weeks' holidays with around 9 hours free each of those days.
Add to that 6 hours of generous free time every weekend day.
We get a grand total of 7688 hours of free time.
Remembering the total 8,760 hours in a year is all we have, it means that only *12% of Jen's year, or 1072 hours, (45 days' worth of time) is free.*

Again, that's a generous estimate. Breaking it down like this, we can see how every action takes away a percentage of our lives. Imagine Jen takes a holiday for 11 days, but later she regrets it as a waste of time. Those 11 days gone are almost one quarter of her free time for the *entire year.*

Let's take this a step further, and look at Jen's entire life. The average life expectancy in her country, the United States, is about 79 years. Assuming that she continues spending time as she does now then…

25-year-old Jen has 7 years of free time left.*
40-year-old Jen has 5 years of free time left.*
60-year-old Jen has 2.5 years of free time left.*

Numbers above have been rounded.
(Life expectancy – current age = ____ x by percentage of free life = years of free time left).

The above is still generous as we'll soon see, for we are guessing she'll live till 79, but what if she doesn't? As people near "retirement age," they tend to lighten their workloads to get more free time. This may boost the number of days' worth of free time they have, but for most, health problems and checkups start to eat up this newly found free time. Likewise, life expectancy is only an average age of death. If you want to be on the side of reality, deduct 10 years from the life expectancy number. Yes, we may live till 90, but we may also be hit by a car at 30. Let's use Jen as an example in our graph below, which will then help you work out the percentage of your life that's free. Send a quick email to vitojgrigorov@gmail.com or go to www.prosperism.org and get this graph, ready for you to fill in, and all other bonus material.

FREE LIFE TIME GRAPH

ACTIVITY	MON	TUE	WED	THU	FRI	SAT	SUN		HOLIDAY Avg. hrs over 4 wks
WORK? Clothing, lunch, travelling, etc…	8h	8h	8h	8h	8h				
BASICS? Sleep, eat, wash, toiletry, etc…	9h 40m	9h 40m	9h 40m	9h 40m	9h 40m	9h 40m	9h 40m		9h 40m
MISC.? Fitness, friends, family, etc…	5h 20m	5h 20m	5h 20m	5h 20m	5h 20m	8h 20m	8h 20m		5h 11m
SPENT HOURS?	23h	23h	23h	23h	23h	18h	18h		14h 51m
FREE HOURS?	1h	1h	1h	1h	1h	6h	6h	**TOTAL** 17h	**9h 9m**

FREE HOURS PER WEEK? × 48 weeks including 4 wks (28 days) holiday	17h × 48 = 816h 9h 9m × 28 = 256h Total = 1072h
FREE LIFE TIME PER YEAR? (Free hours per year / 8760 hours in a year to get %)	1072h / 8760h = 12%
N.O YEARS LEFT TO LIVE? (Subtract your current age from the life expectancy of your country)	Jen's age is 25y (– 79y) = 54y
SUPRISE EVENT LIFE LOSS (Minus 10+ years due to the unpredictability of the future)	54y – 10y = 44y
TOTAL FREE LIFE LEFT ON EARTH (Years left to live × % of free time)	44y × 12% = 5 years & 102 days

For holiday weeks, the "Work" box may be empty, but most people make plans that fill up that time.

If you're unsure of an activity, put it in the hours spent in "Miscellaneous". This box covers all activities the others don't. The "Basics" box covers all the daily habits we often forget about but which suck a good amount of our time.

To locate your country's life expectancy, you can check it out at wikipedia.org/wiki/List_of_countries_by_life_expectancy. Keep in mind to edit the numbers in the table as your life and time changes for most accurate results.

No matter the number you arrive at, it's likely lower than you'd hoped for. Do you now have a different outlook on time? Again, if you didn't subtract 10 years from your estimate do it now. A trip down the stairs, a random car crash, or a bite of food can send you to your grave. No, this is not to scare you, but to be realistic. This should be a reminder to anyone young who's reading this that the statistics show that you have less chance to be diseased, and so more chance to make a difference while alive. This time window is short and rare, and distractions will creep up to suck it away, robbing you of smiling and saying to yourself when on your deathbed, *"I know I did my best."* Partners, parties, purchases and all the rest, if not chosen wisely, will melt year on year *your chance to leave something behind.*

For Jen, it turned out that many things didn't matter as much as she used to think they did. Eating out, going on dates, binge watching TV shows. Now, she sees how as much as 80% of her actions were *time crimes* which wasted away her life. Does a similar pattern show up in your life?

Maybe now you're also starting to see some of your usual activities are after all "wasteful"? Most of us can find something. What does that mean, exactly? Wasteful… *compared to what?* This question only makes sense if we know what a "meaningful" life looks like.

You may have been shocked when you saw the numbers above showing how little life there is left. That's why knowing the meaning of life matters so much. Read on. Let's not waste time guessing which direction to go. Let's use a map instead.

Back in Middle Ages Europe, people wanted to know what *summum bonum* was. Translated from the Latin, it means "highest good".[5] John Locke, the 17th century libertarian philosopher, had this to say: "The philosophers of old did in vain inquire whether summum bonum consisted in riches, or bodily delights, or virtue, or contemplation."[6] Going back to 6th century BC China, the philosopher Lao-Tzu wrote, "The highest good is like water. Water gives life to the ten thousand things and yet does not compete with them."[7]

This gives us a promising path to answering our question of the meaning of life, which in other words asks us to answer... *for what main reason do you live?* What is the highest good a human can live for? If the highest good exists, shouldn't we devote the bulk of our limited time to it? "Man," as French author of *Nausea* and philosopher Jean-Paul Sartre wrote, "is nothing else but the sum of his actions."[8] While David Allen, author of *Getting Things Done*, writes, "You can do anything, but not everything."[9] Yet, many of us step off the path that leads towards the meaning. *We let distractions rule us.* We invite the common ills that have plagued humans for centuries – hopelessness, aimlessness, depression, despair, dependency. If we don't know the "why" of our life, nearly nothing will fill the emptiness long enough. Most of us get so caught up in our day-to-day tasks that we don't think about our lives. Oscar Wilde, poet and author of *The Picture of Dorian Gray*, once said, "To live is the rarest thing in the world. Most people exist, that is all."[10]

This way of living life may not be familiar. It is not the way we relate to things around us, like a car. The car has a clear meaning. It lets us travel long distances. A mobile phone lets us talk with others. Food means we survive and thrive. Finding the meaning in things around us is quite simple. We mostly base it on *usefulness*. However, when we ask about the meaning of life itself, we hit a dead end. So, over the years, we have guessed at the same question in different ways. We ask, "Why are we here? What's the point of my life? Where am I going?" But no direct answer comes our way. Today, even one of the world's top learning institutions, Stanford University, has little to say on the matter. Stanford's encyclopedic website even suggests that if no meaning to life has been agreed upon, perhaps "none exists."[11]

If you ask most people about the meaning, they'll also be at a loss. They may react as if you had asked about UFOs or the Loch Ness monster. Isn't it meant to be unanswerable, like a myth or mystery? No.

Common Excuses for Not Thinking About the Meaning of Life:

1. The sun will explode in a few billion years, so nothing we do matters anyway!

Many debate this, but let's say it's true. It then completely ignores the reality of scientific progress. Thanks to human creativity, most of the world today is very different than it was 200 years ago. Who is to say that at the rate we're progressing, that in just a *million years*, we won't find a solution? Luckily for us, our world was not built by such pessimists. If it had been, we'd still be using crushed insects for anesthetic and crocodile dung as a contraceptive.[12/13]

2. We can't discover the meaning of life, because the concept itself is meaningless!

Instead of seeking the truth, many have looked for a way out. They hide behind *word definitions* and even question what "meaning" is. Yet most people have a general idea of what the words refer to. Funding for research studies continues all the time even in areas where there are no agreed word definitions. There is no single standard for what the word "healthy" means, but that doesn't stop billions of people trying to improve their health.

3. Life is controlled by a Matrix-like computer, making everything pointless!

Life could be a dream, or a hallucination. Sure, it could be a computer simulation, as in the *Matrix* movies. This would be a costly project, if it were only done to trick us. It is possible? Yes. But is it likely? No. Why waste all that computing power generating the evolutionary process over billions of years when a few thousand years as the holy books suggest would have been less costly?

4. Who cares? We will all eventually die, so live each day like it's your last!

The idea of having fun goes back to the 4th century BC Greek philosopher Aristotle, whose ideas are best read in *The Basic Works of Aristotle*. He referred to the highest good as *Eudaimonia,* or "happiness".[14] This gave hedonists who didn't bother reading him closely the excuse to live selfishly, thinking this is what life is all about. Sadly, they got the idea all wrong. *Eudaimonia,* more accurately translated as "human flourishing," does not refer to personal enjoyment. Rather, it points to the public act of striving to make *something unique.* According to author Umair Haque, this value is measured "by what you've lived, what it's worth to you, and what that's worth to humanity".[15] Individual pleasures are a speck of sand on the beach of world history. The world only sees *what you give it*, not what you take from it.

You and I can believe all we want, for instance that we are kind and good people, but as Rachel Dawes, childhood friend of Bruce Wayne (Batman) said in the movie *Batman Begins*, "It's not who you are underneath, but what you do that defines you." Actions speak louder than words. Karl Marx admitted that, "Philosophers have only interpreted the world... The point, however, is to change it."[16]

Like those who misread Aristotle, many people today have plunged into the shallow search for pleasure. They crave the quick delight found in sex or drugs, and may claim that they are happy. Yet this is a happiness coming from an *addiction*, not by a testable process found in the real world. Aristotle reflects that, "It would, indeed, be strange if the end were amusement, and one were to take trouble and suffer hardship all one's life in order to amuse oneself."[17]

No, if we are to find the meaning of life, we must deal with our existence as it is in the real world. We cannot hide in the *comfort and bias* of our minds. This book will aim to answer the question by applying the scientific method. As we search, we will try to disprove the results we find. Like a car or a watch, humanity may not seem to be easy to take apart to be understood. Yet once we start peeling the layers back, we will reveal the core beneath. The chapters in this book follow that peeling process, so they are best read from start to finish.

Most people don't go looking for the truth. It's not an easy path, and the answers you find may change how you look at life. This book may not be easy for you. I'd rather you know now than later that I'm not going to be sugar-coating anything. *If you have the guts, keep reading,* but if you want to keep living in a comfortable fantasy world not wanting to challenge yourself, then throw this book away *right now.* It gets harder the older we are to accept the new, yet those open to it will benefit the most. Like the unborn generations to come, unshackled from past beliefs, they have less blood to spill in changing themselves than their parents and grandparents. Now if you're still keen, remember that most people don't finish what they start, even when it would help them. I hope you're *one of the few that finish.* If you care about the truth, then now is the time to prove it.

Lastly, before we begin our answer, allow me to answer another question. "Why should I read what you have to say?" The answer may surprise you. You should read this because...I'm a nobody and nobodies have more reason to *tell you the truth as they have little to gain or lose by doing so.* What is a nobody? It's a person who depends little or not at all, on someone or something to let them do what they do. Fewer bosses to show off to, fewer professors to suck up to, fewer sad weaknesses like seeking fame. It's when we let others make us think we're somebodies that we're less likely to do what may upset them. They may be those who pay us, who give to us, or who praise us. See what's happening? If we allow it, we become more dependent on money, greed and fame. When our freedom and time are controlled by others we're likely to stop taking creative risks, to stop being honest with others, and to stop speaking the truth. Who loses? You do!

A nobody tries to not let this happen. They don't make what a crowd wants now for a quick buck, but they make what a crowd should soon want and shows them why. At first, it's uncomfortable, it's challenging, and it even angers the crowd. How come? Because you risk showing that there is another way to see the world. Many of the most influential works that are still making an impact to this day were left by those who lived as nobodies most of their lives. Johannes Gutenberg made the printing press, Gregor Mendel discovered genetics that later led to cures and medicines, and Leonardo da Vinci did more than the *Da Vinci Code* by Dan Brown tells you: sculpting, building and experimenting with innovations that would only be made centuries after his death. "But hold on, don't you need a degree to do this?" you may ask. Well, do you hold any opinion on religion, politics, or anything else in life? Where then is your degree for each opinion you hold? Human progress depends less on degrees, and more on us not being afraid to be a nobody.

The above is to show a point... not to compare this small attempt to the greats. The point is that with no crowd to please the nobody doesn't waste time on things that don't matter, but they use the short time they have, as all we humans have, to make more things. Boosting the chance that one of those things will live on to give value after the nobody's bones turn to dust. It's as if what they make is not for the distracted who are living today, but for the yet unborn generations to come. We humans aren't timeless, but what we make can be. It's what's called original, unique, or special. It still matters centuries later. We can be somebodies and please today's crowd. It's exciting for a few months or years, but then forgotten, replaced by the next new thing.

Be a nobody, make the irreplaceable, and always ask, "Who will care in 100 years?"

As you read, you'll see places that have bonus material that ask that you simply send a quick email to vitojgrigorov@gmail.com or go to www.prosperism.org. If any thoughts/improvement tips come up when emailing, I'll be most grateful to you for letting me know, as it will help me make future work better for readers. Likewise, if you enjoyed this book, our friend here has a message:

It'll only take a minute or two
Go to the link below to leave a review
www.originofwhy.com

Some housekeeping as we begin. The first-person pronoun "I" is nearly unseen. In its place, the inclusive "we" pops up, which includes me as the author, and you, the reader, as we take this journey together. Also "they" or "their" and other such words are used to be inclusive of everyone and all genders. As will be obvious, quotes from the past have been used, some from times when gender neutrality was not a concern.

Any dollar amounts where the currency is not made clear are in U.S. dollars. Also, though this book has been written with a broad audience in mind, many facts' and figures' sources are most related to developed nations.

Finally, every effort has been made to contact and appropriately acknowledge copyright owners for any third-party work appearing in this book.

CHAPTER ONE

All Questions Come Back to This

"The longer you can look back, the farther you can look forward."[1]
Winston Churchill (British Prime Minister,
author of *A Gathering Storm*)

"We know what we are, but know not what we may be."[2]
William Shakespeare(playwright of *Romeo and Juliet,
Hamlet, Macbeth* and more)

Have you ever found yourself asking, "Why?" over and over again?

Maybe someone looked at you in a weird way, or an answer in a textbook was different than yours. It's common to get stumped, to reach that dead end in our guessing where it doesn't matter how many times we ask, "Why?"—our answer is still the same. When this happens, it may mean that the answer is not a means to an end but *is an end in itself*, possibly a truth.

How often do you take problems or concepts to their dead end to gain complete understanding of them? If we witness a car crash or the failure of a business, we rarely ask, "Why?" to dig deeper but we stop at the first answer that comes to mind.

He was a young psychiatrist from Vienna before he was forced to endure the horrors of Nazi concentration camps—mass graves, starvation, senseless beatings. His name was Viktor Frankl.[3] All the while, a question troubled him—why did some prisoners live, while others died? Remember that most were given equal rations of food and many suffered the same horrible conditions. Seeking the answer, he gathered scraps of paper left by Nazi officers and ended up writing what would become the best-selling book, *Man's Search for Meaning*. The answer Frankl found was that "those who were oriented toward the future, toward a meaning that waited to be fulfilled—these persons were more likely to survive." Similar answers were found in studies done on concentration camp survivors in Japan and Korea. We see it also in Louis Zamperini's survival story at sea in WWII as told by Laura Hillenbrand in *Unbroken*. Frankl would go on to say, "A man who becomes conscious of the responsibility he bears toward a human being who affectionately waits for him, or to an unfinished work, will never be able to throw away his life. He knows the 'why' for his existence, and will be able to bear almost any 'how'."

What's the first question of human existence? *"What am I living for?"* With no decent answer comes the opposite of life. Anxiety, suffering, depression all leading to an end result, suicide and death. Though billions of humans are different in their beliefs and backgrounds one standard is agreed on by the fact that anyone can witness it. That is, if you're alive right now you have a reason to live that wins over the reason to die. That reason, as foggy as it may be, impacts every question you face in your life. From what foods you eat, will you have kids, where do you work, to what brand of dishwashing liquid you buy. People live life as buddhists, adrenaline junkies, wealth seekers, drug addicts and the list is endless. Whatever they and you are doing now, remember, it all began with the answer or lack of one, to the question "What am I living for?" Answers to such questions go by many names like worldviews, belief systems or ideologies. We will call the answer, a philosophy.

Throughout history, people have often turned to philosophy for advice on how to live life, as it's the one subject that asks repetitive "Why?" questions. In the words of Errol Morris, filmmaker of *A Brief History of Time*, philosophy aims to know "the underlying order in the world,"[4] or as Victor Cousin said, "It describes and establishes what is."[5] In doing so, it acts as the one subject from which all others spring. As Wilfred Sellars writes, "Philosophy in an important sense has no special subject-matter which stands to it as other subject matters stand to other special disciplines." This is why we have the philosophy of science, the philosophy of politics… even the philosophy of philosophy! Sellars continues, "The aim of philosophy… is to understand how things in the broadest possible sense of the term hang together in the broadest possible sense of the term…It is therefore, the 'eye on the whole' which distinguishes the philosophical enterprise."[6]

Philosophy for this reason gives us a unique way to come up with answers which may lead economists, historians, and even mathematicians to look at their work differently, even though their own fields limit such an exploration for these answers. Knowing this, it's little surprise that philosophers, as a profession, *lead the top 10* of the most influential people who ever lived as seen in MIT's pantheon list.

Sadly, many today see philosophy as outdated and useless. Using complex words and jargon makes it sound like it's from an alien civilization. Religions have priests to help explain any unclear messages in their holy books, but philosophy lacks such teachers. It also doesn't help that philosophers use unrealistic thought experiments that are unlikely to ever happen in the real world to make their point. For example, "If you don't hit and kill the mother with a baby in her pram then thirty people in the bus you're driving will die, what do you do?" Such questions have only black and white answers, which forget other real world options, like hitting the brakes to stop or beeping the horn to warn the mother.

However, for those who think philosophy has no effect on their lives, it's wise, even if you're not fond of her books, to listen to what author Ayn Rand had to say, "You might claim—most people do—that you have never been influenced by philosophy. I will ask you to check that claim. Have you ever thought or said the following? 'Don't be so sure—nobody can be certain of anything.' You got that notion from 18th century philosopher David Hume and many, many others, even though you might never have heard of him. Or, 'This may be good in theory, but it doesn't work in practice.' You got that from Plato."[7] Jeff Olson, co-author of *The Slight Edge,* breaks it down further: "Your habits come from your daily activities compounded over time. And your activities are the result of the choices you make in the moment. Your choices come from your habits of thought, which are the product of your thinking, which comes from the view you have of the world and your place in it—your philosophy."[8]

Even economics was once linked to the philosophy departments in colleges and universities the world over, being called "Political Philosophy." As prominent economist of the 1930s, John Maynard Keynes, writes, "The ideas of economists and political philosophers, both when they are right and when they are wrong, are more powerful than is commonly understood. Indeed, the world is ruled by little else. Practical men, who believe themselves to be quite exempt from any intellectual influences, are usually the slaves of some defunct economist. Madmen in authority, who hear voices in the air, are distilling their frenzy from some academic scribbler of a few years back."[9] German poet Heinrich Heine once chillingly wrote, "Philosophical concepts nurtured in the stillness of a professor's study could destroy a civilization."[10] We've since come dangerously close to achieving this in another area of study, formerly known as "natural philosophy," and which we now call, "science".

As with economics, though, there is now a barrier between the subjects. As philosopher Massimo Pigliucci says, "A scientist is still separate from a philosopher as science can only explain what is, while it takes philosophy to say what should be done with what is."[11]

Let's now put philosophy to good use. When we were young, we started life in the driver's seat with only a third of our daily tank used up by basic activities, like sleeping and eating. We then start driving, with little idea of what the destination (*the meaning of life*) will look like. Along the way, we have doubts about the road we've taken (*our purpose in life)*, and sometimes we skid off the road to get to other roads. A car crash (*life-changing event*) may make us see how fragile life can be, leading us to seek another road. All the while, we burn fuel (*time*), causing us to stop before we get to the destination.

Now, if you're wondering what the difference between "purpose of life" and "meaning of life" is, that's a good question. They may seem like the same thing, but they're not.

Meaning is the "final cause", "main reason" or "highest good" that we live for, of which there is only one.

"Purpose," on the other hand, as Charles H. Parkhurst writes, "is what gives your life meaning."[12] It's our way of reaching the meaning. *Purpose can and should be different for each person.*

In what's to come, some quotes will mistake these two, so be mindful of this difference.

If you hear someone say that the meaning of life, for them, is to become a banker or scientist or world record holder, they've fallen into this common trap. Those are all purposes, whereas meaning, to quote Jack Canfield, co-author of The *Success Principle* ™ is "the why behind everything you do."[13] Why be a banker? Why be a scientist? Here we can lean on our trusty "Why?" questions until we reach a dead-end answer. Let's explore this with an imaginary lawyer:

Q: Why did you want to become a lawyer?
A: It's something my grandfather did, and I saw he made a decent living, it got me interested.

Q: Why does a decent living matter to you?
A: I could afford to do what I want, have a large house, swimming pool, kids...

Q: Why is that so important to you?
A: Well, don't most people want something like that?

Q: Why would most people want that?
A: Isn't that what life is about to most people?

Q: If you're correct, then is it the meaning of life?
A: Um, maybe not the meaning, but a part of life, I guess...

See how, after a few "whys," our lawyer hit a dead end? He's unsure of linking what he does with the meaning of life. Moments like these are rare, as Elizabeth Gilbert in her book *Eat, Pray, Love* shows.

We can only truly judge a purpose by how it fulfils the meaning. So, knowing the meaning is crucial as otherwise we may be busy, but going nowhere. With meaning, all our busyness moves us towards a direction.

---

1. PURSUIT: Does the meaning explain our reason for seeking our chosen purpose?

Once we know the meaning, it will become the map from which we can choose the purpose that will best seek it. Below, we will draw the criteria, adding to the first point above, from which we locate our meaning of life sentence. But first...

This is What Happens When You Don't Know Life's Meaning

"What man actually needs is not a tensionless state but rather the striving and struggling for a worthwhile goal, a freely chosen task."[14]
Viktor Frankl

What would you guess is the most common deathbed wish? It isn't for one more puff of a cigarette or even to see family. No, it's, "I wish I'd had the courage to live a life true to myself, rather than what others expected of me."[15] Sadly, as we saw with Jen, many of us may be suffering that same silent desperation. According to the U.S. Center for Disease Control, four out of ten Americans have not discovered a satisfying life purpose.[16]

Best-selling author Robert Greene of *48 Laws of Power*, offers a possible cause for this. "What we lack most in the modern world is a sense of a larger purpose to our lives. In the past, it was organized religion that often supplied this. But most of us now live in a secularized world. We human animals are unique—we must build our own world. We do not simply react to events out of biological scripting. But without a sense of direction provided to us, we tend to flounder. We don't know how to fill up and structure our time."[17]

Does this sound like you? How do you view the meaning of life? A test made from the teachings of Viktor Frankl can show where you are right now in your life. Send a quick email to vitojgrigorov@gmail.com or go to www.prosperism.org to get this test and other bonus material.

Ever thought to yourself, "I don't know what I want to do?" It's happened to all of us. Often it strikes soon after finishing school, when students seek to take just about any job, mostly the best-paying one, which can then put them on a treadmill to an unfulfilled life. The limitless dreams of childhood collapse under the daily mud crawl of routine, creating an inner conflict that Tony Robbins, world-class speaker and author of *Money Master the Game,* describes as when "life doesn't match your blueprint and you feel powerless to change it."[18]

Studies over many decades have found that knowing the meaning and purpose of one's life is vital to the *well-being of a person*. The lack of it is one of the most common problems explored by psychotherapy, psychoanalysis and other methods. Carl Jung, the famous Swiss psychiatrist, found that there wasn't "sufficient meaning" in the lives of most of his patients.[19] Today it's less surprising that this is a problem with new science showing that the human mind is "obsessed with purpose," as Richard Dawkins, biologist and author of *The God Delusion*, said.[20]

1. Depression and all other related illnesses.

Depression is a broad problem usually overused as an umbrella word to explain a range of unwanted states of mind. It's likely you've heard someone you know describe themselves or others as depressed. It has been linked to rising suicide rates that today claim *a life every forty seconds*.[21]

Betty Friedan wrote in her bestseller, *The Feminine Mystique*, about "the problem that has no name". This problem was happening strangely to middle and upper class women. As one woman said, "I ask myself why I am so dissatisfied. I've got my health, fine children, a lovely new home, enough money... Then you wake up one morning, and there's nothing to look forward to."[22] According to the World Health Organization, a shocking three hundred and fifty million people are touched by depression, making it the *number one cause of disability* in the world.[23]

A recent study found a "definite relationship of meaning in life with depression and psychological health". The lower the score in meaning of life tests, the higher the rate of depression, and vice versa. A study of mature people showed over time that 33% of people with low "subjective well-being," died, compared to only 9% with the highest levels of well-being.[24]

In response to the problem she found, Freidan wrote, "The only way for a woman, as for a man, to find herself as a person is by creative work of her own." With the growth of depression, it's no surprise that only one in four people polled believe they're living to their creative potential. When creativity is missing, boredom sets in, which is why repetitive work saps so much from human life.[25]

2. Addictions, neuroticism, and materialistic behavior.

People who don't know the meaning can find strange ways to make up for it, like buying all they see, desperately searching for a partner who'll solve all their problems, or binge eating or drinking until they nearly pass out.[26]

Drugs and alcohol, the twin disciples of the devil, addict tens of millions of people this way. *Narconomics* by Tom Wainwright explores how governments spend billions to try to combat drug based addiction, yet studies have found that knowing the meaning of life can give us the real solution.[27] In a study by Stanley Krippner, every single addict said that "things seemed meaningless". A similar study by Annmarie von Forstmeyer found that 90% of alcoholics suffered from an "abysmal feeling of meaninglessness".[28]

Boredom is used to describe the same feeling. Studies have found that bored people have a *40% higher death rate* than non-bored people.[29] Without meaning, boredom breeds the need to escape, which leads some to fill their lives with the superficial scum of degrading reality TV and sensationalist gossip pages. This "trash media" is made to make us feel like we're missing out on something. The ad break shows us the product to buy to fix it. This conflict of interest leads to unrealistically fake beauty standards for men and women, as mostly all images are touched up. The money spent trying to remove a frown line by those who have been culturally brainwashed could feed a war-ravaged village for months. This media manipulation plays its part in turning women surveyed into walking bundles of insecurities, *with*

98% saying they were not beautiful.[30] As Howard Beale said in the movie, *Network,* "You're beginning to believe the illusions we're spinning here, you're beginning to believe that the tube is reality and your own lives are unreal… You dress like the tube, you eat like the tube, you raise your children like the tube, you even think like the tube. This is mass madness, you maniacs… you people are the real thing, we are the illusion."[31]

Q.   What problems have you faced which go back to not knowing the meaning of life?

A.

This "hedonic well-being," offers only a short-term feeling and sucks people onto an addictive, ever-shrinking rope of materialistic and bodily pleasures which eventually snaps. To avoid falling off, the person constantly chases that next shot of excitement – from laughing at slapstick comedy, popping pills or gossiping like a giggling goose. A vampire needs more blood to survive, *these people need more thrills to live.* As author Annie Dillard of *Pilgrim of Tinker Creek* writes, "The life of sensation is the life of greed; it requires more and more."[32] These people become the *space wasters of society,* seeking loudly on the outside what they fear finding silently on the inside. A fear to sit silently for between 6-15 minutes has been shown in a study to be so hard for some that they'd rather give themselves mild electric shocks.[33]

3. Loss of a healthy and longer life.

In addition to better health and well-being, those in touch with a meaning show lower rates of Alzheimer's, anxiety, neuroticism and other medical conditions.[34/35] Even heart disease, the most common killer in the U.S., is less common—*by about 50%*—in those who know their life's meaning.[36] According to the lead doctor for the study, "If you find purpose in life, if you find your life is meaningful, and if you have goal-directed behavior, you are likely to live longer." Seeing each day as a connected string toward reaching a greater goal gives us the inner drive to keep going even when problems pop up.

What Meaning are You Living?

"What is the use of living, if it be not to strive for noble causes and to make this muddled world a better place for those who will live in it after we are gone?"[37]
Winston Churchill

Know it or not, you are right now living some meaning of life, though if asked, you might not think of it this way. When you think about lifestyle choices, your view of the world, or simply how things seem to you, they are all filtered through a meaning of life sentence you've told to yourself. Even if you think you haven't, you're likely living some autopilot meaning of someone else's. Otherwise without this you'd have committed suicide long ago.

Take food for example. Though nature has never posted a sign telling us to eat fruit instead of rocks, we all get the idea. Likewise, even though nature doesn't openly tell us what the meaning of life is, we should accept that there can exist *a right and wrong meaning.*

According to Kate, Ned seems normal. He doesn't appear to have mental health issues, and he survives on charity handouts by his own wish.

While it's true that he doesn't physically harm anyone, most people would say that the purpose he has chosen lacks meaning. What is the point of picking up leaves, anyway? Almost no one in society benefits from it. We don't have leaf collecting listed with science or engineering as a possible future path for a child. Instead, we support children to seek something more "valuable" (a critical but murky word we will explore). To devote one's life to looking at leaves would be wasting the potential we all have to do more for society.

Some, inspired by writings of John Stuart Mill, such as *On Liberty* and *Utilitarianism,* might say that if someone feels happy doing what they do, let them do it. If they are not hurting anyone, we have little reason to say that what they do is worthless when compared to other people. Does it matter what other people think about the meaning of someone's life? Doesn't Ned's own experience decide the value of his leaf collecting?

This all sounds good, but it forgets an important point. To accurately judge his own meaning, Ned must have a decent understanding of other activities *that people consider "meaningful."* Only then would he be able to see why others call what he does "trivial." Few would argue that a human should strive to become the best that they can be, yet we aren't seeing that with Ned if we compare him to others.

Ned, of course, would disagree. "Isn't what I think what matters most here?" he might ask. It's a dangerous line of thinking, for if it were true, criminals could easily *defend all the horrors* they inflict on other people. Though Ned isn't physically harming anyone, he is harming society by not contributing to it as much as he could be. His way of living would be fine if he were stranded alone on an unknown island, but not in a society with other people.

Living among others gives you rights, but with them come responsibilities. The ancient Greek philosopher, Socrates, famously made this point when he killed himself instead of running away when a seemingly corrupt court sentenced him to death. We aren't promoting blind faith in the government here, for laws and policies can always be improved. When a person has a choice though, to either live in one society or another, they should know the responsibilities that come with that choice.

Yet here lies the challenge. We may let Ned go on his merry way picking up leaves, but if asked for our views by, say, a news reporter, we'd likely say that action should be taken to prevent children from becoming leaf-pickers.

What if there was a scientific way to show the consequences of Ned's actions?

---

2. EVIDENCE: Can the meaning be agreed to by others and its results found in the real world?

Even though we have lists of vague answers to our question "What is the meaning of life?" by some of society's most prominent individuals, a decent direct answer still seems hard to pin down. Popular ones include, *"life is a mystery,*" "*life is absurd,*" "*life is a joke,*" and, "*life is meaningless.*" Pretty uninspiring, and if true, would mean the suicide rates worldwide will likely continue to grow.

In our younger years, we may have thought the meaning was, "*To be cool, I'll drink and test out drugs.*" After graduation, that often changes to, "*I need to get promoted at work so I can earn more money to buy more things.*" As we've found out, these aren't meanings. They are purposes that others, such as the media, try to turn into meaning.

Do you see how these turn our focus inward? Thinking of yourself as the center of your meaning often leads to the neglect of others. Ned does this, and though he might delude himself into happiness, his disregard for others is what leads us to see his meaning as useless. He does not seek to give anything back to society and cares less about the people in it.

> **Q.** **What's the meaning of life you've led so far if put into a sentence?**
>
> **A.**

Sure, focusing on yourself is needed at times, but it's not healthy if done all the time. Think about it. When you make someone else happy, you can't help but feel happy as well. People who live for something other than themselves know this. They're the ones able to go through the ups and downs of daily life without letting it get them down. This is because when you seek to improve the lives of others, the worries of your own *life shrink in importance.* You feel you have a larger mission above and beyond the smaller things.

Let's look at some single sentence meanings found online, which many people live their lives by:

- "Getting rich." The obvious question here is, "What are you getting rich for?"

- "To become an expert at _____." We'd ask, "What's the end goal of learning all that?"

- "Falling in love." Not only is this meaning focused on you rather than the rest of the world, it begs the question of what is next? It lets us keep asking, "Why?" over and over. Depending on another person for your happiness shows that you have unresolved inner questions that you think a stranger will answer for you.

All the above cannot be ends in themselves. For the meaning of life answer to make sense, it needs to not allow for more "what's next?" questions, but by the same token it needs to be open ended in its possibilities.

---

3. FINAL: Is the meaning of life sentence an end in itself? Does asking, "What's next?" make little sense?

Meaning is Not Within You, but Found Outside in the Real World

Biased emotions like happiness can't lead us to a more precise meaning of life, as happiness for *one person may be agony for another*. Any "truth" searched inside us will never be universal for all. The universal can only be found *outside our minds*, and in the real world around us. The more people agree on something, the closer it crawls towards truth. Otherwise it's as good as a personal fantasy.

Studies of mental health can shine a light on this for us. They refer to life's meaning as that which is "positively oriented toward final value beyond one's animal self," and that which can "fulfil a life goal that's constructive and vital to the advancement of humankind."[38]

Likewise, it's easy to mistake the things that we do "in" our lives, with what we want "out" of our lives. It's easy to let our meaning be held hostage by useless distractions. Just walk outside your home and you're likely struck by limitless sounds and movements. As Von Goethe, German poet and author of *Faust*, warned, "Things which matter most must never be at the mercy of things which matter least."[39] After all, how many people have on their deathbed celebrated being able to squeeze in an extra round of drinks each Friday night? Or were pleased with how well they knew what each of their friends was up to on social media?

Humanity's most celebrated minds don't think the meaning lies in those places either, as we can see below:

Aristotle (384 BC–322 BC) – Philosopher and Polymath
"Where your talents and the needs of the world cross, lies your calling."[40]

Will Durant (1885–1981) – Historian, Writer, Philosopher
"To have a great purpose to work for, a purpose larger than ourselves, is one of the secrets of making life significant, for then the meaning and worth of the individual overflow his personal borders and survive his death."[41]

Albert Einstein (1879–1955) – Theoretical Physicist
"One knows from daily life that one exists for other people—first of all for those upon whose smiles and well-being our own happiness is wholly dependent... A hundred times every day I remind myself that my inner and outer life are based on the labors of other men, living and dead, and that I must exert myself in order to give in the same measure as I have received and am still receiving."[42]

Bill Gates (1955–) – Innovator, Philanthropist, Microsoft Co-Founder
"The final measure of your life is not how well you live but how well others live because of you."[43]

Mahatma Gandhi (1869–1948) – Leader of Indian Nationalism
"Man becomes great exactly in the degree in which he works for the welfare of his fellow men."[44]

Reid Hoffman (1967–) – Co-Founder of LinkedIn
"Part of what I think the meaning of our lives is, is the impact we have on other people."[45]

Steve Jobs (1955–2011) – Innovator, Designer, Apple Co-Founder
"When you grow up, you tend to get told that the world is the way it is, and your life is just to live your life inside the world. Try not to bash into the walls too much. Try to have a nice family life. Have fun, save a little money... That's a very limited life. Life can be much broader, once you discover one simple fact, and that is everything around that you call life was made up by people who were no smarter than you. And you can change it. You can influence it. You can build your own things that other people can use."[46]

Helen Keller (1880–1968) – Activist, Lecturer, and Author of *The Story of My Life*
"Many persons have a wrong idea of what constitutes true happiness. It is not attained through self-gratification but through fidelity to a worthy purpose."[47]

Martin Luther King Jr. (1929–1968) – Leader of the Civil Rights Movement and Author of *Why We Can't Wait*
"Life's most persistent and urgent question is: 'What are you doing for others?'"[48]

Dalai Lama (1935–) – 14th Dalai Lama, Co-Author of *How To Practice: The Way to a Meaningful Life*
"Our prime purpose in this life is to help others."[49]

Horace Mann (1796–1859) – Education Reformer and U.S. Politician
"Be ashamed to die until you have won some victory for humanity."[50]

Karl Marx (1818–1883) – German Philosopher, Economist, Historian
"If we have chosen the position in life in which we can most of all work for mankind, no burdens can bow us down, because they are sacrifices for the benefit of all; then we shall experience no petty, limited, selfish joy, but our happiness will belong to millions, our deeds will live on quietly but perpetually at work, and over our ashes will be shed the hot tears of noble people."[51]

John Stuart Mill (1806–1873) – Philosopher, Economist, Civil Servant and Author
"Those only are happy (I thought) who have their minds fixed on some object other than their own happiness, on the happiness of others, on the improvement of mankind, even on some art or pursuit, followed not as a means, but as itself an ideal end."[52]

Alfred Nobel (1833–1896) – Engineer, Chemist, Inventor, Weapons Manufacturer
"To those that shall have conferred the greatest benefit on mankind."[53]*

*This is one of the criteria by which applicants are judged for a Nobel Prize.

Barack Obama (1961–) – 44th President of the United States and Author of *Dreams from My Father*
"Focusing your life solely on making a buck shows a certain poverty of ambition. It asks too little of yourself… Because it's only when you hitch your wagon to something larger than yourself that you realize your true potential."[54]

Larry Page (1973–) – Computer Scientist, Innovator, Google Co-founder
"I want to invent things and get them to people and get them to use them, and to benefit the world that way."[55]

George Bernard Shaw (1856–1950) – American Playwright of Stories like *Pygmalion*
"This is the true joy in life, the being used for a purpose recognized by yourself as a mighty one; the being thoroughly worn out before you are thrown on the scrap heap; the being a force of nature instead of a feverish selfish little clod of ailments and grievances complaining that the world will not devote itself to making you happy."[56]

Arnold Schwarzenegger (1947–) – Bodybuilder, Actor, Governor, Co-author of *Total Recall*
"For me life is continuously being hungry. The meaning of life is not simply to exist, to survive, but to move ahead, to go up, to achieve, to conquer."[57]

Martin E. P. Seligman (1947–) – Psychological Scientist, Author of *Learned Optimism*
"You use your highest strengths and talents to belong to and serve something you believe is larger than the self."[58]

Leo Tolstoy (1828–1910) – Russian Author of Works Such as *War and Peace* **and** *Anna Karenina*
"The sole meaning of life is to serve humanity."[59]

Mark Zuckerberg (1984–) Innovator, CEO of Facebook
"I believe that over time, people get remembered for what they build."[60]

Anyone can make a quote but the above are from those whose life reflects what they say in words. Comparing the quotes, we see words like "help" and "serve others" pop up, with a focus on doing something "larger than yourself." By "building" and "creating" a "victory for humanity," we make the world better for ourselves and for others.

---

4. **BROAD**: How many people will the meaning seek to affect?

Think back to our example of the car on the road to meaning. What do we want to get out of the car during its lifespan? We don't want it to go to waste, throwing away all the time and money we have put into it. We want the car to move us, and others, as much as we need without breaking down. If the car does this, it is then performing its function best. But what about us humans?

What is the Unique Human Function?

To find this out, we need some help from Aristotle. Long ago he remarked that, "Every art and every inquiry, and similarly, every action and choice, is thought to aim at some good and for this reason the good has rightly been declared to be that at which all things aim."[61] He called this good *eudemonia,* which is often wrongly said to link to the word "happiness." In *Personal Destinies: A Philosophy of Ethical Individualism,* philosopher David Norton deviates from the past in suggesting that *eudemonia* is best translated to "meaningful living."[62] But how do we live like this?

The human is best when doing the function that is unique to them, as Aristotle said, "Just as for a flute player, a sculptor, or any artist, and, in general, for all things that have a function or activity, the good and the 'well' is thought to reside in the function. So it would seem to be for man, if he has a function. Have the carpenter, then, and the tanner certain functions or activities, and has man none?"[63]

He used the example of a knife, saying that its function is to cut well. But what is the human function? To find it, we need to contrast what in the widest scope sets us apart from all other species we share this earth with. What's the *largest difference*? Let's see what Abraham Lincoln, of all people, had to say about this: "Beavers build houses; but they build them in nowise differently, or better now, than they did, five thousand years ago. Ants, and honey-bees provide food for winter, but just in the same way they did when Solomon referred the sluggard to them as patterns of prudence. Man is not the only animal who labors, but he is the only one who improves his workmanship—by discoveries and inventions."[64]

Add to this what Socrates writes in *The Republic,* "…end of anything would be that which could not be… so well accomplished, by any other thing."[65]

With the help above, we find that the distinct function of the human being is to **innovate.** Charles Darwin alludes to this as well, "It has been asserted that man alone is capable of progressive improvement."[66] We alone can build on the work of those who came before us, and then pass it on to future generations to do the same.

5. FUNCTION: Does the meaning involve the unique human function to innovate?

Innovation is linked to survival. If we don't innovate, we over time lower our own life expectancy and that of our fellow humans. Asking "why?" comes to a dead end if we're questioning survival itself.

Indeed, as we'll later see, innovation defines what it means to be human. Other related words also pop up like "creativity", "genius," and "invention," all of which for us fall under "innovation."

Pt. 2 BUILDINGS OF LOST DREAMS

THE UNIQUE HUMAN FUNCTION IS TO INNOVATE
Improve upon what we have

Kate works as an accountant. Seeing how slow the accounting process takes, she attempts to use her coding skills to make a program to do it faster.

6. CRITERIA: Does the meaning sentence give us clear goals so we can see if our purpose is achieving it?

Let's take a slight pause here. We're now close to revealing the meaning of life sentence we've laid the groundwork for below.

1. PURSUIT: Does the meaning explain our reason for seeking our chosen purpose?

2. EVIDENCE: Can the meaning be agreed to by others and its results found in the real world?

3. FINAL: Is the meaning of life sentence an end in itself? Does asking, "What's next?" make little sense?

4. BROAD: How many people will the meaning seek to affect?

5. FUNCTION: Does the meaning involve the unique human function to innovate?

6. CRITERIA: Does the meaning sentence give us clear goals so we can see if our purpose is achieving it?

Does any existing meaning tick these boxes? There are plenty of unfocused meanings sitting in the minds of billions of people, directing what they do every day. Some are a mash of those below:

...to chase dreams... to live a life of honor... to seek happiness and flourish... to be an authentic human being... to live forever or die trying... to learn as many things as possible in life... to give more than you take... to end suffering... to treasure every enjoyable sensation one has... to seek beauty in all its forms... to have fun... to strive for power and superiority... to rule the world... life sucks and then you die.

None of the above meaning sentences match the criteria above. But hold on. Aren't there other major influences in our world, which act as the meaning of life for billions? Let's see...

RELIGION

1. PURSUIT: There are thousands of religions, each with their own set of rules. Many religions also have punishments. A common one is that you're destined for hell if you're a non-believer. So, *no matter* which religion you choose, in the eyes of all the others, you're already damned for eternity.

2. EVIDENCE: Many key "historical" events in the holy books cannot be proven. Take Christianity for example. You may have been moved by the *Passion of the Christ* movie, but the earliest discovered writings of the four gospels about Jesus date from 40 to 100 years after they supposedly took place. It's debatable whether they can even be "primary sources" (written by those who lived at the time).[67] Also, can we ever know that a believer of any religion is really living by its teachings? Anyone can wear a necklace with a religious symbol, but still lie, steal, and murder. They may claim they are a religious or spiritual person because they silently pray, but who's to know that they do? There is no way to know if they're ticking all the religious rules. Even if they say they are, how can we know they're not lying?

3. FINAL: Having so many religions would mean that we're dealing with many meanings. Take the obvious one, "To live by what's written in the holy book." This still begs the question, "How do I know what in the holy book matters for my life?" Thanks to how old the books are and the ancient language they're written in, the "important" lessons are open to never ending interpretations.

4. BROAD: Most religions do focus on serving others, but as said above, that serving can be narrowed to only focus on yourself in prayer, collecting donations, or converting non-believers to the cause.

5. FUNCTION: There is nearly no mention in religious texts of the human function to innovate.

6. CRITERIA: Religions have rules for life. Some are very detailed. Yet without an agreed standard among religions there is no way to say that a rule in one is better than the rule of another.

BIOLOGY

1. PURSUIT: For biological sciences, the meaning of life is to have more children and continue the species. In humans, this is tied to the *well-marketed concept of "love."* This meaning makes perfect sense if we happily forget that some time back, humans escaped the instincts controlling all other species, taking us away from hanging on trees to sending satellites into orbit.

2. EVIDENCE: Babies are born and children are raised. Yes, evidence exists for this meaning. Unlike other animals, though, humans uniquely can choose to not have kids. If we didn't have the ability to resist this impulse, all our skills and ambitions would melt away at each sexual urge. Each hour would be filled with having sex or preparing for it, lowering us to a kind of pleasure-seeking sloth-like creature.

3. FINAL: If a horrible accident happens and your children die, does it extinguish the meaning of life? As terrible as it would be, we know that life does go on. Do most people who are unable to have children commit suicide? No.

4. BROAD: We cannot ignore the chemical pleasures of sex, which when not controlled result in the birth of children. It's easy to give in to sexual temptation in the heat of the moment, though humans can and do resist it. So, let's be clear. This is a personal pleasure to satisfy oneself and perhaps your partner, *not one with the benefit of the world in mind*. In the past, having and raising children was promoted, especially to women, as being the main reason they lived on earth. Thankfully women's fortunes have changed, but without an alternative meaning, both sexes can still be fooled into finding sole reason for their existence in having children. Decades later, having not done much with their lives, they defend themselves by saying that their kids are their greatest achievement. Yet if each person who ever lived thought and did this, we'd still be back in the jungle not having progressed, as children would be the sole focus of our lives.[68]

5. FUNCTION: Unlike innovation, having children or offspring is seen across all species, whereas innovation is only found in humans. It's sad to hear people with a lack of meaning in their lives refer to their children as "achievements." Fantasies aside, this supposed achievement has happened billions of times in history—the survival of humanity depended on it. But what if the kid turns bad? Hitler, Stalin, Pol Pot? Certainly, they can't be seen as achievements from a parents' viewpoint. Sure, having children can be an amazing experience, but it must never *be misused and claimed to be the meaning of life*. There are many who perform this "noble deed" only so that the children later care for them in old age, and this guiltily blackmails the child who is meant to robotically do as the parent wishes.

6. CRITERIA: Here, the metric for success would have to be the number of children one has, which rules out women for biological reasons. This leaves this meaning only open to men like Moulay Ismail ibn Shairf, who is alleged to have fathered over 800 children.[69]

Lastly, let's remember that new technologies now mean that the birth and care of children can happen in many ways, eliminating the argument that humanity will die out if we don't jump into bed together anymore.

MEDIA

1. PURSUIT: It exists to be consumed, or else it dies. It pushes us to watch and listen to it. Advertisers mostly pay its running costs, and so the buying of their products and services is promoted everywhere.

2. EVIDENCE: As it is profit-driven, it is more *entertainment than fact*. The "truth" shown is dumbed down, and sometimes made up, slicing away context and reporting accuracy. The dying breed of traditional media, instead of innovating, is copying the barely profitable new media online, *spitting out outrageous articles with little fact-checking*, trying to boost the readers or viewers so enough advertising money can trickle in. To do so, they encourage rather than challenge beliefs, and spread scandal instead of balance. As one judge said in the trial over the crimes committed by reporters of the shut down *News of the World* newspaper, once owned by Rupert Murdoch: "I accept... there was considerable pressure on journalists at the *News of the World* to obtain stories to sell newspapers," and "that may have led to a belief that the ends justified the means."[70]

3. FINAL: Media exists due to a lack of finality, like a cliffhanger ending to the latest episode. There is always a sense of anticipation for what's to be revealed next time. So much of media is meant to stimulate questions, rather than answer them, "How can I get that?", "Why is that not me?", "What will happen next?" But there is no end goal for all these never-ending questions. Impressionable people turn on the TV and are told what they should be doing or thinking. To remove the bad mood it puts them in, they listen to some pop music, which helps further dampen their mind, with lyrics about drugs, drinks, and sex.

4. BROAD: The broadest subjects the media covers focus on *creating dependency*, as that's how they make money. A global freak show of songs, movies, magazines, and TV shows leads people to obsess over things that make little to no difference in the world. Addictive lyrics make fans obsessed with chasing the perfect partner instead of chasing their dreams. Millions of young, impressionable fans of the song "Only Girl (In the World)" by Rihanna, may walk away thinking unrealistically that their future partner must adore them like a goddess.

Pop musician Lady Gaga, known for her albums like *Born This Way*, had similar lyrics in songs she sang, but seemed to have had a change of heart towards the media industry she was a part of. In 2015 she said, "I don't like wasting my time spending days just shaking people's hands and smiling and taking selfies. It feels shallow to my existence. I have a lot more to offer than my image. I don't like being used to make people money. I feel sad when I'm overworked and I just become a money-making machine and my passion and creativity take a back seat. That makes me unhappy. So, what did I do? I started to say no..."[71]

5. FUNCTION: Themes coming from old media companies rarely refer to innovation. Instead, given increased online competition from new media, they now need to promote the most sensational and outrageous stories to grab attention to earn advertising dollars. The full menu of delights from drinking, drugs, violence, and sex, all digested by hundreds of millions of impressionable fans who adore all the singers, actors, performers, and show hosts who, worse than little children, will do anything to get seen by the media monster that made them. It's unsurprising to find side effects to all this. A study done of 959 ninth graders in the U.S. found that students who listen to music with the most references to marijuana are almost twice as likely to have used the drug compared to their peers who don't listen to such music.[72] Some researchers urge less exposure of violence in movies and video games for kids, due to it influencing impressionable kids to take the shooting on screen into the classroom.[73]

6. CRITERIA: There's no set of rules, but a mix of messages from various magazines, songs, and movies. Most media copy and paste the same stories from one another anyway. Based on the rate of word use, a pattern appears of the type of things the media knows are sensational and so pushes most into peoples' minds. The use of words like "sex," "body image," "weed," "hate," "kill," and other variations, have grown more common in songs since the 1980s.[74] In a 2005 study, rap music took the top spot with 77% of songs studied having lyrics on alcohol and drug abuse. This is a 600% jump in drug mentions in rap songs from 1979.[75]

It would seem that such lyrics are aimed at the scum of society – the borderline criminals, yet the base of listeners are *young impressionable teenagers* of all backgrounds.[76] At least one thing you can't hold against such "stars" is that they're mostly well-trained in what they're singing about. Many are drug addicts, alcoholics, ex-criminals, even rapists and murderers, or have close ties with those that are.

All the above influences fall short in many ways in acting as life's meaning. So, let's now find the meaning sentence that can best tick the boxes. Humanity benefits when each of us has a chance to innovate, which in the long run lifts everyone's standard of living. As author Will Durant of *The Greatest Minds and Ideas of All Time* writes, "A man feels significant in proportion as he contributes physically or mentally to the entity of which he acknowledges himself a part."[77] This entity could be our society, our nation, or the entire world. There's a reason humans of any country are attracted to heroes. From James Bond in *Casino Royale,* to Batman in the comic *The Complete Hush*, they mostly try to save the world, and to make things better for a lot of people. In their actions, they seek the best for the most, from stopping a nuclear bomb explosion to capturing someone who'd happily detonate it. A part of us wishes we could do a sliver of what they have done, but then the reality of our repetitive lives returns to us.

Time is short to live in fantasy because "A man who dares to waste one hour of time has not discovered the value of life," wrote Charles Darwin.[78] To do so we first must know what time is best used for.

> Which of these two has left a greater impact on the world?
> Bill Gates OR Joe (Jen and Kates office manager)

Who'd you choose? Even office managers reading this would have to agree that the choice is obviously Bill Gates. Because of his achievements, we can put nearly any occupation opposite his name and the result would be the same.

This shows a very important point. Most humans can see and *rank the value* of someone's actions in comparison to others. It follows then that the world would be better off if there were more people who made an impact of the size Bill Gates has. Walter Isaacson's book *The Innovators* explains the story of this impact very well.

You must have thought it at some point, but by just being alive you're impacting others, even in the smallest way. We can impact even more people by doing something useful for them. We were so quick to choose Gates as he's touched billions, whereas Joe maybe touches a dozen or so people in his life.

As a philanthropist, through the Bill and Melinda Gates Foundation, Gates has donated money to causes the world over, leading to hundreds of thousands of people being employed and an estimated 6 million + lives saved.[79] *Outliers* author, Malcolm Gladwell, predicts that "there will be statues of Gates across the Third World."[80] How did he make this impact? By co-founding and growing Microsoft Corporation. As Gates' co-founder, Paul Allen, wrote in his autobiography *Idea Man*, "Microsoft arguably touches more lives on earth than any other corporation on earth. More than a billion copies of Windows are in use around the world."[81] The software Microsoft makes and sells allows people to do many things easier and better than before. This book, like others, was typed mostly using Microsoft Word software.

Office manager Joe might be solving some problems at work, but the questions remain, "Is he living to his *full* potential? Could he be making *more* value and impact for the world by doing something else?" Well, you've already answered that question when you chose Bill Gates. Joe, in response, agrees that he could be doing more but that his current job doesn't let him create a Gates-level of impact.

Sure, life circumstances might stand in Joe's way, but they also stood in the way of many who have made an impact. Without taking action, Joe, like others, will join our saddened friends buried underground. The graveyards of our world hold the lost dreams of those who did not change their lives in time. At least Joe can celebrate having a larger impact than Ned the leaf collector!

Now, what if we ask the "What's next" question? "What purpose can eclipse that of Bill Gates?"…We hit a roadblock.

As with before, when we hit such a dead end, we see that we must be near some truth. If Bill Gates, through his purpose, has made some of the *broadest ever impact* we can imagine, the next logical question is, "What was the result of his purpose?" or "How do we describe it?" The answer is found in the sum of his actions and in the combined effect it has had on the real world. Thomas Edison wanted as many people to use the light bulb as possible. Scientists wish that cures for disease could reach everyone. We all can dream that one day we'll make a difference to as many people as possible.

So, what's the broadest sentence based on the above, as seen through the different purposes we each choose?

To Seek the Greatest Good for the Greatest Number

If we are to live to our full potential, our actions must pursue the greatest good for the greatest number of people. Leaving the result for *future generations* to benefit and use *after we die.* This sums up, in the broadest way, many other meanings mentioned, while importantly laying out the criteria for how one is to seek it. We tried to make sure each word mattered in the meaning sentence above, for like David Deutsch, physicist and author of *The Beginning of Infinity,* said, the best explanations try to fit so tightly that to change any one detail will affect the whole explanation.

Let's scrutinize this meaning and see how it fits.

1. PURSUIT: Makes clear the end goal that all purposes should seek.

2. EVIDENCE: Points to real-world evidence, rather than to a person's opinion.

3. FINAL: Uses words such as "greatest" to make its point final and never ending.

4. BROAD: Includes as many people as possible in the "greatest number".

5. FUNCTION: Implies by its criteria the human function to innovate.

6. CRITERIA: Gives us a way of measuring fulfillment of the meaning.

Have you heard people say, "It's a means to an end"? Now with the above you know what the ultimate "end" is. Knowing this, we can better find a purpose that has the best chance of seeking the meaning. Indeed, the above meaning sentence, like anything, is not out of the blue. The "greatest happiness for the greatest number" was what utilitarians of 19th century Britain suggested as a rule for all government policies. Yet as we explored, happiness for one person is different to happiness for another.

Pt. 3 BUILDINGS OF LOST DREAMS

THE MEANING OF LIFE
To seek the greatest good for the greatest number

Kate has found a way to finish clients' tax returns faster than before. It also means she and her co-workers will get a bonus, but someone is not happy...

See how our meaning of life has no stopping point? It doesn't aim at creating good for say just 42 people, just as a doctor wouldn't stop after vaccinating a dozen patients. It's never-ending. The more people impacted by your purpose, the better. Continuing after your death, if the impact is large enough it can spread to the unborn millions to come. Thomas Edison died in 1931, but one of the companies he co-founded, General Electric, lives on to this day, headed by past CEO's like Jack Welch, well known for co-authoring *Winning: The Ultimate How-to Business Book*. Since Edison the business has grown to around US$650 billion in total assets with over 300,000 workers at time of writing.[82] Not to mention Edison's many innovations that helped build new industries and inspired other people to innovate to this day. His phonograph (like a sound recorder) alone gave rise to the audio recording, home entertainment, and music industries.

Most of what we find helpful today is thanks to folks having devoted their lives to what they believed in. George Washington risked his life many times for the independence of an infant United States government. Albert Einstein worked on his theory of relativity when others thought it was nuts, and Charles Darwin kept researching evolution his entire life.

Successful enterprises, once only the daydream of the founder, can grow to include many people working toward a common purpose, popularly in the form of a company, organization, or political movement. At the time of this writing, Apple employs nearly 115,000, Wal-Mart 2.2 million, and the U.S. government around 2.6 million people.[83-85]

Historians might argue the effect a person has on society, but what's closer to the truth is, if you have a light bulb in your home, that's "in part" thanks to Edison. Democratic government is "in part" thanks to Washington. That GPS on your phone is "in part" thanks to Einstein. We cannot honestly give each one of them all the recognition, since they had *assistance from many others*, many of whom went on to be inspired to innovate themselves.

Henry Ford worked for Thomas Edison, who encouraged him to make his engine. Innovator Nikola Tesla once worked in Edison's New York office, as explored by author Sean Patrick in *Nikola Tesla*. Edison once even said that Tesla was the hardest worker he had ever seen.[86] The young Edison himself worked for Western Union, which was co-founded by Ezra Cornell, himself having worked earlier for Samuel B. Morse, the maker of the telegraph.[87] When the purpose of an enterprise inspires its workers to then make their own purposes, society benefits most. A well-known example is the "free time" policy for workers which the company 3M started and which Google later took on. It gives employees free time to make their own purpose at work, which could then be funded by and made by the company.[88] Besides workers, we must not forget "stakeholders", the investors and suppliers, who give the money, materials, and services needed to make all these purposes possible.

Profit is the usual reason given for why people make their purpose, but the answer is not so black and white. To make profit, which mostly helps a purpose survive and live on, you need to first make more good for people than they already have. Good comes first, profit follows. Many of history's great makers (Plato, Leonardo Da Vinci, Isaac Newton) died without much money or the wish for more of it. Just knowing that they may have left something useful to the human race seemed enough for them. Maria Popova of brainpickings.com says it well: "To create wealth is not to give people what they want, but to help them figure out what to want by making sense of what is worth having."[89]

Society wins, not by what these people make in their pursuit (conscious or not) of the meaning of life, but also what they earn from it and give away. We've talked about the philanthropy of Bill Gates, thanks to his Microsoft fortune, but it may not be known that he's pledged to give nearly all of it away to charities when he dies. This is part of the "Giving Pledge," created by Gates and investor Warren Buffet, which at the time of writing has over 150 billionaires signed up and growing.[90] Such pledges can better promote giving back to the less well-off, rather than giving to fast-spending family members. Governments can encourage this by giving awards and titles to promote more giving. This comes at a relevant time. A recent Oxfam study showed that the wealth of the 85 richest people in the world is equal to the total wealth of half of the world's population. Around 3,500,000,000 people.[91] In the future, those uninterested to sign up for such pledges may be rejected by many for not giving back to the society that let them gain their wealth in the first place.

In the lead up to the 2012 U.S. presidential election, then president Barack Obama was criticized for saying, "You didn't build that," when talking about business owners.[92] Yet his point was that, if you've been successful, you didn't get there on your own, as society helped you *directly or indirectly*. Having fair laws, an unbiased justice system, and safety nets to help those who cannot help themselves brings out the best in more people. We can't dismiss the sad reality that a lot of people in many countries don't have the same opportunity to seek the greatest good for the greatest number. As journalist George Monbiot writes, "If wealth was the inevitable result of hard work and enterprise, every woman in Africa would be a millionaire."[93]

It's an obvious truth that if there are few services in society to provide for basic needs, like shelter, food, and hygiene, then there is *less free time* open to devote to the meaning of life. People in developed nations have more *opportunity* to seek the greatest good than those in developing nations. They're in the position to make what has not *existed* before in the entire world. Developing countries rarely can do that, and are forced into using *existing solutions* from developed countries to fix their problems.

This is one reason why, as adjunct professor Brad Keywell said, "We all have a moral responsibility to challenge ourselves and reach our highest potential."[94] Once we get outside of our comfortable bubble, we see that most people still live like the developed world itself did centuries ago. More than 3,000,000,000 people live on less than US$2.50 per day, 22,000 children die daily due to poverty, a quarter of all humanity lives without electricity, and over 1,000,000,000 people are unable to read, write, or even speak well.[95]

I know. Numbers can quickly make the horror seem distant. But try to put yourself in their shoes—which many of them don't even have. These people are someone's children, parents and friends. All have dreams and emotions. Yet they suffer more than some will ever have to. If you've never seen it before, a video on YouTube would show you. If these were *people you knew*, there would be no limit to what you'd do to help them.

If you advance the meaning of life you can, in part, assist in the removal of this misery. When we seek the greater good by what we make, we are able to help those who cannot help themselves. Knowing about this suffering, it's easy to see why some think that if we don't hold ourselves to a higher standard, we are failing not just ourselves but all of humanity. If you have a habit of defending what you do by saying, *"you only live once,"* just remember what it really means. A greedy accumulation of memories in your head, which you'll realize on your death bed mean nothing to the world or to you, as you *won't be alive to remember* them anyway.

Some, understandably, say we should focus more on helping the developing nations and not the developed. Let's not forget the fact that creating value for people in developed nations is likely to result in faster success, which can then be used to create value in developing nations. Bill Gates could not have earned his fortune if he had founded Microsoft in Africa, but today a lot of that fortune is going there. Yet we have something missing here. How do we know an impact is being made when we haven't explained what it is?

Measuring the Meaning

"When you can measure what you are speaking about, and express it in numbers, you know something about it. But when you cannot express it in numbers, your knowledge is of a meagre and unsatisfactory kind. It may be the beginning of knowledge, but you have scarcely in your thoughts advanced to the state of science."[96]
Lord Kelvin

Humans like to think there is something out there that would let us confirm the value of our existence. The criteria found in a meaning sentence is crucial for this reason. For us though, any attempt to measure needs a unit that is found in the real world, and not a fantasy of someone's mind. Only then can the meaning of life make better sense than just being a sentence.

Sciences like astronomy, meteorology, or geology work well as they are based on predictions which are seen repeatedly in the outside world. The same is needed for our meaning of life if it is to be able to show how everyday actions and historical events seek the meaning or do not.

Humans understand the world through the senses, it's the single standard that nearly no belief can deny. If we see a piece of furniture and know that the word "chair" describes it, we don't call it a "banana." Would you answer "yes" or "no" to the following question: "Am I reading at this moment?" If you answered "yes," then you're showing that you understand reality. The common reply that, "nothing can be known since everyone interprets things differently," quickly crumbles by using the word "nothing," which by definition, would also include the very sentence itself. We gather truth from fact, and fact comes from *observations in the real world that are agreed* to be so by others.

The way a courtroom works is much the same. Facts show what happened in the past. As former U.S. politician, Daniel Patrick Moynihan, said, "You are entitled to your own opinion but not your own facts."[97] What's mentioned above is what in philosophy jargon is called "epistemology," the definition of what is reality.

Say you want to grow the size of your biceps at the gym. To track your progress, you need to measure them often, using a tape. Or else you're guessing if they have grown or not. The ability to measure and test every guess has let us progress to where we are today. Ideally, a measurement should be so easy that any person can do it themselves. Our meaning, to seek the greatest good for the greatest number, has in its wording, a *measurement* other meanings lack. It's similar to what author of *Death by Black Hole* and scientist Neil deGrasse Tyson, said: "We're not who we say we are, we're not who we want to be—we are the sum of the influence and impact that we have, in our lives, on others…"[98]

It's true, we've not been very kind to subjective feelings so far. Given Ned's example, we hope we made the case that feelings can fool us. But changes in the real world, outside of our mind, can't. We're not saying that feelings don't have any use, they do. The most sought-after feeling is likely to be happiness, and it is important. Studies direct us to the fact that it best comes from seeking meaning. Feelings can also help push you towards what you most wish to change in the world. Next time, remember what makes you most *angry*, and then see how that same thing *affects other people* and how you can solve it for them. But if we choose to solve what we can't measure then no matter what we try it'll likely not make a difference, not even as a footnote in the pages of human history.

As shown earlier, it's hard to confirm that other "meanings of life" are working. Let's look at a common one: "Living for God." A catholic nun is likely to measure this differently than a cross wearing Italian mafia boss. It's the same with other meanings like, "to expand one's perception of the world" or "to know and master the world". They cannot be measured by anyone but the person experiencing them and each person likely will give a biased answer that suits them. Unlike a court room, we personally aren't going to be collecting evidence to prove how many people they say they are helping is true. It'd be simpler to give free hugs on the street, as we could easily video record to prove those accepting hugs got some value.

Only once a *real world criteria* is defined will the subjective monster be locked up in its prison. To find out how our meaning does that, we must break down the two parts of the sentence. The "greatest good," is the value given to others as a *result of our purpose*. Using Gates and Microsoft again we see the value they made came from products/services. This covers the "greatest good" part of the statement. The "greatest number" part is answered by the fact that billions of people the world over have been measurably impacted.

To be scientific and reduce our own human bias, when making our own estimates we should not add people we *personally know* into the "greatest number" total, as most friends and family will, out of kindness, praise whatever we give them. The strongest evidence comes from people *we don't know*, who show their approval with our purpose through a purchase, membership, sign-up, consumption, or something similar.

When the result of your purpose is adopted by a large and rising number of people in society, then we can start to agree that what you've made has *given value to them*. By doing this, it lets us connect with people we don't personally know. Any guess how many people you see every day? Depending on what you do, you may see hundreds or even thousands, yet you could never have enough time on earth to get to know all of them. There is a gap between you and them, "alienation" as some would call it. Most of these people become *instant memories* the moment you see them, your paths wont cross ever again. The religious are taught to love these neighbors, yet there are 7+ billion of them. The most practical way to help them is to give them something *they can use to better their own lives*. Indeed, our meaning of life may be for some believers the broadest most practical way of fulfilling the sacred biblical mandate given in John 15:13 "Greater love has no one than this: to lay down one's life for one's friends."

MONDAY 7AM: SAME TIME - SAME PLACE- SAME SUNKEN FACES...

WHY DO ALL THESE PEOPLE GOING TO WORK LOOK LIKE THEY'RE SUFFERING FROM SOME *DISEASE* ?

STRANGE, I SEE THESE SAME PEOPLE MORE THAN MY GRANDPARENTS, YET I DON'T INTERACT WITH *ANY* OF THEM.

Every day on her way to work, Kate sees the same people. These people mostly ignore one another. They appear tired and zombie-like. They are the walking dead, or more precisely, the *working dead*. Like cogs in a wheel, they don't seem to be living the meaning of life, but instead, living lives of quiet desperation.

We bridge this gap with others in the world by fulfilling a worthy purpose, which by its results gives value to those who use it, making their lives and society better off. This "greater good" we make can then be measured by *counting the number* of people impacted. Paul Graham, co-founder of start-up business program, Y Combinator, and author of *Hackers and Painters,* was onto this. "You can envision the wealth created by a start-up as a rectangle, where one side is the number of users and the other is how much you improve their lives."[99] Ben Silbermann, CEO of Pinterest says pretty much what we've talked about, "What would make me really happy is to… see someone that I don't know using something that I made, and have it be useful."[100]

Our measurement of how someone is seeking the meaning of life can be shown in the following:

**Millions of people affected
by the Innovation**

This "value meter" shows an estimated range, using reliable sources, of how many people have been impacted by a purpose. There's no place on the meter for other metrics that people often use to measure their "success"— no bank balance or number of sports cars collected. Our reason for measuring "millions" in our meter is that it matches the ambition found in our verbal meaning of life, *"to seek the greatest good for the greatest number."* Such a large number is not used to scare you but to encourage you to be ambitious regarding how big your impact can be.

Below, let's look at value meters of some people through history, some known and unknown.

WHO	PURPOSE AND ITS RESULTS	PEOPLE AFFECTED
Marie Curie	Discovered radium, leading to x-rays	1-2 Billion people[101]

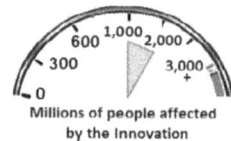

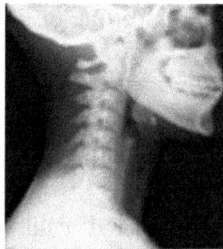

**Millions of people affected
by the Innovation**

*Source: nobel.se website, public
domain // Jmarchn*

Karl Landsteiner

Source: Wikimedia Commons,
public domain //Magnus
Manske

Discovered blood types
(A, B, AB, O), leading to
safe blood transfusions

1-1.2+ Billion
people[102-103]

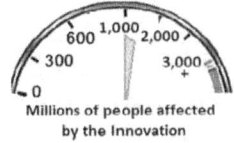

Millions of people affected
by the Innovation

Steve Jobs

Source: www.photoree.com,
Creative Commons
Attribution License //Rama

Co-founder and CEO of
Apple, NeXT, Pixar

1.5-2 Billion people+[104]

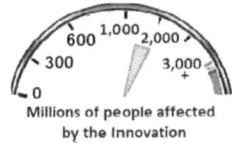

Millions of people affected
by the Innovation

Mark Zuckerberg

Source: james5smith, Creative
Commons Attribution License
//munhuu94

Co-founder and CEO of
Facebook

1-1.5 Billion people+[105]

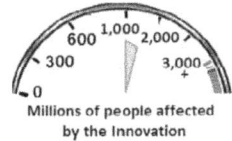

Millions of people affected
by the Innovation

Paulo Coehlo

Source: Marcello Casal Jr./ABr, Creative Commons Attribution License //Lin Christensen

Author of over 30 books, many bestsellers

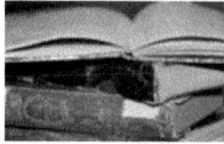

210 million people[106]

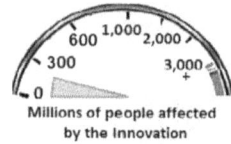

Millions of people affected
by the Innovation

YOU!

(Write ideas for your purpose)

_____

_____

_____

_____

_____

Like others, you start off small, and by improving your purpose, more people can be impacted by it.

Millions of people affected
by the Innovation

As we said earlier, many who've made a large impact didn't need to *earn much profit or financial success*, like Curie and Landsteiner, to have the impact they had. We will show near this books end how you can try tilting the balance in your life so to begin work on your own purpose. Now again, don't let the huge impact numbers discourage you. Sure, it may seem that we're setting the bar very high, but each of these people didn't act alone. Each of them organized others to help them build their purpose, and they all built off the work of those in the past.

Take Mark Zuckerberg, for instance. He'd obviously have been unable to build Facebook had Tim Berners-Lee and others not built the foundational tools for the Internet. Imagine if former U.S. vice president Al Gore, later to be presenter of *An Inconvenient Truth,* had not campaigned with his team to pass legislation opening the Internet for commercial use in the early 90's. The takeaway here is, if you seek the greatest good through your purpose, and that touches others, even just a few dozen, then it's possible that those few may be inspired to build their own purposes in part due to your example.

> **Q.** Estimate how many people you have given value to up till now?
>
> **A.**

Purposes today are mostly formed around an enterprise, such as a company, non-profit organization, movement, or government department. In the legal jargon, all these are "entities" as they are owned or managed by a person or group of people. For simplicity we'll refer to them all as "enterprises" or sometimes as "companies." Setting up such an "enterprise" broadens the number of people impacted by your purpose as we break it down below.

1. ADOPTERS – People who've opted to use the innovation. Customers, users, members etc.
2. EMPLOYEES – People employed to make it. This includes suppliers etc.
3. SHARE/STAKE-HOLDERS – People who've invested, and anyone else who has assisted.

Most of those above are not forced but are voluntarily part of your purpose and can cut their connection to it at anytime. Like selling off shares, quitting their jobs, or not using your product. If they don't, it's good evidence that your enterprise is giving value to them.

If your purpose say is a website, its impact is mostly measured by the number of "active users" it has. A retail product's impact would be the total number of units sold. The impact of a movie would be seen by ticket sales, purchases, downloads, illegal downloads, and other types of viewership, like TV broadcasts. As you spread your purpose it's likely more people are impacted than you think. Parents end up watching a TV show, or using a new tech device because their children are fans of it.

Steve Jobs is a well know example of the above who built several enterprises by which he was able to touch a large number of people. From the Academy Award-winning animation studio "Pixar," to the computer and software maker "Next," to his most well-known enterprise, "Apple." The Apple iTunes store alone houses over 800 million accounts and is growing daily.[107]

As with many parts of life, an opposite exists. There are also those who have destroyed value for many people.

Timothy McVeigh

*Source: FBI Lab forensic
artist, Public domain*

Carrying out the
Oklahoma City bombing

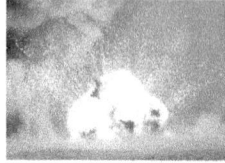

168 people killed and
600+ injured[108]

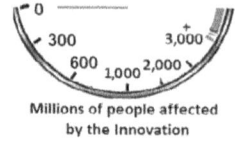

Millions of people affected
by the Innovation

Joseph Stalin

*Source: Wikipedia, Public
domain //jgaray*

USSR, a police state.
Ignorance in WW2 caused
huge loss of life

24 million estimated
killed. Hundreds[109] of
millions impacted

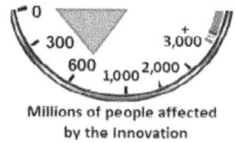

Millions of people affected
by the Innovation

Adolf Hitler

*Source: Wikipedia, Public
domain // fornax*

Nazi Germany, a police
state. Led the world into
WW2

48 million estimated
killed. Hundreds of
millions impacted[110]

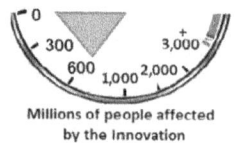

Millions of people affected
by the Innovation

In light of the dark side above, one might think that Twitter leads to more suicides as bullies can easily attack others, but Twitter is not to blame here. Would you *blame the postal service* for the death of a lady who inhaled poisonous anthrax when opening a letter? The destruction of value seen in the actions of McVeigh, Stalin, and Hitler are due to evidence of their direct actions which led to murder and suffering on a mass scale.

Simplicity in the value meter is helpful but more details can assist, if say we need to measure complex historical figures. Check out the expanded value chart after you've read the book as it will then make better sense to you. Send a quick email vitojgrigorov@gmail.com or go to www.prosperism.org to get the expanded value chart and all other bonus material.

Pt. 4 BUILDINGS OF LOST DREAMS

THE PURPOSE OF LIFE
What you do to seek the meaning

Fearful of anyone stepping beyond his wide shadow, Joe is angry that Kate worked on the software while she was on the clock for her usual work.

Many people will see their jobs as the main way they can impact society, so it becomes to them their purpose by default. Yet, most work for their weekly wages under a boss of some kind, who can *restrain their creative freedom*. This mostly will lower the number of people they can impact. What if they quit and pushed ahead with their own purpose? It's unlikely that taking the chance would lead to even less people impacted. More lottery tickets bought lead to more chances of winning, and the same goes here. As more people take the challenge, *the chance* of more impact increases overall. Sure, not everyone will end up touching billions of people in their lives, but if hundreds of thousands or millions of people try to together, they can benefit billions of people when their collective impacts are combined.

You may now be thinking what 19th century Russian novelist Leo Tolstoy did when he said, "Is there any meaning in my life that will not be annihilated by the inevitability of death?"[111] Or in other words he may have asked what we did in the introduction, "Who'll care in 100 years?" We may not think it, but 99% of what we do and worry over won't matter in a century's time. Yet Tolstoy's books are cared about to this day, tens of millions have read and continue to read and be moved by them. His skull may crack a smile in seeing that he lives on today through that purpose. Without leaving something useful for others, in a hundred years after your death, there will be little proof that you even lived on this planet and likely no one alive bothering to know. Think about it... besides your grave, government records, and some buried family photos and videos, *it's as though you never existed at all.* So, we must not be afraid to be honest with ourselves and ask, "As my time is short, what can I make now that has the best chance of leaving behind the greatest good for the greatest number?" Though extreme it may seem, we can now see why many in history say they'd die for what it is they are making. As what they're making is the proof of their existence on this earth.

Such questions push you to seek what's broad and most impactful like a cure for cancer, a cheaper way to grow food to feed the world, or a faster way for poor children to learn with a software app. But let's be clear, nearly every person starts making their impact on a small scale, with larger scale impact likely to come later. And even if it doesn't, we celebrate each person's attempt to give value to others, for when we multiply it, then everyone is a part of a shared broader impact.

Solving the Reverse of Life and Meaning: Suicide

You may now be more convinced by what's in this chapter, but still you feel like something is missing? Same here, and it comes down to this: We can best find the answer to a question when we explore its reverse. The opposite of life, and so of the meaning of life on a personal level.... is suicide. It's the most self-destructive action a person can take against themselves for it deletes them from this earth. Statistics from WHO (World Health Organisation) show that close to a million people do this yearly worldwide with tens of millions attempting it, but surviving. It's likely over a hundred million living people have tried taking their life at least once in their past. Choosing to take one's life is the clearest example of the failure to answer, "For what reason do I live?" It's the meaning of life that provides that answer and as a result decreases suicide, yet how does seeking the greatest good for the greatest number pull it off?

Psychologist Abraham Maslow wrote, "Peak experiences can make life worthwhile by their occasional occurrence. They give meaning to life itself. They prove it to be worthwhile. To say this in a negative way, I would guess that peak experiences help to prevent suicide." Later on, psychologist Mihaly Csikszentmihalyi would relabel these peak experiences as "flow". Whatever the name, these experiences are the most personal to someone who is on the path to fulfilling the meaning. Steve Kotler explored in *The Rise of Superman* how Csikszentmihalyi discovered in his studies that "the happiest people on earth, the ones who felt their lives had the most meaning, were those who had the most peak experiences". It was not by chance either that "they didn't just have the most peak experiences; they had devoted their lives to having these experiences". And no, this did not mean popping pills at a rave party, but rather, as Csikszentmihalyi wrote, these peaks "didn't come when they were relaxing, when they were taking drugs or alcohol, or when they were consuming the expensive privileges of wealth. Rather, it often involved painful, risky, difficult activities that stretched the person's capacity and involved an element of novelty and discovery."

It's in the act of innovating that we find this effect, when our body and mind are fully absorbed in making something for the outside world using our inner creativity. While we're doing this, our mind is unable to think negative thoughts, for it's on constant alert for the next idea to pop up to help improve our innovation. Remember the times when you've had those "aha" moments? They give us a joy like we used to have as kids, when we found something unique, a "treasure" buried under the ground. What if you had more of these moments each day? Innovating captivates our mind in the most natural and human ways by immersing us in the action that separated us from all other species.

As a study titled *Not Just a Hobby* points out, creative hobbies help "reduce anxiety and depression rates". Why could this be? By attempting to innovate, which is making something new with your entire self absorbed in it, is by definition the opposite of boredom which has long been shown to be linked to suicide. This was explored in *Boredom*, a documentary by Albert Nerenberg, while social psychologist Roy F. Baumeister wrote that "suicidal people resemble acutely bored people" in his classic paper *Suicide as Escape from Self.*

So what's the collected result of all the research to date? It was distraction that was found to be key in reducing the risk of suicide, as explored in a recent study titled *What Interrupts Suicide Attempts in Men.* In other words, do something besides thinking about your boredom. And what's the most impactful and rewarding way of doing something? It's innovating! Further, once we also realise that innovating is the unique human function, and that it fulfils the meaning of life, it then takes on an even greater (if not the greatest) importance in the life of someone who before was on the edge of falling off the cliff.

If we can reduce suicide and so cut the root of the problem first we can eliminate years of damage and decay building up from those early warning signs like moodiness, anxiety, panic attacks, etc. Instead of moving from bad to worse, we fix the worse and the bad is solved as a result.

We've only scratched the surface of the meaning of life, focusing largely on the "greatest number." For us to fully grasp our meaning, we need to dig deeper into what makes the "greatest good".

Chapter Summary

\#   **Free time is the definition of life. This refers to the amount of time you have to do what you want with few or no distractions.**

\#   **The signs of those missing meaning in their life are:**

1. Depression and all other related illnesses.
2. Addictions, neuroticism, and materialistic behavior.
3. Loss of a healthy and longer life.

\#   **Criteria for a sentence to best describe the meaning involves:**

1. PURSUIT: Makes clear the end goal that all purposes should seek
2. EVIDENCE: Points to real-world evidence, rather than a person's opinion

3. FINAL: Uses words such as "greatest" to make its point final and never-ending

4. BROAD: Includes as many people as possible in the "greatest number"

5. FUNCTION: Implies by its criteria the human function to innovate

6. CRITERIA: Gives us a way of measuring fulfillment of the meaning

\# Aristotle's function question asks, "What is the broadest thing that humans do best?" When we compare humans to all other species, we see that innovation is what most sets us apart. To "innovate" is a uniquely human function.

\# The broadest way a person can innovate is with a purpose that seeks "the greatest good for the greatest number."

\# It's not your opinion which shows if you're seeking the meaning of life, but the *real-world impact* you have on others, which is seen by others using the result of your purpose.

\# A purpose can live long after the death of whoever built it to continue to benefit people.

\# Unlike other meanings, we can see a person progress in seeking the meaning of life through the value meter. The top 3 groups of people impacted are "adopters," "employees," and "shareholders."

CHAPTER TWO

Who Knows What Is Good?

"All sciences must, from now on, prepare the way for the future work of the philosopher: this work being understood to mean that the philosopher has to solve the problem of values and that he has to decide the rank order of values."[1]
Friedrich Nietzsche (*On the Genealogy of Morality*)

"The question of value is fundamental. Almost every speculation respecting the economical interests of a society thus constituted implies some theory of value; the smallest error on that subject infects with corresponding error all our other conclusions, and anything vague or misty in our conception of it creates confusion and uncertainty in everything else."[2]
John Stuart Mill (*Principles of Political Economy*)

Why do you check your mailbox and inbox? Seriously, why do you do it? Let's ask "why" long enough to see if we can come close to the truth.

Q: Why do it?
A: To see who's trying to get in contact with me.

Q: Why does that matter?
A: Say I missed paying a bill. It could be bad.

Q: Why could it be bad?
A: The power could be shut off and who knows I may go to court if it continues.

Q: Why is this bad?
A: Isn't it obvious!? *(Aggravated)* How would we survive without electricity? How would my kids eat if I was put in jail?…What pills are you taking to ask such stupid questions?

The dead end we reach offers a clear answer. In this case, we check our mail to *survive*. More "why?" questions won't go deeper. If we didn't want to live, we'd likely have found a way to be dead by now. Survival is the *bedrock of everything else*. Death melts any and all future actions into the air.

We are all born with an urge to survive. If we are not suicidal, we will do almost anything to stay alive. Most of us wouldn't bite our tongue off, jump off a cliff, or stab ourselves. But people with no meaning have done those things. This is why the theory that humans seek pleasure and avoid pain *does not stack up*.

Frankl writes, "Man's main concern is not to gain pleasure or to avoid pain, but rather to see a meaning in his life."[3] The pain of travelling to work does not result in everyone quitting. The pain of giving birth doesn't stop all mothers from having more than one child. The pain that happens in sport doesn't make sports less popular.

Survival is the source of "value". We don't talk about it that way, but instead we make value unclear. Voters say that politicians don't value their rights and freedoms. A partner in a marriage says that the other doesn't value their opinions. Stock market analysts advise buying stock in companies that are more valuable. What happens if we put all the above under repeated "why" questions, as we did with the mail example? We always end up with "survival" as the end point of all these supposed "values".

For most people and most dictionaries, the words "good" and "value" are nearly the same. Both refer generally to that which is of "the importance, worth, or usefulness of something." For us here, value is the "good" in our meaning sentence "the greatest good for the greatest number." So, let's find out what this word is all about.

Abraham Maslow, psychologist and author of a *Theory of Human Motivation* wrote that all humans need a value system. Without it, our psychological state would be damaged.[4] Yet it doesn't help that different professions see "value" in different ways. Psychologists may think it's "well-being." Accountants may think it's "money." Economists speak of "utility."

David Ricardo, a 19th century economist, put it this way: "From no source do so many errors, and so much difference of opinion in the science of political economy proceed, as from the vague ideas which are attached to the word 'value.'"[5] Economist Adam Smith, as seen by Russ Roberts in *How Adam Smith Can Change Your Life* shows an ability to find answers to tough questions. To explain value, Smith asked why diamonds are valued more highly than water.[6] We cannot live a week without water, but most of us go our entire lives without owning diamonds, however water is much more common than diamonds. It's nearly unlimited in supply and so it's free. Diamonds are not, thanks in part to diamond company monopolies. Yet just a bag of them can be exchanged for an amount of *money some can live off for a lifetime*. Have you ever thrown out jewelry when cleaning your home? Almost no one does, but we do throw out everything else.

The natural sciences (biology, physics, geology… etc.) rely on the solid foundation of evolutionary theory. No similar theory for social sciences (history, psychology, economics… etc.) exists that can give decent explanations. Many hoped it would be the reliable sounding "Standard Social Science Model" (SSSM), yet even that has been shown to have huge holes. Without agreeing on value, we see little common focus. Say your friend lends you $100. A psychologist may say that your friend wants to be loved to make up for their childhood loneliness. An anthropologist may say that lending money is a common tradition in your society. An economist may say that your friend was driven by greed to earn interest or a future favor from you. One seemingly simple act, but many possible explanations.

To find value, we need to first find something social sciences agree on: the existence of human actions. This may sound obvious. Actions, or what we humans do in the real world is what lets value exist. If all humans froze into statues right now, all value would vanish. Natural sciences study the actions of nature. Social sciences study human action. What exactly are "actions?" Let's break it down.

What Are Actions?

i. The foundation on which history is built*

"The preamble of thought, the transition through which it passes from the unconscious to the conscious, is action."
Ralph Waldo Emerson (*The Essential Writings of Ralph Waldo Emerson*)

Human history shows never-ending change which needs action to take place, be seen and recorded. By the way, the * above means that this will pop up and be explored later in the book.

We will use the word "action" broadly to cover "behaviors," "habits," "traits," "characteristics," "opportunities" and other similar words. Anything concerning movements of the human body.

Simply, an "action" is "doing something." Every single second, from the moment of conception until our death, we are involved in some sort of action. Below we define "actions" and how they will be used in this book.

1. **MOVEMENT**
    Actions refer only to the movements of the human body that can be observed by others through the senses. We must be able to see, feel, hear, touch, smell, or taste it for it to be an action. Take smoking, for example. It's an action. When we smoke, we move a cigarette, or similar object, to our mouth and inhale smoke into our body. The cigarette is clearly influencing these movements. It is not an action itself. It is an object. The things we use offer us a range of different actions. The more things there are, the more actions are open to us, and so we say more "opportunities" exist. Some things give us actions we never had before. Take the ultra-sound machine. It shows a baby's actions in the womb. A century ago this would have been unheard of. Remember, thoughts are not actions. They cannot be observed by another person until new technology pops up letting us mindread. We can glimpse the thoughts of others by their actions, but we can't know their thoughts for certain.

2. **DELIBERATE**
    Actions are under your control. We *don't include actions which are biological reflexes* like breathing, sweating, sneezing, sleeping, or what you do in the restroom.

3. **DEGREES**
    Actions have degrees of detail. They are, at the same time, part of a set of smaller and larger actions. Take the action of running. In that action, there are dozens of other actions. The runner sweats into their clothes. They push their shoes off the ground. They turn to follow a path or cross a street. Gather a group of runners doing this, and you have a larger action, a marathon.

Pt. 5 BUILDINGS OF LOST DREAMS

ACTIONS
Movements that you can control

Joe doesn't seem to have much control over his actions. He's always been this way, but his excuse lately is that it's hard managing his terrible workers.

With the explanation above, we see *it's in our actions* that value can first be seen. Value is linked to our survival. Question is, which actions support life and which don't? Humans mostly act in ways to *grow and extend* life and avoid actions that will *weaken and destroy* it. But we don't always know the effect our actions, or those of others, will have on us or them.

A friend of yours who is drinking alcohol at a club on a night out may think that they're just relaxing, and that this is good for their health after a tiresome week. However, science has shown that such drinking is hurting their health. Also, they are in a spot where they are 90% more likely to be robbed than if they went across the street. Numbers like these help us choose which actions to take in different areas of our life. Sam Harris, author of *Waking Up* and *The End of Faith*, explores in his other work, *The Moral Landscape*, how science may soon show how we can bring about more well-being much like it does now with finding the cause and cure for diseases. Lee McIntyre's book, *Dark Ages: A Case for a Science of Human Behavior*, gives a strong reply to those doubting that a single approach to human behavior is possible. Many think it's dangerous. We can't deny that scientists can also be blinded, contributing to some of the worst horrors in human history. It's for this reason that new ideas need to be tested many times to find the closest path to truth, rather than being believed blindly. It's by this method that many societies, after a long and bloody process of trial and error, made laws to stop certain human actions. Why? Because *most illegal actions weaken and destroy human life* while most *legal actions do the reverse.* Imagine if you lived in a society where neighbors were murdered weekly, being a robber was the most common job, and arguments were decided with bullets. Such an existence is one step above being suicidal for the dangerous conditions prevent a person from living and fulfilling the meaning.

Robert Skidelsky, a British economist and co-author of *How Much Is Enough?* has a sad forecast, that if we are not "under the control of an objective concept of the good. Unless that control is achieved, we are a doomed civilization."[8] Nazi Germany and the USSR showed how different concepts of value decide the future of a nation and affect the larger world. Novelist Albert Camus wrote, "Belief in the meaning of life always implies a scale of values,"[9] whereas author of *The Inevitable*, Kevin Kelly, writes that "The urge for self-preservation, self-extension, and self-growth is the natural state of any living thing."[10] Philosopher John Ruskin noted long ago what we're repeating here, saying that which is "truly valuable... is that which leads to life with its whole strength. In proportion, as it does not lead to life... it is less valuable". Indeed, the same thought was known as natural law in medieval times and was considered obvious by such thinkers as the influential theologian St Thomas Aquinas.[11]

Even cells act like this. Scientists have long seen this pattern in human cells in a Petri dish. The cells always move away from poison endangering their existence, but move toward nutrients that are beneficial to survival.[12]

So, what does all this mean in practical terms? We have the value meter for the "greatest number." What do we use to measure the "greatest good?"

Life Expectancy is the Measure of Value

"Try not to become a man of success, but a man of value."[13]
Albert Einstein

If survival drives our actions, the most obvious measure of survival humans have come up with is life expectancy.

In the last 100 years, human life expectancy has more than doubled. The global average a century ago was 31 years; now it's 71 years.[14] It's hard for anyone, unless they're suicidal, to say this is not good.

Life expectancy is easy to see in the real world, unlike other measurements. Just pick a time period. Add up all the ages at death. Then divide them by the total number of people who died. The life expectancy number you get is likely a reflection of the combined lifetime actions of those people in the area or country they live in.

With it we can accurately compare groups of people with one another with none of the foggy bias of those subjective slippery questionnaires asking, "How happy are you?" It's obvious, but easily forgotten, that nations with longer life expectancies have people with healthier lives. Our age can only increase if we cure or slow down disease, and lessen wear and tear on the body, and yes that includes our mind as it's within our body. Some may like to point out that longer life is pointless if you live unhealthily with a disease. These are exceptions, not the rule. For it to be the rule then all who have ill health would have had to turn to suicide. The fact they don't shows that they consider their life is still worth living. It is why life expectancy is the most commonly used measure of health we have so far.

Beneath the statistics, you may not know that some people with disease may be better off than you think. Why? They may have a purpose to fulfil the meaning of life, or even the hope that a cure may pop up soon to help them. None of us have the same life, but it's broadly agreed that longer life is encouraged by nearly all otherwise more people would be killing themselves. By staying alive, in even the most horrible situations, people show us that they agree that *longer life is better than shorter*. They hope the future will be better. For this and other reasons in this book, we'll disagree

with Peter Singer, philosopher and author of *The Most Good You Can Do.*
His view is that parents should abort a child which has physical and mental
disease. Imagine if 20 years after aborting medicine had improved to the
point that a cure had now been found for the exact problem the parents had
aborted their child over. Finding this out would crush them. Also, if all
parents abort, then no problem would exist to push science to innovate and
find a cure, which as it happens, can spill over to cure other diseases also.

Today many poor nations still only have life expectancies of around 30
years. Developed nations have more than double that. Populations with low
life expectancies mostly have high infant mortality rates. 100 infant deaths
per 1000 births usually means that 1 in 10 die before their 5th birthday. This
lowers the nations' life expectancies dramatically. A life expectancy of 30 years
does not mean that no one lives past 30 in that country, but it does mean
that your chances of a long life as a newborn baby are lowered as you may
die following birth or soon after. Most developed nations have fewer than
10 infant deaths per 1000 births due to better medicine and technology.

Let's take a look at how life expectancy has changed over time.

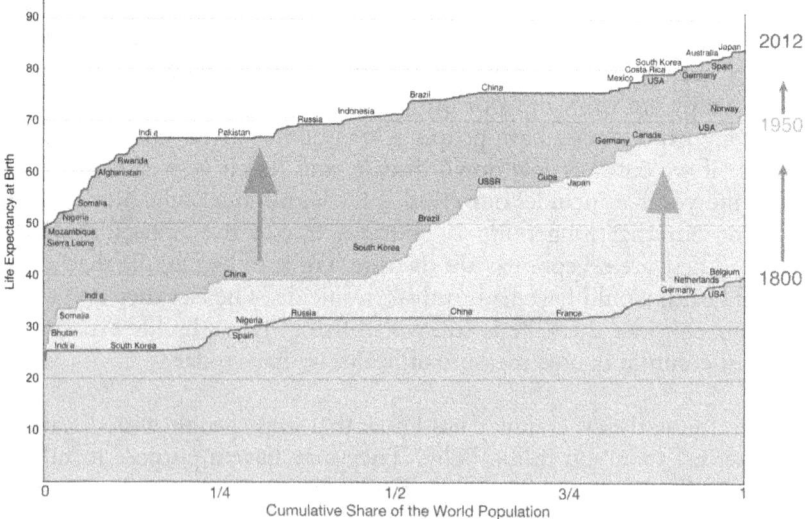

Life Expectancy of the World Population in 1800, 1950 and 2012
Countries are ordered along the x-axis ascending by the life expectancy of the population.

Source: maxroser.com, Creative Commons

Better medical technology leads to the most obvious changes in life expectancy, but so do simple choices such as what you eat, listen to, or read. Life insurance companies can better estimate your risk of death the more they know about you. Take smoking, for example. When we sign up for life insurance, we check a box asking if we smoke or not. The evidence is clear up to today that smoking shrinks life expectancy. When friends smoke near you, called second-hand smoking, it has nearly the same effect. Drinking alcohol has similar effects. In Russia, alcohol is linked to a shocking number of deaths. 25% of male citizens die before age 55, and the average life expectancy is just 64 years for men.[15] Far lower than 79 years for men in the U.K, and 80 years in Australia.[16,17]

Clearly, smoking and drinking affect our life expectancy. It was not so long ago that smoking was thought of as harmless. We now know better today, and the same may happen for *so many other things we do* as science moves onwards. Watching violent films, listening to degrading songs, or just staring at photo shopped plastic people on the screen may affect our life expectancy more than we know. Sound strange? Insurance policy checklists today include smoking, and enough evidence may soon cause them to include other questions about how long you watch TV, what websites you visit, how often you read, and factor all these and more into a life expectancy estimate. For example, reading books lowers stress levels by 68% and cuts the risk of depression by 50%.[18]

Could an app calculate this? Perhaps, when enough studies have been completed. A life expectancy clock could show us the average life expectancy result of any action we type into it. Data from the app could help actuaries and statisticians analyze the life expectancy of each person in more detail. Smart clothing that checks your momentary body signals already exists and is being improved. It could check stress levels, emotional moods and the heart rate caused by each action on millions of people and average out the results. We might get a text message from software in our clothes telling us to take deeper breaths or drink some water to lower our heart rate. Such advances are likely to lead to a rise in life expectancy over time.[19]

Life Expectancy Clock

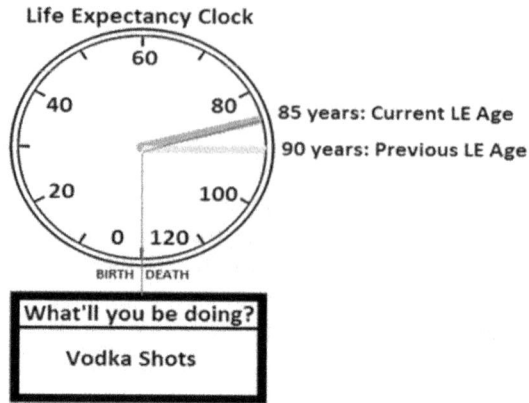

85 years: Current LE Age

90 years: Previous LE Age

What'll you be doing?
Vodka Shots

You may be trading those vodka shots at the New Year's party for 5 years of your life.

What about genetics? Science has shown that for most people, only a small fraction of life expectancy is set by genetics. For most of us it's *our combined actions* which determine how long we live.[20]

If we know and seek the meaning of life, it follows that each action of ours will be filtered through it so as to best achieve it. If actions don't follow our meaning of life, then we'll likely lower our life expectancy. How so?

The Four Value Factors of Life

ii. Criteria for Selection*

*"It's not about winning or losing;
it's about doing something that's valuable."*[21]
Mark Zuckerberg

Do you track the amount of time you spend on your phone? Or budget your money? Maybe you try to eat healthily or do puzzles to keep your mind sharp?

Actions, or lack of them, show how we adapt to life to best survive. Life expectancy is how we measure the sum of our actions. So what is it about actions that affect how long we live?

The answer is what we call "value factors." They also show us why we, consciously or not, do certain things and not others. The value factors apply to all actions on every degree, big or small. Those at home, school, business, politics, military, everywhere. The action of your reading right now and the action of army generals deciding to go to war all fall *under the same value factors.* Sound ambitious? Let's see if we can pull it off.

Below, we've defined each factor broadly to save space. We've given some examples to show you how to apply each of them to situations in your life. It's a flexible not a rigid guide, as we're dealing with areas of life that can change based on new information and discoveries as time ticks on.

Be aware, we're going to use some very exact terms below to define these value factors.

1st Factor: HEALTH

What is it exactly?

Health is when the body functions with *ease*, yes that includes the mind as it's within the body. We move and get what we need done with the least physical effort and mental energy.

How does it affect your actions?

Ever had food poisoning? You were likely unable to do much the next day. Or have you been in an accident? Better health leads to *less actions* needed to get a result, while worse health leads to more actions.

Here are some examples:

- Melinda, a neighbor of Kate's, injured her legs in a car accident. She can do all the things she once did, but it takes more effort, and more actions to do so. Driving, showering, or walking the stairs now demand that she move her legs carefully. Sure, we have technology to lessen some of Melinda's new challenges. However, no solution yet takes away the fact that she must now perform more actions than before.

- Joe likes to drink and smoke. He once could easily remember names, but not anymore. He could sleep without waking up coughing, but that's in the past. He's heard that drinking and smoking damages brain cells and leads to lung cancer, but he still continues puffing.[22]

- Kate's group is doing accounting work for a mobile phone company which is building a new cellular tower. However, studies have shown that the tower could lead to disease for those who live nearby, negatively affecting their health.

Questions you can ask:

- What's the healthiest action?

- How does this action affect my health now? And into the future?

- Will this action affect the health of others? Who are they... friends, family, co-workers, the population?

- Where can I learn more about how this action will affect my and/or others health?

2nd Factor: INTELLIGENCE

What is it exactly?

Intelligence is our ability to *choose* what actions to seek and what motions our body will perform. We do this by understanding information collected with our senses and use reason to pick out what we need. The less thinking (actions in our mind as brain scans show) needed to get a result, the more we can use our mind to focus on other things.

When we have better quality information, we are more likely to make *better* choices. The amount of information we deal with is called "cognitive load."[23] Our minds only have *so much* processing power. When we fill our minds with too much worthless information, we become overwhelmed, holding it all like a juggler given more balls than they can handle. Memory is most at risk from this. With enough distractions, we can forget important information from the past, which would've helped us with our present choices. Distractions lead to "switching costs". When we switch back and forth between actions, we do *a little worse* at all of them. Generally, the fewer distractions, the better our decisions will be. It's little surprise we get ideas when showering, as for most people it's the only time they're free from random distractions.

How does it affect your actions?

Remember a time when you could not understand why someone did what they did? Or maybe you were surprised when you reacted by shouting at someone?

- Kate doesn't want her dog, Benny, to sleep under her chin at night. She worries it may cause her to get fleas from him. Yet one morning she wakes up with him under her chin. She is shocked. How did it happen? She realizes that she got caught up thinking about work the night before. She forgot to set him aside.

- Joe is angry. He is distracted by drilling on the floor below. He hasn't thought about putting in earplugs. If he had, he'd block out the sound. He would have *one less thing* to think about.

- Take any situation. Add some heat, noise, bad smell, and visual distractions and you have a recipe for tragedy. Your mind is distracted. It must perform more actions to keep focus. People who want results try to avoid distractions. The sound of text messages, email notifications or the thinking up of random thoughts. Studies show that making lots of tiny choices lowers our self-control.[24] Even unread email can have an impact. In one study, workers with just one unread email were so distracted by it that their effective IQ dropped 10 points.[25]

Questions you can ask:

- Can this be done more intelligently?

- How can I remove all these distractions?

- Am I making the best choice given what I know right now?

- Can I find information that might improve my choices?

3rd Factor: TIME

What is it exactly?

Time is how we measure change and relate it to our lives. It's one of the most universally used practical measures humans have come up with. Ticking away everywhere worldwide.

How does it affect your actions?

Each action we choose affects our short time on earth. We prefer actions that get us the result we want in *less time*.

- Kate goes with Benny to the park each day. This takes about 30 minutes. Kate does this after work. By doing this, she shrinks the time she can spend at the gym.

- Given how little free time we have, we often try to find shortcuts. Joe spends money hiring a cook and maid for his home.

- Enterprises which offer time-saving products and services are in demand. Email can save you months of time due to the speed of sending and receiving. Paper mail would do the opposite.

Questions you can ask:

- Can this be done faster?

- Do my actions take more time than the results are worth?

- Could I get the same result if I spent less time on them?

- If aiming at a long-term goal figure out how much time per day you should devote to it?

4th Factor: MONEY

What is it?

Freedom to choose one action over another is what this factor is all about. Money is how humans have come to do this by trading almost everything.

How does it affect your actions?

Many actions depend on money. With money, we can use the latest smartphone. We can live in a safer place. We can get healthcare that heals us faster. Without money, all these actions aren't in reach, or if they are they demand more actions from us, more hours working to afford their cost.

- Kate earns money from her job. It lets her pay for other things in life. Like owning Benny and taking him to the park. Even that action costs money. Going to the park every day causes wear and tear on her shoes and Benny's leash. Kate could instead stay to work overtime, but by walking Benny she is choosing to sacrifice money, just like she sacrifices not spending more time in the gym.

- Most seek to save money where it makes sense to do so. Joe likes bargains, but buying the cheapest electronics means they mostly stop working sooner, or if it's cheap food it's likely bad for his health.

- Like most businesses, the cafe near you may seek to lower its prices. So, if they can buy machines to lower the cost to make their food, they can pass on this saving to you.

Questions you can ask:

- Can what I do be done cheaper?

- How much money does the action cost me?

- Could a cheaper action give me the result I want?

- Would delaying the buying of the item lead to a drop in its cost and a saving for me?

All above factors can be mixed in useful ways. With them, we can rate which actions are best in different situations, both for ourselves and for others. It'd be great to have a way to know we've reviewed each action from each angle, but not all questionnaires out there let this be done. One way of getting there is the personal value test table below, which like its name suggests is best used for personal situations. You won't see it popping up later in the book, as our tests later on will be impersonal, as they try to find broad facts not personal opinions. Both tests use the same principles. Below we see that each factor is scored out of +/-10 points. In each box, you can choose to explain the reason for your score, which helps you to explore your thinking. Put in your own time dates for the 3 periods at the top. Once done, add up the scores on the three vertical time period (short, medium, long) columns. In the bottom rightmost column, you can average out each value factor score to get a more accurate picture. Below the graph, we further explain the filtering steps to keep in mind when scoring each factor. The table down here is an example in action, with manager Joe testing if it's worth using a new product to see if it will help him lose weight. Send a quick email to vitojgrigorov@gmail.com or go to www.prosperism.org and we'll send you this graph and other bonus material.

Q. DRINKING SHAKES *INSTEAD* OF PAST DIET

	SHORT (in 4 weeks)	MEDIUM (in 2 months)	LONG (in 6 months)	Total Score
MONEY	−8 I'll lose money upfront but it may be worth it in the end.	4 If it works, then I'll stop paying for that personal trainer.	4 But hold on, at this point can't I learn to just eat healthy, and stop spending my money on it?	
HEALTH	1 It's like there's a multivitamin in each shake!	4 But why such a great taste? Maybe it has preservatives?	4 Will I become addicted to it forever?	
TIME	2 I save time not needing to buy or make my meals.	3 I've got more time to do other things.	4 But will I spend more time later with doctors to cure my addiction?	
INTELLI-GENCE	2 It's pretty easy to use.	1 But will I forget how to cook?	−1 Will I start thinking about drinking it all the time?	
Period totals	= −3	= 12	= 11	20/3 = +6.66

= VALUE CREATIVE ACTION

Overall, Joe's scores point to the probability of the action being positive. Below, the above scores are put into an easy to see visual graph.

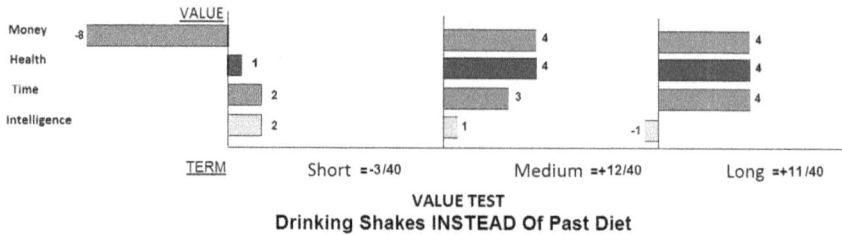

VALUE TEST
Drinking Shakes INSTEAD Of Past Diet

The 9 steps below will help us filter and point score each factor so we can run any action past it.

1. **QUESTION** – WHICH ACTION IS BEST?

It's the foundation of all that you do next, so it's best to word this question as accurately as you can. You're mostly comparing two actions, one against another. The word "instead" is the divider of these two actions. Adding more than two actions is confusing, so it's best to make the comparison to either do the action or not to do it. For Joe, it's drinking shakes or sticking to his current diet. Joe knows he's way overweight. So, he tries out the "shake the fat" milkshake product he saw on TV. Joe loves the taste and spends a lot of money on them monthly. He drops a few pounds right away and thinks this will continue. He maps out his action scores and averages them out. Of course, this is biased as it's only done by Joe, and not by a group of 1000 people or more.

2. **SCARCITY** – WHAT ARE YOUR LIMITS?

Each factor in your life has *limits*. There is a limited amount of time. Eventually, we'll die. There is a limited amount of health. We all age. Neither do we have unlimited amounts of money or intelligence. Same goes for each day, week or month. Earlier you hopefully figured out how much free time you have per day. Same goes for money, health and intelligence. Do you know how much money you can spend per week without going broke? What feeling makes you know you're tired and irritable? Or do you get stomach aches from eating a certain food? For Joe, he has to limit the Money factor as he already has a massive credit card bill.

3. **CONNECTED** – HOW FACTORS AFFECT ONE ANOTHER?

Factors are mostly interconnected. For example, if the price of food jumps, you may be unable to afford healthy eating anymore, leading to possibly more health problems in a decade's time, which will lower your life expectancy.

Cycling on the road may be good for our health, but at the same time it may put us at risk of being hit by reckless drivers. After doing a point score the solution may be to exercise on a stationary bike. By checking off each action against each factor, new and better solutions may be found. Probabilities are what we're playing with here, and both honesty and research can help us choose the best actions to take. Joe realizes that though he is saving time in the short run, if his body becomes addicted to the shakes, more time will be spent later curing him of the addiction.

4. **EVOLVING** – ANY NEW INFORMATION?

Information changes daily. This happens all the time with a factor like health. Studies may come out saying it's healthy to eat more fat than we did before, leading us to rethink what foods we gobble down. Or perhaps you're about to take out a home loan. Then interest rates jump from 3% to 6%. This affects the money value factor. Can you afford the increased monthly payments? You now need to decide. We mostly always need to change our actions as information changes. Ben Franklin did this a lot in life as Walter Isaacson's biography *Benjamin Franklin: An American Life* explored. Franklins pro's and con's list is a good classic way of weighing different pieces of information. Another is "Bayes' net" as seen in computer programming where it recalculates probabilities automatically when information changes. It uses Bayes' theorem which simply says that new information should be included to update choices. Sounds simple but we don't always do it. Take the following: Is this person riding on the train a male or female?

We start with a 50/50 chance as this is the male/female split in the population. Now let's add more info. This person has a bag full of blankets, which they just bought at a knitting festival. The festival had $2/3^{rds}$ of all tickets sold to females. So, we may up the chance that the person is female from 50% to say 62.3%. Later they drop a purse, which is mostly used by females, and this boosts that probability to around 83.9%. Finally, lipstick rolled out of the purse, so we boost that number to 90.0%. Of course, it's still possible that the person may be male and wish to be seen as female by others so 100% certainty is not given. All information, especially past information, can usually help us get closer to an answer. It took a few weeks but Joe found online that some people were claiming that an ingredient in the shakes was addictive. He asked his local pharmacy about it and they said they'd get back to him about it.

5. TIME PERIODS – HOW MUCH TIME IS AVAILABLE FOR EACH PERIOD?

Each action nearly always causes effects over the short, medium, and long-run. Short run for one person may mean 2 weeks, but for another 2 months. It's up to you, but when labeling dates be as realistic as you can. Same goes for point scoring. A good action today may, unlikely as it sounds, lead to huge problems 10 years in the future. It's hard to predict the future but we can still predict our response to different future paths. As Joe has done above, he has estimated point scores based on what may or may not happen. If you were in his shoes, you might end up with different scores. With new information, you may change the time periods durations on the graph. Even Joe's chart might change if he doesn't start losing weight. It would also change if he learns that the shakes are harmful or addictive. Later in this book we will see how everyday things could be affecting the actions of billions of people.

6. IMPACT ON OTHERS – HOW ARE THEY AFFECTED?

It's not just about the person doing the action, but we also need to include in our score how it impacts other people. Friends, customers, enterprises, and even the entire population may be impacted. As can animals, plants, and the environment. This all may be tough to calculate. Sometimes we have the information, but most times we don't and may need to guess. Accounting is a good example. Kate knows that a mistake made on a client's tax return may lead to problems. It may even prevent a tax refund, leading to no bonuses paid to workers. Or it may lead to fines from the tax office. Joe knows that he is less likely to suffer health problems if he gets his weight down, otherwise he may be unable to work.

7. NEXT BEST ACTION – WHAT OTHER ACTION/S CAN GET YOU THE RESULT?

Value factors let us see deeper into our actions. They also help us *test actions against* one another. To do this best we should use the next best action. For Joe's value test above it was "Drinking shakes *instead* of past diet." Now let's say you drive a car to get to places, but your bike is your next best choice if your car breaks down. Cycling may mean more time lost vs. using the car. Also, because of the type of work you do, you need to answer your mobile throughout the day. The intelligence factor drops at this point. More cognitive load means you're likely to crash the bike with one hand away holding the phone. You realize it may be best to get a taxi instead. You think harder and see that if you can afford it, a wireless ear piece may be better, but after testing it you realize that talking distracts from hearing the sounds of cars and pedestrians, putting you in danger of crashing anyway.

When the next best action offers us less value, we know that the original action is the best one, so far, to reach our goal. Ideally, most of your actions will support the purpose you've chosen with which to seek the meaning of life. Knowing this we can try to guess why others do what they do. Like when we wonder "Why would he do that?" or, "How does that make sense to her?" we can use value factors to test and see if we can find the answer ourselves.

8. PURPOSE AS A STANDARD FOR COMPARISON – WHAT IS YOUR PURPOSE?

It's harder to make the right choice between actions if you don't know *the end result* you want. The purpose you choose to seek the meaning of life assists us here. Actions more closely related to your purpose are more important to you than other non-related actions. Comparing both will give you a chance to confirm if the non-purpose related action matters as much. Say you research that you can raise money to launch that recycling business you've long dreamt off to rid the world of rubbish. But needing money you fear public speaking in front of investors. The little money you have saved can be spent on educating yourself to speak confidently, but the money is also enough to fulfil another longtime dream to travel to Asia. Knowing your purpose and that you're not on this earth for long, you make the choice to educate yourself. Without your purpose, the holiday may have won out, delaying a solution to a big problem in our world. Joe, as we know, doesn't have a purpose, and so small daily problems can eat away at his motivation to lose weight, whereas a purpose to be fulfilled would keep his motivation up as it would be a long-term goal that with less weight he would more likely be able to achieve.

9. PERSONAL AND IMPERSONAL VALUE – WHAT'S FACT AND WHAT'S OPINION?

A personal value test is where you decide its best to sell your car, and save more money per week, letting you leave your job for a few years to test out your chosen purpose in life. Can all people do this? No, that's why its personal not impersonal. For some, selling a car is not an option. They may be unable to walk well, or their family may live in isolated towns with no transport. Using other alternatives, like a bike, train, or bus will lead to larger losses than gains in their value test. But even so, it is possible to find patterns that may fit a impersonal value test for all, even if people have different situations and purposes. Empirical experiments and controlled trial studies when done with proper methods, are examples of what we call impersonal value tests that we can use to find out which transportation will give *most people* the best value factors in *most situations.*

It's a fact that a car does travel faster than bikes, buses and sometimes trains in most places around the world. So to get closer to the truth we'd do best to study a large sample size of people over a long time period to see if most agree the car is faster for them. Say we did and 79% agree and 21% disagree. Only then we can say that, overall the study shows that the car is the fastest form of transport.

In other areas such studies have and continue to reveal the negative side effects of junk food, smoking, drugs and more. As the *Sherlock Holmes: The Ultimate Collection* shows the master crime solver saying, "You can, for example, never foretell what any one man will do, but you can say with precision what an average number will be up to." Joe's own value test will show his own opinions, but only an impersonal value test can come close to showing facts.

The quality of most news articles with headlines reading "studies show" are based on how well journalists understood a studies results. If they get it wrong, then so will millions reading who don't have time to explore the study itself. The trouble is that all kinds of impersonal value tests are yet to breakdown their results into value factors. Most studies wish to reveal a truth, like Zimbardos Prison experiment, as seen in *The Lucifer Effect* which aimed to see how everyday people change if put into roles (i.e gaurds or prisoners). Without a standard metric though, like the factors above, experimental studies like these lose their power of answering what everyday people ask: "What's in it for me?" Because of this, the hard work of millions of studies ends up forgotten.

Our Appendix A shows a more detailed "Private value test" that will help you view your everyday actions in a new light. With the aim of assisting you to think broadly on decisions you make in your life. Send a quick email to vitojgrigorov@gmail.com or go to www.prosperism.org to get Appendix A and·all other bonus material.

Don't be scared, all the above does not mean that every action you take should aim only towards your purpose. We're human, after all. Yet the majority of your life's actions should though. Health and wellbeing results we explored earlier point this out. You may have heard of various values like moral value, cultural value, societal value as though they're all different. We're saying no. There is a *single value criteria* as actions are the basic unit on which the real world is based on. By finding out the differences, between the best and worst actions through the value factors, humanity can best progress.

All other things being equal, given that we will die and the small number of years of free time we have, humans will mostly default to seeking the best mixture of the below factors in nearly every action they can.

- Money – Use less now = More to spend later on what's important

- Time – Use less now = More to use later towards your purpose

- Health – Use less now = More left as less pressure was put on the body in the past

- Intelligence – Use less now = More available as the mind is less exhausted to decide

Bodily Damage

As the above shows us, the boost of each value factor mostly helps lower the number of actions our bodies take to get a result. What does this mean? *Less wear and tear on the body.* Call it "stress", "uneasiness", "inflammation", "bruising" or "torn ligaments" to remember the concept. And yes the mind like all other organs is inside the body so it's also at risk of damage. By dragging hundreds of kilos through the mud every day you break your body and mind down, especially when you don't want to do it. That's why we got stronger horses on farms to do it for us, long before tractors replaced them. When we want to talk to a friend in another suburb, why don't we walk to their door and knock? Too many actions. So, we call them on a phone instead. It's easier. Indeed, we may save on the actions of walking but the never ending phone calls lead to a headache if we don't set limits. Most of what you do in life, the things you use, the words you say, and even the thoughts in your mind, are all your own way of doing the least to get what you want. Sure, some people seem to do more than others think is necessary. Like writing letters not emails. It may be they think that letters are better for a reason, like being more memorable, or they guess the time to learn how email works is not worth it. Education and being open to learning is crucial to finding new ways to do more with less. We must remember, daily doses of bodily damage add up over time. And as we'll soon learn, this impacts our life expectancy.

> Q. What would you change in your life now that you know the value factors?
>
> A.

Two Kinds of Actions

"Do you know that one of the great problems of our age is that we are governed by people who care more about feelings than they do about thoughts and ideas ?"
Meryl Streep (Playing Margaret Thatcher in *Iron Lady*)

Whenever we have two of anything it's a little unfair, the world is not black and white, there is a lot of gray. Our actions sit *on a scale*, with value destruction on one end and value creation on another. Many actions will fall in between, so remember these are guidelines not golden rules.

Value-Destructive Actions

Value-destructive actions are likely to lead to:

i.   LIFE EXPECTANCY shortened
ii. VALUE FACTORS wasted
iii. SHORT TERM thinking
iv. PAIN vs. PLEASURE mentality
v.   INNER selfish focus

We used to define such actions as "evil." A word so removed from daily life it mostly pops up in storybooks or movies. Now, with our value factors, evil can be explained in all its darkness. Its the sucking of free time, the shrinking of life expectancy, the waste of doing what isn't necessary. All these are features of value destructive actions.

They waste time and money, weaken our health, and lower our intelligence. They set value factors against each other. Smoking, drunk-driving, eating junk/processed food we've earlier explored, but there are many others like keeping the wrong friends, listening to scum filled lyrics, and doing illegal crimes. These and other actions harm our body, lower our life expectancy and hurt society. They lead us to take costly, wasteful actions and so lead to bodily damage where it is not needed.

Society has banned actions like murder, robbery, and kidnapping for a reason, mostly because society would not exist if such actions were allowed or encouraged.

Pt. 6 BUILDINGS OF LOST DREAMS

VALUE
Four Value factors form your Actions:
Time, Money, Health, Intelligence
Leading to either
Value-creative actions / Value-destructive actions

Another day, another tragedy. Joe doesn't care for the meaning of life. He chooses pleasure. He does things differently from Kate. As we've seen, she finds *happiness in actions that connect* to her purpose and which seek the meaning of life.

Some destructive actions don't seem that bad. Take the example of going out to a nightclub. We don't see that as a terrible idea. It's better than taking illegal drugs. But nightclubs are some of the most dangerous places in most cities. Many people inside and on their way to them, are more likely to take drugs and drink alcohol. Everyday people act in unpredictable ways there. Fights break out, leading to stabbings and other bloodshed.

Yes, violence can happen in the safest places, but the chances are much lower. Take the story of an 18-year-old man in Sydney, Australia. His very first Saturday night out to a club led to his death. But he wasn't drunk. He wasn't alone. He wasn't even in a club. What happened? He was walking past clubs in Kings Cross with his girlfriend and her friend. They turned a corner, and he was punched for the fun of it by a drunk, drugged-up thug.[26] How the minds of such freaks work is under research, and soon we'll need to consider how what they watched, read, or listened to during their life affected them.

Viktor Frankl talked about value-destructive actions. He said people do them when their lives lack meaning, "People fill the resultant void with hedonistic pleasures, power, materialism, hatred, boredom, or neurotic obsessions and compulsions."[27] American economist Thorstein Veblen has a similar take, "Under hedonism, the economic interest is not conceived in terms of action. It is, therefore, not readily apprehended or appreciated in terms of a cumulative growth of habits of thought."[28] The *love of comfort* is the enemy of meaning. Comfort kills the drive to seek the greater good. It turns people into couch potatoes of inaction, or human hyenas with drug-filled brains. At the extreme, we become parasites seeking only caveman-like pleasures. Of course, we aren't saying anyone who likes to relax is "sinning" against society, but those who devote the *bulk* of their lives to blind pleasure are.

There are key differences between people who live to *feel* good, and those who *do* good. Studies have shown different effects on genes between the two groups. People who do good deeds are more resistant to sickness. People who only find joy in pleasing themselves were less resistant. A life filled with value-destructive actions catches up with your genes as we'll soon explore.[29] Roy F. Baumiester, co-author of *Willpower* and a social psychologist asked this, "Do people go out looking for stress in order to add meaning to their lives? It seems more likely that they seek meaning by pursuing projects that are difficult and uncertain. One tries to accomplish things in the world."[30]

We all know the feeling when we see a fancy car drive by. Mostly it's not envy. Though those driving may like to think it is. The feeling is different. It's shock that someone *wasted so much money* on a car. *Selfish spending* is its name. Why spend ten times more money than what a basic car costs, when all you need is to get from point A to point B? It leads us to wonder how many war-torn starving children have been sacrificed in buying that car. Car thieves may not have that thought in their minds, but it is obvious from data that expensive cars are attacked and broken into most often even when nothing inside is stolen.[31]

When we buy expensive cars, throw lavish parties, and showoff designer clothing, we sacrifice the chance to help others in the world. We have to draw a line somewhere, but many don't. A wedding for most is a rare event to overspend, for others each weekend is a splurge. Just one expensive piece of jewelry can cost what an entire impoverished village couldn't even earn over their combined lifetimes. Today 3 billion people live on less than US$2.50 per day. 1 billion of them have no plumbing, electricity, decent food, education, or health care. If they did, just think how many *hundreds of millions of potential innovators* we may have, but most people in developed nations don't even know of these problems thanks to living in their own self-absorbed cocoons.[32] A visit to a poor nation, as a volunteer, may be the best education for all those who are confused over the meaning of life.

Have you ever given in to short-term pleasure? We all have at some point. Many times it causes long-term pain. Science can show the results in studies which are the impersonal value tests for us all. Take smoking again. It hooks some of us when we're young, and are hoping to look cool, but smoking leads to a 10-year drop in life expectancy.[33] We all can overeat at times, but obesity leads to a 14-year loss in life expectancy.[34] Addictions, obsessions and other slime-like habits grow more the more life they suck. Worse, they lead some to let their flaws *define* their daily life and destiny. Forgetting that, we humans change as we *learn* from our errors over time.

We can all sometimes fall prey to value destructiveness, but to endlessly repeat this destruction, we must give up meaning. It's only then, like we said back in our introduction, that we commit *time crimes*. Those that do, end up living for the next "hit" of pleasure from drugs, sex, music, or the snobbery of putting themselves above others. Even the Bible refers to a "proud look" as a sin. All such things do is reveal how insecure the proud really are to waste time on such trivial trash.[35] The result is humans sucked down to the same level as blobfish and flatworms.

It's true that over time, humanity has learned to do better. Ancient value-destructive actions, or "rituals" as cultural relativists may call them, get dumped, as we come to know that such actions *shorten* our lives. Like human sacrifice, foot binding, cannibalism, ceremonial rape, and slavery. Even so, some destructive traditions still exist. With evidence as our reason we don't always have to let people do as they please. Donald Symons says it this way, "If only one person in the world held down a terrified, struggling, screaming little girl, cut off her genitals with a septic blade, and sewed her back up, leaving only a tiny hole for urine and menstrual flow, the only question would be how severely that person should be punished, and whether the death penalty would be a sufficiently severe sanction. But when millions of people do this, instead of the enormity being magnified millions-fold, suddenly it becomes 'culture,' and thereby magically becomes less, rather than more, horrible, and is even defended by some western 'moral thinkers,' including feminists."

Now by us linking up actions with life expectancy and value factors, we finally have a way to show which actions are destructive to life instead of giving respect to each one which calls itself a "cultural tradition." It's no surprise that slaves, prostitutes, and criminals have lowered life expectancies.[36] The more of them in society the more it's likely to lead to a slow but dropping life expectancy spread throughout a nation.

The interesting fact about cultural relativism is when you look deeper you realize the practices it explores (human sacrifice, foot binding, infanticide, etc.), are all done with the false belief that they *boost value factors so to increase overall life expectancy* in that society, today or in the future. Aztecs sacrificed thousands of people for weeks in the belief it will prevent future famines killing even more. Eskimos killed their children, but only as a last resort after trying adoption and then only if there's so little food to share, that it risks the death of the adults, without whom no food can be caught. Child marriage is mostly in societies with lower life expectancies, where people die young, so to them it makes sense to get married at 11 not 21.

What about suicide bombers who die and kill others? They believe in life after death and that the best rewards will come by killing enemies of their faith. Suicide then is the only way to have a good life *after* this one and for their families too. As many times the terrorist group pays money in thanks for their relatives' sacrifice, the money likely boosting the family's life expectancy. Likewise, ordinary people take their lives knowing their life insurance pay-out will help their family pay off stressful debt and their children's education costs. Then we have physical punishment in school which many countries have banned. The goal, like above was a false belief, punishment would create discipline, helping the later grown adult in life. Data collected showed it leading to trauma, drug use, and crime later on.

Any one-sided belief system can pull people back into the stone-age. Take the supposed golden rule, "Do unto others as you would have them do unto you." So much detail is missing that it's dangerous to even think this as a rule at all. Some people want to be left alone. Should we all then leave each other alone? Unleash this golden rule into other societies and you give permission for some tribespeople to go back to the ritual of ripping out a child's heart. Remember, this is meant to "please the gods." When all tribespeople were young, they went through this ritual. The ones who are alive today are sad that they "missed out" on the glory those sacrificed got from the gods. Take the famous saying of Jesus, "If anyone slaps you on the right cheek, turn to him the other cheek also." This saying deeply touched Mahatma Gandhi. He is praised for using it as a rule for life, but he took it so seriously that he suggested that Jews pray for Hitler, and then give themselves up to be butchered rather than try to escape.[37]

As we learn more we hopefully change our false beliefs. In 2012, Australia launched compulsory plain packaging on cigarettes. The hope was that it would decrease the appeal of smoking by removing the attractive graphics and branding from the boxes. Likewise, surveys show support for banning junk/processed food commercials during children's TV shows. The mix of added sugar, salt, and fat has near zero nutritional value, and in large amounts have an affect like heroin does on the brain.

Governments are also waking up to the way that dying breed called the media, manipulates photos it publishes. We see value-destruction in making people look so "perfect" they appear inhuman. Israel now demands media place symbols below photos that have been touched up. In 2016 France banned very skinny models at fashion shows, while London has banned public transport advertising with unrealistic body images. Adults may be harder to trick, but the minds of children and teenagers are easier targets. Like studies show that when images of anorexic models are searched online this later leads to web searches for "how to become anorexic."[38]Value destruction even turns up on the side of cars. A camper van rental company known for spraying sexist slogans on the outside of their rental vans wrote, "In every princess there is a little slut that wants to try it." A confused 11-year-old girl saw this, leading to a mass petition, with the company removing the slogans.[39]

Some might think the above is an attack on free speech. John Stuart Mill argued that people should have the freedom to seek their tastes. His guideline was that actions should not harm others, even if they are deemed "immoral." The issue here is a *murky* definition of harm. Take second-hand smoke. It is indirect, but it leads to nearly the same effects in non-smokers as seen in smokers. What would Mill think? In a similar way, song lyrics, movies, or photos can poison our minds and actions, and so *lead to harm*, shrinking our own and others life expectancy. Some music listeners use the excuse that they somehow *don't hear* the awful lyrics, using some superhuman power to only listen to the rhythm and beat of the music. We don't believe such fraud. Indeed, science shows otherwise, as each word heard forms pictures in our head.[40]

Of course, indirect harm seems *less urgent*. We don't have to react as fast to it as we do to a shotgun-waving-maniac, but what happens if we just let indirect harm float through, like passive smoke? *We let it silently breed and spread like a virus.* In the end, more are killed from it than from the shootings of the maniac. As the often-misattributed quote to Edmund Burke says, "The only thing necessary for evil to triumph is for good men to do nothing." Parents would riot if they found out teachers were telling students to lie, get drunk, and have unsafe sex, but children get these messages all the time. The "poetic" lyrics of rappers, images from sexualized music videos, and booze-soaked stories of their idols are burned into their minds.

Mills' version of "harm" is not clear enough, but with life expectancy and value factors we get a clearer picture. If an action shortens life expectancy, we must check it closely and ask if it should be stopped from spreading. We shouldn't risk sacrificing millions of lives in the decades and centuries to come. When study after study over decades showed the dangers of smoking, governments did nothing but accept political blood money from tobacco companies. Credit is due to Peter Singer who said it best, "We are responsible not only for what we do, but what we could have prevented."[41]

> Q. **What value-destructive action/s can you start removing from your life?**
>
> A.

Value-Creative Actions

Value-creative actions are likely to lead to:

    i.   LIFE EXPECTANCY increased
    ii.   VALUE FACTORS used best
    iii. LONG TERM thinking
    iv. MEANING-DRIVEN mentality
    v.   OUTER giving focus

We used to define such actions by the word "good." To most people eating well, exercising, and learning may come to mind. Depending on our purpose these actions likely improve our health, save us money, help us use time well, and boost our intelligence. Our body breaks down less than it would have, and this increases our life expectancy.

Value-creative actions move us closer to the meaning of life. It's not surprising that many who seek the greater good care less about pleasure. In the words of economist Joseph Schumpeter, they have "indifference to hedonist enjoyment."[42] Value-creative actions are driven by meaning, rather than pain or pleasure. Obviously, it helps to have a purpose in order to do this.

Some may see exercise as a value-destructive action, their muscles hurt so they want to avoid it, but short-term pain likely leads to long-term gain, if exercising correctly.

Value-creative actions help open up value factors in all else that we do. Say you save 5 hours by not playing video games during the week. You can use that time to visit your grandmother in the nursing home. Slow down when driving and you're likely to reduce the chance of injuring others and shortening their lives. Broader value-creative action includes governments simplifying laws and companies giving employees flexible work hours if targets are met.

Take the use of crop fertilizers as an example. Some are harmful, but many aren't, and these allow hundreds of millions of people to be fed who otherwise would starve. Machinery helps us better farm food and trucks ship it to supermarkets. This has reduced back-breaking farming work of centuries past and helped increase life expectancy. Today fewer people spend all day farming. We have more free time to put toward value-creative actions. Or take medicine: a few cures and vaccines, mass-produced for the world, have added billions of years of life for the worlds population.

The car has likely saved hundreds of billions of combined years of time. A car gets you from point A to B in 30 minutes each day compared to 60 minutes on public transport. You save 3.5 hours per week multiplied over 50 years. That opens up 379 days of free time, an entire year and more of life. We can now use this time to better seek our purpose. It was in 1873 that Jules Verne wrote the book, *Around the World in 80 Days*. Today's aircrafts let us travel round the world in 24 hours.

Technology plays a major role here. With fridges, we can save food we didn't finish instead of throwing it out. We have light bulbs instead of dangerous gas lamps. We can turn light on at night without fear of fire from the spark of a dropped lamp. Billions more hours have been unlocked thanks to the light bulb letting us continue the day into the night.

A mother puts her life on the line so her child can survive. An overweight man struggles to finish the race he started. A poor single father starts a business to give others the value of his design skills. All these actions call us to go through pain for meaning. We may suffer in seeking meaning, but by *suffering we grow*. We can now better understand Friedrich Nietzsche's famous quote, "That which does not kill him makes him stronger."[43]

A little test can show this to us. Say we ask a smoker what they want to achieve by smoking. They'd find it tricky to answer. *Little, if anything, can be achieved.* However, someone who's studying, working, or programming could give a variety of answers such as, "I'm learning a skill so I can use it to make something valuable."

Author Dean Keith Simonton put it this way, 'The gregarious who fritter their time away at cocktail parties, social outings, and family get-togethers are less likely to leave enduring impressions on posterity."[44]

Q. What value-creative action/s will you now focus more time on?

A.

What does it mean to leave "enduring impressions on posterity"? At this point, we know that the "greatest good for the greatest number" is the meaning of life and we know how to measure it, but how do we give value through the unique human function to innovate? How do we reach the greatest number of people?

By asking and answering the question on the meaning of life we got in return a sentence length answer. Such a sentence is the icing on the cake, *beneath it are all the other ingredients*, which together make the meaning matter and take it to its ultimate conclusion as we will see next.

Chapter Summary

\#   Survival is at the bottom of everything we do.

\#   Value is how an action changes life expectancy.

\#   Life expectancy is found by looking through four value factors: Time, Health, Intelligence, Money.

\#   Action is the observable, deliberate movement of the human body. Unlike the biological, i.e. sleeping, eating, sneezing.

\#   Bodily damage is the effect actions have on the wear and tear of our body and mind. Typically the less actions to reach a goal extends life expectancy, more actions to reach the same goal reduces it.

\#   We judge actions using the value factors. Helping us decide which action is best.

\#   There are 2 kinds of actions in the world:

  - Value-creative, that which increase life expectancy.
  - Value-destructive, that which decrease life expectancy.

CHAPTER THREE

Why Innovations Matter?

"Man's dearest possession is life. It is given to him but once, and he must live it so as to feel no torturing regrets for wasted years, never know the burning shame of a mean and petty past; so live that, dying, he might say: all my life, all my strength were given to the finest cause in all the world—the fight for the Liberation of Mankind."[1]
Nikolai Ostrovsky (**Author of** *How the Steel Was Tempered*)

"To yield to every whim of curiosity, and to allow our passion for inquiry to be restrained by nothing but the limits of our ability, this shows an eagerness of mind not unbecoming to scholarship. But it is wisdom that has the merit of selecting, from among the innumerable problems which present themselves, those whose solution is important to mankind."[2]
Immanuel Kant (**Author of** *Critique of Pure Reason*)

Take a look at all the things around you right now that were made by humans. How many different things can you count? Too many?

It's an unavoidable fact that nearly all that we use was *made or impacted by humans*. The built modern world did not magically pop out of thin air. It was the purposeful result of the unique human function to innovate. From the trains that move millions of people each day to the thousands of tiny parts and tools that built the screen you may be reading from right now. To the humble desk on which many us get work done, everything man-made came from the purposes of different people combining what already existed.

This is what I found a while back. In one photo, there are centuries old stories behind much of what we use. Exploring the items in this image could fill entire bookshelves if we researched deep enough into the history of how they were made.

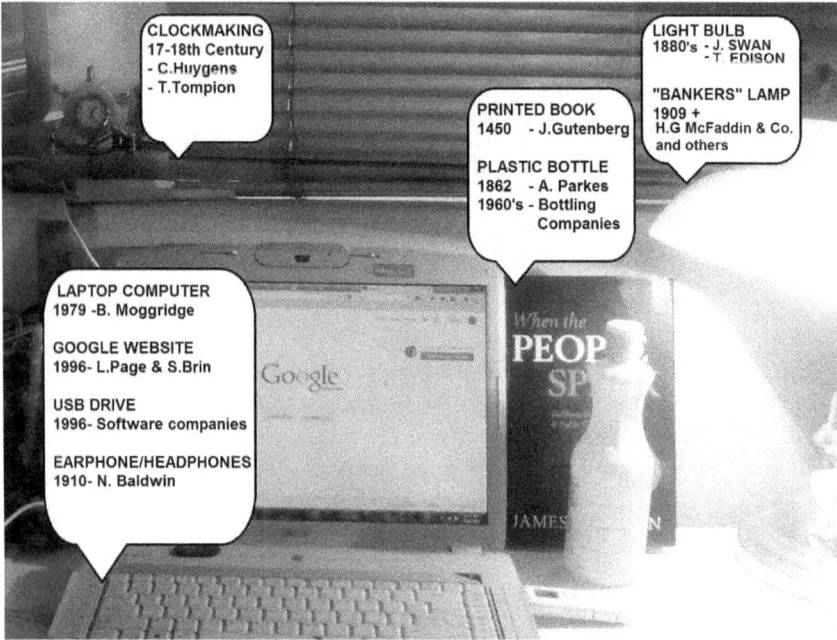

Now imagine, tomorrow you woke up and everything made over the past 500 years had vanished. Your mobile phone, toilet, stove, the bed you slept on, the electricity you used, all gone. What you'd see is a world thrust back into the Middle Ages. *Frontier House*, a TV series produced by PBS in the early 2000s, showed exactly that. Modern American families tried living in a 19th century country house with the same food, clothes, and tools as the people of that time.

Not only would there be fewer human-made things the further back you go in time, the dictionaries you'd find back then would be a lot thinner than today's. Why? When we look in the dictionary, we can see that *words broadly fit into two groups*. One group, let's call them *innovation words* describe things of human making, like "car," "paper," and "alcohol," along with words describing the human actions which arise from the use of those innovations, like "drive," "write," and "drunk." The other group, *non-innovation words* describe what is of natural origin, like "ocean," "air," "water," and the linked human actions, like "swim," "breathe," and "drink." All words found in dictionaries fit in one of these two groups. Every innovation made and used by humans has needed to be described, *bringing a new word into existence* and slowly fattening the dictionary over time. Take google.com, the search engine product of the internet company, Google

Inc. The human action that it produces is known as "googling," which means searching the Internet through the Google search engine.

In 2014, the Merriam Webster dictionary announced it was adding 150 words to the dictionary, including "hashtag," "unfriend," and "social networking." Most of these words emerged from the use of websites like Facebook and Twitter. Innovations you may use daily, like the sofa, the keyboard, and the car respectively produce new actions as words in the dictionary, such as couch-surfing, typing, driving, and there are millions more examples like this.

Unsurprisingly innovations have also changed human actions over the centuries. Though unhealthy, humans are sleeping less with every passing decade.[3] It sped up with the industrial revolution in the late 18th century, spreading innovations which later Thomas Edison and others would combine into a fought over electrical network to let us use light after dark as the Graham Moore novel, *Last Days of Night* explores. People, who would before simply stay at home, could now thanks to street lighting, go out to a cafe, and push two sleeps into one long one. This is one of many examples showing humans are the adaptable animal, most of what we think of as fixed instincts are just habits which can be changed. With each innovation, more options popped up to get us a result we want, and the *more options, the more chances of survival,* but where did this come from? This unique human function to innovate we talked about earlier? It didn't pop up out of thin air. It begins with evolution.

In 1859, Charles Darwin published the *Origin of Species,* a book that held a dangerous idea—that humans evolved from less intelligent life forms and that all species on earth descended from a common ancestor. This process took billions of years. Evolution showed that living organisms that best adapt and survive end up reproducing, while those unable to do so die out. Darwin called this process "natural selection." We see it in the traits of an animal, like skin color, running speed, or its size, that help it to survive to have offspring, who then inherit those traits and pass them on again. It's mostly the *genes inside that lead* to these traits, influencing who survives and who dies.

Let's remember this took place over 4.54 billion years, the approximate age of the earth.[4] Let's imagine all that time on a 100-meter rope. Modern humans came on the scene along the last 4.41 millimeters of the rope, or the last 200,000 years. Our journey started like all other species, from a single-celled organism that evolved over time into what recently was found to be one of the ancestors of all modern mammals, including us—*a squirrel-like insect eater.*[5]

Source: Gould, Public domain

Knowing this, readers of Spencer Johnson's *Who Moved my Cheese* may now better relate to the main mouse characters in his book.

All this even goes back further to 13.7 billion years ago, which is when the universe began, possibly starting from an energy field. For all we know, we could be the only beings in the entire universe with the ability to realize our own conscious existence. Earth, our "pale blue dot" is just one of the estimated trillions of planets in the universe.[6] It's a dot which once looked like hell, with scorching sandstorms and exploding volcanoes,[7] but ever so slowly, this once vast wasteland has spawned the music of Beethoven, the works of Shakespeare, and the journey of humans to the moon.

Our need to remember this evolutionary journey from microscopic cells to astronauts is well said by various images shared online, "You are the result of billions of years of evolutionary success. F*#%^@g act like it!" It's easy for us to forget how slim the chances were 40,000 years ago that the right female and male would come together to start in motion actions that would lead to your eventual birth. A freak virus, falling tree, rotten meat, or wrong turn, and those chances would melt into the air. We should be grateful knowing that *we beat the odds to simply be born*, versus the billions of others who weren't so lucky. It's a gift to motivate us to make the most of our short time here.

Have you ever thought about all of this? Sadly, evolution is seen as having little practical importance to our daily lives. Engineering, architecture, and a crowd of other fields are thought to be more important for the here and now. It's simply not true. For evolution is uniquely important in our understanding of every area of life including the meaning of life and the purpose we choose to seek it with.

Evolution's importance lies most clearly in the "natural selection" process, which has let our species to evolve and survive to the present day. This process will be crucial in understanding what we'll be exploring in chapters to come. So, let's briefly simplify below how natural selection works.

1. **Small differences exist within a species.**
   Take an island, home to a group of birds. Most of the birds have short beaks, as do their young. Yet there are also a *few* rare long-beaked birds.

2. **Changes in the environment lead to a struggle to survive.**
   After some harsh weather, the amount of food, like insects and nuts, shrinks. Survival pushes the birds to *compete* against one another over the food left.

3. **The difference that helps those survive is passed on to their young.**
   The long-beaked birds have a *better chance* of surviving as their beaks can reach in between rock cracks to catch food that the short-beaked birds cannot. Short-beaked birds die off, unable to find food for themselves or their young. The longer beak becomes valuable for survival and since their young inherited their genes, the islands birds become mostly long beaked over time.

This process repeats and is always in motion as weather, predators and food supply changes.

You may ask, "How did the first few birds have long beaks to begin with?" *It was random.* Called a *mutation.* That's the key to understand biological evolution, it's not controlled. Mutations happen by chance. Like the randomness of what's in any garbage bin you open. Without long beaked birds, it's likely then that *all birds* would have died out. Odds are there will be something "different" in a small percentage of any species. Like being born with an added eye, ear or finger. In some species, this may prove an advantage for survival. Differences are important for this reason.

Today in many cases, humans have impacted this natural process. Now those same long beaked birds may die from oil leaking from a sinking ship nearby, unable to use their wings, they then drown in the sea.

We humans unknowingly also pass on genes to our young, which long ago helped our species survive. Some genes gave our muscles more fast-twitch fibers, boosting our running speed and helping us hide from the lions. Some helped develop vocal cords to let us speak, while others helped us use our thumbs to make things with our hands. Similar changes can be found in any other species, but there is one change that isn't, a change that would be the key to why we became the dominant species. Darwin briefly touched on this, yet never went into great detail, when he wrote, "The formation of different languages and of distinct species, and the proofs that both have been developed through a gradual process, are curiously parallel...The survival or preservation of certain favored words in the struggle for existence is natural selection."[8]

So What's Special About Humans? Instinct Elimination by Innovation

"We are nothing else than evolution become conscious of itself."
Julian Huxley

In 1871, Charles Darwin published another book, *The Descent of Man*. In it, he writes, "Man has great power of adapting his habits to new conditions of life. He invents weapons, tools, and various strategies to procure food and to defend himself. When he migrates to a colder climate he uses clothes, builds sheds, and makes fires, and by the aid of fire, cooks food otherwise indigestible. He aids his fellow men in many ways, and anticipates future events. Even at a remote period, he practiced some division of labor."[10]

The evolutionary progress of humans followed a similar path to nearly all other species until around 150,000 years ago. That's when humans became **self-aware.**

This is critical. No other species has the same amount of self-awareness as human beings do. You know this, as you can recognize yourself in the mirror. All other species run mostly on *instinct*. Yet humans run on *reason*, we question, doubt, and think. This gives us a lot of power, as well as, responsibility. As Richard Dawkins, author of *The Magic of Reality* said, "The human brain provides possibly…the only engine of departure from Darwinian principles," which we used to *escape* the cycle of evolution which created us.[11] This lets us make our own evolution as best seen when developed cities today are compared to those hundreds of years back. While most other species can feel pain, their actions still remain mostly instinctual, but humans can *disobey* instinct. We gamble to say that this self-awareness arose from innovation, when we saw we could change the "fixed" world around us. It's then that we started asking, "What if?" for the first time. We started to try new things and create more options, leading to different results then from the past. Can we go back in time to prove this happened? Almost, just look at one of our closest evolutionary relatives, the gorillas, who have been seen using sticks near ponds to test how deep they are, and Senegalese chimps using sharpened sticks to kill other animals for food, just like we once did.[12] But we got to the finish line first, by making innovations like our cranes, drill machines, weapons and explosives we've taken it further, we can change and destroy entire environments and other species.

It is innovations that led us to break free from instinct and progress beyond other animals. Instinct is a confusing word to use to refer to humans, for only the basics of survival can claim to be instincts for us, like food, water, air, sleep, and warmth. All else is covered by the word "*dependency*" because it contains all actions we have shown ability to control and say "no" to until our death, if we wish. It's only in lacking a clear path to meaning that we let dependency suck our lives away. It's when we *confuse dependency for instincts* that we descend into the dark Stone Age, when we obey the inhumane. We're most human when we *resist and overcome dependency* as our history shows. When we weakly surrender to them, as seen with bursts of anger, sexual arousal, or jealousy, we slip ourselves into the chaotic muck of the barbarian past, *we uncivilize what we struggled millions of years to civilize*, we tumble into the wilderness with the jackals. History shows we can and have disobeyed our dependencies and even our supposed instincts. The true believer can choose to burn until death than reject his beliefs, ignoring the "instinct" to survive, while others will control their sexual urges so to live religiously, ignoring the "instinct" for sex. We can even go without sleeping and eating to the point of death. It's this human capacity to conquer instinct that is on full display in the transformation of the landscape around us. Take for example Sydney, Australia.

BEFORE   **AFTER**

(Painting by Thomas Watling 19ᵗʰ century)
Sources: State Library of NSW, Public domain – Merbabu,
Creative Commons Attribution License

How is it that such a change has *repeated itself* in countless places the world over? Go back in time to almost any spot humans have settled, and years later we find evidence we were there. Why? We change each environment we touch, no other species does it like humans have. During this process, nature may suffer damaging changes, but like many human overreaches, it will *likely be fixed with a creative innovation* in the future.

Before, it was differences in genes that used to control our evolution and survival, as they still do for other species, but today genes are mostly *useless* in their impact on us. Humans now control our own evolutionary path and have sped it up with each year that passes. We're in control not just of the environment but also of the life and death of every species on the planet.

All this is not to say that our genetic evolution doesn't continue—it does. This can be easily seen in children born with diseases mostly inherited from genes of family members, like Huntingdon's, diabetes and many others. Due to the long time it takes for natural selection of genes to spread through such a large and diverse group as humans, we likely won't be around to see what next great evolutionary trait our genes will produce. Hopefully it will be something more useful than the tailbone (coccyx), corner wisdom teeth, or male uterus.[13] Babies born with more fingers, legs, or eyes, which may have proven useful to survival long ago, are instead removed with surgery.

This capacity to control ourselves and what's around us goes back to one of our first humanoid ancestors, Homo habilis, meaning "handy man". They were the first to change the environment with innovation and bring about *self-awareness*. Our gamble remember, is that modern human *consciousness started to form when we innovated,* when we took control of something in the real world i.e. tools, farming, animals. Only then did instincts chokehold on us start to loosen as we humans realized that we could now control what had always controlled us.

We then used these tools to destroy enemies to our survival, such as predators, competing tribes, and eventually the weather and food shortages. We turned nature from a feared mystery into a tool for our use. The sea was a barrier until boats were made, animals had to be hunted until we started farming, and coal was a useless lump until it eventually was burned to make power. The wheel was used to move goods, scissors to cut, and lenses to read. Today with cloning, we can even bring back extinct species, like the Pyrenean ibex, a wild mountain goat.[14]

Alfred Russel Wallace, who co-originated the theory of evolution with Charles Darwin, seems to agree: "From the moment when the first skin was used as a covering, when the first rude spear was formed to assist in the chase, the first seed sown or shoot planted, a grand revolution was effected in nature, a revolution which in all the previous ages of the world's history had had no parallel, for a being had arisen who was no longer necessarily subject to change with the changing universe—a being who was in some degree superior to nature, in as much as he knew how to control and regulate her action."[15] This event gave us the first glimpse of a reality unshackled from instinct, giving us as humans the *power to control something outside of ourselves.* Before that moment, it's safe to say that human actions existed without innovations to affect them, something that is *near impossible* to find today. The crucial point, as Wallace's quote highlights, is that human actions and innovations are joined at the hip—unable to be understood separately from each other. Most explanations of humanity and its society fail to recognize the importance of this link.

All of today's innovations stretch right back to that first ape ancestor of ours who had that eureka moment when they found that a bone could be used as a weapon to kill prey, as seen in Stanley Kubrick's film, *2001: A Space Odyssey* based on Arthur C. Clark's book of the same name. Of course, we don't know how that exact moment unfolded, but Kubrick's demonstration works well.

From that eureka moment to today, the impact of genes on humans has been *slowly overtaken* by innovations. It was supposedly Benjamin Franklin who first called man, "a tool-using animal."[16] Philosopher Thomas Carlyle followed him, adding, "Without tools, he is nothing; with them, he is all."[17] To sum it up, *innovate or die* is the path humanity has taken. Medicine is a great example. Medicines and antidotes for a crowd of diseases have given life to hundreds of millions of people who otherwise would be dead. Ever hear of penicillin? It's the original antibiotic, which has, according to some sources, saved 80 million lives and counting.[18]

Through innovations, humans have struck back at evolution's twisted game of chance, where some people get good genes and are healthy while others get bad genes and die of disease. This continues to be a battle—we haven't escaped yet. Recently, the World Health Organization has been seeing common infections become resistant to antibiotics, with WHO Director-General Margaret Chan saying, "Things as common as strep throat or a child's scratched knee could once again kill."[19] Yet in early 2015, scientists discovered new antibiotic strains which may prevent bacterial resistance from growing at all.

Years ago, British zoologist C. Lloyd Morgan observed, "Evolution may leave the faculty of the race at a standstill while the achievements of the race are progressing by leaps and bounds."[20] We are innovating faster in the physical world than the speed of evolution inside of us in our genes. Now we can better understand Richard Dawkins in his classic work, *The Selfish Gene,* "...as each generation passes, the contribution of your genes is halved. It does not take long to reach negligible proportions. Our genes may be immortal, but the collection of genes that is any one of us is bound to crumble away. Elizabeth II is a direct descendant of William the Conqueror. Yet it is quite likely that she bears not a single one of the old king's genes. We should not seek immortality in reproduction. But if you contribute to the world's culture, if you have a good idea, compose a tune, invent a sparking plug, write a poem, it may live on, intact, long after your genes have dissolved in the common pool."[21]

How sad life would be if, like some believe, all the hard work and accomplishments of women and men are done just to attract the best partner to have kids with. Thankfully the dependency to leave behind children *has less hold on us today* than it once did. Like the Greek hero, Achilles, who chose to leave his mark through his deeds than by raising a family. Humans today can more clearly see that it's their innovations, not their children that can give that immortality after death that Achilles sought. In time, as more people realize this the religious' monopoly on "life after death" will melt away, replaced by humans living on in the innovation they leave behind. An engraving may show up on tombstones of the future like below.

Akiro Endo discovered statin drugs which have saved the lives of 5 million people and counting, yet he never earned a dollar for it. He said, "I did not start the research to make money or become a big man. Since I was born as a human in this world, I wanted to leave my mark before I die. I want to die after I do at least one thing useful for the world."[22]

Kate sees that Mike, like many, seeks a relationship with her in order to become happy, rather than be happy with himself first before the relationship. Yet Kate is happy, even without him, as she is making something of her own.

Philosopher David George Ritchie continues what we can now see is an obvious truth, "An individual or a nation may do more for mankind by handing on ideas and a great example than by leaving numerous offspring."[23] Sir Francis Bacon, statesman and author of *The Essays*, takes this one step further, "He that hath wife and children hath given hostages to fortune, for they are impediments to great enterprises, either of virtue or mischief. Certainly, the best works, and of greatest merit for the public, have proceeded from the unmarried or childless men. Both in affection and means, they have married and endowed the public."[24]

Indiana Jones might come to mind when you hear the word "archaeology," but few know that the field studies all that humans have made and left behind from the first recorded innovation to now. Starting an estimated 4 million years ago, with new discoveries regularly pushing this date backwards.[25] Even the names of the different stages of human historical development are linked to the materials we innovated with: Stone Age, Bronze Age, Iron Age…

Today similarly, we tend to group people by "generations"…X, Y, Z based on their birth year. This label overlooks the fact that its *innovations that define generations*. Innovations people grow up with impact all their actions, like habits, personalities, behaviors which older people then generalize. The innovation of the TV could be said to have defined Generation X, while the innovations of the internet and mobile phone did the same for Generation Y.

Morals Change with New Innovations

It's the same case with those foggy concepts of morality and social norms. *As innovations change, morals change.* Most claim that humans over time become more "moral" so that's why slaves became free, but not so fast. Why would slavery, defended as far back by the ancient Greeks, the Bible, and the Koran, and said to be a key part of the human condition, simply change? It's innovations that gave a practical real world reason to do so. As author Christopher Fettweis touches on in his book, *Dangerous Times,* slaves up until the 19th century were seen as essential because most farming tools were still unchanged since the Medieval Ages. Progress on the farm did not move much, the work hours per acre stayed nearly the same every century.[26] To eat you needed to work daily for your food like your ancestors did, but if you had slaves you had *a life of free time* opened up.[27] Though work conditions are hugely different, housemaids and servants perform similar roles for wealthy families today.

But in the 19th century there came new innovations like McCormick's reaper and Deere's steel plow, among others, which grew productivity on the farm to the point *that they didn't need slaves.*[28] Only then did most people stop seeing slavery as "natural". As economic collapse was now unlikely to happen, the mass freeing of slaves became more justifiable, as seen in Britain and the U.S. in the 19th century. Millions of freed slaves now had control of their actions, and they in turn could put their actions to use in jobs which were becoming more productive to society, such as the factories making the farming machines that helped free them. The same is the case with feminism. If innovations had not developed to the point where women could do the same work as men, like remote controlling machines to make products in factories the world over, equality is unlikely to have changed. How so? Well what happens if you remove machines, which anyone, man or women can control? We go back to farming, and even before that hunting. It's here that men have a size and strength advantage over women, and so are more likely to survive to kill the prey and bring food back to the tribe. This same size and strength also means men are very likely to overpower a woman in a fight as shocking domestic violence statistics the world over show. Now guess what happens when machines spread? Women don't need to depend on men to bring back food. They can earn money to buy it by doing a job that men do and be even better at it. The result? They don't need to depend on, be in relationship with, or marry men. They can finally live by themselves if they choose to.

The opposite of the last few paragraphs is best known as Moral Relativism, which is the idea that truth is different for everyone so we can't know what's right or wrong. But innovations over time drive a knife into the heart of the relativist argument. Where before relativists could hide behind thought experiments like earlier explored, pointing out that people react differently when asked to choose how should the speeding bus driver react, in a few decades to a century the question won't even exist. As an agreed real world answer would likely be established by then, written into the code of the driverless bus. As computers will be in control, our vehicles will have preset reactions to all sorts of situations. Brake hard if pedestrian jumps out, Accelerate away if car to the side is within an arms length.

Innovations are Controlled, not Random

Remember our example of those longer beaked birds? Random mutations as found in genes don't happen in human innovation as some think. Just because we cannot find exactly who made the first wheel or the first stone tools, doesn't mean they popped out of thin air as some, who have little experience in making innovations would think. All it shows is a lack of record-keeping, not randomness. Today we have patents, trademarks, and copyright databases showing the history of mostly all innovations we use. Entire books have been written researching the history of the television, telephone, light bulb, and many others. We can pinpoint on a timeline their story, who assisted in them becoming part of our lives and which companies were involved. It takes a self-aware and "prepared mind," in Louis Pasteur's words, the modern father of germ theory, to know an innovation for what it is and may become.

As Steven Johnson points out in, *Where Good Ideas Come From,* the long-held view that people randomly have a spark of genius is not only *historically incorrect but also near impossible.* We never see a spark as much as a *combination* of what already exists, from a knowledge base of what came before. A random person from the street would not think twice looking at a growing mold, yet Alexander Fleming, as a biologist and pharmacologist had the past experience to see its potential to write a paper on it, and Howard Florey had the experience to read and see that it could become penicillin. Johnson rejects as a myth that the 15th century printer, Johannes Gutenberg, had a flash vision of the moveable type mechanism when he made his printing press. Instead he knew many wine press workers whose methods he put into printing. One of history's most celebrated innovators, Thomas Edison, even said, "None of my inventions came by accident. I see a worthwhile need to be met, and I make trial after trial until it comes."[29]

Of course, the innovator *cannot always predict* the result of their creation. Edison knew his phonograph had many uses, such as recording voices of people who would soon pass away, but he never expected its popularity to be in recording and playing back music, helping make the music industry we know today.

It would be a disgrace to the memory of all these people to say they "randomly" came upon their innovations as one does finding money lying on the street. It took Darwin decades to make sense of his theory of evolution by linking up patterns and evidence to make sure he was not fooling himself. Darwin himself even made the point that, "man can and does select the variations given to him by nature, and thus accumulates them in any desired manner."[30]

Anything of Human Creation is an Innovation

To better understand the rest of the book we need a description to cover all the others words we have to describe innovations. Like "human creation," "improvement," "man-made," "artificial things," "material things," "objects," and "built environment". Our word for all these and others is simply, *innovation.*

Innovations

iii. Unit of Historical Change*

1. Innovations are physical and so can be observed by the human senses.

All forms of matter are basic energy as a scientist would say. Humans observe the physical world through our senses, mostly sight, hearing, touch, smell, or taste. As most of us sense the world and its innovations in nearly the same way, it lets most of us *agree on rules for how the world works.* You can easily see this on the road, as most car drivers follow the same paths, signs and directions.

Innovations include every single thing that's *physical* in human life, such as buildings, cars, language, books, songs, laws, enterprises, clothing, and poetry. Yes, that phone bill you have been waiting to pay is an innovation, as are the words you're reading right now and the language you're reading them in.

2. Innovations come from and/or have been improved by humans.

Regardless of its shape, form, or appearance, as long as an innovation *comes from and/or is improved* by a human, and can be observed by our senses, it is an innovation. Yes, we're repeating ourselves on this definition, as it's easy in the moment to slip and forget that almost anywhere you lay your eyes you're seeing innovations. In philosophical jargon, this is the "ontology". We define and categorize what's found in the world as mostly filled with innovations or what can be used in making them.

You may now ask, *Is the road I walked on an innovation?* Yes, it is. It was made by humans. *Are the subjects I learned at school all innovations?* Yes again, made by humans. *Are the laws that the government proposes an innovation?* Yes, they were made by humans. *When people yawn, is that an innovation?* No, yawning is an involuntary reflex of our body. *But when the human ape ancestor in, 2001: A Space Odyssey, picked up the bone and used it; was the bone an innovation?* Yes, it became one. Though the bone was from nature, the use of it by the human ape holding it, and then smashing it against the skull of an enemy as a weapon, changed its shape and turned it into an innovation. This is the same as when we use anything from nature: wood from trees, minerals from mines, or oil from wells. When we come in contact with it and better it for our use, we turn it into an innovation.

Here's a sample to see the differences:

Nature (Natural origin)	Innovations (Human origin)
Instincts	Economic institutions
Weather	Social systems
Species	Products and services
Minerals	Law and customs

3. Thoughts are NOT innovations.

Except for superheroes, humans can't yet read minds. Thoughts in the head cannot be known to others until they are *released* into the world, by speaking, writing, recording, or any other way. This is important, as many mistake unreleased "ideas" for innovations. An idea that sits in the mind of a person is a crucial starting point on the path that leads to the making of an innovation in the real world. Intellectual property law confirms this, as it does not protect ideas in someone's head unless they're ready to take them out and put them into *physical recordable* form that another human can observe.[31] So, for example, speaking the idea makes it an innovation, if another person is listening and if needed, can remember and repeat it if, say, the person who spoke it is to die. Writing ideas down better protects them but it won't matter if they are lost and unread by anyone.

4. Actions are NOT innovations.

Actions are the *deliberate movements* of the body that we make as living beings. They existed without innovations before humankind's first eureka moment. Today it's nearly impossible to find actions that are without the influence of innovations, unless off course you grow up among the wolves on some isolated island.

Actions without innovations have very little value as our ancient human history shows. It's only *when actions come into contact with innovations* that those bodily movements can be compared to each other through the four value factors earlier mentioned. Take the action of swallowing something. The mouth is opened, and you place something inside. The action is neither value-creative nor destructive until we know *what we are swallowing*. Let's say it's either ecstasy pills or vitamins. Now that the layer of innovations has been added, we can find out which action is value-creative and which is value-destructive. We find this out by comparing the *observable range* of resulting actions that both innovations produce. As done earlier, we then filter each action by the *estimated change* scored by the value factors which then shows us the *likely increase or decrease* in life expectancy it may lead to. Below is an example and results for a group if done as a study/impersonal value test:

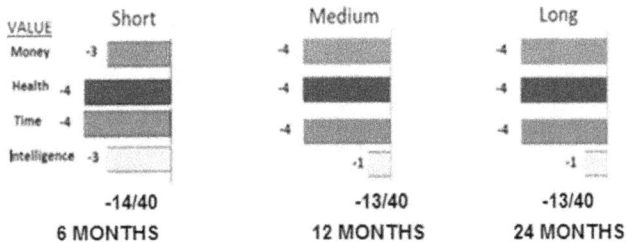

Action involved =   Swallowing

⇕

Innovation/s used =   Ecstasy pills

⇕

Resulting Actions =
- Memory loss
- Increased body temperature
- Increased blood pressure
- Blurred vision

⇕

Impersonal Value test =

VALUE	Short	Medium	Long
Money	-3	-4	-4
Health	-4	-4	-4
Time	-4	-4	-4
Intelligence	-3	-1	-1
	-14/40	-13/40	-13/40
	6 MONTHS	12 MONTHS	24 MONTHS

⇕

= VALUE-DESTRUCTIVE ACTION

INSTEAD OF

Action involved =   Swallowing

⇕

Innovation/s used =   Vitamins

⇕

Resulting Actions =
- Lower stress levels
- Increase in energy
- Increased nutrients to strengthen skin and hair
- Increased protection against cancerous cells

⇕

Impersonal Value test =

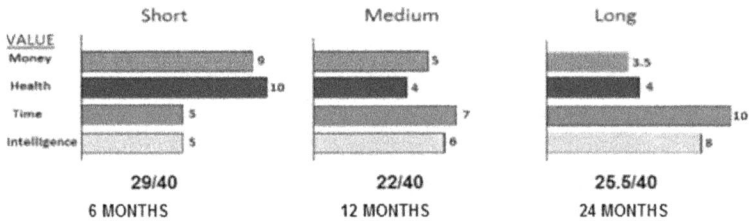

VALUE	Short	Medium	Long
Money	9	5	3.5
Health	10	4	4
Time	5	7	10
Intelligence	5	6	8
	29/40	**22/40**	**25.5/40**
	6 MONTHS	**12 MONTHS**	**24 MONTHS**

⇕

= VALUE-CREATIVE ACTION

You may now see how powerful an innovation can be in your everyday actions. This flow chart can be used to compare how innovations influence actions. Not just two innovations, as above, but as many as needed can be judged against one another, as humans have made many competing solutions for most problems. In the future, apps and software may help us calculate value like above for nearly every choice we make. You'll also see the above value graphic pop up in other sections of the book. To score any innovation well, evidence and studies are best found beforehand. Sometimes you'll need to wait for such information before scoring.

5. Innovations are both separate and part of other innovations.

An innovation can be *split into smaller innovations* that it contains within itself, which we'll call sub innovations for simplicity, and nearly all innovation are themselves *sub innovations of larger innovations*. Glass is a part for light bulbs which are in turn part of the electrical grid. The grid is full of millions of innovations like cabling, switches, and electric substations. A city can be said to be a sub-innovation of the national government, which itself is a sub innovation for international government bodies, like the U.N. The car, computer, court system, and government are built from countless sub-innovations that have been mixed over time.

6. Innovations let us do more with less action, and the opposite is also true.

Many innovations *decrease* the number of actions we need to do to get the *result* we want. People in most developed nations buy their food rather than farm it, opening up more time to have a hobby, start a family or help a charity. Sam Walton explored this in his book *Made in America*. His own Wal-Mart supermarkets, among many other innovations, led to such decreases in action. If we all had to grow our own food, then there would be *little free time* to do anything else, and so innovation would suffer. The opposite is also true, innovations can create more actions as well as fewer of them. If a nuclear explosion forced surviving humans to go back to picking berries in the woods to survive, we'd have turned the *clock back on progress* and added more actions than fewer to achieve our goals.

7. Innovations are our purposes of life.

You may have picked up on this by now. Our purpose is what we do to seek the meaning, and what we do needs to be observed by the senses of others to make any difference in their lives. Innovations cover all that is of human making, and so innovations cover all our different purposes.

8. Innovations combine and add up over time to make more innovations.

Nearly all innovations are combinations of past innovations. We, ourselves, are the result of combined evolutionary changes. Anything we call "new" in this world is simply *a different mixture* of what already existed. It looks new, but we already had the parts to do it. As Einstein observed, "Combinatorial play seems to be the essential feature in productive thought" which is seen in his own life as explored by Walter Isaacson in *Einstein: His Life and Universe.*[32]Thomas Edison combined 1,000+ experiments to find the longest burning filament to power the light bulb. Over 30,000 pages of notes from the thousands of books he read during his life were combined by Karl Marx, to write his own books.[33] Combinations are innovations.

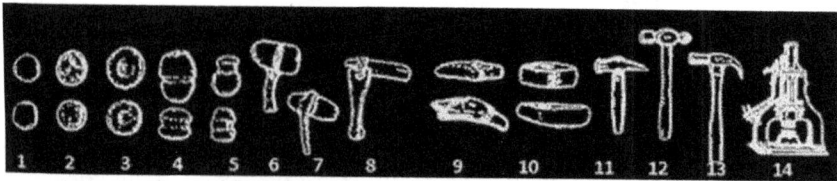
Source: Hough, Public domain

It may not seem obvious at first, but each innovation creates new actions which the next innovation aims to make better in some way. To get the picture, one simply needs to look at the evolution of the hammer above to see how it evolved over time from stone tools to a machine. Every innovation around you has a similar evolutionary path.

Economist Joseph Schumpeter understood this when he talked about innovations being "combinations," as did William Fielding Ogburn, who wrote, "When the material culture was small, inventions were few, and now, when the material culture is large, the inventions are many."[34] Philosopher Karl Popper thought that the "mainspring of evolution and progress is the variety of the material which may become subject to selection."[35]

Imagine you're on an island which represents early humanity. You and other islanders over time make 10 innovations, such as knives, pottery, beads, clothing, and stone hammers. Now all that needs to happen is for 1 of those 10 innovations to be mixed with the others to form a "new" innovation. You're the lucky one who, for the first time put a sharpened rock on top of the hunting stick to make a spear. Someone else then put two knives together with a handle, making scissors.

Not all combinations will be useful, but the more attempts we make, the more the chances increase and so with 10 innovations, we have 45 possible combinations.

1st combines with:	2, 3, 4, 5, 6, 7, 8, 9, 10	= 9 combinations
2nd combines with:	3, 4, 5, 6, 7, 8, 9, 10	= 8 combinations
3rd combines with:	4, 5, 6, 7, 8, 9, 10	= 7 combinations
4th combines with:	5, 6, 7, 8, 9, 10	= 6 combinations
5th combines with:	6, 7, 8, 9, 10	= 5 combinations
6th combines with:	7, 8, 9, 10	= 4 combinations
7th combines with:	8, 9, 10	= 3 combinations
8th combines with:	9, 10	= 2 combinations
9th combines with:	10	= 1 combination
Total combinations		= 45

Say in another 20 years, we see 50 more innovations added to those original 10 above, bringing the total to 60. Now the combination number *jumps dramatically* from 45 to 1,770 potential innovations. The bigger the pool of innovations to mix, the greater the chance of more useful combinations.

Now, say in 2000 years, the island has advanced to now hold 1.5 million innovations. This gives us the extraordinary number of 1,124,999,250,000 potential innovation combinations. Like above, many nations today have trillions of potential innovation combinations awaiting human creativity to combine them.[36]

Besides it being familiar, we use the word "innovation" for another reason. It stems from the Latin *innovare*, joining together the meanings "into" and "new"—essentially, "the introduction of something new." This, as we have explored, comes from what existed before. Bows and arrows were replaced by guns and bullets, the campfire replaced by the stove, and sharing spoken stories replaced by the written. This is why the word "invention" is confusing. It brings to mind something *mysterious*. It leads to a person being called a "genius." This word unsurprisingly originates from the Roman "genii", which are the spirits chosen for you at birth. To those in the past, inventions seemed to happen randomly; they were a spark of magic revealed by the gods. *Unseen to most* was the hard work and experiments behind it all that turned that ugly block of marble into a beautiful sculpture. Like the novel, *The Agony and the Ecstasy,* which reveals the unseen life of the artist Michelangelo who said, "If people knew how hard I worked to get my mastery, it wouldn't seem so wonderful at all."[37]

In recent centuries, as innovations have been mixed faster to solve more of our problems, it has been clearly shown that human life expectancy has grown. It's estimated that since 1840, a 3-month increase in human lifespan has been added for every year up to today.[38] This is no accident as we'll soon see, as it's through fulfilling our purpose that we can increase life expectancy for all.

Actions are Reactions to Innovations

"It is not the consciousness of men that determines their being, but their social being that determines their consciousness."[39]
Karl Marx

Our actions are our responses to the innovations we come into contact with. Psychologist Mihaly Csikszentmihalyi may be better known for his book *Flow: The Psychology of Optimal Experience*, but with Eugene Halton he earlier co-wrote, *The Meaning of Things,* in which they made a curious observation: "To understand what people are and what they might become, one must understand what goes on between people and things. What things are cherished, and why, should become part of our knowledge of human beings. Yet it is surprising how little we know about what things mean to people. By and large, social scientists have neglected a full investigation of the relationship between people and objects."[40]

As historian and author of *Auschwitz*, Laurence Rees says: "We massively underestimate the power of the culture that we are in to shape us." His work has shown how ordinary people can perform evil acts as he documents examples from Nazi Germany. But how does culture do this? To begin with innovations are culture. So if you throw in the wrong type of innovations, value destructive actions start to spread and time crimes multiply. Innovations include everything, from what we're taught at school, books we read, what the media says, the laws of the state and country and, yes, everyday objects. Studies have put people at "business" desks, with briefcases and leather portfolios, and saw only 50% of them split money with another person when playing the ultimatum game. The same game played at a "neutral" desk with a backpack, cardboard box and wooden pencil led to all 100% of them splitting money. Depending on where you live, it may be hard to change the innovations in your society, especially those that give value destructive actions. Ignoring them is one option, but most migrate away from those innovations to another country that doesn't have them.

While it's true that we can and do choose which actions we'll perform in a given moment, we can't disagree that where we are, our environment and the type of innovations it contains, shapes the *number of actions open to us to choose from*. We can't dance and shout in a library like we would at a party. We can't do a bench press while driving a car, or talk on a phone with no signal.

If we remove innovations, we mostly *lower the number of actions* open to us. Take the mobile phone away from your desk, and you stop the action of texting during work. Put the phone back, and that action becomes possible again. When innovations are missing, not only does the number of actions we're open to drop, but it may *force us* to choose an action we may never have done so before. Marie Kondo shows this in *The Life Changing Magic of Tidying Up*. Say Kate has lost her phone and laptop, and she wants to rush back to see if she can find them at the shopping center, but before that she must cancel the coming dinner with her frail grandparents. Strangely, she can't find their new mobile number saved anywhere, they don't use the internet, and she doesn't have a car, so she decides to ride her bike 20 minutes across town to knock on their door to let them know what she'd otherwise say in seconds on the phone.

Months later, when she is so close to finishing her software, her laptop is unable to connect to the internet. She now needs to bike 15 minutes to get to the library to go online to find a fix to a problem in her software code. We can see how taking away some innovations can lead to an increase in the number of actions needed to get a result.

What if you never knew of the existence of an innovation in the first place? You'll never know *how many actions it could save you* in getting a result. For example, what would you do with this?

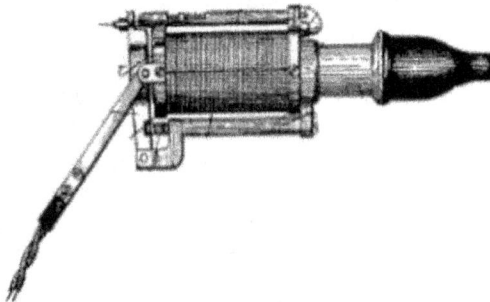

The above illustration shows the knowledge problem humans have. With so many innovations in the world combining constantly, unless one knows where to search, it becomes tougher to find the *best innovation to use right now* to solve a problem. Putting people together can lead to solutions. Take the 20-year old family mystery that was solved in just 14 minutes with a simple blog post online. A grandson copied the mixed jumble of mysterious letters found on index cards left by his speechless and dying grandma in her final days. Once he posted them online, where many people could think it through, an answer was quickly found.[41] More people solving problems thanks to innovations like the internet, mostly leads to faster and better answers.

This point brings to mind an example from cognitive scientist Steven Pinker, author of *The Better Angels of our Nature* and *The Sense of Style*. In another book of his, *The Blank Slate*, he used an example about a man named Rex, who got off the couch and walked to the phone to call his friend, Cecile. Pinker writes, "How might we explain why Rex just walked over to the phone? We would not say that the phone-shaped stimuli caused Rex's limbs to swing in certain arcs. Rather, we might say that he just wanted to speak to his friend Cecile and knew that Cecile was home." This may be true, but had *Rex not known what a phone was or how to use it*, he would have had no chance to move his limbs in certain arcs to talk with Cecile. The same could be said if he did not have a phone, like many of the world's poor. But let's say Rex's phone had stopped working days back. With the action of calling now gone from his range of actions, he may then *not even think* to contact Cecile in the first place. With his health as it is, walking to Cecile's home may lead to bodily damage and lowered life expectancy.

Why then shouldn't we blame the phone company when a wife commits suicide after a verbal clash on the phone with her husband? Doesn't the innovation used determine the actions taken, even when they are deadly? The phone, unlike the cigarette, gives *multiple actions* to the user. A call to anyone in the world is possible if you know their number, and anything can be chatted about. The phone that was found on the wife who committed suicide could have been used to dial any number, not just her husband's. She had a choice, as we all usually do, but the range of choices to pick from is determined by the innovation. *The more actions an innovation provides the more responsibility falls on us, the less actions the more the responsibility falls on the innovation and those who make it.* Like the cigarette, it gives us just *one action*—a mouthful of addictive toxic air. A cigarette does not have any *practical use* beyond this. Unlike the phone, the cigarette's existence rests on it addicting people to repeat value-destruction on themselves. Another example?

The CEO of ashleymadison.com defended his dating website, saying that it doesn't encourage, but "merely facilitates", marital infidelity. "We're just a platform. No website or 30-second ad is going to convince anyone to cheat." Wrong. Anyone knows that if you let people *easily do what was once difficult, more will do it*. Making any action easier promotes use of it. Hold on though – this website is no charity, it's a business. To grow and survive a business needs more people to use it. Does their own motto sound like it doesn't encourage? "Life is short, have an affair."[42]

To find value in an innovation like the telephone, we must compare its actions to earlier actions that would have happened before it was made. A century before, without a phone, Rex likely would have *written a letter* to Cecile instead. Today, many people text message one another in seconds vs. days spent waiting for the mail.

Does this help explain everyday life? Let's break down what happened when Kate walked to the library to use the internet. Walking is of natural origin, humans did it before we innovated, but *what motivated her choice to walk were other* innovations of human making. When she walks, she has clothes on to shield her from the weather and the elements, and her shoes protect her feet, while footpaths, streets and pedestrian crossings provide safe areas to walk. If many of these innovations were gone, as seen during wartime, then like Rex, Kate may not even think about going outside in the first place. There would be too large a risk for damage to her body and, therefore, her life expectancy.

Now imagine you're a fly on the wall at the home of Kate's boyfriend, Mike, where you see him and Kate arguing. Could their actions be moved by innovations? One innovation already mentioned is Mike's home, which protects them from the weather. They are clothed, have food, and a toilet. If just these innovations were deleted, then Kate and Mike may not be having the conversation in the first place. Now, you as the fly see they're talking about money matters. They are reacting to the innovation of the financial system humans have built over time. After the fight, you see Kate sitting silently in thought. Which possible reaction to innovations could be happening during silent thought though?

She is most likely thinking with *language*. The words popping up in her mind are causing other different words and sentences to do so also. Language has physical existence as it can be spoken, written, heard, and read. The definitions of words can affect how we think. Kate also likes to picture her thoughts, but all those images can't help but include innovations... like the food stained car Mike picked her up in on their first date.

It follows then that society, defined by some as a group of people who interact with one another, can only exist if *innovations are in between* those interactions. Innovations let us, in humanity's earliest days, relate to one another beyond our deep grunting. We see then that society exists based on the type of innovations that are in between people. Which affects how they trust, hate or cooperate with others, most of whom they meet for the first time. A country using the internet has websites which show ratings of how trustworthy businesses are, which boosts confidence in customers that they won't be ripped off. Another country bans the internet, and so its people are more suspicious, being unable to know who is trustworthy.

All this we call *innovational determinism* or in other words... *innovation filtration*

1. As innovations have evolved with humans, all we think and do is filtered through innovations.

The often debated "free will" concept becomes pointless as no human action or thought is immune to innovation filtration. We can't go back to a free "state of nature", to a time *before innovations arose.* We can't change much of the source code we've grown up with.

2. We can, *to some degree*, predict possible future scenarios by comparing the most likely to be combined innovations into the future. The 2nd movie in the series *Back to the Future* shows how we humans can try to predict the innovations of the future, sometimes accurately.

To be clear, our "determinism" is different from "technological determinism." The word "technology" doesn't *cover all* material human creations as our definition of "innovation" does. This shortcoming is one of the major reasons why technological determinism has not been given much thought.

Let's see innovational determinism at work: Mike tells Kate he bought a car. He says to Kate, "I compared the features and prices online and chose the best." What Mike forgets to add, as its obvious to Kate, is that he had past experience with using the internet. Before even knowing that he needs to know how to read, do basic math, and negotiate. He knows what website to use to find the best deal out of thousands listed. We all do this in our own way every day. Mike's dad on the other hand doesn't use the internet, but instead he just talks to friends to get advice. This leads him to find only a few deals versus the thousands he could find online. What if an entire nation was like Mike's dad? We could predict quite well that they'd likely all be unable to get the best deals, as few would know how to find them.

The internet today and over time may grow to become the closest practical example of "perfect knowledge," that mystical dream of being able to know all there is.

Now, though the range of actions may be known in most cases, it's harder to know the one that will be chosen. Take the example from the comedy classic, *The Gods Must Be Crazy*. The film starts with a glass bottle dropped from a plane which lands in the Kalahari Desert. Not knowing what the bottle is, the local tribe uses it for all sorts of things, like making music, playing games, and even as a weapon against one another.

"Sure," some might say, "The glass bottle can make tribespeople perform new actions, but that's thanks to human nature, not because of the bottle!" We know that's not true, as humans can and do reject dependency. Once we were told that human nature swayed our actions, but most now agree that if the environment does *not first trigger certain genes,* human nature cannot be unleashed in our actions.

Say a child is born with genes linked to violent behavior, but they grow up in a kind, happy family. They may, instead, focus the *violent urge into sports.* If they grew up in an abusive family, they could have easily become a criminal. Remember your school friends? Did they turn out later in life differently than you or even they expected? This means we're missing something. We're missing what it is that *pushes* a person to choose one action from the many on offer.

Could our guess be …that the innovations we use affect our genes, which then *push* us to choose some actions over others? Could human nature be changed with innovations? In the last 30 years, science has been showing more evidence that this may be the case.

Q.	What innovation/s out there has changed your actions the most?
A.	

We Are What We Use:
How Innovations Affect our Genes

"Many scientific researchers have shown an obvious fact, that the behavior of a human being is created by the environment. If genes predispose a certain behavior but the environment doesn't support it, then that behavior won't manifest."[43]
TROM – The Reality of Me (Documentary)

Did you know that our fastest evolutionary leap happened in the last 3,000 years? It's a gene mutation found in people from Tibet and other mountain areas which stops their blood from thickening at such heights. This lets them live freely without the headaches and sickness that bother and even kill foreign mountain climbers.

Now take the simple book, computer, or mobile phone. Your eyes are mostly at a short distance from the screen. Use it often enough and it can lead to near-sightedness, called myopia. It's common in Asia, with an estimated 70-90% of the people having it. This may be linked to the long history of study in Asian culture, as influenced way back by the teachings of the philosopher, Confucius.

In Africa, the majority of the people have the opposite condition—hyperopia, or far-sightedness. This could be due to their short history of study. Darwin touched on this point in *The Descent of Man*. "It is familiar to everyone that watchmakers and engravers are liable to be short-sighted, whilst men living much out of doors… are generally long-sighted."[44]

We know that both nature and nurture play a role in the way a person acts, and we've explored the nurture side with innovations which make up our culture, but what about the nature side? *What if… nurture affects nature,* and not the other way around? What if innovations influence our genes?

We know of two methods that lead to changes inside humans. The first method is about what sits *inside us* from birth, the genes we inherit from our parents. We may look like our parents, have high blood pressure like our grandfather, or a weak heart like our mother.

The other method is what we use and filter into our body and mind from the *outside*. Like we do with all the innovations we use. For example, drinking lactose, an ingredient in dairy products, was not something our early ancestors could do. They simply had too low a level of the enzyme lactase, which is needed to digest lactose. All human babies are born with enough lactase to drink milk from their mothers, but as they grow into adults, this is turned off in some, stopping them from continuing to drink milk without feeling sick. So how did this change? One theory is that, once cows became part of our farms thousands of years ago, people began trying to drink their milk before killing them and eating their meat. Early on, most who tried this became sick, but a few did not. Those few who could drink milk had a high level of lactase, just like those few lucky birds who'd developed long beaks in our earlier example. Also like the birds, it's guessed that these milk drinkers were able to survive food shortages, unlike the others. By some estimates, those who could drink milk could leave ten times more surviving children than the others. By those estimates, it's no wonder then that the "turned on" lactase enzyme has spread to hundreds of millions today.[45]

Before this discovery, scientists had never seen a human innovation (domesticating cows and consuming a once foreign ingredient, lactose) lead to a biological change that was passed on from parents to children. John Cairns, a British molecular biologist, tested this by placing bacteria that could not produce lactase into small dishes with lactose as the only food source. The unthinkable happened as days later the bacteria were *eating* the lactose, meaning the DNA of the bacteria had changed in response to *starvation*, seemingly confirming that in times of famine, milk can be digested to survive.[46]

Today an estimated 98% of people of European ancestry can digest lactose. In Hispanics, its 20-50%, African Americans, 20-40%, and 5% for people of Asian ancestry.[47] Here is where it gets interesting, though. You've likely heard of "lactose intolerance"? It's when people who can drink milk and eat dairy can't anymore—the gene gets switched off.[48]

What if our other genes could switch on and off like this? The same genes that control our mood, personality, behaviors, and all the rest? If this is possible, then something else is affecting our genes and doing it at a faster rate than the thousands of years it's taken the lactase gene to switch.

Epigenetics is the field that studies how genes can be turned on and off.[49] Explored in books such as *The Epigenetics Revolution*, this new field shows we all have a switch in our genes, which certain actions will trigger. This happens through "chemical tags" (which glue onto our DNA and sit on top of the genes) which turn the genes' ability to express themselves either on or off. Scientists simplify this by saying that the gene is the *hardware* and the chemical tag is the *software*. The gene does the work, but the tag tells it what to do.[50]

The trigger for the switch can seemingly come from *all and any actions*, from emotions, daily stress, what we watch, read, our beliefs, the foods we eat, chats with friends, nearly anything imaginable.[51] All of these daily actions are affected by innovations.

In *Epigenetics: The Ultimate Mystery of Inheritance,* Richard C. Francis PhD talks about the story of twin brothers, both suffering from Kallmann syndrome. This means they have lost the ability to smell and have underdeveloped sexual organs. Both brothers have the lack of smell, but one is fully sexually developed while the other isn't. According to all the science, their problems should be *identical* given they're twins and share the same DNA. A similar story is seen in another set of twins, this time with the same genetic fault in chromosome 15, one has Angelman's syndrome and the other Prader-Willi syndrome. This also should not happen according to genetic laws. A fault in the chromosome should result in the same disease, not two different ones.[52] So how could all this be possible?

According to epigenetics, the actions that you, your parents, and even your grandparents make, can *affect you and your children* through the on/off switching of the tags. Russian scientist Ivan Pavlov showed some of this over 90 years ago. He is best known for his experiments of ringing a bell to show it's dinnertime for his dogs, who would salivate at the sound as they expected food to be close by. However, it's another of his bell-ringing experiments, this time on mice and their young, which showed curious results. The first generation of mice, the parents, took 300 lessons to link the bell-ringing with feeding time; the second generation, their kids, only 100 lessons; the third, grand-kids, 30 lessons; the fourth, great-grand kids, 10 lessons; and the fifth, great-great-grand kids, took only 5 lessons. This old data seems to support what modern epigeneticists are now finding, that mice and arguably all other species experience "memory-like" changes to their genetic tags which are then passed on to their offspring.[53]

Harry Potter had magic memory passed on by his dad as seen with how quickly he learned to ride on a broom. But in the real world, genetic memory means that children may be at risk of inheriting the value-destructive actions of their parents who use *certain innovations* in their lifetime. A recent study showed that a third of all babies who were born to mothers who had smoked during the first trimester of pregnancy had changes in 100 gene regions. Some regions were linked to fetal development, nicotine addiction, and the self control failure to quit smoking.[54]

Research shows that the eating habits of parents may have a direct effect on the life expectancy of even their unborn grandchildren and possibly generations beyond that. Take the embryo of a baby in a half-starved mother, who as a result has a smaller pelvis size. Epigenetic tags would send instruction to prevent the baby fetus from growing to a healthy size to keep it small enough to push through her narrow birth canal. This results in an underdeveloped baby, likely to have health problems as an adult.[55,56]

When electricity was cut in Canada during the Quebec ice storm of 1998, "signatures" in the genes of unborn children were later found showing the stress of the experience in the pregnant mothers.[57]

It may be wise, not only for yourself but for your children's sake to take more value-creative actions and *avoid value-destructive ones*, as the epigenetic switches they inherit could push them to be inclined to smoke, eat poorly, watch trash TV, and other value-destructive actions.

Remember that these switches are not set in stone. *They can be changed.* New switches can also happen for the first time. Say a child comes to worship a singer by replaying their songs, with lyrics about drugs, depression, and dangerous sex. This can lead to an epigenetic switch and a change in the child's actions. This isn't just limited to song lyrics. It's the same for all innovations we use or come in contact with.

On the flip side, the "genius" of a child prodigy often comes from early exposure to an innovation, which flicks another epigenetic switch. The book *Beethoven: Anguish and Triumph* explores how Beethoven was taught from a very young age by his father, who unsurprisingly was a music teacher. A little earlier, the exact same thing happened to Mozart.

With DNA sequencing getting cheaper each year, more people can now find which genes they have that make them "likely" to get health problems. It doesn't mean it's certain they will develop a disease, but it does mean they're more likely to if they don't put a stop to some actions. We have more control than we like to think, as some scientists say *that around 80%* of how we age and our potential for chronic diseases come from our actions.[58,60]

This raises some sticky issues. If parents, by using some innovations and not others, seek selfish pleasure over the health of their future children, should society stop them from using those innovations to prevent future suffering? In the future, newborn babies may even *have their DNA checked* and saved in order to find genes that could lead to health problems later in life, letting parents prepare the child's upbringing to lessen the chance of triggering the troublesome genes. This opens the door then for science to find gene patterns that may cause or correlate to violent criminal behavior later in life. Deleting the names of the babies will be crucial to protect privacy so that when they grow up they won't be stereotyped as potential criminals.

There's still plenty about epigenetics that hasn't been confirmed. For example, how exactly do innovations turn these markers on and off? Our bet is that it appears that this happens through the information our *many senses collect* of every action we get up to. And as we know, the innovations we use play a crucial role in what actions we most end up doing.

We see this pop up with nationality. People have long grouped others, not only by how they look, but also by their habits and cultural beliefs. Rather than genetics, it's the innovations people from different nations use over time that shape their actions on an epigenetic level. Some may point out that a society's cultural beliefs prevent the use of certain innovations, like African nations that have banned birth control pills or condoms, but that's not quite accurate. Cultural beliefs as we know are innovations, as are birth control pills. *They are not separate.* Both, like all innovations, are made of matter which can be observed through the human senses. Remember, cultural beliefs only exist if they are spoken, written, or recorded in some way. How do we discover a good innovation from a not so good one? We will soon explore this for without knowing that, no one can hope to change people who are brainwashed from a young age to think that birth control pills came from the devil.

Darwin, long ago, had similar thoughts to what we are now learning with epigenetics. "Now, if some one man in a tribe, more sagacious than the others, invented a new snare or weapon, or other means of attack or defense, the plainest self-interest, without the assistance of much reasoning power, would prompt the other members to imitate him; and all would thus profit. The habitual practice of each new art must likewise in some slight degree strengthen the intellect. If the new invention were an important one, the tribe would increase in number, spread, and supplant other tribes. In a tribe thus rendered more numerous there would always be a rather greater chance of the birth of other superior and inventive members. If such men left children to inherit their mental superiority, the chance of the birth of still more ingenious members would be somewhat better, and in a very small tribe decidedly better."[61]

Like a cell that moves away in its Petri dish from what's attacking it, so do we, as our bodies are but giant groups of cells. A drug addict may try to tell themselves that they enjoy drugs but that *won't convince* the cells in their body to stop dying out. The same for our life expectancy, which will be affected by the on/off switches happening from our actions, which either improve or destroy our lives, based on which innovations we use. Innovations leading to body-deteriorating, value-destructive actions will in time be less favored by the epigenetic process than their value-creative opposites. The four Value factors show us why, pointing to bodily damage, sometimes slow and indirect, that many popular innovations can have.

Pt. 7 BUILDINGS OF LOST DREAMS

PRODUCTIVITY
When you do more with less Action

KATE!

SORRY JOE I GOT EVIDENCE THAT MY PROGRAM IS GOOD FOR THE COMPANY. IT COMPLETED THE TAX RETURNS 75% FASTER THAN OUR CURRENT METHOD!

NO NO NO! YOU USED WORKTIME AGAIN!

SLAM

IF HER PROGRAM GETS OUT THE 200 HOURS WE CHARGE FOR TAX RETURNS WILL DROP TO 50, LOSING US TRUCKLOADS OF MONEY!

Kate tries to show Joe that her software can save the company from missing its deadline but Joe refuses to hear her out, because if tax returns are completed faster they'll earn less money.

If we apply this to all other innovations, it could result in *policy-making challenges* for governments. Especially if studies can show unhealthy epigenetic switches, like those that *aggravate cancerous cells and tumors* being switched on with the use of certain music, magazines, foods, TV shows, gadgets and websites.[62,63] Take horror movies, for example. Some adults may think they do little harm, but how many billions of nightmares have they led to which *sucked precious free life time*? Horror is uniquely focused on the extremes of death, torture, and fear. All these decrease life, and unsurprisingly most people want to get the images they've seen out of their heads.[64]

We've now talked about the what and why, but *how* does life expectancy really change and how do we choose which innovations to use based on this?

Chapter Summary

\#   Evolution is how we and the natural world evolved, separate from innovations:

   1.   Small differences exist within a species.
   2.   Changes in the environment lead to a struggle for survival.
   3.   The difference that helps those survive is passed on to their young.

\#   The difference between humans and all other species is that humans are self-aware, and this came about when we first innovated.

\#   Morals change with new innovations

\#   Innovations come from a controlled, not a random process.

\#   Anything of human creation is an innovation. An innovation contains the following:

   1.   Are physical and so can be observed by the human senses
   2.   Come from and/or have been improved by humans
   3.   Thoughts are not innovations
   4.   Actions are not innovations
   5.   Are both separate and part of other innovations
   6.   Let us do more with less action, and can do the opposite
   7.   Are our purposes in life
   8.   Combine and add up over time to make more innovations

\#   Our actions are reactions to innovations.

\#   The type of innovations we use may switch our genes epigenetically, leading to increases or decreases in our life expectancy over time.

CHAPTER FOUR

How Does Life Expectancy Change?

"No empire, no sect, no star seems to have exerted greater power and influence in human affairs than these mechanical discoveries."[1]
Sir Francis Bacon (speaking of the magnetic compass, gunpowder, and the printing press)

"The power to question is the basis of all human progress."
Indira Gandhi

To answer the question of how life expectancy changes, we need to remember what we touched on earlier. That we can tell if an innovation give us more value-creative or a value-destructive action by the bodily damage it inflicts. Typically, the more actions needed to use an innovation, the more damage; the less actions, the less damage.

When we use an innovation, our mind gets information from our senses and this can then *trigger an epigenetic switch*. Feelings may be a sign of this, like pain or unease, but likely it happens even without them. Have you ever had a song stuck in your head? If that song were to sit replaying in your mind, then depending upon the lyrics, it may lead to epigenetic switches over time.

How does that change our life expectancy? Each cell of the trillions found in our body contains DNA, which holds our genes.[2] The on/off epigenetic switch on top of the gene should influence the *telomere length* of the cell. Telomeres are the *protectors* of our cells, and given that we are a bundle of cells at the microscopic level, the longer the telomeres of our cells are, the longer we will live.[3] In contrast, shorter telomeres result in a shorter lifespan. As Elizabeth Blackburn, the 2009 Nobel Laureate in Medicine and author of *The Telomere Effect* writes "DNA is not supposed to change. You've probably heard that the DNA we are born with is the DNA we die with". She discovered the opposite, what we do and what we use in our daily life can grow our telomeres, not just shorten them. Last chapter showed that what our parents did before having us can impact our genes and unsurprisingly that includes the telomeres we are born with. Shortened telomeres at birth pushes you behind the starting line in the race of life and this is likely from the counterproductive innovations your parents were using.

While more research is needed in the long run, studies have found that diet, exercise, and our environment play a role in the length of our telomeres. Think of a cell as shoes with holes in the bottom. Wearing them would make your feet wet, while fixing up the holes would stop that. If our actions, swayed by innovations, lead to damage and inflammation of our body and mind, like being tired, stressed or diseased, then our epigenetic markers may switch, leading to shortened telomere length, and *exposing* the cells to more damage.

Obvious examples are the damage our liver cells get from too much alcohol. Smoking damages cells in our lungs, leading to trouble breathing. Antidepressant drugs alter our brain cells.[4,5] Could some Websites, Apps, TV shows, Music, and other innovations have similar affects?

As Blackmore's book explains, on average babies at birth have 10,000 telomere base pairs, but bodily damage crushes this down by more than half to 4,800 base pairs by our 65th birthday. Mothers with the highest stress in the year before giving birth had babies with telomeres that were shorter by 1760 base pairs. Stress as we know is the wear and tear of our bodies that's influenced by the innovations we surround ourselves with. So how do we reduce this bodily damage?

"Occam's Razor," comes from medieval monk William of Ockham, who said, "It is idle to bring about through several means what can be brought about with fewer."[6] This concept is generally talked about as "productivity," and for this book we define it as— *to do more with less action*. When this happens, value is made. When we do the opposite, we destroy it. When less is done with more actions, stress is placed on our bodies, likely leading to damage to our cells over time. We talked about this earlier in the section on bodily damage. Less done with more actions was the story for most of human history—backbreaking farming work led the average life expectancy to be very low. Once we started to *remove that stress with animals and then with machines*, we saw jumps in life expectancy.

Various thinkers through history like Spinoza, Hegel, and Marx all referred to being "productive" as one of the fullest expressions of a person.[7] Whenever you read words like "progress," "growth," and "success" they boil down mostly to the aim of doing more with less action. It's a near-universal response that people, when seeing something more productive, will *gravitate* towards it. We tend to embrace anything that helps us do actions in a faster, cheaper, healthier, and smarter way.

What does productivity look like in the real world? Consider a factory making 1,000 TVs in 10 minutes for $20 rather than 800 TVs in 40 minutes at $30. The first example is clearly more productive than the second. Looking to the internet, the websites that become leaders are mostly ones which need fewer clicks to get a result. Twitter.com does this for communication, as explored in *Hatching Twitter*. Its co-founder and former CEO, Evan Williams, explained, "Take a human desire, preferably one that has been around for a really long time… and use modern technology to take out steps."[8] Just like Aaron Levie of Box.com who asks, "What steps can we cut out of this process to automate it?"[9] Removing actions that once were needed to finish the same task leads to freeing "more" of the four value factors for use in other areas of our life. Remember a time when you wore sunglasses? Ever ask yourself why you did it? With health, they protected your eyes from the harm of the sun's rays. With money, wearing them protects or delays needing costly eye surgery decades later. With time, they save us countless hours with an eye doctor. With intelligence, they remove the cognitive distraction of the sun's glare, letting you focus on what's in front of you.

Few studies are done with a fair criterion to see *how innovations change those for whom they are made – the consumers*. Most, instead, focus on the impact innovations have on companies, governments, and other forms of enterprise. Also, these studies, instead of looking at what innovations do best, like grow knowledge, remove pain, or create relationships, focus mostly on cost. But cost is money, and money is just one of the four factors. The others are forgotten. It's the innovation that *gives more of each* of the four value factors that is likely, but not always, to be the most used and adopted innovation.

The Forgotten Importance of Productivity – Unlocking Free Life Time

Let's try put an end to the Loch Ness Monster of economic mysteries: why do most customers over time choose one innovation over another? For instance, what phone brand do you use and why? The most profitable companies, like Apple, Inc. are in most cases making innovations, like iPhones, that are the most productive to the consumer versus the others, like Nokia phones. iPhones dominate as *they give more actions* than old feature phones. Remember, profit is the slave of value as Google and Facebook have shown. Losing money in their early years so *to make more productive innovations to attract income* in years to come.

Economists have long looked at productivity as the way to improve an economy, and the key driver of productivity they found was…you guessed it… innovation. Gary Banks, from the Australian Productivity Commission writes, "Productivity is virtually synonymous with innovation,"[10] while another study continues, "Innovation is synonymous with change, and a high capacity to deal with change allows the nation to be resilient and prosper."[11] Innovation is the main method for growing wealth, for *if nothing new or different comes into existence, then value cannot increase.* Governments can cheat by printing money, but living standards of people are unlikely to move up. It's little surprise to find that "ninety-one percent of Australian businesses report a benefit from innovation and this can be as high as 97.6% for large Australian businesses. These benefits include increased revenue, lowered costs, gaining a competitive advantage, and improved customer service."[12]

In fact, the single most important statistic we know of boosting standards of living (Which is an average measure of the wealth, material goods, employment, housing, health care, and education, in any nation) is by *increasing productivity.*[13.14] Politicians like to repeat the word "productivity" but don't explain what it means exactly or why it matters until one of them finally says they wish to cut traffic times by 30 minutes, the Time value factor, so people can get home sooner from work.

As innovations improve living standards and boost life expectancy, what's crucial to realize is that people slowly get more days, months and years of free life time with which they can go on to make their own innovations. We can see this most clearly by looking at the increases in productivity from innovations in medicine.

Imagine for a moment that you were a rich king or queen from the 18th century with everything at your fingertips. You may think that such a life back then would be better than it is for you today, but you'd be wrong. Even as a ruler, your risk of illness would have been higher than *that of a poor person in a developing country today*. Mary II of England died of smallpox, for which almost all babies are now vaccinated at birth. Her husband, William III, died of pneumonia, which today could have been cured quickly with antibiotics. It doesn't matter how much money you have either, you could be dead quickly if the right innovations are missing. Industrialist billionaire, Nathan Mayer Rothschild died long ago from a blister-like abscess, which today can be cured for a few dollars at your local pharmacy.[15,16]

Humanity eventually succeeded in innovating its way out of this mess. Edward Jenner helped make the innovation of vaccination, which is estimated to have helped save 530 million lives and counting.[17] Louis Pasteur removed the pain of millions, along with the belief that disease was spread to those who sinned against God by showing that surgeons spread it by not washing their hands. As *Ghost Map* by Steven Johnson showed, cities could now grow larger, as the spread of disease was shut down. Every survivor of such innovations not only was given life, but also had a chance now to *make their own innovation*.[18]

You are likely to have added 10 years to your life just by living in a country with a decent healthcare system. For those not so lucky, other innovations are today filling the gap. Mobile phones can now help doctors heal patients. Apps like "Figure 1" lets pictures be sent to doctors to check for problems.[19] These apps, if spread wide enough, will have a large impact in countries like Niger that don't even have a single doctor per 1,000 people.[20] If the app shows a life-threatening diagnosis, the information is sent to the nearest hospital to get treatment prepared and a doctor sent out. Such use is likely to spread to developed countries where costs for treatment and drugs are growing.

Professor Frank Lichtenberg from Columbia University has found that new medical breakthroughs made up for 40 % of the growth in life expectancy during the 1980s and 1990s alone.[21] Medicine is most visible in how it saves people from death, and heals bodily damage, but the combined effect of all other innovations we use plays a larger role. If his figures are accurate, it leaves another 60 % of the healing to the rest of our innovations. Other studies suggest that medicine has far less impact than Lichtenberg's estimates, leaving a larger gap for other innovations to fill.[22]

Pt. 8 BUILDINGS OF LOST DREAMS

LIFE EXPECTANCY
The average age of death in society

Joe doesn't want to admit it, but those cigarettes he smokes are doing something to him. If the scans of his lungs are true, he thinks he may soon be in a grave if he doesn't stop.

Take Infrastructure innovations that get built by governments, and are taken for granted by many, all help decrease incidents of bodily damage and the number of unhealthy people. For example, clean running water, toilet piping, sewerage systems and roads. The simple fact is that for modern medical innovations like drugs, imaging machines, clinics and hospitals to be made, used and spread, a huge bunch of non-medical innovations, like computers, scanners, printers, and electrical systems *need to exist first.* If these non-medical innovations are not around, we can say goodbye to the medical ones.

That's been the major problem for those hoping to help impoverished countries. But some breakthroughs in innovation are happening like the fridge-sized, "Slingshot," which may lead to a huge jump in life expectancy. It promises to reverse the lack of clean drinking water for millions of people, making up to 1,000 liters out of any water source, whether it is salt, sewage, or bore.[23]

In the past, prisoners paid for their crimes by working on government infrastructure projects. Developed nations can today donate not just money, but prison labor to work as removalists, shifting things on projects, like the set up of electricity grids in poorer nations. By such work prisoners can gain an *appreciation for the society they sinned* against by seeing the real problems most of the world's people are forced to suffer daily.

Donations are not the only answer to poverty as authors Abhijit Banerjee and Esther Duflo discuss in *Poor Economics*. Other authors like Paul Polak and Mal Warwick say in *The Business Solution to Poverty* that what will most help is for poor people to earn more money. The money most earn now is not enough to get them out of the poverty cycle they are in. Yet, if useful innovations are made at lower prices, things can change. Coke knows this as it sells its drinks for around 0.25 U.S. cents per bottle in many of these poor nations; or else no one could afford to buy them. Taking that example, some enterprises have together helped more than 20 million people escape poverty and increase their life expectancy by growing their income for the first time by using the simple innovation of a treadle foot pump like the one pictured below.

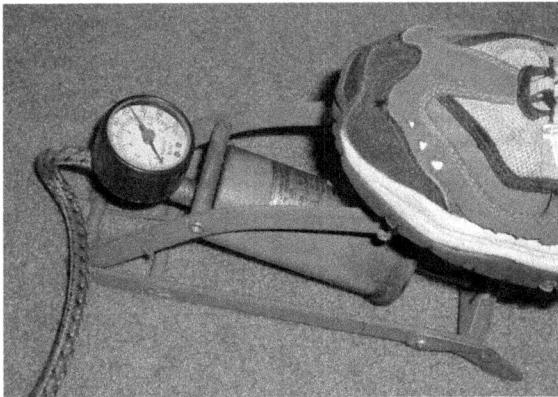

Source: Scott Ehardt, Public domain

Poor people in the developing world have been pressing their feet onto these pumps and lifting their families out from near starvation and death. How so? The foot pump is like a water hose, sucking water from a nearby lake and splashing it onto corn, wheat and other crops. It's shrunk the time spent on the backbreaking daily work of carrying in buckets and splashing round the same amount of water. This is like a mini industrial revolution. But the foot pump is one of many innovations needed before increasing growth can occur to lift developing countries out of poverty. How so?

As the pump lets more liters of water be pushed out to a larger area, so more food crops can be grown for the family—the *extra crops are then sold for profit at the markets*, and for the first time more money can be earned. Keep this in mind when donating to charities. The ones who help give out such innovations are likely to lead more quickly to the shrinking of poverty while simple cash deposits can lead to billions of donated dollars landing in the bank accounts of corrupt government officials.

Seeing the above, we realize how all innovations beyond just medicine can push our life expectancy in even the smallest way upwards by helping us do more with less actions. Changes in life expectancy may be so small as to seem almost worthless, but they *add up over time*, we just have to track them. Imagine a tribe living almost the same way it did a hundred years ago, with life expectancy holding steady at around 35 years of age. As most of their time is focused on survival, little free time exists to think and make new innovations. Also, their low life expectancy is mostly caused by actions that they *don't know* are value-destructive, like drinking dirty water that gives disease. Yet, say we gave them the innovation of a pot for boiling water to make it clean, we'll see that over time the 35 year average jumps to 43 years in a single generation. Give the foot pump, and it goes to 48 years. Bring in the Slingshot, and it goes to 52. Launch electricity, and they're up to 59. You can see where this is heading. It's a story repeated in most nations throughout history. Add schools, health care, roads, supermarkets, and in time, life expectancy is at developed world levels.

If you take this example and apply it anywhere in your life, you can see how small but obvious a fact it is that innovations *change* life expectancy That footrest in your living room could be saving you years by lowering the risk of blood clots gathering in your legs. Your use of credit cards removes the need to touch cash and coins, one of the dirtiest disease carriers in the world. And innovations like the internet give you quick information on how to do more with less action in minutes not months, such as the fastest path to take on the road tomorrow, the best and cheapest health insurance or what foods best prevent cancer.

Productivity

iv. The measurement of the value that an innovation gives to our actions*

To reword physics, we may call what we've just covered the *special theory of productivity*. Now we're ready to show the *general theory*. How productive an innovation is can be seen when one explores how much value-creation or destruction is found in the actions that the innovation affects. As we know, when an innovation lets the least number of actions get the same or better result, then bodily damage is reduced and this leads to increases in life expectancy and standard of living over time. The more such innovations are made, spread, and used the more life improves for those using them.

One innovation may increase life expectancy by 2 years, another by 280 days, the third by 40 days. Add them up and it's a decent amount of life time. The more productive innovations society uses, the *longer its members are likely to live*, giving more free life time for them to make innovations for others.

The criteria we attach to each definition below are like those from previous chapters. We look below at the electronic book reader, or e-reader as an example. Let's see how it compares to the next alternative innovation, the printed book.

An e-reader can connect to the largest library of books thanks to the internet. On it, you can search any book to buy and then search anything within the book you want to find. You can copy and paste text directly out from the book, again saving time not needing to retype. Each of these actions is done faster on an e-reader than with a printed book.

The cost of the e-reader may be above $100, depending upon which brand and where you buy it. But this larger upfront cost shrinks with the long run saving of each e-book purchase being in the $0.99 to $9.99 price range. Compare this to $24.99 for an average hardcover book and you can see how you can read many e-books for the price of one hardcover.

Many innovations built into the e-reader lower the number of actions you'd need to remember. For example, the e-reader keeps track of the last section read, saving you from needing to rely on a bookmark which may fall out. The *search function* lets you quickly find anything in seconds. A printed book means more time spent searching the index, which even then may not have listed the keyword you're after. The end result is more cognitive use of your memory with a physical book than an e-reader.

Whether reading off a screen is worse for the eyes than reading off paper has yet to be determined. Yet one health difference is that an e-reader stays at a light weight no matter how many e-books are stored in it. You could have 10,000 e-books, and the device would still *weigh less* than one printed book. Just ask any school student with a backbreaking backpack full of textbooks which they'd choose. Printed books also need paper made from cut down trees which impacts the environment and the many species that call it home.

Action involved =	Reading on a screen
Innovation/s used =	E-book reader
Resulting Actions =	• Time saved as the search function allows information to be easily found
	• Money is saved as books cost less
	• Health is improved as carrying heavy books don't crush your spine
	• Intelligence is boosted as more relevant information can be read

INSTEAD OF

Action involved =   Reading on paper

Innovation/s used =   Standard print book

Resulting Actions =
- Time wasted flicking through book to find information
- Money is lost as books are more expensive
- Health is at risk long term if many books are carried in backpacks
- Intelligence affected from the delay in finding right information

Impersonal value test   Reading on a screen Vs
total   Reading on a printed page

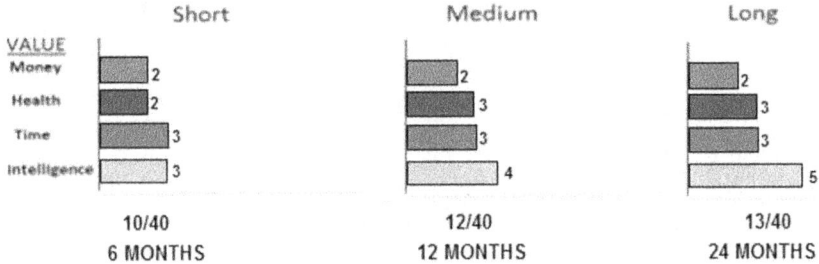

	Short	Medium	Long
VALUE			
Money	2	2	2
Health	2	3	3
Time	3	3	3
Intelligence	3	4	5
	10/40	12/40	13/40
	6 MONTHS	12 MONTHS	24 MONTHS

You've likely seen people walking on the street, robot-like with earphones plugged in and their eyes glued to their phones. But why? Sure, some may be listening to music, but others now can listen to podcasts, audio books, or streaming radio. We can't deny these innovations now give people more choice of actions. Radio hosts are being replaced by podcast hosts such as Joe Rogan, Stephen J. Dubner, and Ira Glass.

Many have limited free time, so it's obvious that they will try to listen to useful information on their regular route to work and back. Faster access to innovations in the form of audio leads to more innovation combination happening in the mind, *leading sooner to an idea for an innovation* they'd hope to make themselves. So, what's the point? This highlights a near universal rule that we humans forget…

Deleting Distraction with the Path of Least Action

Why do most drivers switch to the less busy car lane? We guess we'll save time and be able to beat the red light. Like most things in life, we seek the *shortest route to get the results we want*, which means we remove as many steps in between. Authors Thaler and Sunstein write about this affect in *Nudge* while in *Thinking, Fast and Slow* psychologist Daniel Kahneman similarly says that it "applies to cognitive as well as physical exertion… if there are several ways of achieving the same goal, people will eventually gravitate to the least demanding course of action."[24] The important word here is *eventually*, as it takes time for humans to change their habits, yet by repeatedly seeing the benefits we will ultimately move to value factor testing of our actions. Until this time comes our actions will likely be split between the impulsive System 1 or logical System 2 habits we've grown up as Kahneman has explored.

In economics though, there are two versions for this which really should be one. Some economists say that *maximizing*, getting the greatest return, and *satisficing*, getting a return that's just enough, are the extremes in which people behave. As we know, though, black and white thinking leaves a lot out, and it's the gray in the middle where most people fall. That means seeking the most with the least action. Whenever we find a shortcut we will likely take it.

Humans by default seek productivity in what we do. That which we call *the path of least action* to get a result. European hotels slashed the number of guests forgetting to return their room keys on leaving. How? By attaching a large metal block to the keys, its weight and size was so annoying that few guests could mistakenly put it into their bags.[25] Animals also take the path of least action; it's called optimal foraging. Electrons do the same, taking the path of least resistance in circuits. Light crosses the shortest path, as air does when flowing from one place to another. For now the path of least action is perhaps the closest we may come to *a theory of everything*.

Remember, even if we get the *same* result with less action, not more with less, we still achieve more at the end. How? Say our goal is to walk to the train station as we do each work day. Instead of taking the usual 10-minute path, we find a shortcut that gets us there in 4 minutes, freeing up 6 minutes of time. The result is the same but we have more time now to leave home later and add a light morning exercise, meditation, or reply to emails or texts.

> Q. **Name 3 daily actions where you can get the same result with less action?**
>
> A.

On the flip side, as Jen showed us earlier, we forget to be aware of how many such small 6-minute time sucks pile up as habits in our day, reducing the already low free life time we have. We should be on the alert for new innovations which try seducing us to use them. Why? Lacking value, many enterprises promote their innovations by playing on our *instincts, making it harder* for us to say no. Like eating take away food which is made to be as tastily addictive as possible with chemicals like MSG. Yes, it's cheaper and faster to eat, but lacking nutrition in the long run you may be seeing doctors for diabetes medications each month. Just like buying cheaper batteries usually means they run out sooner, you get what you pay for, goes the saying. Or take a dripping tap. Not turning it off leads to distraction from your work like all *noise pollution* has been shown to do in countless studies.[26]

We can take it further back into our younger days and ask, "Why did I waste so much time on _____?" Knowing the meaning of life would have helped back then, but it's likely that you wished to test what you'd been taught about the world. Humans like to check if what we're told really works, so we use *trial and error*, especially when young, to test things once reserved for grownups. Without the meaning, though, we can slip into letting "life happen" to us, instead of the other way around. In what seems like a blink of an eye, we have a child on the way, then a family we need to work to feed and never-ending emails to clear.

FRONT OF CLASS

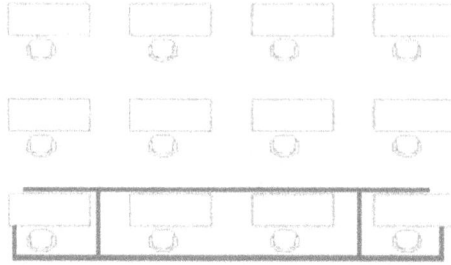

You may remember this seating layout from your school days. The red lined seats at the back, and those at the corners mostly get the top demand. But why? It's productive. The corner seats don't let anyone *see what you're doing* from behind or to one of your sides. Fewer people nearby means *distraction is less likely and so cognitive load* improves. Also, these seats give full view of the entire room, which can aid the health factor. How? When a question is asked, people mostly turn to face the questioner, but you need to turn your neck less if you're seated at the back. Trivial as this might be, these neck turns add up over time.

Below we see how the smallest things in the background add up into big things without our even knowing it.

1. WORDS

Imagine you're writing a story and trying to choose between using "overfed" or "full," to show how a character is feeling after a big meal. Let's test this using the value factors. Say both words have nearly the same meaning to your reader. The word "overfed" has 3 syllables, compared to 1 for "full." Less time is spent reading and/or saying "full" than "overfed." If you made this a rule for all the words in your 600-page book, you may cut 100 pages or more, as fewer syllables mean fewer letters and words. A shorter book is likely to be read and finished by more people, leading to more readers and reviews, and faster improvements in people's lives and maybe even their life expectancy along with it. We do this with nicknames as well. Shortened and made up words let us call on a friend with as few sounds as needed. In the 20th century Francois Richaudeau was one of the first to point out that humans do this, and later, Harvard linguist George Kingsley Zipf would show in tests that humans are bound, as an average, to favor *shorter words than longer ones*— "math" vs. mathematics, "plane" vs. airplane, and "bye" vs. goodbye, itself shortened from "god be with you."[27] Fewer words do what symbols, like the cross, circle, and question mark, have always done—

give us more information with less effort. Yet we are generalizing this into a suggestion not a rule for anyone writing. As too many great works are long when they could be short, but we'd never say that they should not be read because of the length. Given our time on Earth is limited the below should not be too surprising.

Action involved =   Reading

Innovation/s used =   Book with fewer words

Resulting Actions =   • Time saved which can be put
                               towards other activities
                             • Money, health, intelligence factors
                               likely to increase

INSTEAD OF

Action involved =   Reading

Innovation/s used =   Book with more words

Resulting Actions =   • More time spent so less can be put
                               towards other activities
                             • Money, health, intelligence factors
                               likely to decrease

Impersonal value test   Reading shorter book Vs Reading longer
total   book

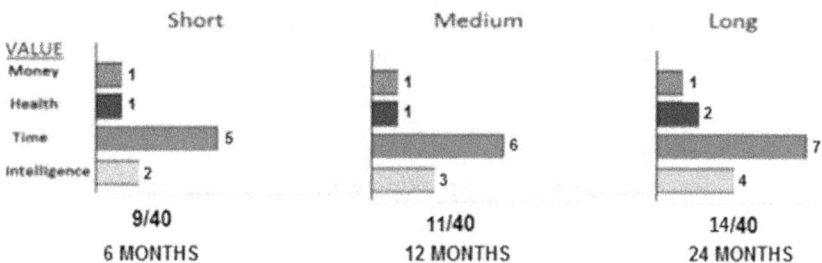

Short — VALUE: Money 1, Health 1, Time 5, Intelligence 2 — 9/40 — 6 MONTHS

Medium — 1, 1, 6, 3 — 11/40 — 12 MONTHS

Long — 1, 2, 7, 4 — 14/40 — 24 MONTHS

2. TYPING

What about innovations which ask for more actions rather than fewer? Take the QWERTY keyboard that most of us type with as an example. The layout of the letters on it was first put that way to actually slow down writing speed. In comparison, speech-to-text software increases writing speed, yet is not widely used. Why? If an office full of workers all began speaking what they want written, the noise level would likely increase, distracting other workers and cutting overall productivity. The biggest reason is that moving from typing to speaking is like learning a new language, for some— *it's too much effort*. It may be weird for people to say out loud, what before, they thought in their head and typed by hand. The short-term pain trumps the long-term gain.

Action involved =	Speaking
Innovation/s used =	Speech to text software
Resulting Actions =	• Less work done due to learning new method leading to loss of income • Less ability to think due to increased noise in the office

INSTEAD OF

Action involved =	Typing
Innovation/s used =	Word processor software
Resulting Actions =	• More work done in less time due to past knowledge of typing • Higher quality of thinking due to less noise in office
Impersonal value test total	Speaking words vs Typing words

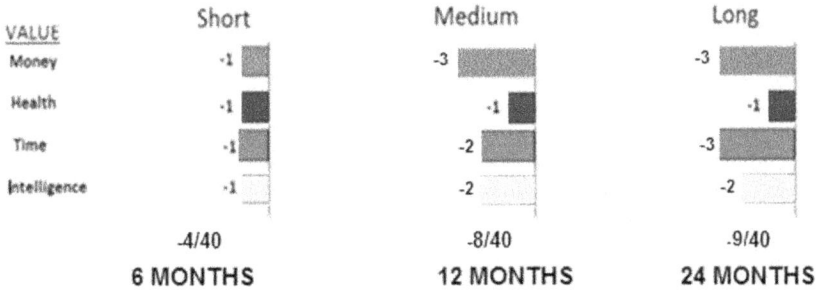

VALUE	Short	Medium	Long
Money	-1	-3	-3
Health	-1	-1	-1
Time	-1	-2	-3
Intelligence	-1	-2	-2
	-4/40	-8/40	-9/40
	6 MONTHS	**12 MONTHS**	**24 MONTHS**

3. WEB DEVELOPMENT

Millions of web specialists the world over aim to cut "friction." This refers to almost anything that adds more actions than needed for a visitor to get what they want, like longer loading times, messy writing, broken links, and distracting colors.

Below we see a donation page for the 2012 Obama re-election campaign.

Removing the bottom part of the form as seen on the left side, led to a 5% jump in donations. Why? Less clutter leads to it *looking simple and easy* to use as seen on the right side version. Every day millions of websites are tested to remove such unneeded actions.

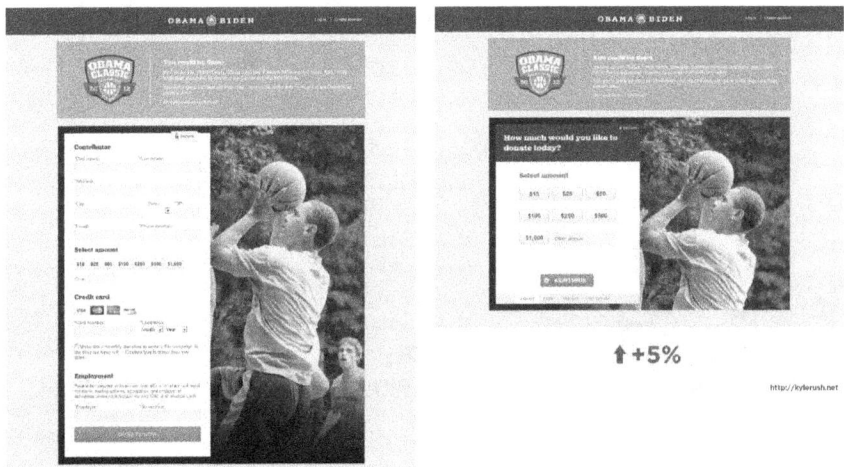

⬆ **+5%**

Source: Kyle Rush, used with permission

Action involved =   Viewing/reading webpage

Innovation/s used =   Shortened donation form

Resulting Actions =   • Less cognitive load needed to see
                                   and act upon donating
                                 • More donations lead to less
                                   fundraising time needed
                                 • Health is conserved as volunteers
                                   have more energy to go door
                                   knocking

INSTEAD OF

Action involved =   Viewing/reading webpage

Innovation/s used =   Longer donation form

Resulting Actions =   • More cognitive load needed to see
                                   and act upon donating
                                 • Less donations lead to more time
                                   needed to hit fundraising target
                                 • Health is spent and less energy
                                   available for volunteer door
                                   knocking

Impersonal value test   Simplified donation form Vs Previous
total   longer donation form

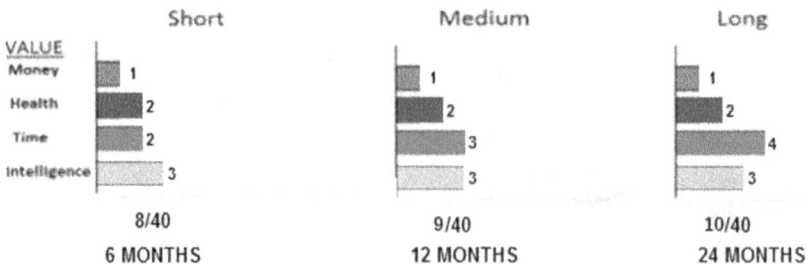

VALUE	Short	Medium	Long
Money	1	1	1
Health	2	2	2
Time	2	3	4
Intelligence	3	3	3
	8/40	9/40	10/40
	6 MONTHS	12 MONTHS	24 MONTHS

What clothes do you wear each day? It may seem unimportant, but it takes
actions to pick them. Barack Obama stuck to one of two colored suits –

blue or gray. Mark Zuckerberg wears different pairs of the same clothes, saying, "I'm in this really lucky position, where I get to wake up every day and help serve more than a billion people. And I feel like I'm not doing my job if I spend any of my energy on things that are silly or frivolous about my life."[28] By opening more time to focus on his purpose, Zuckerberg may be better able to select new innovations which we may soon find, could grow the life expectancy of Facebook users.

We earlier explored whether physical books were better than e-readers. But what about the type of book you read? Books can mostly be grouped into fiction or non-fiction—imaginative stories or factual explanations. We mostly look to the practical world to find truths, and so non-fiction *may hold* more useful information compared to the made-up world of fiction. That healthy eating book could show you how to lower your high blood pressure right away. Or you could find stretches for the body which in years to come save you a lot of pain and money. All this can help boost your Life expectancy. The MIT pantheon project shows us that most of the top 100 influential people in history had teachings classified today as non-fiction or semi non-fiction. It's true, stories do fascinate people, especially when they're claimed to really have happened, as religions claim of their holy books. Fiction has its place, but its ability to sway the workings of the real world, as seen historically *seems less stronger than non-fiction*. Combining both is an option and reading either genre seems to have the effect of lowering stress levels down by 68% and depression risk by 50%.[29]

What about actions which deal with that tricky word "morality"? Why protect someone we don't know from having their wallet stolen and beaten up by drunks by putting ourselves at risk? Because it's not hard to picture ourselves as being the victim getting attacked. If we don't help stop it then the drunks may do it again, harming others, and eventually harming us. Take this logic further and let's ask how you would best try to understand a world event. Newspapers? Nightly news? Perhaps 140-character Twitter posts online? The path of least action shows that people wish to get things faster, cheaper, quicker, and more intelligently. Yet if you want to "understand" what's happened rather than to simply "know" it did, we need to move beyond 10-second sound bites. To do this, reading books becomes arguably the most productive way to understand nearly anything due to their *capacity to hold and organize a lot of information*. Language is the most productive innovation for communicating the actions of others. Writing has the *most information density* of any other medium, unlike visual TV or audio. Just a few pages read over 5 minutes may contain more words and facts than those spoken in an hour-long documentary on the same subject. Knowing how the world works lets us best live in it without needing to relearn lessons it took our ancestors millions of years to figure out. Like the image below shows, books give us timeless explanations beyond the simplistic stories we watch and hear on the surface.

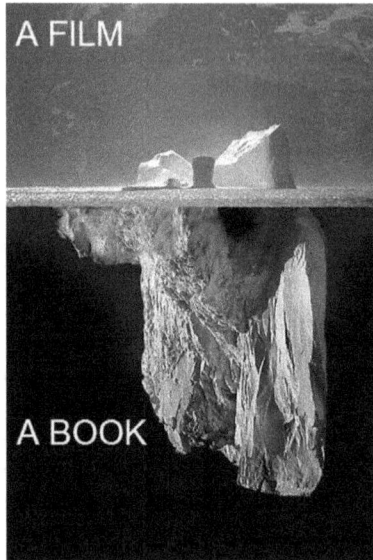

Source: Uwe Kils and Wiska Bodo
Creative Commons Attribution License

Take the comparison of classical with rap music. In studies, listeners of rap music had increased blood pressure, which comes before a fight or flight reaction when danger is near.[30] Rap music, like most songs, have lyrics which fight for your attention, making it hard to think of anything else. Classical music which has few or no lyrics, is shown to boost creativity and lower blood pressure.[31] The music of Mozart has been shown to reduce pain and relax people, and some guess that it increases intelligence.[32,33] Listening to music with lyrics prevents our mind thinking as we're forced instead to think about what the singer is saying. In 2004, British train stations began playing the music of Bach, Handel, and Mozart, and this correlated with a drop in the rate of robberies and other crimes by one-third. Travelers also said they felt safe when such music was played. In time we may see music like rap being held as evidence in court as a proximate cause for crimes. Many would say that, in the right place, listening to rap music makes sense. For instance, getting mentally prepared before a football game, but the question is why get prepared by hearing some ex-criminal sing about rape? These songs are already played in movies, TV shows, commercials, and inside shops where people are forced to hear them. The songs are made to be addictive, and the artist and music company want you to repeat them in your head and out loud. They make more money the more friends you spread the song to.

Rock and roll music pops up here also. Take a genre of it called "grunge," which can sometimes sound like the insane screaming you might imagine if you visited hell. A study found that grunge music leads to boosts in hostility, sadness, tension, and fatigue, with drops in caring, mental clarity, and vigor.[34]

Plant experiments in the 1970s tested classical music against rock. Plants grew strongly, with stems bending toward the speakers that played classical. Plants being played rock music were stunted, lost leaves, and had gangly stems bent away from the speakers. The rock music plants *died on the 6th day* while classical music plants continued to grow and flower.[35]

Below let's see how documentary films do against music videos:

Action involved =	Watching and listening
Innovation/s used =	Television documentary on ideas that changed the world
Resulting Actions =	• More wonder at how the rest of the world works
	• Likely greater interest in reading the books on topics discussed
	• A deeper understanding of why the world is at it is

INSTEAD OF

Action involved =   Watching and listening

Innovation/s used =   Popular music videos

Resulting Actions =
- Repetition in the mind of addictive lyrics with rude words and degrading sexual themes
- Repeating attention-seeking behavior like copying the body movements of singers and wearing similar clothes like them
- Risky behavior during social events

Impersonal value test total   Watching Educational content Vs Entertainment content

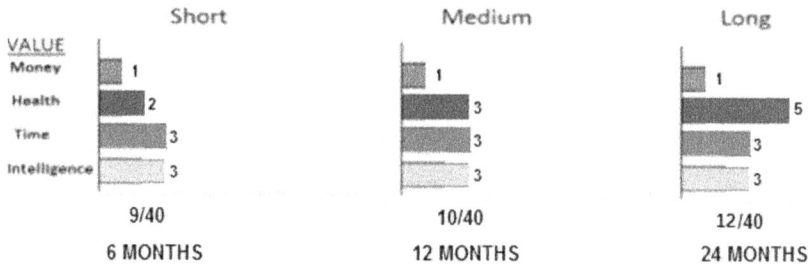

	Short	Medium	Long
VALUE			
Money	1	1	1
Health	2	3	5
Time	3	3	3
Intelligence	3	3	3
	9/40	10/40	12/40
	6 MONTHS	12 MONTHS	24 MONTHS

You can likely guess which innovation has a higher chance of increasing life expectancy in the person and also those they touch in their lives. But each innovation does this differently and now that we've shown the basics we can figure out the groups that most innovations belong to and how that impacts on the collective actions of society.

The Many Faces of Innovation

As you may have guessed, innovations are not all created equal. Using productivity as our map, we can divide them into three groups: *Productive, Unproductive, and Counterproductive.* Not all innovations will fit snugly into just one category, and they can and do move between them. The following criteria will help us as a guide:

Pt. 9 BUILDINGS OF LOST DREAMS

INNOVATIONS
Everything humans make fit into three groups:
Productive, Unproductive, Counterproductive

Kate's co-workers can't see why her accounting software is being rejected by the managers, especially when they see what Joe uses work time for.

---

i. MADE FOR WHOM?

"Who's the market?" is a repeated question heard in business. Kate's accounting software is "productive" for enterprises doing tax returns, but she later needs to adapt it for personal tax returns, if she is to reach a *larger number of people* with her innovation.

ii. REAL WORLD PROOF.

Like we explored earlier for how to measure the "greatest number", we need evidence showing the number of adopters using an innovation. Again in business, the "market share" pie chart is useful, with the best-selling innovation and enterprise mostly winning 50% or more of the adopters. Take for instance how landline phone use has dropped, while mobile phone use is growing worldwide. Today, we have as many mobile phones used as there are people on earth, 7+ billion. Landline phone use, on the other hand, is dropping yearly, and is now below 1.1 billion.[36] Mobile phone use would not grow like this if it did not give us better productivity over the landline.

iii. CHANGING FACTS.

Here's a tricky one we need to keep in mind. In the early 20th century, many medical experts liked to say that cigarettes were healthy, and they were even advertised as cures for everyday health problems. The darkest humor may now come from old advertisements like the one below, which claims that they cure "all diseases of the throat." This would be illegal to say today, as the facts show the direct opposite. At least it was thoughtful to recommend that children under 6 not smoke. In the United States, it took until 1964 for a Report of the Surgeon General to finally say that smoking had a definite link to the surge in lung cancer. With that in mind, hopefully we can forgive James Bonsack's 1881 innovation, a rolling machine that was able to make 12,000 cigarettes an hour, versus 240 per hour if done by hand. Bonsack, like many others, just didn't have enough facts like we do today. "Tempus edax rerum," or loosely translated to "Time conquers all," wrote the Roman poet Ovid, for in the future we may know more, but today, we can only look at everything based on the facts we have.

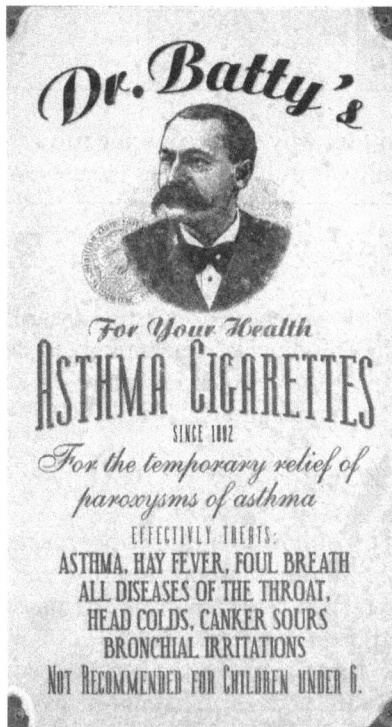

Source: Stanford School of Medicine, Public domain

iv. HOW MANY WAYS CAN IT BE USED?

As explored earlier, besides being smoked, a cigarette cannot be used say as a fertilizer for your garden, nor are you able to draw or write with it. It has almost no range of actions. So what? With facts showing that smoking lowers life expectancy, the cigarette's value-destructive actions can't be replaced by any value-creative ones.

Take a car running on petrol. We know that petrol pollutes the air, but we also agree that the car has many uses besides polluting. A car's range of actions are mostly value-creative: get from point A to B faster than other methods and move goods and people on the way. However, the actions resulting from the petrol exhaust system are not value creative, as people end up breathing more polluted air. On balance, more actions from a car are value creative than destructive. Soon the exhaust system, being *a counterproductive innovation* is likely to be removed by a productive innovation. Electric cars are the front runners to fix this problem. They may be more expensive to buy now, but having to spend almost no money on petrol can save more in the long run.

Productive Innovations

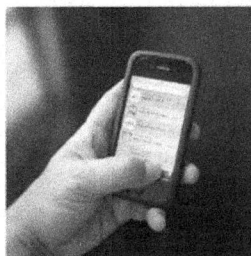

Source: wpclipart.com, Public domain
The Land, Creative Commons Attribution License

Create More with Less Actions

"The hand mill gives you society with the feudal lord; the steam-mill, society with the industrial capitalist."[37]
Karl Marx

A productive innovation gives a larger range of actions, mostly value-creative. Using them lets a result be reached with *faster, cheaper, smarter, and healthier actions*, moving us to a likely increase in our life expectancy. In exploration of actions earlier, we noted that time periods are important to remember. Productive innovations in their early days can give huge productivity boosts to the market with previously unseen value-creative actions, and as a result they become popular and profitable. Other innovations quickly pop up to compete to try give even more value-creative actions to take that profit away.

Let's take a look at how the now outdated technology of the landline telephone scored when it was still considered cutting-edge:

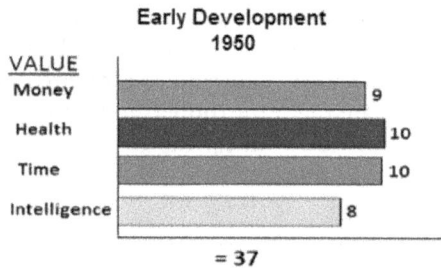

Early Development
1950

VALUE		
Money		9
Health		10
Time		10
Intelligence		8

= 37

In 1950, telephone growth in the United States became widespread after its humble start in the late 1800's. The telephone gave more productivity than other alternative innovations, like the telegraph, letters, and physical meetings. This is seen in the value score above.

With this in mind, let's check the three elements of most productive innovations:

1. They replace current innovations being used by adding more productivity.

Websites like amazon.com boost productivity by giving more choice, cheaper prices, and faster and more accurate search results. There is even a one-click checkout button which buys the item without any more clicks needed. Items bought are then posted to your door so no time is lost having to pick them up in a shop. Some may remember what you had to do before the internet to find some uncommon product, like a rare music album? You'd have to call record stores to check their database, search in many mail-order catalogues, and maybe go to a few garage sales. If you traded stocks, you'd have to call and place orders over the phone or else do it by posting your instructions. Now, most people buy or sell stocks instantly on a website, like etrade.com. Money can be sent in seconds with internet banking, rather than taking an hour to make the trip and stand in line at a bank branch. Yes, many productive innovations are expensive when they first come out, like the original cars, but as more people use them, the more are made, the cheaper they get.

As more innovations combine, the speed of change grows. For an innovation to stay productive, which to some means it's "popular" or "important", the enterprise making it needs to replace it *with even more productive innovations*. It's an uncomfortable thought for those managing the enterprise as doing so risks *killing off their original* profit-making innovation. Many enterprises have done this over time, such as Ford, General Electric, and IBM, which is one reason they've been around for over 100 years, and still offer productive innovations. *Good to Great* by Jim Collins explores this with detailed statistics. We may soon see such companies in the same way as author of *The Effective Executive* and management thinker, Peter Drucker did, as being some of humanity's great achievements. Political parties are in the same boat, needing to replace innovations that don't do well – like their parties rules and policies or else they'll lose more votes at the next election.

Q. What 3 innovations would you take to an island? (They're likely to be productive)

A.

---

2. They increase competition which boosts productivity, leading to increased life expectancy in society.

If the nation's economy allows for fair competition, a productive innovation will attract competing innovations from other enterprises who will try to better it. This leads to a *never-ending* ping pong game of improvement for us, the adopters and consumers. Take yahoo.com, one of the first search engines set up in 1994. Yahoo poured a lot of money in to stop users from leaving their website, by showing the weather, news, classified ads, and seemingly everything to grab attention. In contrast google.com, started in 1998, gave only a single innovation—the best search results—unlike Yahoo, they wanted people to find what they were searching for and then leave. Besides the superior search results, Google's site was clear of any distractions, being almost fully white in color with only a search box. This lowered the cognitive load on the user, unlike yahoo.com which confused them with clutter.

3. They make new actions which did not exist before.

Innovations may not be seen as important early on, but they win this status as more people start to use them, going from being seen as a gimmick to something useful. Also productive innovations, as they create many actions in society, can spill over to impact other industries.

The making and driving of cars led to accidents with pedestrians, which led to innovations like crosswalks, traffic signs, and street lights. The innovation of car insurance, and auto mechanic shops to service cars popped up in each suburb.

The typewriter boosted productivity by making writing readable from the jumbled scrawl of handwriting, and along the way made the Qwerty keyboard layout a standard. Later the computer improved this with word processing software, further boosting productivity and putting writing onto a digital file that could be saved, stored, and printed. The "backspace" button was seen as *a miracle* to many typewriter users, who before had to retype the entire page or mark out their mistake with white goo.

Most visible today is Facebook, which has created many new actions, like posting, liking, replying, and messaging. It has also made around 4.5 million new jobs as people make apps to be used in its store. The same can be said of the Apple iTunes store, with over 1 million jobs created, and YouTube which has some video creators living off the videos they post online.[38,39]

The careful reader would realize by now that if our purpose is also our innovation then it's the *productive innovation that best grows our chance* to create the greatest good for the greatest number of people and unlock free life time for them all to try to innovate.

Unproductive Innovations

Creates the Same with the Same Actions

*"The definition of insanity is doing the same thing
and expecting different results."[40]*
Narcotics Anonymous Handbook
(Wrongly attributed to Albert Einstein)

Unproductive innovations mostly leave productivity unchanged, neither adding nor taking it away. The range of actions they give are nearly the same as those of similar innovations. Life expectancy doesn't move. Actions aren't much *cheaper or expensive, faster or slower, dumber or smarter, healthier or unhealthier.*

Productive innovations may have started as unproductive innovations and then were improved. An entrepreneur may open a car wash—nothing new to most people as there are many of them. After washing some cars, liquids get mixed and a new liquid is found that removes almost all car stains. The car wash evolves into a liquid selling business, helping millions of car owners to save money and time by removing the toughest stains without costing thousands of dollars.

Productive innovations as we know can also quickly become unproductive. The landline telephone gave a lot of productivity until *mobile phones, and the internet* came knocking in the 1980s and 1990s. Below we see how its productivity dropped, as did its use, leading to falls in the number of units manufactured to this day, much like the vinyl record player which is, unless as a collectors' item, extinct from production.

Say you use a map to guide you when you're driving instead of using a GPS navigator. You still *need to guess which route is fastest by distance and with less traffic*. Your guess is not perfect so this action is likely to lead to fuel and car wear and tear costs in the long run. The GPS, instead, will calculate the path of least action, with least distance and traffic.

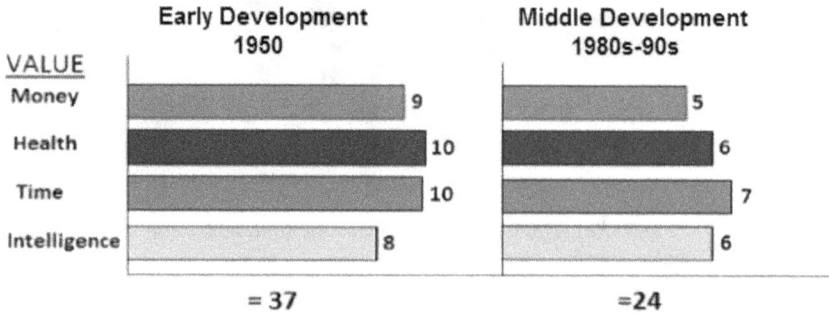

	Early Development 1950	Middle Development 1980s-90s
VALUE		
Money	9	5
Health	10	6
Time	10	7
Intelligence	8	6
	= 37	=24

Now you may think, *A map is still useful so why is it considered unproductive?* It's only unproductive because another innovation exists which beats the map on many value factors. The GPS right now is the most productive innovation for the action of finding the best path to take towards your destination. But context is king here. If you don't have enough money to buy a GPS, then a map makes sense, but for that you sacrifice hours which add up to days or weeks of lost time and petrol money. Likewise, if GPS signals stopped working suddenly, then the forgotten map would again become a productive innovation for most drivers.

Below are the three elements of an Unproductive innovation.

1. They copy other innovations, sacrificing productivity.

Swapping a blue color garbage bin to a red color doesn't change the actions the bin gives to people. What about that new burger shop that opened down the street from you? True, it gives a different burger than McDonald's, but it's doubtful the ingredients used are a new combination that will boost value factors or increase your life expectancy. Like the different names of dry cleaners, this is only *a minor difference,* as most of the services they offer are the same.

This goes for most innovations out there, and it's not said to offend any enterprise but warn them that they are easily replaceable. Remember, we're not saying these innovations aren't useful – but that they *don't improve on anything that already exists* in the world. Take the example below:

Imagine a hair salon with two competitors within 1km of its location. How does this one hairdresser differ from the others? Sure, they have different names, logos, advertising, and shop layout, but these are small changes, and so productivity to clients is nearly the same. Why? They all use the same innovations, scissors, dryers, and hair products, and so all three end up giving the customer near the same range of actions when they visit. Unless a hairdresser changes the innovations they are using, they will be at the mercy of slippery customers. So let's say one of the hairdressers adds a new innovation, a hard to find spray for the head that strengthens hair and saves people going bald. Most customers would see this as more productive than what the two other hairdressers offer, especially if scientific studies confirmed the improvement the spray gave to the hair.

Likewise, you may be tricked into thinking that given the attention celebrities receive that they are changing humanity in some deep way. Yet interestingly enough, no one from their professions has ever been deemed worthy enough to even *be near the top of lists ranking the most influential people that ever lived.*[41,42] Century old music from Mozart, Beethoven, and Bach timelessly pull our imagination with their sounds and so are replayed to this day, unlike modern songs full of lyrics made for the quick buck which are then forgotten in years or decades time.

Oscar Wilde, author of *The Importance of Being Ernest*, said back in his day, "All art is quite useless." While economist Tyler Cowen, author of *Average is Over* writes, "Art is not that important to us, no matter what we might like to believe."[43] This depends on your definition of art. Let's assume it's sculpted or painted art. Harsh as these criticisms are, they appear to come from the fact that many people are annoyed that they can't measure any practical *real world value out of art*, particularly modern styles of it. Art writer John Kouwenhoven says this, "The mind's characteristic employment is the discovery of meaning," and that if "we perceive no patterns of relationship, no design, we discover no meaning."[44] Art cannot instruct people viewing any image with how-to advice they can easily *copy and put to use* in their life. Instead it mostly creates confusion, while books by using words, can instruct and relaxing music can lead to creative breakthroughs. It's one of the reasons why Einstein adored playing his violin.

Remember that mystery object a chapter ago? It was meaningless to you. If you don't know what it is, how can it be of any use to you? Much of today's art is like that, being mysterious, secretive and puzzling. An art museum today may display a rock you can find in the local park, and it's stared at by people asking themselves, "What must the artist have meant?" The answer is likely…nothing, other than winning attention with a sensational distraction to get a media headline. This slippery slope for attention gets steeper each year, as art becomes more outrageous to get a headline. Some may argue that what matters with art is that an artist can express themselves how they wish. Then why show art to an audience when it wasn't made for them to understand in the first place? Isn't such art best hung on the artist's home wall instead? But what about famous art? The Mona Lisa is considered most famous and so there must be a good reason, right? Nope.

Few cared about it for hundreds of years, until it was stolen from a French Museum and then rescued. Rather sad that it was a sensational event that is the hidden cause behind it becoming famous, than say what you'd expect, like the way the painting was drawn. Take this: "You run into a burning house, would you save the Van Gough painting enjoyed by millions or save the baby in the crib?" It's a common thought experiment, and yes, we don't like them. But what do we realize from it? Though his life and artwork is riveting, as read in *Van Gough: The Life* by Steven Naifeh and Gregory White Smith, the child if saved can grow up to make innovations saving millions of lives, while a painting cannot. Off it goes to the flames.

2. Price is the main difference, not the other value factors.

If you were to compare the wheat harvested from one manufacturer with wheat from thousands of others globally, you'd likely not find much difference. When this happens the term "commodity" is used. We see this in grains, coffee, oil etc. All have prices set by the trading happening on the world's exchanges. Price becomes the only difference between such innovations. Money, though, is only one value factor out of four.

Productivity best comes when all factors are improved. Say you put your heart and soul into opening a cafe. If it didn't go well and was to shut down it likely wouldn't change the lives of your customers all that much. Even if there wasn't another cafe nearby to attract them, the customers could simply go and buy coffee from the supermarket and *make it at home*. Why then, if one of these same customers were to lose their mobile phone, may it drive them to emotional breakdown?

A mobile is more productive, and it's being used daily by a person. Its photos, data, and messaging make it complex, unlike a commodity.

Does this mean that the shops you see in most town squares use unproductive innovations? Most likely. It's hard to argue that humans don't have *greater potential to do more complex actions* than wash clothes, serve food, and drive taxis. Machines are slowly starting to do all this for us. So what stops many from trying to do the complex? It's that there is little explanation of how to do it. This we'll soon explore.

3. They're easily replaced by other innovations.

A productive innovation can quickly replace an unproductive one, starting its slide into the *relic heap of history*. Candlelit lamps, papyrus paper, and earlier versions of almost any innovation have been thrown away, or are in antique shops. What once sat selling for a sky-high price behind locked glass now sits on the street corner awaiting pickup by garbage collectors. Here are a few modern-day examples you will likely know about:

a. Feature phones.
The first mass produced mobile phones, now called feature phones, cut landline use and are now having their own use cut by smart phones. Unable to fully use the internet and with no touch screen, they *restrict all the actions available by millions of apps*. Today over 50% of all mobile phones are smartphones.[45] In 2013, smartphones started out-selling feature phones for the first time.

b. Desktop computers.
Notebooks, tablets, and mobile phones have led to the drop in the use and purchase of desktop computers, which are heavy and hard to move. PC sales are stagnant worldwide, while sales of mobile devices are increasing.[46] Also, history shows us that most software and applications move to the *most used devices*. As we see, the low use of Nokia and Blackberry phones also means they have fewer apps, compared to Apple and Android phones. Soon the same game will play out with wearable devices, like glasses and wristwatches.

c. External disk drives.
Some may remember saving computer data onto floppy disks and CDs. Both of those we know were overtaken by USB and external hard drives. Today, cloud storage has overtaken that, as it automatically saves online what you made moments ago on the computer. An internet connection is all you then need to check your files anywhere and on any device. The year 2011 saw the first drop in the shipments of external hard drives as online storage got easier and more popular.[47]

The timing of when an innovation comes out is also important. Many unknown innovations are unproductive by *being ahead of their time*. In them, we may get a taste of the future, but to be useful they *need other, yet to be made innovations* in order to spread to everyone. Over a decade before Apple gave us the iPhone, they released the Newton, one of the first PDAs, personal digital assistants, promoted as a digital diary. It had no mobile phone functions, like calling or texting, nor internet access. It didn't give enough new value-creative actions to justify its high price versus the paper diary most people were already using.

But how would we explain a mobile app like Angry Birds? Played by hundreds of millions of people the world over, we'd say *it straddles the border* between productive and unproductive. However, this is only if we're comparing it to other games and game playing in general, like the Xbox, PlayStation, Nintendo, etc. Most of these gaming consoles demand more actions like a desktop computer does, for you cannot take and play them on the go. The mobile phone lets you play the game anywhere and with fewer steps. Sure, this example is simplified, but you get the point. The fewer steps to get a result, the more people move towards it. Remember, though, we're here only comparing Angry Birds with using other gaming innovations, not comparing it to the innovation a person makes to fulfil the meaning of life. If we were, then the game innovation melts into the counterproductive, as work on our innovation would take top place given the small amount of time we have on earth.

Ideally the innovations we surround ourselves with, mobiles, cars, computers, books, conversations, should *best be used to help us* make our own innovation, so we can seek the meaning of life. They help by letting us do more with less, unlocking more time and value factors. Yes, each person's innovation will be different, so we can't predict yet how well the innovations they use will help their own pursuit to innovate, but we can caution that many innovations give little or no help. Kate from our comic seeks the meaning by making the accounting software program, which could help millions worldwide to do more with less action. If she started playing the Angry Birds game, it's very unlikely to help her finish the software. So, when she's plays she admits it's a "weakness" of hers. Many of us have those, and its best we work to get rid of them rather than be their slave. Others say that the distraction of the game may help her relax, letting her program better afterwards. Why do other programmers not need such "relaxation," though? Instead they relax during involuntary actions, like bathroom breaks, eating, and sleeping.

"Each person is different" is the typical answer, but we are all human, and what's different is that one person has made a consistent habit that another is too lazy to try out themselves. Given shortness of life, its best we try to *remove weakness so to focus best on our innovation*. Kate is then best off imagining the worst. Would she regret her months' long addiction to game playing if she was suddenly in an accident making her unable to program, or worse, on the edge of death? Yes, is her answer and so she throws the game playing to the flames.

Counterproductive Innovations

Source: wpclipart.com, Public domain
Xwomanizerx:, Creative Commons Attribution License

Create Less with More Actions

"Because some men aren't looking for anything logical, like money.
They can't be bought, bullied, reasoned, or negotiated with.
Some men just want to watch the world burn."
Alfred Pennyworth (Batman's butler in *The Dark Knight*)

A counterproductive innovation removes productivity by giving actions that are mostly value-destructive for the person and/or society. These actions tend to be *expensive, slower, unhealthier, dumber*, and likely to lower life expectancy. It's possible for productive and unproductive innovations to sink to the counterproductive level if a *problem is found in them*. Like a super drug cure for depression that later is shown to cause suicide, or a shopping center whose badly built roof crumbles onto shoppers below. Unproductive innovations are likely, over time, to slip into the counter-productive group, as cigarettes did when enough evidence was collected. Many counterproductive innovations are also *addictive*, lowering people's ability to say no with *self-control*. As free life time is at such low levels for many people, innovations which help reduce bodily damage are immensely useful. The electric car, replacements for alcohol, patches for cigarettes, or non-lethal bullets are likely to lead to more free life time. Below, we hope to make clear the criteria for the most damaging innovations in society, especially the indirect ones which silently breed *time crimes* and which few suspect are risks in the present moment.

Our landline telephone example wraps up here. It may seem hideous to some to put the telephone alongside drugs and cigarettes, but there's little arguing that it is now a waste of productivity, given the mobile and internet innovations out there.

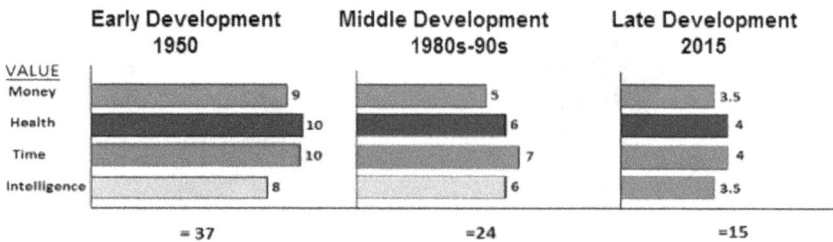

VALUE	Early Development 1950	Middle Development 1980s-90s	Late Development 2015
Money	9	5	3.5
Health	10	6	4
Time	10	7	4
Intelligence	8	6	3.5
	= 37	=24	=15

Using what's old and outdated may have the same harmful effects as using counterproductive innovations, particularly those which are addictive. A society where email is banned, *we propose has less development* and likely a lower life expectancy in the long run, then one that doesn't. Below are the three elements of a Counter-productive innovation.

1. They give value-destructive actions for society and its people.

Many counterproductive innovations gained a grip in society long before science could show the toxic plague they were spreading. Drugs and junk/processed foods are the obvious examples here. It's horrible to see that the total deaths from smoking over the past century are more than the lives lost in all of WWII.[48]

A U.S. judge recently ruled that cigarette companies had to use their own money to put out advertisements saying, *"Smoking kills, on average, 1,200 Americans every day."*[49] Junk/processed foods aren't far behind. They don't only cause health problems but social ones as well, as found in obese people, who have a lower chance of getting a job, which then limits the amount of money they can earn.[50]

Let's check into minor crime which is the early training ground for major crime in the life of a criminal. Shouting, playing loud music, or spitting out rude words lowers value factors in those abused and the abuser, which over time drops life expectancy for all. It's why in the U.K., actions that some may think to be wrong, but the law does not cover, are curbed under the Antisocial Behavior Order (ASBO). Signs are put out on streets with the writing, "Antisocial behavior will lead to a fine from police."[51]

Entertainment can add to the growth of borderline crime in people's actions, particularly of young children.[52] Video games let kids virtually mass kill, bomb cities, rob, torture, urinate, and even rape—all depicted by graphics that are looking closer to real life every year.[53-54] Many of today's mass murderers in the real world have been shown to have been mass murderers in the virtual world as well.[55-56]

Children's minds are shaped by what they're *shown*. In reading the classic poem, *If*, by *The Jungle Book* author Rudyard Kipling, a child may grow to live up to ideals like, "*If you can wait and not be tired by waiting… Or being lied about, don't deal in lies… Or being hated don't give way to hating.*" Such poems are today replaced with songs like, *Die Young*, by Ke$ha, with lyrics about dying, living wildly, and seeking pleasure. It would be hard for a child listening to this to not think that death seems to be positive and to link the sexual words with sexual images.

The song was pulled off many radio stations for having unacceptable lyrics after the Newtown School shootings in the U.S in September of 2012, where 20 children and 6 adults died. The singer herself said that she had been "forced" to sing the lyrics, before denying it, later saying that she was worried about adding the words "die young." It's likely that the music company executives liked the lyrics as they were controversial, so were a perfect path for a lot of media attention and sales.[57] The question remains, why would these lyrics not always be seen as wrong for the young target audience of listeners? If murders of children need to happen until radio stations remove such songs then by that point the horror has already happened. Removing such lyrics makes society know that it has left no stone unturned in making clear it does not support or promote value-destructive actions in any way. It's these indirect violent and sexual messages that Peggy Orenstein brilliantly explores in her work *Girls & Sex* showing how slowly and silently destructive thinking can spread to young minds.

Unlike standard firearms, automatic guns shoot more bullets in a shorter time span, growing the chance of people being hit by them. Australia outlawed guns after the Port Arthur massacre in 1996, and it led to a drop in gun crime.[58] Like the phone, a gun can be used in a variety of ways, to shoot and defend against a robber, or to protect against predators when camping. The problem most explored is what happens when a gun gets in the hands of someone who has little control of their own mind? The path of least action means a human will seek the innovation which *best gets them the result they want*. If it's to kill as many people as possible, then an automatic gun fits the bill. As countries like the U.S. politically seem unable to change gun laws, they'd best approach it the way electric car companies did so in innovating on the counterproductive sub-innovation of the polluting exhaust system. But how?

Compared to other weapons, it's simple to injure or kill anything at a distance with a gun. Why? The degree of harm is affected by the *type of bullet* which hits the target. Put in laws to make and sell bullets with non-lethal materials, softer rubber as an example, and fewer people would be dead after being shot. Also the law can demand gun barrels be made to accept only softer bullets so to slowly make extinct older lethal guns. The gun then goes from being a killing device to a self-defense device, which is what most people wish it to be.

Outright bans on cars have long been called for due to their effect on pollution, but go back 100 years and more, and we see horses were the main way to travel and move things. Little is it known, that horses were a *public health risk* of massive proportions, especially in cities. As the population grew, so did the number of horses. Mini mountains of horse manure piled up on street corners as just one horse produces between 15-30 pounds of manure a day.[59] Houseflies, liking manure, invaded city streets, spreading a range of diseases to humans. The solution to this plague-like disaster was none other than… the car. Strange as it would sound to environmentalists today, the automobile was praised back then as an *environmental savior*. True, the car has its own manure problem with exhaust fumes, which some would argue have added to deaths across the world. In return, though, the car has saved untold millions of lives in getting sick people to hospital quickly for care, and moving things that would lead to breaking backs and bodily damage.

Like the internet or the phone, the car gives a broad range of actions with its many use cases. It's led to boosts in life expectancy, and soon the removal of its counterproductive sub-innovation, exhaust fumes, will lead to further increases in life expectancy. As explored before, the counterproductive sub-innovations of productive innovations are *mostly removed over time*, as the electric car shows by having no petrol exhaust system. Next, self-driving cars may reduce the counterproductive actions of pedestrian deaths and car crashes, and let people do more productive things, like working on a laptop, while being driven by the car.

The fact that cars aren't all electric at the moment doesn't mean we should seize and remove all motor vehicles like some would like, leading to a freeze of entire industries and everyday life. Such thinking forgets the reality of making such a massive change, as it will lead to unpredictable and likely worse problems. Slow but steady change on the other hand does the trick. *A small change gives time to fix the unseen problems that pop up.* Solutions we forget, create problems which then create better solutions. Perfection doesn't exist. Only pursuit of perfection does. It sounds messy but this is how we increase life expectancy. We must constantly creatively think up new explanations to test instead of sitting thinking that things will magically just get better.

2. They mostly create or support dependencies / addictions in people using them.

What's common among liquor, cigarettes, junk/processed food, drugs, and sensationalist media? They are all addictive in some way, distracting the person from the deeper *dependency or insecurity within them, likely a lack of meaning and purpose in their life.* Addictions stick like a parasite, sucking the marrow of society, living more the more productivity they suck. As we've seen with epigenetics, the genes can only turn on or off if the actions from innovations bring it about. Say you're worried for your best friend who seems suicidal. To prevent the worst, you remove kitchen knives, ropes, sharp objects etc., all which could help them take their own life. It's obviously easier to cut with a knife than without one. The same goes for removing foods that are unhealthy and not watching shows that dumb you down, promoting pointless pleasure along with stupid and risky behavior.

On a larger level, government laws are the same if they lead to dependency and breed lazy and corrupt enterprises. Take farming, which in countries like the U.S., is protected by government tariffs, so local farmers don't have to compete with cheaper foods from foreign farmers. This leads to shoppers in supermarkets paying more for a product, that they otherwise could buy cheaper if it were imported. Another result... is that poor farmers in nations like Africa can't sell their foods to the U.S., leading them to lose out on earning money that could lift their family, and in decades the entire region, out of poverty.

3. The innovations and their actions are often illegal and/or opposed by society.

Some governments try to reduce the spread of drugs, alcohol, and smoking and when they succeed they can help boost the standards of living. In return, this helps them raise more taxes as more people are healthy enough to work more or start new enterprises. We see this in the U.K's Sugar Tax plan to start in 2018, with the aim to further shrink the grams of sugar in drinks. The more sugar a company's products contain the more tax it has to pay. Mexico has already started its own sugar tax. The Philippines, India, and South Africa are aiming to do the same.[60]

Can you imagine a society where robbery is legal, killing is allowed, and hacking computers is normal? Would it survive? As history shows, *a good chunk of the population would leave* to find a better life in another country. It's one of the reasons politicians need to react faster to catch up and put laws in place when innovations change for the worse or else risk seeing a chunk of their population flee elsewhere, reducing the total taxpayers in the country.

Before it plunged into bankruptcy and sucked others into its value-destructive flood stream, Lehmann Brothers had been covering up large financial problems. Its accountants used tricky methods, like "repo 105", where a short-term loan is shown as a sale, all while executives continued to be paid millions of dollars.[61] As explored in the book and documentary *The Smartest Guys In the Room*, before its bankruptcy, the executives of former energy giant Enron were pushing its energy price traders to call their own Enron-owned power generator plants in California to tell them to shut off the power for "maintenance." This let traders profit from rapid price bounces that flowed from news of "energy blackouts" across California in 2001.[62] Think of the damage this caused to everyday people and the possible deaths in hospitals that might not have had enough reserve power generators. More recently, in 2007, Standard & Poor's and other credit rating agencies gave the highest grade investment rating of AAA to collateral debt obligations (CDOs), which in part, contributed to the global financial crisis. The U.S. government later launched a lawsuit against Standard & Poor's, accusing them of lying about the risk posed by CDO securities. In early 2015, Standard and Poor's agreed to settle the case for US$1.5 billion.[63] Adding fuel to the fire was the poor lending rules used by banks which led to loans being made to people unable to repay them. The next financial crises is likely to be caused by the misuse of innovations by people applying for such loans unless banks improve their own screening software. Ever improving picture editing means that the income and tax report documents that banks rely on to approve trillions of dollars of loans for houses, businesses and governments, could all be faked on a simple computer. When this is discovered, all these loans would become invalid, wiping away billions of dollars and erasing once again the confidence in the financial industry.

Former Attorney General for New York, Elliot Spitzer, when asked why technology companies don't appear to have the same levels of criminality as the financial services industry, responded by saying that tech companies are a "fundamentally creative business. The value generation and the income derives from actually creating something new and different."[64] Curiously, financial services may make new innovations, like CDO's, but they won't achieve productivity as they are *seeking to make money out of money. As we now know, value must be created first through innovation, money comes after.* Sadly, the culture in the financial industry sets up desperate workers to seek huge bonuses by breaking the law and risking millions and billions of hard earned dollars invested by everyday people.

Chapter Summary

\#   Innovations and the actions they give to humans may turn genes on and off epigenetically, leading to changes in life expectancy. The type of innovations within a society determine the type of actions of people inside it.

\#   Productivity ("do more with less actions") is simply how much change happens in the value factors of actions that an innovation allows us to do. Ideally the value factors become faster, cheaper, smarter, and healthier.

\#   There are 3 types of innovations:

1.   Productive – An innovation that does more with less actions (e.g. mobile phone, computer, car).
2.   Unproductive – An innovation that does the same with the same actions (e.g. cafe, toy shop, hairdresser).
3.   Counterproductive – An innovation that does less with more actions (e.g. drugs, fast food, crass lyrics, sensationalist news).

CHAPTER FIVE

The Entrepreneur – Playing the Greatest Game on Earth

"When we treat man as he is, we make him worse than he is;
when we treat him as if he already were what he potentially could be,
we make him what he should be."[1]
Johann Wolfgang von Goethe

"Great minds discuss ideas; average minds discuss events;
small minds discuss people."
Anonymous

Holding up a finger, he says, "One thing. Just one thing. You stick to that, and everything else don't mean shit."[2] This is the moment in the 1991 movie, *City Slickers* where Curly the rancher (Jack Palance) tells city worker Mitch (Billy Crystal) what the secret of life is. The one thing, as we've come to know, is the making of our productive innovation for the greatest number of people. Many of life's problems melt into the air when the bulk of our actions focus on this.

Now it's time to explain these actions. What is the best word for our one thing? It's *entrepreneurship*, and it's the closest concept we have that bridges together the meaning of life with the real-world action that makes it happen.

It's true, another word could be found, but it would not be as well-known. Yes, the word entrepreneur can be overused, but in some ways, that's a result of many not fully understanding what it means. If we were to look at what entrepreneurs do, we would see that they play not just an interesting game, but the greatest game on earth. Instead of moving a ball forward; it moves the *human race forward*. So, what is an entrepreneur? The generalized definition of the word is: "A person who organizes and manages an enterprise… usually with considerable initiative and risk."[3]

Sadly, the word entrepreneur has been kidnapped into meaning something it doesn't. Indeed, "innovator" is a word which better shows the actions of seeking and making a productive innovation. Yet it can only be used *after* someone has proved they created value for others. That's why it mostly describes those who are dead but who left something of value behind. You don't use it for yourself. Few, if asked what they do, would say, "I'm an innovator." Anyone hearing it would think that guy or girl is dreaming. As we see it, to be called an innovator by others, while living or dead, is the highest honor one can reach in society, high above all the "sir" or "madam" honors given out by governments.

Before *we become innovators, we are entrepreneurs*. As a word, it's as flexible as the people it describes, as entrepreneurs adapt themselves and their innovations to the changing conditions around them to survive and create value. They show to us that the unique function of humans is to innovate. As Peter Drucker, whose work can be read in *The Essential Drucker* noted, "Innovation is the specific function of entrepreneurship."[4]

It's what got us out of the caves and trees to build the world of today.

An entrepreneur, like any label, refers only to the actions of a person. A quick definition so we can tell if people are one or not.

An entrepreneur makes and gives a productive innovation to society.

The key point is that the innovation should aim to be productive, if not now, then in the future. Those who make and use unproductive or counter-productive innovations *do not add productivity* to society and so do not come under our definition of entrepreneur. This is not so new, as Clayton Christensen, Jeff Dyer and Hal Gregersen write in *The Innovator's DNA*, "When someone opens a dry cleaner or a mortgage business, or even a set of Volkswagen dealerships or McDonald's franchises, researchers put them all in the same category of being an 'entrepreneur,' as well as the founders of eBay (Pierre Omidyar) and Amazon (Jeff Bezos). This creates a categorization problem."[5] A quick read of *The Everything Store* book can easily show how different Amazon is from other enterprises it's typically grouped with.

We aim to remove the confusion. The dry cleaner, mortgage business, McDonald's franchises, and Volkswagen dealerships all fall under the unproductive category and so are removed from our exploration of entrepreneurship along with a big crowd of other business enterprises.

Finding gaps of missing productivity in the world around them, entrepreneurs plug those holes with productive innovations. To do this, in most cases, they start and run an enterprise that owns and holds the productive innovation. This is mostly, but not always, in the *form of an enterprise*. As explored earlier, this can be an organization, political movement or party etc.

Unlike the wide-eyed inventor experimenting in the loneliness of their basement, an entrepreneur gets advice from the outside world on what people think of their innovation. In the list of activities that humanity has made to meet and beat its survival needs, entrepreneurship is the only one that has *no set rules*. It's not a job that can be advertised or hired for. It's the opposite of a job, *as its many actions can't be squeezed into a single category*. Like philosophy has the freedom to comment on any subject, so too can entrepreneurs make innovations for any area of life. With few rules, they uniquely can risk going too far, and so find out how far one can go. In the words of Abraham Maslow, they can seek to be "all that they can become."

As tech blogger Michael Arrington writes, "If I was a lawyer right now, even a rich lawyer, I'd always have wondered if I had what it takes to do something a little more exciting with my life than work for someone else."[6] Oprah Winfrey says in her work *What I Know for Sure*, "The biggest adventure you can ever take is to live the life of your dreams."[7] Drew Houston, CEO of dropbox.com says that entrepreneurs "work hard because working on an exciting problem is fun."[8] This is similar to what Kevin Rose, former CEO of digg.com., said. "If you believe in something… it won't feel like work."[9] In his first speech as the 32nd President of the U.S., Franklin D. Roosevelt said, "Happiness lies not in the mere possession of money; it lies in the joy of achievement, in the thrill of creative effort."[10] His own life is an example of that as the book *No Ordinary Time* by D.K Goodwin showed. Even Karl Marx wrote, "Real wealth is the developed productive power of all individuals."[11]

According to a global study, "Entrepreneurs exhibit relatively higher rates of subjective well-being in comparison to individuals who are not in the process of starting a business or owning-managing a business."[12] Such research is showing what we talked about earlier, that *eudemonia* is linked to the human function to innovate. Religions of the world unknowingly give high praise to creativity, as many of their gods had to be creative to make humanity. Likewise, the common actions of an entrepreneur are the ones that most lead to a creative and flourishing life. Many psychologists name creativity, independence, and mastering something as some of the key signs of a healthy life. Some may think this is strange, as the hardships an entrepreneur may face in making their innovation can seem to lower their well-being. Not so as a further study showed that people who got joy from having a greater purpose and meaning had higher protection from sickness than those seeking joy by pleasuring themselves.[13] The point here is made clear in George Halas' quote, "Nothing is work unless you'd rather be doing something else."[14]

People with a purpose to seek the meaning, love what they do, and crave to do more of it not less. It's play, not work for them. "Why would you want to stop playing?" they ask. Those without a purpose, who've never experienced play, frown and say that "balance" is needed. *That's a worker's mindset, as a worker fulfils someone else's purpose* and so is less excited about what they do as they have less control to make it as they'd like. The stress from this builds up, making them want to escape to find this undefinable "balance", which is really a disguise for what that they truly crave: freedom to make what they want.

Steve Jobs in his dying days appeared to understand what it meant to be an entrepreneur. Walter Isaacson recounts him saying in his biography, "What drove me? I think most creative people want to express appreciation for being able to take advantage of the work that's been done by others before us. I didn't invent the language or mathematics I use. I make little of my own food, none of my own clothes. Everything I do depends on other members of our species and the shoulders that we stand on. And a lot of us want to contribute something back to our species and to add something to the flow."[15]

How entrepreneurs do this has been unclear to many, making entrepreneurship seem magical to some. Media articles don't help as they don't define or separate what it is to be an entrepreneur from the millions of jobs out there.

The entrepreneur is unoccupied by any occupation, has the most freedom of any, and is open to innovation in any category. He or she has no job requirements, no minimum work hours, no work contracts to sign. *Entrepreneurs remake the world in their own image*, like the highest act for the religious is of God making man in his own. When others ask, "What do you do?" a question essentially about your purpose, the answer of "entrepreneur" mostly draws a blank stare and a second question, "An entrepreneur of what?"

Few, if any, other answers lead to such a question, since mostly all occupations give us an easy visual image. A carpenter works with wood, a plumber fixes pipes, an architect draws buildings, but an entrepreneur? It's a fuzzy image, and many steer clear of it as they don't even know its meaning. Its origin is French, from the word, *entreprendre,* meaning "to undertake."[16] Some nations who've recently began using "entrepreneur," have done so as no word before could describe entrepreneurial actions. Lack of visible entrepreneurship and innovation in some societies,[17] like Japan for example, mistake an entrepreneur for a person who can't find a real job.[18] Sadly to some the word is stained thanks to lying salespeople, get-rich-quick seminars, and flashy crooks who throw the word around.

Our definition aims to clear this up. It's the creative act which separates entrepreneurs from the rest. To do this, the entrepreneur has to *mix the actions* of many, like the accountant, lawyer, marketer, designer, and many others, mostly by learning as they go along.

Entrepreneurship, unlike other activities, doesn't discriminate against a person's education, background, or race. It only asks that the entrepreneur adapt to ever-changing events so to find the best way of making their innovation better. It's well known that Bill Gates, Steve Jobs, and Mark Zuckerberg all dropped out of college to start their productive innovations, but a lot of entrepreneurs make their innovations later in life. Michelangelo, for one, began work on the Sistine Chapel at age 75 as detailed in *Michelangelo and the Pope's Ceiling.*[19] As Austrian economist and author of *Human Action* Ludwig von Mises writes, "In order to succeed in business a man does not need a degree from a school… A man becomes an entrepreneur in seizing an opportunity."[20]

Higher education may help those seeking specialized jobs, like doctors and lawyers, but in a world of rapid change, *general knowledge* may be more useful. Learning the actions of an entrepreneur can help those in all other occupations become better at what they do.

An entrepreneur doesn't need to have expert knowledge of the innovation they are working on, though it doesn't hurt if they do. Instead, they need the ability to find the right blend of innovations, and then figure how best to mix and then promote them. Thomas Edison said that he was no expert in the theories beneath the innovations he made, even bragging that he had not even passed algebra in school. Instead, he hired the smartest people in science, engineering, and other fields, mixing their innovations to help him. He used to say, "I can always hire mathematicians, but they can't hire me." This is a liberating quality of an entrepreneur versus the control of other occupations.[21]

Author of *Banking with the Poor* and 2006 Nobel Peace Prize winner, Muhammad Yunus, who helped millions of poor people through micro loans, says, "All human beings are entrepreneurs. When we were in the caves, we were all self-employed... finding our food, feeding ourselves. That's where human history began. As civilization came, we suppressed it. We became 'labor' because they stamped us, 'You are labor.' We forgot that we are entrepreneurs."[22] Below we will define the entrepreneur for future clarity.

Pt. 10 BUILDINGS OF LOST DREAMS

ENTREPRENEUR
They experiment to find productivity others have missed

Kate can see that an entrepreneur should be someone who has made something more productive than what is already out there. She hopes the software she's made does that.

The Force of Creative Destruction

v. Agent of Historical Change*

"The reasonable man adapts himself to the world.
The unreasonable man adapts the world to himself.
Hence, all progress depends on the unreasonable man."[23]
George Bernard Shaw

Innovations are mostly owned and run under an enterprise, like a company, organization, club, etc. Almost every enterprise was originally founded, grown, and taken care of by an entrepreneur(s). Remember, it is actions that define an entrepreneur, not their job title. So, when an entrepreneur moves on or passes away their actions in the enterprise are passed to others who become the entrepreneurs. In this way, *all jobs can have entrepreneurs in them as we can find entrepreneurial actions* if we look close enough. Politicians do this through parties, Scientists through laboratories, and generals through the military. Entrepreneurial action can exist in any place at any time. Ron Chernow's *Washington: A Life* shows how George Washington had to use a lot of entrepreneurial actions to keep his army from defeat. Today, *managers, directors, or CEOs* are some of the different names given to those taking the role of the entrepreneur. In that their *decisions shape how productive* the innovation will or won't be. As explored earlier, those employed, if given the chance, can also be entrepreneurs by making further productive innovations within the enterprise.

To not confuse, we must remember that the enterprise is itself an innovation even though it houses innovations inside it. Much like the government is an innovation even though it oversees every other innovation in society. As we remember from our definition, innovations are seen as both separate from, and part of, larger and smaller innovations.

Let's quickly check below on the types of entrepreneurial roles which are most visibly seen within the common "company" enterprise (the definitions may differ between countries).

1. Founders.
These entrepreneur(s) made the innovation and/or brought it to the market. Learning lessons and using skills like determination, seeking advice and learning from failure help a founder make their innovations last. A classic book to help us explore these skills and more is Stephen R. Covey's *The 7 Habits of Highly Effective People* as is Simon Senek's *Start with Why* and *Find Your Why*. Visible founder entrepreneurs in the media spotlight include Larry Ellison, Richard Branson, Marc Benioff, Evan Spiegel, and Donald Trump, before he became U.S. president.

2. Executives, board members, and other leadership positions.
Enterprises don't work well without someone making decisions. It's those decision-makers who are taken to be entrepreneurs as they perform the actions that the founding entrepreneurs previously did, such as asking the tough questions, showing leadership, and increasing the value of the innovation. Most well-known here is the position of Chief Executive

Officer (CEO), who could be the original founder or even a person hired from outside the company.

3. Employees and those connected with the enterprise.
Letting employees innovate rather than robotically do boring tasks shifts actions from being those of a worker to that of an entrepreneur. Enterprises hire people to only get work done, forgetting that they are *missing out on the next big innovation* under their noses. With a 20% free-time rule (1 full work day letting employees be creative), Gmail was born in Google, going on to become the world's most used email service.[24] To make it fair, an enterprise would best give an employee an ownership share of the innovation they make and support the making of it within the company.

As the above does not happen often in companies, the trend is for most productive innovations to come from an entrepreneur free to start their own enterprise, with no job description to follow, rules to fear, or boss to bother them. With increased competition, more enterprises may soon realize that to survive they need more new innovations to come from their employees.

No matter which group an entrepreneur comes from, the skills of determination, adaptability, and leadership are crucial in making and spreading an innovation. Thankfully, many books have been written on the entrepreneurial process to help. *The Lean Startup* by Eric Reis, *The 4 Steps to the Epiphany* by Steve Blank, *The Alliance* by Reid Hoffman and Ben Casnocha, *Hard Thing About Hard Things* by Ben Horowitz and *Zero to One* by Peter Thiel and Blake Masters.

To better understand the entrepreneur and confirm the important role we're giving them, we need to see what their effect has been in the past, present, and future.

For this, we turn to the field which in its past has given only the smallest mention of the entrepreneur. It's nicknamed, "the dismal science," but it rarely makes accurate predictions like a science should. Economics is its name. Broadly, it's described as the study of all the actions that go into making and spreading goods and services in a country.

As we've seen, at the center of these actions is the entrepreneur and their enterprise, which makes and spreads new, and hopefully productive, innovations. As Harvard economist Joseph Schumpeter wrote, "Without innovations, no entrepreneurs; without entrepreneurial achievement, no capitalist returns and no capitalist propulsion. The atmosphere of industrial revolutions—of "progress"—is the only one in which capitalism can survive."[25]

The economic growth which comes from this is tied to *how fair the rules are*, and those rules affect the number of innovations able to be later combined. Remember a time when you saw a referee rule unfairly in a sports game? Entrepreneurs, like anyone else, leave if they are treated unfairly. As von Mises said, "In eliminating the entrepreneur, we take away the driving force of the whole market system."[26]

Most of the debates in economics become pointless if you don't have entrepreneurs in the economy to begin with. Governments many times have tried to step in to fill the shoes of the entrepreneur with bad results. Why? *Governments can't compete with themselves*, unlike entrepreneurs, who need to always add more productivity so as to not be beaten by other entrepreneurs. We saw the results of government experiments in the USSR right up until its collapse in the early 1990s. With no entrepreneur, productive innovations faded from society, with unproductive and counterproductive copies taking their spot, sucking life expectancy downwards.

As Joseph Schumpeter said, the entrepreneur is the "Pivot on which everything turns." Like Von Mises, he saw the entrepreneur as the key force that constantly lifts the living standards of the people. This is done through what he called, "creative destruction," where the old and rusty (unproductive and counterproductive) innovations are replaced by the new and improved (productive) ones.

Let's look at a real-world example:

In December of 2000, Microsoft was the most valuable company in the world at US$510 billion. At the time, Apple was valued at only US$4.8 billion, not even 1% of the value of Microsoft. Nearly 12 years later, as of June, 2012, it was Apple holding that top spot at US$541 billion and Microsoft cut down to US$249 billion. What happened? Innovation. Apple stopped selling unproductive innovations and released productive ones, which replaced others in the market, such as Microsoft's. The well-known example of the iPhone, launched in 2007, had in one quarter (end of March 2012) collected more revenue for Apple (US$22.7 billion), as a single product, than all of Microsoft's products and services combined (US$17.4 billion).[27]

Without forgetting the abuses of capitalism, as there are many, we can still say that since the fall of the USSR in the early 90s and the economic shift in China, the positives of a "freer" market have become more accepted across the world. Just like entrepreneurship's link to the unique human function, capitalism is evolutionary in its ability to change and adapt. Geoffrey A. Moore, author of *Crossing the Chasm*, writes in his other book *Dealing with Darwin,* "Free market economies operate by the same rules as organic systems in nature." This echoes economist, Thorstein Veblen, who in 1880 wrote an essay entitled, *Why Is Economics Not an Evolutionary Science?* Adding to this, Schumpeter says, "The essential point to grasp is that in dealing with capitalism we are dealing with an evolutionary process. It may seem strange that anyone can fail to see so obvious a fact."[28]

Compared to other systems, capitalism changes fast. The rules of the past are flipped upside down. In the words of Karl Marx, "All that is holy is profaned."[29] Likewise, *democracy is capitalism's political twin*, replacing laws, policies, and political parties as they become unproductive or counter-productive. The left hand of democracy wrestles with the right of capitalism, limiting the abuses that capitalism creates and giving help to people who fall under its speeding wheels.

In capitalism, the blacksmith shop is set up, only then to be wiped out by the factory. The horse and buggy are paired, only to be later deleted by the car, and the print newspaper is replaced by the online newsfeed. These entrepreneurial actions upset the magical "equilibrium" (balance) of the economy that neo-classical economists wish existed. These are the economists who are writing most high school and university textbooks today. Tough to grasp for many, *Economics in One Lesson* by Henry Hazlitt simplifies such textbooks well.

In short, neo-classical sees an economy as a set of rules, *even if unrealistic,* which they think will at least help them to guess the future. These guesses have directed trillions of government dollars worldwide, yet as many point out, most of their "rules" can rarely be found in the real world. Take the rule of "perfect competition," which says that, "All companies have access to the same information." It's true if you believe that secrets don't exist. Another rule says that purchasers, like shoppers in a supermarket, buy and sell products through an auction. So, when you're buying milk next time just let the manager know you want to offer a lower price. But the best rule might just be that all similar products sold have the same quality. Well, maybe so in a world where all products are made by the state like it was in the USSR.[30]

Yes, rules help make sense of the world, but those rules need to link to reality.

We mustn't forget that the world is unpredictable, but most economists don't like that. Unsurprising then to see that neo-classical economics has no rule made for the existence of the entrepreneur and their unpredictable innovations. All the models and charts they make to explain the world assume that all innovations popped out of thin air. Even Nobel Prize-winner, former chief economist of the World Bank, and author of *The Price of Inequality*, Joseph Stieglitz, said, "Anybody looking at these models would say they can't provide a good description of the modern world."[31] Another Nobel Prize-winning economist, Douglas North, said, "Neo-classical theory is simply an inappropriate tool to analyze and prescribe policies that will induce development. It is concerned with the operation of markets, not with how markets develop. How can one prescribe policies when one doesn't know or understand how an economy develops?"[32]

If we don't know what the disease is, how can we cure it? Without the entrepreneur, *we can't understand how economies develop*, wasting hundreds of billions of taxpayer dollars on policies that band-aid the bleeding, but never fully stop it. Sadly, "Austrian school" economists who see the importance of entrepreneurs are less represented and so have little effect on government policies. Saying that the world is unpredictable is not comforting to politicians who need to show that they "know" what's going on to get elected.

Let's explore and see if there is an answer to Douglas North's question.

Productivity Reflects Prosperity

GDP Per Capita, 2011-2015
Source: © World Bank.
http://data.worldbank.org/indicator/NY.GDP.PCAP.CD/countries?display=map
Creative Commons Attribution license (CC BY 3.0 IGO)

Why is it that the 30 richest nations by GDP per capita (Gross Domestic Product, or the combined $ money value of all goods and services a nation makes divided by its population) as seen above (darker color) are nearly the same ones that held that position going back 50, 100, or even 150 years ago? Japan, Singapore, and South Korea have recently joined this group.[33]

The answer lies with productivity, which we covered a chapter ago. Nobel Prize winning economist and author of *End this Depression Now*, Paul Krugman, writes, "Productivity isn't everything, but in the long run it is almost everything."[34] It is humanity's best known way for improving its standards of living. By doing more with less actions we can move away from shortages of anything, that state of struggle, bloodied red in tooth and claw. Though most societies look peaceful, just remove the basics, like food and homes, and the peace melts into violence and robbery. Developed nations, with more productive innovations, have less chance of this. Sadly, billions of people the world over face the horror of such shortages every day.

The problem begins with economists today mostly measuring productivity based on how innovations improve enterprises, forgetting that the more important improvement is in the lives of adopters/consumers as seen in the value factors. Both measures need to be mixed to find the full picture of productivity.

But first, what leads to productivity for a nation?

The Productivity Commission of the Australian government says that the two major causes are:

1. *Innovation,* and though they don't label different types of innovations, they do say, "The innovation that counts is a much richer concept than the exogenous technological advances espoused in economics textbooks." An example they give, is "electricity, as it has multiple applications,"[35] or a large range of actions, which as we talked about, is common of productive innovations.

2. *Creative destruction,* which Schumpeter said is the removal of old innovations by new, more productive ones.

You've seen this yourself when products and brands vanish from the supermarket and are replaced by new ones. What makes all this important is when we learn that *for each percentage point jump in productivity we see the standards of living rise over time in response.* Nothing else effects standards of living like this, helping shrink the poverty of a nation and boost its well-being and prosperity. It's like an economic holy grail from which a nation drinks to cure its ills. It's not so long ago that 500 million people were lifted out of poverty between 2005-2010,[36] mostly in China and India. Never before have so many people escaped poverty in so short a time. That success is mostly thanks to new laws that have let entrepreneurship flourish and by doing so, boost productivity. By changing the "rules," it changes how people play the game.

As Liu Chuanzhi, the founder of Chinese computer giant Lenovo, said, "I remember that it was in 1978. There was an article in the People's Daily about raising cows. I got so excited upon reading it. During the Cultural Revolution (1966-1976), every newspaper article was about revolution and class struggle, non-stop, only editorials. At that time, raising chickens or growing vegetables were viewed as capitalist tails to be cut."[37]

This is why donations to poor nations don't do much good *if they don't help people help themselves.* Effective altruism (donating a regular percentage of your income) and other movements risk wasting money, by fixing the symptom and not the cause. Abraham Maslow even stepped out of his area of psychology to say, "The difference between the great and good societies and the regressing, deteriorating societies is largely in terms of the entrepreneurial opportunity and the number of such people in the society. I think everyone would agree that the most valuable 100 people to bring into a deteriorating society, for instance, Peru, would not be 100 chemists, or politicians, or professors, or engineers, but rather 100 entrepreneurs."[38] Even Bono, the lead singer of U2 and a campaigner for charity donations for the poor admitted, "Entrepreneurial capitalism takes more people out of poverty than aid."[39] In 1948, half of the world's people lived in poverty; today we've cut that to 21%.[40] Aside from dealing with dire emergencies like starvation, charities will do best by teaching local people how to do things themselves. Giving food or clothes for free is not as helpful as showing people how to make and sell it themselves. *What's given for free creates dependency*, and in the long run does not improve living standards. It may sound like we're saying entrepreneurship is the silver bullet to all the problems of the world. Not so, there are many roots under the tree, but if there is a root cause, entrepreneurship is it.

Give a village that sews clothes by hand a sewing machine and we see a boost in the quality of clothes, a drop in their price and more income to pull the workers out of poverty. If more villages get a sewing machine then they can all compete leading to better quality clothes for the people. But aid instead dumps free clothes (like unwanted branded clothing donated by people in the U.S) and instantly no one sewing can sell anything as no one will buy it.

As Brynjolfsson and McAfee, authors of *The Second Machine Age*, said in their other book *Race Against the Machine*, "If labor productivity grows at 1%, as it did for much of the 1800s, then it takes about 70 years for living standards to double. However, if it grows at 4% per year, as it did in 2010, then living standards are 16 times higher after 70 years."[41]

Given what we know, the more productive innovations are, the higher the standards of living are likely to be. More innovations spread and sold means more tax revenue flowing to the government for improved roads, health, schooling etc. This in time all pushes up life expectancy.

Ancient Rome and Medieval Britain had life expectancies of 28 and 30 years respectively—less than half that of the developed world today.[42] Between then and now, an untold number of productive innovations have been made which have increased life expectancy to the global average of 71 years today. Are we so sure we're right? Is this able to be proven wrong? Is it "falsifiable" as some scientists would ask?

How do we test this? Earlier we talked about a method. *Spread a productive innovation in a population that doesn't have it and record life expectancy changes over time.* Take a recent experiment: iPads were randomly dropped into Ethiopia where people could not read or write. They found that the children were soon able to figure out how the iPads worked. Using the educational apps found in them, they learned how to draw letters and eventually how to read.[43]

So, if we recorded the life expectancy of the village before the iPads were given and then the life expectancy in a few decades' after, it's likely we'll see some change in the length and quality of life. With this we can test to see the effect that almost any innovation has on life expectancy. True, we'd need to make note of all other innovations introduced and removed from the village during the study period to get the most accurate picture of the iPad's effect. We already know that the logic of this works, as we've seen life expectancy shoot up when innovations in infrastructure and medicine are brought to poorer areas.

We can also see this working by reversing the experiment. We can also remove an innovation from a village and see its affect. Anthropology studies have shown this to work countless times. Removing cigarettes from a village is more than likely to lead to a jump in life expectancy, or replacing old cookware with new pots and asking villagers to boil disease ridden water before drinking it. Most prisons prevent inmates using any innovations, and studies find that every year in prison leads to nearly two years lost from life expectancy.[44]

Q. **Which innovation do you think has increased your life expectancy the most?**

A.

The more stress removed from people's actions by productive innovations, the less bodily damage, the longer they are likely to live. Prisons are made to do the opposite.

Remember we pointed out that productivity for economists today, incorrectly, measures enterprises but forgets consumer productivity? Before we explore a solution to this we must find out how they measure enterprise productivity. It all starts by finding the number of working hours needed to make a set number of innovations. How does this work? When Henry Ford saw that he could make an assembly line, which saved time by passing car parts to the workers instead of having the workers fetch the parts, he grew the number of cars built per hour. As more cars were built, fewer workers were needed, less wages were paid, and so the price of cars dropped lower. In many ways, it's very similar to our value factor examples earlier. Economists, however, would measure it based on *output*, how much was made, and *input*, number of hours worked, what's missing here are the deeper details of time, money, health and intelligence.

Consumer Productivity

Using our value factors, we can measure the missing "consumer productivity" that economists forget. Our measure can also apply to the enterprise productivity that economists do measure as we described just before with the Ford example. To best measure consumer productivity, we'd need to gather the answers, using an impersonal value test, like an empirical study of a selected sample of consumers reviewing the innovation. The more people in the study, the better the accuracy of the answers. Yes, such tests are subjective, but as explored earlier we can average out answers from say 1,000 people quizzed on the effect of the drop in price of Ford cars to gain insights. Below is an example of those considering purchasing a car, with the average point score (+10/-10) and most common responses from people. As you'd expect, the results are positive. But even though the car is made for consumers, economic statistics don't show this data, even though it reveals for the first time the real productivity effect of the assembly line. Which is that it made cars affordable, leading to more people purchasing them and experiencing the below effects to their value factors.

TIME +2 = More time as an average 4 hours is saved per week using a car, not taking the train.

MONEY +3 = More money can be made as more work can be done with faster travel.

HEALTH +2 = Less damage to the body as faster travel to doctors and hospitals.

INTELLIGENCE +2 = Less Cognitive load with near silence in the car thanks to closed windows, unlike the noise from walking among traffic and people.

Below we apply the same impersonal value test as above to study the enterprise. Here the results are less subjective if the enterprise can measure changes in its manufacture process. Below we look at how adding the assembly line assisted Ford in the 1900s compared to before the assembly line. Enterprises wishing to use the value test may need to set up specific methods to measure such changes in innovation. Point scores here are subjective, but the stats do the scoring for us. A time period (12 months or so) before the innovation is introduced needs to be selected to show the most accurate before/after changes that have taken place.

TIME +3 = 2 hours saved to make a single car compared to a year back. 50 minutes less work time needed per average worker.

MONEY +3 = $21 million saved with 982 more cars made compared to a year back.

HEALTH +2 = $1.1 million saved on worker injuries compared to a year back.

INTELLIGENCE +2 = Workers can be moved to do more complex tasks.

But the old productivity measure would instead include mostly the *Money factor and time factor statistics.* But as we can see above it will *miss reporting the health and intelligence factors.* Without that the full picture is not known. Hopefully in the future all factors become reportable. Yet for all its faults, the money and time factor statistic is all that enterprises and industries have data on. Due to this where needed, we'll be referring to and using the old productivity measure.

Moving on we see clearly below that productive innovations like the assembly line have been very good at cutting working hours in the long run. Add up all other innovations like the assembly line over the centuries and the result is that working hours have dropped even though living standards have risen across developed nations. The same trend is slowly occuring in developing nations.

Hours of work per week, 1870–2000 – Max Roser[2]

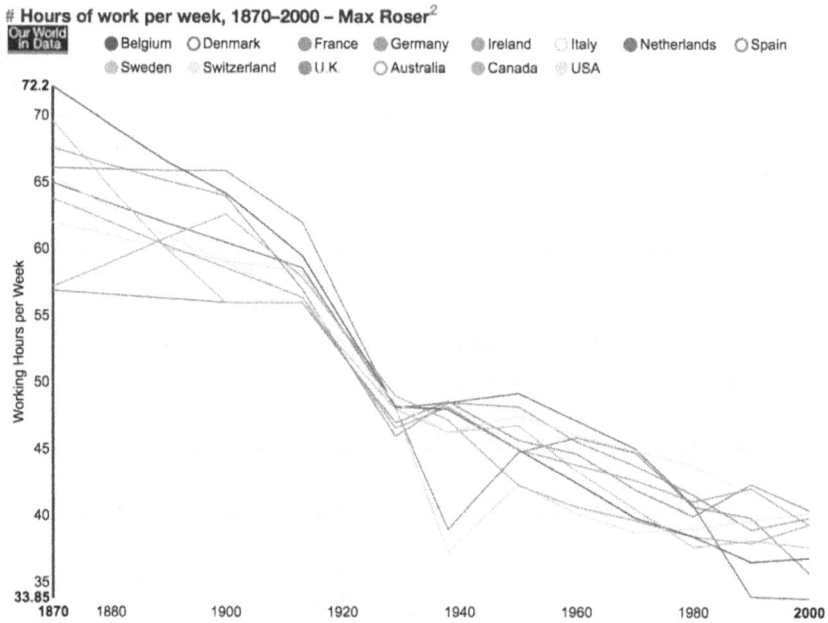

Source: Max Roser (2014) – 'Working Hours'.
Published online at OurWorldInData.org.
Retrieved from: http://ourworldindata.org/data/economic-development-work-standard-
of-living/working-hours/. Data source: Hubermann & Minns (2007).

Without productive innovations inside the enterprise, output per worker (the number of products made by them over the same amount of time) cannot grow. Their weekly pay therefore can't increase and neither does the price of the innovation drop, it even may rise preventing new people from buying it. This increases bodily damage and lowers life expectancy if essential items like food, clothing and housing are caught in this cycle.

The old productivity measure when used by economists to measure government data becomes known as "GDP normalized to purchasing power parities (GDP PPP)". It's a per hour measure of an entire country's productivity. To compare countries, this GDP per hour number is mostly converted to US dollars.[45]

Below we see the top 20 most productive nations according to GDP (PPP):

Rank ⬍	Country ⬍	GDP (PPP) per hour 2013 ⬍
1	Norway	75.08
2	Luxembourg	73.22
3	United States	67.32
4	Belgium	60.98
5	Netherlands	60.06
6	France	59.24
7	Germany	57.36
8	Ireland	56.05
9	Australia	55.87
10	Denmark	55.75
11	Sweden	55.28
12	Austria	54.83
13	United Kingdom	51.38
14	Canada	50.29
15	Iceland	50.01
16	Switzerland	49.88
17	Spain	49.59
18	Finland	48.79
19	Barbados	46.19
20	Italy	45.04

Sources: Wikipedia,
https://en.wikipedia.org/wiki/List_of_countries_by_GDP_(PPP)_per_hour_worked
(Creative Commons). The Conference Board Total Economy Database – Output,
Labor, and Labor Productivity, 1950 – 2013 (Excel). The Conference Board. January
2014. GDP per Hour, in 2013 EKS$. (Public domain), "Labor productivity per hour
worked (ESA95)." Eurostat. (Public domain).

It's no surprise that many of these nations are also on the previous map with the highest GDP per capita. In Appendix B, we select the national statistics we find that will best assist the increase of life expectancy in a nation. As nations boost these statistics in the right directions by encouraging more productive innovations, the more likely increases in life expectancy will occur. Send a quick email vitojgrigorov@gmail.com or go to www.prosperism.org to get Appendix B and other bonus material.

Making the Game Fair

"The end of law is not to abolish or restrain,
but to preserve and enlarge freedom."[46]
John Locke

To know how economies develop, we need to know the rules they develop under. Just as no one will want to play a game with unfair rules, no entrepreneur will care to do their best if someone can easily steal their hard work. What does this mean for government? Being itself the *largest innovation* within a country and *referee of* all other innovations, governments need to do their best for the people who are innovating by *promoting the rule of law, making fair laws, and applying them.* For simplicity, "law" covers all similar words and concepts like, "regulations," "policies," "rules," etc. Laws as innovations themselves are the foundational bedrock of a nation, and governments cannot exist without them. To figure out why something has happened in a nation we can ask, "Why" many times over and as we'll see the trail tends to lead to a set of laws which have roots going back into the past.

1. RULE OF LAW

Two online social networks took off a few years apart from each other in different parts of the world. Facebook.com took the lead in the U.S. and later expanded globally, while vkontakte.ru took the lead in Russia. The leading co-founders of these companies share some similarities. Mark Zuckerberg and Pavel Durov were born in the same year, both have become very wealthy, and both, as expected, have similar views on the free sharing of information. But as of this writing, one controls his company, mostly free to run it as he wants, while the other claims the legal system failed him as he was fired and forced to flee his country.[47] Unfair laws can lead a lot of people to migrate out of a country, reducing its population.

For a country to function, laws are passed by politicians for each area of life. Governments over time establish enterprise-like departments of health, education, finance, environment etc., usually run by elected politicians, to oversee if the laws are being followed.

Laws work like *filters* in which all innovations of society pass through, being accepted or rejected. Acceptance means you can continue doing what you want, but rejection may mean you get a call from a health and safety regulator, tax inspectors, or the police.

Many books are written trying to find out how best to encourage societies, and more importantly, governments, to obey the rule of law. If a government obeys its own laws, the people are more likely to do so too and be less distrustful. Remember when your parents told you not to drink out of the milk carton but then you saw them doing it? Did you get angry that they were a hypocrite? Did you aim to disobey them next time? The same reactions come from everyday people who are fooled by their own government.

2. FAIRNESS OF LAW

A nation's constitution is the document which should show what can and can't be done by a government. Most governments are not stupid enough to pass laws that encourage value-destructive actions or counterproductive innovations. But some politicians have a creative way of "interpreting" their laws in a way that lets them and their friends get rewarded first.

Take Ukraine in 2004, where one of the largest steel mills in the country was sold for US$400 million to a group that innocently included the son of the country's president. The next year, Ukraine's new president undid the deal and sold the mill to the highest buyer for US$4.8 billion.[48]

Then there's Shakhbut bin Sultan Al Nahyan, who ruled over Abu Dhabi, Saudi Arabia, for nearly 40 years from 1928-66. As authors of *Why Nations Fail*, Daron Acemoglu and James Robinson explore, he spent freely on his own private projects while banning all other construction that he didn't personally approve. Schools were almost non-existent during his time, preventing the country's youth from learning about the innovations of the world.

On the other hand, Sierra Leone's president, Ernest Bai Koroma, built luxurious schools and houses that resemble those in developed nations. Sadly though, this was all to house the children of the ministers of his government while the majority of the people lived in huts, uneducated and poor.[49]

Corruption, as we can see, is like being forced to play a game in which, no matter how many times you score, your opponent as a rule will always be 10 points ahead of you.

3. ENFORCEMENT OF LAW

Now let's say that some politicians and their buddies in business have broken the law. The people see this and protest. When nothing happens, some of the brave ones take it to court, where the case is rejected on some minor detail which makes no sense. Calls to the media get no response.

Angered, more protestors then push for another party to win the next election. Opinion polls show it running close, but then the current party wins in a landslide. Slowly the protestors get given strange criminal charges, like tax fraud and stealing mail from neighbors.

Such stories may not happen to everyone, but others may hear them and wonder, "Do I want that to be me?" Fear freezes them from trying to fix problems, all seems hopeless. Standards of living drop, more people have less money and so more start taking bribes to survive. A struggling new business owner may have to pay "protection" money to a gang, but mostly this payment protects him from the gangsters themselves smashing up his shop. *When the police, instead of protecting people, stop and fine them unless a quick bribe is paid, society starts to distrust the government.* Ever spoken to a rude call center rep? It takes only a few minutes with one impolite person to make the customer hate the entire company forever. So if the police can be bribed and they represent the most visible arm of the government, what now do people start thinking about the politicians? Their brand is damaged, the law they claim to uphold is worthless. If all laws can be bought by the highest bidder, then productive innovations are risky to make if a wealthy competitor can sue you into fleeing the country.

Some claim that each country is "culturally" different and that the people of "flawed" countries may in fact be "happier," than those in developed ones. If you ever hear this, ask for proof. The best of which is found in the number of *people who vote with their feet and emigrate.* Unsurprisingly, it's those from poor African nations who wish to do so more than anyone else, with developed nations of the United States and Canada being among their top destination choices.[50]

The story of human immigration is one of people choosing which nation will provide the most productive innovations for them and their family. Nations losing people mostly have less productive innovations spread across the population. Entrepreneurs banned from innovating in one country, usually migrate to another one to try spread their innovation there.

According to a Levada poll, 38% of Russian entrepreneurs wanted to leave their country, with 15% of Russia's prison population estimated to be entrepreneurs—around 3 million people. Boris Titov, the spokesperson for business rights at the time, reflected that it is "hard to find another social group persecuted on such a large scale."[51] However, history needs to be remembered, as it's hard to change a planned economy into a market economy. The collapse of the USSR in 1991 led to a drop in the already stressed living standards, as people had fewer basic innovations, like food, heating, and jobs than before. Life expectancy for Russian men dropped a full year in 1994 alone.[52] The new ideas of democracy and capitalism had never existed in the country. A few decades is little time to change centuries' old actions of an entire people. Over a century after its founding, even the U.S. still had the mafia controlling large parts of its economy.

Forbidding the Game for Thousands of Years

It's very easy to spit out what we think is right, but it's best to find out what led nations to be the way they are today. Governments are guilty of forgetting this, when from afar they criticize other nations' actions without putting themselves in the others' shoes. We're guilty of this on a personal level too. We make black-and-white judgments, forgetting that the truth often lies in the gray.

Philosopher Karl Popper thought that societies can be put into two groups, *the open and the closed.*[53] Sounds pretty black and white, right? Yet we'll use his labels to try to find the gray by the level of filtration of the actions and innovations as seen in the making, applying, and enforcement of law.

Open societies encourage their people to create more with less action, by giving fair rules and few filters to most actions so as to let innovations develop, spread, and be used. *More innovations mean more choice*, and more chance we'll get the result we're after with less actions. Most, if not all people, are treated the same under law, decision-making power is spread among many, corruption is low as standards of living are high, and opportunity is more widely spread out. This all leads to an openness to change and to an understanding *that with change problems are expected, but will be solved over time.*

A closed society pushes its people to create the same or less with more action. They put down unfair laws for the entrepreneur, heavily filter actions, and block what is not paid for in bribes. Decisions are made by the few, your rights are decided by your bank balance, and who you know matters more than what you can give to society. *Fewer innovations means less choice which makes it harder to get the same result with less actions.* The elite fear change and use the laws to prevent loss of power by continuously removing people's access to innovations.

Most nations will have features of both types of societies. It's a gray matter of degrees, and every year, decade or century, a nation can change itself for better or worse.

Ancient Rome was an example of the shift from open to closed. In its early centuries, it was governed by people elected to the plebeian council and the senate. It was called a "republic" for this reason, the state was represented by the public. The early Romans feared that one person could gain too much power and harm society. That's why their highest office, the consul, was shared by two people. Those elected to consul were limited by law to serving only one year per decade. Also, they had to be 43 years of age or older, rather elderly given the low life expectancies of the time.[54] Only an emergency would put a pause on this, as it did when the general, turned farmer, Cincinnatus was given dictatorship by the senate to crush a rebellion.

Otherwise the laws remained untouched until Julius Caesar (100 BC–44 BC) was also given dictatorship in war time, which his great nephew, Octavius, (63 BC–14 AD) exploited after Caesar's assassination. When Octavius' army beat that of Mark Antony and Cleopatra, he took the name, "Augustus" and as dictator started the empire (rule of emperors) by cutting or rewriting most of the laws that had helped Rome for over 500 years. Before Augustus, laws were fairer, as everyday Romans had *social mobility*, and were able to move from being a merchant or soldier into the aristocratic classes. Augustus shut this down, he broke up the Plebeian Council and gave more power to his friends in the aristocratic Senate. The result? A much more closed society than before.

Around the same time, the opposite was happening in Middle Eastern lands controlled by Rome's armies. The high priests had long ruled over Jewish society, as they were the only ones who could read and translate the religious books, making up laws to suit themselves. The Pharisees, as judges on legal matters, resisted this. Instead they wished for all people to have the freedom to study the religious books, and to let everyone have a say in the making of laws. Yet it was only war with the Romans in 70 AD that led to the high priests' downfall, letting the Pharisees spread Jewish study to all society.[55]

Rome's turn to dictatorship let emperors, like the high priests, do almost anything they wished. In 301 AD, Emperor Diocletian introduced price controls making it so that most things sold for the exact same price through the entire Empire. Any merchant who changed their prices would be killed. The guilds of the day (unions) were put under government control, people skilled in a trade were unable to leave it, and their children were forced to be trained in the same job to replace their parents. With little innovation allowed to counter the worsening living standards, Rome saw its population shrink as people fled to find a better life. The result? Rome had fewer people to collect tax money from to pay their armies who were protecting the borders against invaders.

Diocletian's decisions led to food shortages across the Empire. Neighboring barbarian tribes started to get less food than they were promised by the Romans, which among other things, led to rebellion and their eventual invasion of Rome in 410 AD.[56,57]

Rome survived nearly four centuries under direct rule from emperors after Julius Caesar. It helped that many emperors, like other rulers throughout history, used belief in a god to help make people fearful and obedient towards them. In Christianity, rulers found help in the dead literary hand of St. Paul whose words found in the Bible say, "Let every soul be subject unto the higher powers. For there is no power but of God: the powers that be, are ordained of God."[58] This let rulers get the arrogant belief of greatness known as "the divine right of kings." For almost 2,000 years it made everyone think that God gave rulers the power they had. And thanks to the help of the priests, who like salespeople retold this story endlessly, most of the people believed it.

Over time, though, people saw that any king or queen could screw up the job God had supposedly given them. In 1688, England went through one of the first modern revolts, called the "Glorious Revolution," which forced the dictatorial King James II to flee the country. By stripping the rights of the people and wishing to remove the hard-won powers of parliament, James II was seen to be moving England backwards. After kicking him out, the everyday parliamentarians, barons, and those of the upper class hashed out the productive innovation of the Bill of Rights, which William and Mary of Orange had to agree to sign before being crowned, with lesser powers, the new King and Queen.[59] Nearly a hundred years later in America, a group of people with mostly British backgrounds revolted against Britain and wrote another Bill of Rights.

Today, we see the same lessons repeated when political parties don't defend the rule of law. Unfairness spreads which leads to two key problems:

1. Fewer innovations develop within the nation, as there are fewer entrepreneurs.

2. Fewer innovations enter the nation from outside, due to a fear of unpredictable law changes.

When governments stop defending the law, enterprises in that country start to fail and many sell or get out. When money "leaves" a country like that, the value of the country's currency can drop a lot. These are all red flags to outside enterprises and entrepreneurs, who then avoid investing in that nation like the plague, leading to fewer innovations entering that country.

We see this before Augustus came along. Rome was famous for such innovations as aqueducts, pumps, roads, and the water wheel, but once emperors took power, innovation sharply declined. According to one scholar, cement masonry was the only great discovery of the Romans during the empire until its collapse.[60]

When a nation's people have a more diverse set of innovations to use, the boost in productivity gives that nation an advantage over others, be it in trade, sports, or even war. After the Glorious Revolution, Britain passed laws that helped the emerging class of entrepreneurs and gave everyday people new actions to choose from, such as owning a dog, sending their children to school, and printing books. As small as this all sounds to us, the domino effect it had cannot be forgotten.[61] It was through this ever-growing rule, fairness, and enforcement of law that British entrepreneurs could make and import innovations in the areas of vaccination, shipbuilding, guns, machinery, and new construction methods from both at home and overseas. In 1840, the British navy invaded the coastal town of Tingai, China, only to find the locals mostly using spears, bows and arrows. Only a few guns were found. Though it was China that had first made gunpowder and firearms around the 11th and 12th centuries, its rulers' desire to close up society prevented it from innovating in firearms as well as the British did centuries later.[62] As Sir William Petty said, "A small country and few people may be the equivalent in wealth and strength to a far greater people and territory."[63] With a population of only 7 million people at the time, Britain was able to take control of India, Canada, Australia, New Zealand, and many other nations.[64] By the turn of the 20th century, the British Empire was the largest in history by land area, totaling near 13.01 million square miles and including 458 million people.[65] As the character "blood" said in the poem, "The Modern Traveler," by Hilaire Belloc, "Whatever happens, we have got the Maxim Gun, and they have not."

GDP

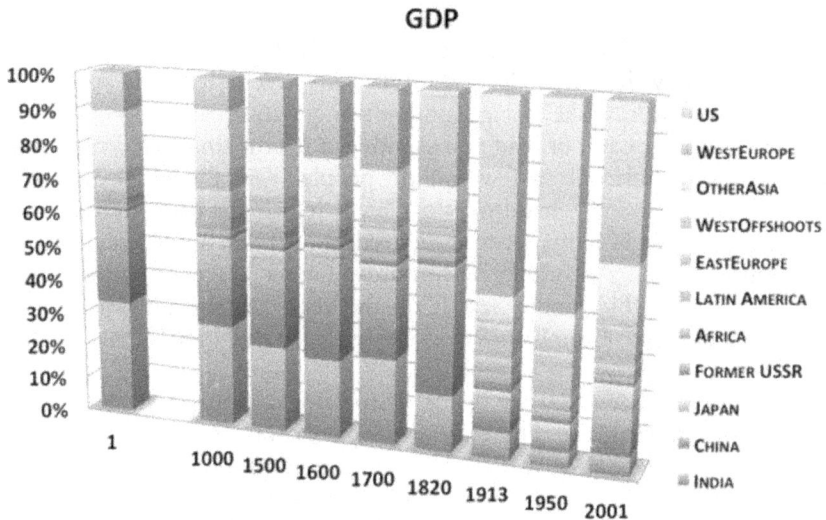

Population

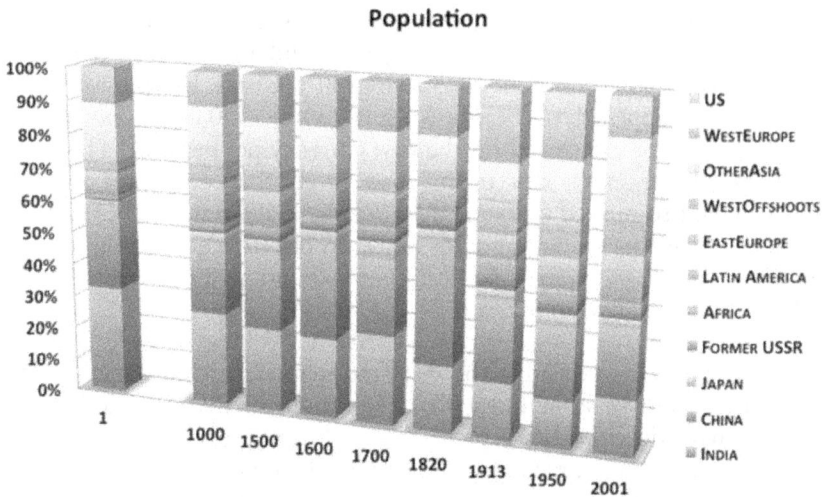

Source: www.theatlantic.com, used with permission

This is no praise for imperialism, but rather an example of how with the spread of innovations we see that *population and land size start shrinking in their importance*. Go back to the time of Caesar, and we see the most populous countries of China and India holding most of the world's GDP as at that time innovations were not well developed. As the years 1913 and 1950 show, the U.S. alone overtook both India, China, and others in GDP though its population was a fraction of theirs.

Today we know better that it's the most productive innovations which decide a nation's share of the world's GDP. The U.S. learned this from the British and now holds the largest GDP share, yet it has only 5% of the world's population. Take Hong Kong, it's only 426 square miles (about the size of New York City) of land and islands but it's the financial center of the Asian region, with only a few million people. Run by the British for a century until the 1997 handover to China, it had for decades one of the highest standards of living, economic freedom, IQ, life expectancy, and low corruption scores.[66] From 1978 onwards, China has taken a new path, unlike its past, which today sees it on the verge of becoming the world's largest economy, as Evan Osnos explores in *Age of Ambition*.[67]

North Korea shows us the value-destructive actions that come from eliminating innovations. The Korean peninsula was once a single country, until it was divided after WWII. The South became a more open society as seen by its high standards of living and access to new innovations, while over the border the North became closed, with some of the lowest standards of living. There, the Kim Jong family of rulers copied well the Roman Emperor Diocletian, for in 2009, North Korea did a currency change. Ever wondered what you'd do if all your savings in the bank became worthless? That's what happened to North Koreans. Only 500,000 *won* (around US$200) could be exchanged for the new currency per person.[68] This made worthless all the extra *won* people had saved that now they couldn't exchange, and so pushed everyone down to the exact same level of poverty. The idea of keeping living standards low is an old strategy, aiming to make everyone *rely on government for their survival* and to prevent them from making large demands on the rulers.

Remembering what we said at the third chapter's start about new words in dictionaries, it may seem likely that the countries that use the English language have developed, accepted, and use more innovations per person than other countries. English has, by most accounts, the most number of words of any language, at between 1 and 2 million with linguists estimating that a new word is added every 98 minutes.[69] How fast words are redefined also shows the speed at which new innovations, along with their actions, are spreading in that society. If some countries ban innovations coming in from around the world, like North Korea does, it doesn't take a genius to see they simply won't have the need for words like "googled," "posted," or "tweeted." It's likely the word "entrepreneur" hardly exists, given how strange the talk of "business" appears to North Korean students on rare student exchange programs to neighboring universities.[70]

In contrast the more open South Korean society has produced huge international enterprises like Samsung and Hyundai, spreading value through the world. The shocking difference can be seen in the below satellite picture of both Koreas at night time, with the North having seemingly one dot of electricity compared to the hundreds found in the South. It's no surprise that South Korea enjoys a life expectancy 12 years longer (80 years) than the North (68 years). The gap may be even larger if independent studies are allowed in North Korea.[71]

This extreme difference can even be seen in more open nations. Mathew Desmond explores the U.S. divide between rich and poor in his book *Evicted*. Studies done for the city of Glasgow, Scotland, show people in the poorest neighborhoods can expect to live 12 years less than those in the richest parts of the city. Why? Researchers boil it down to several factors: material (e.g. basic goods), behavioral (e.g. diet), biological (e.g. blood pressure), and psychosocial (e.g. stress) which call to mind the four value factors we've mentioned before.[72]

Source:www.globalsecurity.org, Public domain

Marx's Malfunction

"The capitalist achievement does not typically consist in providing more silk stockings for queens, but in bringing them within the reach of factory girls in return for steadily decreasing amounts of effort."[73]
Joseph Schumpeter (Economist and author of
Capitalism, Socialism, and Democracy)

We can best see the importance of an entrepreneur, not just by looking at economies whose laws let entrepreneurs exist, but also by looking at economies whose laws don't. Like the USSR, a Marxist nation which collapsed only a few decades ago.

With our past mentions of him, you'd be guessing correctly that Marxism is named after the all-rounder, Karl Marx, who, with the help of his friend, Friedrich Engels, wrote many books and thousands of unpublished notes. His ideas would be cherry-picked and taped together to make up laws for governments best known as being socialist and/or communist. Surprising to some is that Marxism has importance today, as many of its ideas are alive in political debate, and are helping *guide policies of parties from the "left"* side of politics the world over, mostly from parties with names like: Labor, worker, socialist and democrat. Risking simplification, the left seeks more government control in society than does the right. China, Cuba, Laos, North Korea and Vietnam all call themselves communist party states to this day and widespread government influence in society reflects that.

What we find most remembered of Marx's writings is his explanation of both the bad and the good results of capitalism. If we were to define it simply, capitalism is a system of private ownership of innovations. Marx instead called for eventual public ownership of innovations, with the government providing for the needs of most people. What's often forgotten is that he only thought this was possible once enough wealth had been built up from capitalist growth. He saw the importance of capitalism when he wrote that, "During its rule of scarce one hundred years, [it] has created more massive and more colossal productive forces than have all preceding generations together."[74] For most people who know about him, though, Marx is mostly remembered for criticizing capitalism for what it destroyed. Remember the context he lived in, which was 19th century London, which Boris Johnson explores well in *Johnson's Life of London*, which was a time when the *laws were not keeping up* with rapidly changing innovations. This led to counterproductive innovations like company policies letting young children work 18-hour days in mine shafts, with many dying on the job. With no laws setting a minimum wage, companies paid pennies to their workers who as a result lived in poverty no matter how hard they worked. Seeing this, Marx said it was all a result of the capitalist system which was "vampire-like" in the way it reduced people to inhumane conditions.[75] Capitalism let rich landlords and owners sell products and take the profits while paying their workers just enough to survive.[76]

Within one hundred years of his death, half the world's people were ruled by Marxist governments.[77] His teachings are compulsory subjects to this day for each student in China.[78] In Britain, it took 80 years for clause 4 of the British Labour Party's founding constitution, about the Marxist idea of spreading wealth to everyone, to be deleted in the 1990s.[79] Sadly, many of Marx's ideas are forever stained by how governments interpreted them and put them to use. Yet most people have never read his books, and most of what they have heard is based on quotes taken out of context, which mostly make him out to be the spawn of the devil. It's true he promoted political revolution, since revolution back in the 1800s was how dictatorial governments changed. The celebrated American and French revolutions are examples of this. His writings never gave a step-by-step explanation of what should happen after revolution though. He never said that a single party should rule a nation forever. The dead cannot speak for themselves, but their followers do so instead. For Marx it was Vladimir Lenin, the Bolshevik leader, who in 1917 led the revolution that would establish the USSR. He read Marx's known translated writings up to 1920, added his own ideas in his *Essential Works*, and together they became known and taught as Marxist-Leninism. What he read, when we now look back, was only a small percentage of Marx's writings, as more were later found and translated, showing Marx not as a fixed thinker, but who evolved and changed his views on many topics.[80] This incomplete reading led to the opposite results in the USSR to what Marx said would be needed for a country to reach true socialism. How so?

One of Lenin's key plans was to eliminate entrepreneurs as enemies due to Marx's idea of "class struggle." Lenin's successor, Joseph Stalin, would fulfill this wish as explored in Stalin by Khlevniuk and Favorov. Marx talked about society being made up of two main classes in constant conflict with each other, the working class and the capitalists. Marx predicted that the working class, having been exploited for so long, would rise up in revolt against capitalists. This single concept led to all sorts of murderous laws against entrepreneurs. The cruel irony was that Marx never explained the difference between entrepreneurs and capitalists, leaving Lenin and others to think that the two are the same, a common error, even among economists today.

This error had started way back, as few cared to review the original use of the word "entrepreneur", which was first defined by early 18th century French economist, Richard Cantillon, and he very clearly divided the entrepreneur from the capitalist as two different roles. Yet in the late 18th century, British economist, Adam Smith, mixed the two roles into one due to the fact they both involve risk, and in his footsteps so did John Stuart Mill. In the 20th century, Ludwig von Mises and Joseph Schumpeter would bring back, with some small success, the original definition of Cantillon. But thanks to the spread of neo-classical economics in universities and textbooks, the differences between the two would not be fully explored even till today.[81,82]

The difference between the two is rather simple. Capitalists make money from money; entrepreneurs make money from innovation. Capitalists supply capital, entrepreneurs make innovations. Capitalists invest to earn profit without organizing the growth of the innovation their profit comes from, it's entrepreneurs who do that organizing. Marx here seems to realize this as he defines the actions of the capitalist: "It is only in so far as the appropriation of ever more and more wealth in the abstract becomes the sole motive of his operations, that he functions as a capitalist."[83] So if wealth appropriation is not the sole motive, then by Marx's own definition these people cease being capitalists, but what then do they become? Marx gives no answer. But it's clear, they are entrepreneurs.

Modern-day capitalists have started to see that they need to be more than just money shufflers, buying low, selling high. Venture capital funds and angel investors try filling this need, where not only is money invested but mentoring, important contacts, and legal advice is given to help the entrepreneur. As Alice Schroeder explores in *The Snowball,* billionaire Warren Buffet's Berkshire Hathaway does this for many companies it invests in, taking a management role to make the company profitable again.

If you read Marx, you further find out that he points out this crucial distinction between money gain and value-creation that shows the difference between the capitalist and the entrepreneur. In Chapter 4 of *Das Kapital* he writes, "Use-values must therefore never be looked upon as the real aim of the capitalist... The restless never-ending process of profit-making alone is what he aims at." Without boring you, Marx said that two dual values exist, one was "exchange value," the price of an innovation, and the other "use value," what an innovation does that makes it useful. The criteria for "exchange value," is the price, as seen in the money paid for it. Yet Marx never gave an explanation for "use value." Our value factors help fill this massive hole, showing what is gained or lost when our actions are swayed by innovations.

Entrepreneurs seek use-value, as they must innovate first before profit comes, but a capitalist with deep pockets seeks exchange-value, to buy low, sell high and make profit. A capitalist may not care if a counter-productive innovation is made with their money as long as it earns them more profit. Money laundering, drug trafficking, and prostitution, have long been financed by wealthy individuals as the profits are very high. Unlike entrepreneurs, capitalists can easily seek profit-making alone, as easily shoving their millions into a savings account lets them live off the interest alone. Innocent until their actions prove them guilty, an entrepreneur mostly seeks to change the world for the better than have the money transform them into a profit hungry fat cat. Yes, an entrepreneur can become a capitalist and a capitalist an entrepreneur. An executive at a pharmaceutical company may fund a new lab to find a cancer cure while closing down an unprofitable pain-killer helping millions of people. Is he a capitalist? An entrepreneur? Only by seeing the scorecard of their actions until their death will we know with more certainty.

The "interest" that grows on a capitalist's money is called, in economic jargon, *rent-seeking.*

Even in economics, this term is used to describe a set of value-destructive actions.

Trainee stockbroker, Seth Davis, from the 2000 movie, *Boiler Room,* said it best, "I didn't want to be an innovator. I just wanted to make the quick and easy buck." In the 2013 movie *Wolf of Wall Street,* a stockbroker says this about his job, "We don't create shit. We don't build anything." Parasites live off their hosts blood by sucking it and giving nothing back, and we can see some similarity with capitalists. Economist John Maynard Keynes, was hoping this exploitation might not last long when he wrote, "I see the rentier aspect of capitalism as a transitional phase which will disappear when it has done its work."[84] Unfortunately, as the book *The Big Short* by Michael Lewis showed, the system is built so it does not disappear. Many seeing this, leave. Like former Wall Street trader turned author of *The Black Swan,* Nassim Taleb said in a speech that "success" is from "having taken a heroic route for the benefits of the collective".

From the above, we can better see that Marx was quite clear on his definition of who was a capitalist and that it did not include the actions of the entrepreneur.

It's true that near the end of Marx's life in the U.K, the laws helping modern entrepreneurship were being set up. But it's tough to say he should have predicted the changes they would make in the world. Marx is well known for being a champion of the workers, but what's not well known is that he really felt sorry for them. He wished they could be unshackled from backbreaking work to become their best selves. Though those on the left may find it hard to swallow, it appears that the modern entrepreneur is Marx's ideal for what a person should seek in life. As he writes, "A being does not regard himself as independent unless he is his own master, and he is only his own master when he owes his existence to himself."[85] Marx, like many others, saw the creative act as crucial to a person's life.

Marx named it the *species being,* John Stuart Mill called it *individuality.* Abraham Maslow labeled it *self-actualization.* All pointed to the human unique function to innovate.[86] Marx knew that boring work ends up robbing a person's free time, sucking away their chance to make their own innovation in a *life-time spent chasing money to survive.* The result is unhappiness or "alienation," as a worker becomes a "dependent being." This, he predicted, would fuel the workers' revolt against the capitalists. Being held back from seeking the meaning of life, we've suggested, is the root cause of most personal and societal problems. Before the opening of entrepreneurship in the late 70s, Chinese communist party theorists wrote that alienation gave the "most scientific explanation" for most problems of Chinese society at that time.[87]

More recently in *Capital in the 21st Century,* economist Thomas Picketty, touched on the capitalist problem, saying that many wealthy people have never worked a day in their lives because they've inherited their wealth from someone in the family. That someone was likely an entrepreneur, who, with blood, sweat, and tears made an innovation for the greater good of all, only to have the profits flow to fools and frauds in their family. This entrepreneurial ancestor would roll in their grave on seeing what filth of the earth the unproductive and narcissistic use their effort is now spent on. The movie, *The Aviator* may play up the splurging life of Howard Hughes Jr. but compare him to his dad, the innovator Howard Hughes Sr. and you get the idea. *Instead of seeking value, their descendants seek fame.* Silver spoon-fed sloths living off bank interest, who, slime-like, ooze from one burst of excitement to the next, dripping away bucketfuls of money.

This may be what's leading so many billionaires to sign the "giving pledge" mentioned earlier. Fearing their future family will suck away money like a succubus does her victims. When children of entrepreneurs don't struggle, they can't value innovation. A shining example of this is from a Forbes article, *The Gilded Age Family That Gave It All Away* by Chloe Sorvino, which quoted 19th century steel billionaire Andrew Carnegie: "The man who dies rich, dies disgraced." He followed his own advice, as did his family, for he left them just enough to get by, and his daughter even sold the townhouse passed to her, as the cost to maintain it was too high. This meant his great grandchildren of today, like their parents, aren't living off money that they never earned. As one of them said, "Making one's own way in life is a healthy way to be." So, what happened to his $4.8 billion fortune after his death in 1919? It funded 200+ libraries, established what are now the global Carnegie-Mellon University campuses, and the Carnegie Corporation of New York, which has donated billions worldwide for nearly 100 years.

By innovation not temptation, we see those like Charles Darwin, who though inheriting wealth, ended up working towards an innovation which impacted the world many times over. Marx himself could only write like he did thanks to the large salary of his friend Engels, who may be the best example of an angel investor, as he not only gave money but also helped in the making of the innovation. Engels co-authored books with Marx, and after Marx's death he transcribed and published his remaining writings.

It's our actions that show who we are, not the family we're born into. After all, it's not that each action can always be made to seek the meaning of life, but as long as the sum of our actions aim to do this over our lifetime, can we die knowing we've tried to do our best.

The Capitalist Revenge

Imagine you're the CEO of a computer company, hundreds of local people work in your company, but with more competition from overseas your market share is dropping. You're losing money monthly and fear you'll need to fire half of your workers. What do you do? Instead of innovating and making faster and cheaper computers for your customers… you call up the nation's president to ban these "low-quality," foreign computers flowing in. In return, you hint that you'll make a generous donation to the president's re-election fund. Sound fair?

Capitalist "rent-seeking" is alive and well today. The goal is to get money from favors that otherwise would be earned by innovating. *Bribery and corruption are the undercover versions of legal lobbying*, which occurs worldwide. Enterprises try to hide their failure to innovate by crying that laws are needed against their competitors for untrue reasons like to increase public safety, prevent loss of jobs, or comply with regulations.

The U.S. auto industry gives us an example. Being unable to innovate against the low price and high quality of imported Japanese cars, the industry swayed the U.S. government to change the law to drop the number of foreign cars that could enter the country. This forced Americans to pay around $5 billion more for cars during the 1980s than was needed. It took time but Japan beat these barriers by setting up manufacturing plants in the U.S., so now their cars weren't "foreign made". You'd think that the U.S. car manufacturers had bought some time to get their cars into competing shape, yet they did nothing. They continued to run unproductive factories making expensive, inefficient cars. In 1981, U.S. car enterprises had a 75% domestic market share, but by 2012, due to this lack of innovation, it's dropped to 45%.[88,89]

Australia invested billions of dollars of government money to keep factories of the major car companies from closing to save local jobs, but the high cost of wages meant that on any day the same car could be made in an Asian factory for a cheaper price. By 2014, Mitsubishi, Holden, Toyota, and Ford had either closed or announced plans to soon close all of their plants in Australia.[90]

Like the car manufacturers, car dealerships have also been rent-seeking. In the U.S., they got court orders to stop electric car maker Tesla Motors from selling their cars directly to the public, scared this would set an example for other car manufacturers to do the same, leading to the dealerships' extinction as the middleman. No innovation here, the dealerships just wished to protect their rent-seeking retail model which increases the final sale price of any vehicle.[91] Now, imagine your anger if you missed an airline flight or funeral or wedding thanks to a taxi you booked weeks back not showing up. This happens somewhere every day. That's the rent-seeking taxi system that Uber is trying to remove. Or imagine working for years on your book, only to be forced then to give away all rights from now until 70 years after your death to a publisher who'll give you back a measly 10-15% of each book's sale price and demand you promote it yourself. That's the rent-seeking book publishing industry which amazon.com is trying to replace.

The more governments help rent-seekers the more they tend to forget what it is that lets a government exist in the first place. What do we mean? *Nothing gives more to a government's tax accounts than the innovations of enterprises and the actions of entrepreneurs*, both living and dead. In return for giving the rule, fairness, and enforcement of law, entrepreneurs make productive innovations that give the government money from taxing the profit of the enterprise, the income of its workers, sales of its innovations and countless other taxes. This all adds up to form the bulk of all yearly government income. Yet governments *fail to see that these tax monies all lead back to the entrepreneur and can only be sustained with growing entrepreneurship.* Like neo-classical economists who advise them, politicians take entrepreneurship for granted, thinking it will always exist, forgetting that laws need constant updating to make sure the game entrepreneurs play is fair. Even just a small boost in the number of entrepreneurs and enterprises would lead to governments getting more revenue over time. The Kauffman Foundation estimates, if just 30 to 60 out of the millions of U.S. enterprises grew to become worth US$1billion, then the U.S. could add 1 percentage point to its yearly economic growth.[92] Just 1%? Looks small, but it's not when you realize that on average most yearly growth is between 1-3% no more, so an extra 1% is really like increasing growth by 33% on the previous years.

Instead of wasting money giving handouts and saving jobs in industries with unproductive/counterproductive innovations, governments would do well to help industries that seek to make new productive innovations. Politicians are turning taxes paid by productive enterprises into loans for dying industries that then use the money as a weapon to crush the productive enterprises whose tax money paid for it. In the Hierarchy of Misery we see how government repeatedly forgets that the entrepreneur is usually responsible for the money they use to pay for everything else.

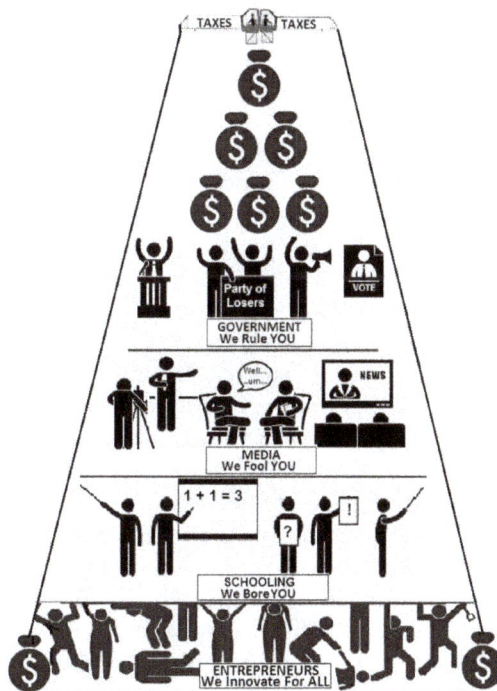

An Economy Without an Entrepreneur

Picture a world of plenty, where all you ever wanted was yours, and you didn't need to do much work to get it. This is the communist dream that Marx said may be possible, but only if societies first went through capitalism to create productive innovations, he called them "productive forces". By wrongly removing the entrepreneur, most Marxist nations were doomed from the start in their effort to reach this utopia. Perfection doesn't exist, only improvement does. What's best today, is not so in the future. This, among other reasons, is why standards of living in the USSR always lagged behind the U.S. and other capitalist nations.[93] Though the USSR was making productive innovations in military and space innovations, the everyday innovations for their own people were missing. There were few phones, TV's, fridges, washing machines, and sometimes food was limited.

The 1917 October Revolution in the Russian Empire, led to enterprises being taken over by the Red Army of the government.[94] Thinking they were capitalists, entrepreneurs were banned. Work for all people overtime became guaranteed by the government, even if many worked on worthless innovations. True, this kind of brute force planned economy can boost standards of living quickly in a previously war-torn nation. Like the growing muscles of a beginner bench pressing, a developing nation can see amazing growth rates of over 10% of GDP because they started off so poor to begin with. But after years of lifting the same way and weight like before, it's harder to add more muscle, like seen when countries become developed and see lower growth rates. It's because they are already rich with productive innovations, but developing nations are still playing catch-up so their growth rates remain high.

Without the entrepreneur and a free market, a planned economy will also stop growing its muscles, because workers are *repeating the same old actions with the same old equipment*. Nothing new is being made. Would you break in and trash a hotel room just to create more work for the cleaners? It would seem stupid, right? Isn't their effort best put to mop up the emergency water leak at the front entrance to reduce the risk of injuries? But the trashed room means more work for cleaners and also police and hotel staff. This example simplifies what many find wrong with governments using "Keynesian economics." Create a problem and pay billions to hire as many people as you can to fix it. Will it lead to the most productivity and innovation? Unlikely, but that doesn't matter to some Keynesians. What's crucial to them is that people get a job and earn money to then spend so enterprises won't lose sales and go bankrupt. Let's remember context. Keynes pushed this concept in his book *General Theory of Employment, Interest and Money* to boost growth after the 1930s Great Depression, but 80 years later it's become part of the medicine box of most governments, who use it to cure unimpressive economic statistics.

Innovation comes from trial and error, *not from creating fake problems* or making government the provider of all innovations.

In the planned economy of the USSR, say a factory made 10 cars a day a decade back and today has improved to 30 cars a day. But during the same time, a similar factory in a free market economy is today making 100 cars. Why the difference? Without entrepreneurs and the competition among them, the planned economy gives little reward for anyone to innovate, to find ways to make more cars in less time with less money. Now in case it's unclear let's break some definitions down:

Planned economy – Actions directed by government.
Free market economy – Actions directed by competition between entrepreneurs.

Picture our Kate working in a radio factory in the USSR a half century ago. She gets an idea for an innovation, to install a Ford-like assembly line, so more radios can be made per day. In the USSR, trying to get approval for that would result in many roadblocks. First, Kate would have to convince her boss to tell his boss about it. This is already difficult, as a manager doesn't want to be outshined by a creative worker below them. It's hard for people to think differently when their pay check demands that they don't.

Let's say Kate gets lucky, and her bosses agree and get her idea in front of a government assessor. Trials then start in a few radio factories to test if the assembly line increases productivity. It works, and so the assembly line spreads to all radio factories. What would Kate get out of this? The grand reward for possibly billions of dollars saved is... a slightly larger apartment (remember all housing was owned by the government in the USSR) or... a small pay increase, but not above what her boss earns. Are these rewards enough for all the trouble? No, is the obvious answer. Strange as it sounds, Kate is allowed to patent her entire idea, but it'd be pointless, as the USSR government owns all patents anyway on registration. No enterprises are allowed, so Kate could not make it herself. Mikhail Kalashnikov is a case in point. He made the Kalashnikov rifle, earning the USSR billions of dollars in arms' sales worldwide for decades. Yet he never received a penny, and has like others just a standard state pension for the elderly.[95]

Would anyone be keen to innovate in a place where government snaps away control of your innovation and does with it as it wishes? No, is the answer again. Instead, the aim of all these workers robbed of creativity was a race to *finish their work day as quickly and easily as possible.* Spying was nothing new during the Cold War as explored well in *The Billion Dollar Spy* by David E. Hoffman. To keep up with the U.S., the USSR poured billions into spying on how productive innovations were being made in the U.S so as to steal designs and recreate them back home. When the Reagan administration discovered this, they on purpose put fake manuals and designs into Soviet hands so they'd waste time and money recreating innovations that didn't work anyway.[96] The computing industry alone showed the huge difference between the two nations. In 1987 there were only two hundred thousand personal computers in the USSR, and almost none were affordable to the everyday person. In the United States, over fifty million, mostly affordable, computers were owned by everyday people. It was years after the fall of the USSR that affordable computers started popping up in the former Soviet Republics.[97] Behind the USSR controlled iron curtain of nations, similar shortages were seen in households of East Germany. In 1989, 24 % had no toilet, 53% had no modern heating system and 84% had no telephone.[98] Picture the number of deaths of people who could not easily call for help.

Guess what else happens when you remove the entrepreneur? *You don't know how much you need of most things.* How many radios do people need to buy next week? How many radios should be sent to each city and town? In a free market, entrepreneurs in each city and town would have accurate answers. Instead, Soviet planners hundreds of miles away in Moscow were trying to be more accurate than any local person. Economist Friedrich Hayek, author of *The Road to Serfdom* and *The Constitution of Liberty*, would call this the "knowledge problem."[99] Say the planners estimate 10,000 radios be sent to sell in Town A, yet only 1,000 would be sold and 9,000 are thrown away when the next model radio is released. They estimate 50,000 winter boots are needed for Town B, yet all of them sell out in a week, and thousands of families are left with old boots with holes for the winter.

The pattern above repeats with all innovations, most importantly food. Sometimes eggs weren't on the shelf, milk was gone, or juice would be back in two weeks due to a mistake by the planners. Shortages like this would mean people lining up for hours before a shop opened to hopefully get just one of the 100 milk bottles due to arrive that morning. The people had no choice, the *government was the only seller of all innovations, it was a monopoly.* People wasted away large percentages of their life time waiting in lines to buy food, which in nations with entrepreneurs was nearly always available on the shelf.

The last General Secretary of the USSR, Mikhail Gorbachev (1985-1991), talked openly about such problems, saying, "In our country, scientific and technical progress is slowing down… mainly because of the economy's lack of receptiveness to innovation."[100] In 1988, an attempt was made to bring the crumbling economy to life by finally allowing entrepreneurship for the first time in nearly 70 years. This "Law on Cooperatives" proved too little too late. The USSR ceased to exist on December 25, 1991 as detailed in *The Last Empire* by Serhii Plokhy.[101]

Before the Soviet collapse, the neighboring Chinese communists, running a similar planned economy, saw trouble ahead if changes did not happen. Under Chairman Mao's rule starting 1949 until his death in 1976, China followed the Soviet model of eliminating the entrepreneur. After Mao's death, the emerging new leader, Deng Xiaoping, moved away from the black or white thinking of Lenin's prediction that "as long as capitalism and socialism exist, we cannot live in peace, in the end, one or the other will triumph."[102] Deng disagreed, "Planning and market forces are not the essential difference between socialism and capitalism. A planned economy is not the definition of socialism, because there is planning under capitalism; the market economy happens under socialism, too. Planning and market forces are both ways of controlling economic activity."[103]

Few things in the world are black and white, and *almost all economies use different degrees of planning and market forces.* Anyone who actually reads Marx would know he wrote that it is capitalism that "creates those material conditions which alone can form the real basis of a higher form of society, a society in which the full and free development of every individual forms the ruling principle."[104]

Though many people believe the Chinese government of today pays lip service to Marxism, the truth is that almost every major reform they've applied has a Marxist theory explained in each policy, as outlined by China's president in his book *Xi Jinping: The Governance of China.*

After Mao's death, party theorists began to see that China, following the USSR's example, had tried to skip over the capitalist stage of development which Marx said needed to first be developed before socialism could arrive, *leaping from a farming economy to the abundance of socialism in one step.* From the outside, the USSR as a model that China aimed to copy seemed to be working, until you went inside to see the frozen living conditions as more productivity couldn't be squeezed without innovating. In 1979, Su Shaozhi gave a thesis at a Chinese party conference called, "underdeveloped socialism," which gave a Marxist explanation that China needed the capitalist stage to get to developed socialism.[105]

On becoming leader Deng started to slowly relax laws, letting entrepreneurship breathe again. His changes are arguably the foundational driver behind China's industrial revolution, bringing hundreds of millions of people out of poverty. As Deng said, "It doesn't matter if the cat is black or white, as long as it catches the mouse."[106] It's the results that matter as only they can show if the state or entrepreneur is best for the job. Previous state efforts at economic growth from 1949 to the late 1970s were deeply carved into the minds of Deng, and nearly a billion Chinese, most of whom suffered horrible famines. With the new experiment in entrepreneurship, the economy bounced back, for the first time showing year-on-year improvements, as slowly did the standards of living. Entrepreneurship was officially approved in 1987 when the 13th Party Congress endorsed the theory of the "primary stage of socialism." It concluded that China needed to enter the capitalist stage to become a fully developed socialist country.[107]

It would seem that the Marxist theorists of the Chinese Communist party have by now understood the difference between the entrepreneur and the capitalist, for after decades they finally gave communist party membership to entrepreneurs in the early 2000s.[108] Entrepreneurs are doing for China, in several decades, what it took other nations hundreds of years. Following China's example, Cuba's new leader, Raul Castro, has relaxed laws for the first time, unlocking entrepreneurship for more than 200 occupations and counting. Today in Cuba homes can be bought and sold from one person to another. Under his brother, Fidel, for nearly 50 years entrepreneurship was banned, and you could not even open up a hot dog stand. Taking the path of the USSR, the Cuban economy grew until no more productivity could be squeezed out of it.[109-110]

Below is a list of measures which together help boost entrepreneurship to spread innovations.

DEMOCRACY:
Many opinions exist about democracy, but surveys worldwide mostly show people's agreement to sentences like, "Democracy may have its problems, but it's better than any other form of government." Results show approval of 81% in the former USSR, 88% in the Middle East, and 92% in Western nations.[111] Like capitalism, democracy has an evolutionary way to adapt, - election method that gives the fairness that dictatorships lack. As each party seeks re-election, each entrepreneurially learns from its mistakes and aims to find out what voters want. Through such small experiments better laws are

passed over time, rather than the daydreams of a distant out of touch dictator. It's this ability to experiment with change using elections that prevents the bloody revolutions that happen in dictatorships. If democracy exists in addition to a free market then the capitalist economy is likely to push money to a minority of the people, while the *democratic government balances this by taxing and redirecting money back to the majority*. A study recently showed that democracy boosts economic growth, increasing GDP by as much as 20% in the long run.[112] Does democracy also link to increased productivity? The world's 20 most productive nations are all democracies.[113]

FREE MARKET:

Poverty is said to be a side-effect of a free market, but *poverty has always existed in human history and on an even more gigantic scale* before free markets emerged. A "free" market needs the rule, fairness, and enforcement of laws by government. Sometimes that fails, as it did in the lead up to the 2008 financial crises, as explored in *Too Big to Fail* by Andrew Ross Sorkin. As long as the nation is open to allowing and encouraging its people to trial and test innovations, they will have more chances to fix problems over time.

We see that the top 20 most productive nations are also called "free" in the 2015 Economic Freedom of the World index.[114] Nations with more "controlled" economies are lower on the productivity list. Such nations have problems like the longest delays in registering businesses, which is one of the crucial first steps an entrepreneur must take. In Zimbabwe, it will take you 90 days, in Haiti it's 97 days, and in Equatorial Guinea, a suffocating 135 days.[115]

MEDIA FREEDOM:

One of the main demands of the Glorious Revolution, and later the American Revolution, was a free and uncensored media. Free thought and disagreement let people not just *know which innovations exist, but also what to think of them, which in turn shapes their actions.*

Productivity is linked with the free flow of information as well. The 20 most productive nations also have high scores on the Press Freedom Index.[116]

HUMAN DEVELOPMENT:

The United Nations' Human Development Index aims to show a nation's standard of living. All 20 of the most productive nations are in the top 30 of this index, showing that increased productivity has a link to boosts in standards of living.[117]

LIFE EXPECTANCY:
As we explored, GDP (PPP) does not measure productivity boosts from a consumer but from an enterprise, but that's still enough to show us that the top 20 most productive nations are ranked within the top 40 nations with the highest life expectancies.[118]

The On/Off Switch of the Dark Ages

"A man may die, nations may rise and fall, but an idea lives on. Ideas have endurance without death."[119]
John F. Kennedy (35th U.S. president and author of *Profiles in Courage*)

Imagine you heard a politician today say, "We do not desire at all that the great masses shall become well off and independent... How could we otherwise rule over them?"[120] That's what British philanthropist, Robert Owen, was told when he sat down with Austrian government officials to talk about helping their people.

So fearful were the Austrian elite that they refused to let factories be set up in Vienna, the nation's capital, saying that the increased population would *bring revolution* to their doorstep. To calm their fears fewer rail lines were built leading to the city. The elites running other closed nations agreed with the Austrians. Their sole wish was to hold onto their power, and to do that, they saw they could not let anything new change the way things were. We've explored that entrepreneurship is the main driver boosting the standards of living of nations, and we've seen that the rule, fairness, and enforcement of law are the foundational innovations to a prosperous society. Below, we will discover what specific law changes are needed to make this happen.

It's often forgotten that the opening up of societies is itself a recent productive innovation. Even before Marx's writings were cherry-picked in the 20th century, the rulers of the past had been silencing entrepreneurs for thousands of years. Laws forbade innovation with penalties of jail or death which educated the young to fear trying anything new. Remember back how the Roman laws changed after Augustus? Author Cullen Murphy said in his research that "the Romans looked down on entrepreneurship," with Roman senators forbidden to engage in shipping and other kinds of trade.[121]

Roman author Pliny the Elder (23 AD – 79 AD), wrote about a glassmaker coming to Roman Emperor Tiberius and showing him the productive innovation of unbreakable glass. How and from what it was made was known only to the glassmaker, who asked permission to be the only one to sell it, like getting a patent today. Instead of rewarding the man or hiring him, Tiberius had him killed in fear that his innovation would lead to a drop in the price of glass.[122] Thirty years later, the trend continued. Roman historian Suetonius (69AD–122AD) tells us how Emperor Vespasian rejected an innovation which would unemploy the large number of slaves moving heavy building pillars saying, "How will it be possible for me to feed the populace?" Without work and payment, the slaves would starve and maybe revolt. Fast forward to 1589, and we see English Queen Elizabeth I also fearing job losses when a priest from Calverton, England, asked for a patent for his new knitting machine. But it wasn't unemployment that was the real fear, it was what it would lead to, a potential revolution.[123]

Just imagine how many millions of entrepreneurs like those above were rejected or didn't even bother trying due to fear? Sadly, the rules of the game set by the rulers at the time meant, as Schumpeter would point out, "The fact that Greek science had probably produced all that is necessary in order to construct a steam engine did not help the Greeks and Romans to build a steam engine."[124] Like the estimated *one percent of all ancient writings which have survived to this day*, an equally small number of innovations succeeded in escaping entrepreneurs' minds and being made in the real world.[125] It didn't help that most people long ago were either slaves or servants, with little chance to make an innovation, fearing they'd be punished or killed for experimenting. The guilds of the time didn't help either, as they protected workers, so like the unions of today do, aimed mostly to eliminate innovations that could put jobs at risk. As they spoke for a large number of workers, rulers listened to the guilds because they didn't want riots. In time, the guilds' power declined which was as economist, Milton Friedman, co-author of *Free to Choose*, wrote in his other work *Capitalism and Freedom* "An indispensable early step in the rise of freedom in the Western world."[126]

The result of all this fear of productive innovations should make humanity kneel in shame. For it was Eratosthenes (276 BC – 195 BC), a Greek mathematician, who first calculated the circumference of the earth almost as well as those who claimed they were "first" to do so a thousand years later. It was Apollonius (262 BC – 190 BC) of Perga, who made the first study on conic sections 1,400 years before Johan Kepler "discovered" the same thing. And 400 years after that we see René Descartes, author of *Discourse on Method and Meditations on First Philosophy* "discovering" again what Apollonius had long ago found.[127] Because these old innovations of Apollonius and others were lost or destroyed, future generations had to waste *centuries of time finding out again what their ancestors had already discovered*. The result? The path for increased life expectancy was delayed for thousands of years, as innovations long ago were stopped dead from combining with others.

Just imagine moving about in the 13th century, not on a horse and cart, but on trains, then in cars in the 15th century. The first moon landing happening in the 16th century and the internet soon after that. By today we'd likely have explored outer space like is imagined in books like *Seveneves* by Neal Stephenson or the sci-fi writing of Lindsay Buroker. This all may have come had the rules of the game been different. What if people had long back noticed Heron of Alexandria's (10 AD–70 AD) discovery that by catching air puffed from a vacuum we could turn it into energy? What if we'd earlier seen that the earth was not flat, and been quicker to agree that our planet went around the sun? In human history, we see too many instances of what German writer von Goethe said, "Ignorant men raise questions that wise men answered a thousand years ago."[128]

Even drawings of the helicopter, a farm reaping machine, and many other innovations of Leonardo da Vinci that we praise today were lost for 300 years following his death in 1519, until they were rediscovered and finally printed, but an estimated 80% of all his written work has never even been found.[129]

To some, the bad luck above was a sign that God disliked innovation, which led rulers to think they were right to suppress it. Strange as it may seem, the holy books of the major religions have moments of dislike for what entrepreneurs do. According to the Hadith of Islam, "Every innovation is a misguidance and every misguidance goes to Hell fire."[130] Sentences like this blocked many innovations in the Muslim lands for millennia.

This was seen in the Islamic Ottoman Empire (14th–20th century), where most decisions were influenced by religious books. Unsurprisingly a member of the elite once warned against the spread of the scientific method by saying, "It's rare that someone becomes involved in this foreign science without renouncing religion." Given that renouncing religion led to the death penalty you can see there was little reason for anyone to risk innovating. Instead of wasting time killing people, a law was passed in 1553 that lasted until the 18th century that smartly tried to stop people ever thinking of innovating in the first place. The law banned the printing of books and it did a good job at slowing down the spread of ideas. The excuse for this ban was that human writing was said to be holier than machinery – "The ink of a scholar is holier than a martyr's blood."

It wasn't until 1731 that the ruler Mohammed the 1st was given a printed book, ironically its topic was on why western nations were so far ahead of the Ottoman Empire. Islamic scholars pinpoint the dislike of innovation to differences in the two major groups in Islam. Unlike the Shia, it's said the Sunnis came to accept the Ulema (clerics), as the heirs of the prophet and sources of truth. The clerics mostly put a stop to reinterpretations of old religious laws to fit modern times. Instead as above, the sentence that each innovation goes to hell became the rule. Innovation stopped and this can be seen in the low standards of living of many Muslim nations to this day.[131]

Western nations at the time slowly allowed some innovations, but banned any which went directly against religious teachings or put government power at risk. While it's famously known that astronomist Galileo (1564–1642) survived execution for his view that the earth went around the sun, it's less known that over a thousand like-minded people were killed during this time. Domenico Scandella was killed for his belief that God was created from chaos, and Giordano Bruno was burned alive for logically pointing out, that our sun is one of many suns, and the earth one of many possibly inhabited planets.[132] Only by silencing those who speak out against it can a closed society survive, and we see this repeat throughout history. Eight hundred authors, printers, and booksellers were found locked up when the Bastille was stormed in 1789, during the French Revolution.[133] Millions of intellectuals were horribly sent to the gulags of the USSR and the concentration camps in Nazi-occupied Europe.[134]

The innovation of Johannes Gutenberg's printing press in 1452 caused an early problem for the Catholic Church. More Bibles could now be printed and spread, yet so could books criticizing the Bible. This led the church to start the "Index Librorum Prohibitorum," or the index of banned books which was updated right up until the 20th century. It included some of the most famous and productive innovations. Books from Victor Hugo, René Descartes, Immanuel Kant, Sir Francis Bacon, John Locke, and ironically Blaise Pascal, who in his work *Pensees* argued in favor of God[135]

In China, the Ming dynasty (1368–1644) was not far behind on its dislike of innovation. As one Christian missionary said at the time, "Any man of genius is paralyzed immediately by the thought that his efforts will bring him punishment rather than rewards."[136] In 1793, the Earl Macartney was sent to China as the first representative from Britain, to show some British innovations for trade, like the small handheld clocks which at the time amazed many and would one day slide around our wrists as a watch. He returned with a letter from Chinese Emperor Qianlong, saying, "We have never set much store on strange and ingenious objects."[137]

Yet turn the clock back to the 11th and 12th centuries, and we see China leading the world in the innovation of compasses, gunpowder, paper, and more. All thanks to the fairer laws under the Song Dynasty. Ironically, in this time an entrepreneur named Su Sung had made the world's then most complex clock. Housed in a 40-foot-high tower, powered by a water wheel, it even showed the location of the planets.[138] These good times continued until the end of the epic sea adventures of the famous Zheng He, after which the Ming dynasty in 1433 put out the Haijin edict which slowed exploration and innovation.[139] Some historians take that year to be the start of Chinese decline versus other parts of the world, as shown in the Chinese documentary "River Elegy."[140]

Besides the rulers trying to protect their power, there was also a strong disbelief within most people that they had control over their lives. As the entrepreneurial process was unknown to them, most innovations popping up were seen as God's work and that it was God who decided what happened. Thomas Bell, the president of the Linnean Society during Charles Darwin's time there, even repeated this thinking in saying that the careers of Sir Isaac Newton and Sir Francis Bacon, "seem to especially be appointed by providence."[141] If it was God who chose kings, the victors of battles, or who lived or died, then surely it was the same with innovations? This is why words like "divine inspiration," "God's grace," or "miracle" are used even by some people today when remembering the early days of an innovation.

In other countries, less of it was God and more the *social class of your ancestors* that affected whether you and your innovation would live. India, the world's 2nd most populous nation, to this day has a visible class system, called "caste", which for centuries, has stopped the social mobility of its people. By just being born into the wrong family, you may always have doors shut in your face because of your surname or the town you're from. The lowest caste is part of the "untouchables".[142] That's 160 million people who are mistreated like some colored and LGBT people are in xenophobic nations. Untouchable children must sit apart from their classmates in school, and even some healthcare workers refuse to care for them.[143]

Every country has had class systems in different shapes and forms. Long ago, France had the three estates, England had its feudal order. Today, it's less your ancestors, but more how much money you have which sets you apart. Though many nations seek more equality for their people, there is still a belief in many parts of the world that failing is horrible and that it harms the reputation of one's family. Such old mental chains first began to be unlocked in today's Britain, with the children of the nobility and the upper classes being given the chance to try their hands at innovation. In other countries at the time they would be kicked out by the royal court and disowned by their families.

The cloth merchant and politician Slingsby Bethel, wrote in 1680, "England has… the advantage of all other countries." It breeds "the younger sons of gentlemen, and sometimes of the nobility, to the ministry, law, trade and physic, without prejudice to their gentility." Remember how ancient Romans stopped senators from being merchants? This belief held strong for centuries as seen in France and Spain, where a nobleman, if found to have involved himself in innovating would be stripped of his rank. But not in England, and later Britain. We even see that the brother of the first Prime Minister Robert Walpole (1721-1742), worked in and ran a factory far away in Aleppo, Syria.[144] This gradual disrespect for the posh life pushed the nobility to invest and help make innovations. By joining their money and contacts with the *skills of the lower classes, social mobility could begin, and the lower could climb higher up the ladder.*

In a country like the United States, the process of trying, failing, then trying again is mostly accepted as the way things get done. Experience from trial and error is a quality most investors look for in the entrepreneurs they invest in. Failure is seen as a teacher, giving lessons that if used wisely can help anyone do better the next time they try.[145] As IBM co-founder Thomas J. Watson Sr. said, "The formula for success is quite simple—double your rate of failure."[146]

So which laws help us change the rules of the game for the better? Let's find out below.

Laws for Prosperity

"Remember that you are an Englishman, and have consequently won first prize in the lottery of life."[147]
Cecil Rhodes (Businessman and Prime Minister of Cape Colony)

1. Lending Laws

In 1049, Pope Leo IX banned loans with interest from any Christian to another, and this spread to most European nations under the Church's influence. Like we saw in the Ottoman Empire, this law was thanks to a few sentences from the Christian Bible. Leviticus 25:37 was the most direct of all, "You shall not lend him your money at interest, or your food at profit,"[148] while the Gospel of Matthew spread the fear of money-making: "It is easier for a camel to go through the eye of a needle than for a rich man to enter into the Kingdom of God."[149] The non-religious got the same advice from Aristotle, who wrote, "money was intended to be used in exchange, but not to increase at interest... That is why of all modes of getting wealth, this is the most unnatural."[150] Long before capitalist rent seeking arose Aristotle foresaw its lack of productivity, but as we know, if the *giver helps grow the innovation,* then rent seeking dies off. Value then comes first, profit after.

A while ago, the fear of roasting on pitchforks in hell led many to abandon their entrepreneurial dreams. Some were brave enough to try, but didn't have enough money. Jews filled the demand as lending was one of the few jobs Christians did not ban them from working in. Sadly, lending only grew the anti-Semitism and attacks that Jews faced. The character Shylock from Shakespeare's *Merchant of Venice* is a classic example. Epigenetic changes may help show how two millennia of hardships led Jews to adapt and thrive to the present day.[151]

With little money to be borrowed we see that most innovations came from those with wealthy backgrounds, like Lord Byron, Lord Rayleigh, or Charles Darwin. Entrepreneurs from lower classes leaned mostly on support of the wealthy and royal families which supported artists like Leonardo da Vinci, Michelangelo, and Donatello. Unable to find support, Thomas Newcomen had to collect funds from his Baptist church in the early 18th century to make one of the first steam engines. But it took more money, as given by Matthew Boulton, to let James Watt advance the steam engine and spark the industrial revolution. In time, as governments separated church and state, the curse of church rules wore off. Venture funds and wealthy angel investors emerged to fund the innovations no one before would touch.

2. Bankruptcy Laws

Would you even bother finding investment for your innovation knowing that, if it failed, you'd be jailed and your family forced into slavery to repay your debt? That is exactly what would happen if you lived in ancient Greece.

In Henry the Eighth's England, you'd be thrown into a prison and have a nail put through your ear to mark you as bankrupt. Genghis Khan's Mongol Empire used a 3 strikes policy—you could have 2 bankruptcies, but a 3rd would leave you dead.[152] Modern bankruptcy law sprung from British changes to the 1869 Debtors Act which was updated with the 1883

Bankruptcy Act. This put an end to the debtor's prison, letting entrepreneurs file for bankruptcy without fear of harm.[153]

A 2010 study found that more *entrepreneur-friendly bankruptcy laws led to more entrepreneurship* in a country. Sadly, debt penalties still exist in some developing nations but modern bankruptcy laws are now spreading to more countries every decade.[154]

3. Enterprise Laws

The year 1555 was the start of the first joint stock company, and its features were to become part of most enterprise structures to this day. Named the "Muscovy Company" it traded between London and Moscow, holding a monopoly on this trade route until 1698. The innovation of this company structure now let governments record the money given by investors to fund a ship's trip to sell innovations across the sea. With the government involved, investors were *more confident that their money would not be stolen by a lying captain.* With this near bulletproof protection, other trade and exploration companies were also born. The Virginia Company was set up for the settlement of what is now the United States. The East India Company was given a monopoly on trade with India and became so powerful it had an army of its own. Next came the Joint Stock Companies Act 1844, which set up steps for how anyone could open a company, and in 1855, the Limited Liability Act made sure that any member of a company could never lose more money than what they put into it. Investors now could breathe easier knowing they wouldn't be taken to court to pay for debts of another person in the company.[155] Everyday people could now start companies by filling out forms and paying the fees rather than needing to kneel and kiss a ruler's hand.

4. Intellectual Property Laws

Just as governments gave monopolies on trade between nations, they also chose who got monopoly to sell an innovation inside the country. Centuries back in England it was common for the king or queen to give their friends monopoly rights to sell an innovation while banning everyone else from doing so. Nearly all household items came from a handful of enterprises.

This all stopped when Edward Darcy, a buddy of the royal family and the only importer of playing cards was taken to court. And for the first time a court ruled against a monopoly, saying that a *monopoly cannot be given on an innovation which does not show some improvement* over competing innovations. No productivity, no monopoly.

Lawyer Edward Coke later built on this case when he wrote down the Statute of Monopolies Act 1623. This act let entrepreneurs apply for a patent in which they had to show that their innovation increased productivity, and if they did so, they'd be granted a 14-year monopoly. No competitors could copy their innovation. After 14 years, anyone could copy it again.[156]

This law, unlike any before it, removed the past threat of royal monopoly which had before banned competitors forever, sinking the productivity and living standards of the people. This new law importantly let entrepreneurs *lock in on public record that they innovated first*, to prevent competitors copying and claiming it was them instead.

Previously, entrepreneurs had feared to innovate, as a larger wealthier competitor would come in stealing away any new improvements they made. Abraham Lincoln, himself a lawyer and patent holder as profiled in D.K Goodwin's *Team of Rivals* would write, "In the days before Edward Coke's original statute of monopolies, any man could instantly use what another had invented, so that the inventor had no special advantage from his own invention… the patent system changed this, secured to the inventor, for a limited time, the exclusive use of his invention, and thereby, added the fuel of interest to the fire of genius, in the discovery of new and useful things."[157]

It took time for other nations to catch up to this innovative patent system, but the infant United States was fast to start, placing patents in the very first article of its constitution and even improving upon the British system. In Britain of 1772, it cost an entrepreneur £125 to file a patent, or the equivalent of US$17,750 today, while two decades or so later in the infant United States, a patent application cost just 50 cents or around US$12 today.[158,159]

Before the French Revolution, the monarchy of France had a patent system similar to the later USSR. All patents were owned by the monarchy, but the difference was that the entrepreneur could make the innovation themselves. If it sold well, the French king was given the right to the income made by the innovation, which is how we got the word royalties. In thanks, the entrepreneur was given a state pension, getting a lot less than the royalties going to the king.

Such unfair incentives in France led to fewer productive innovations. Which is why Britain, with less than half the population of France at the time, issued 743 patents from 1790 to 1800 versus France's 128. The start-up United States, with less than half the population of Britain, issued 309 patents in that same period,[160] and then quickly took the lead in the total number of patents issued.

5. Foreign Trade Laws

It also took time for many nations to see the reward of having open borders, which let innovations enter and spread. In the past, more nationalism meant fewer people bought foreign products, preferring to buy local ones. Today the internet has changed that letting us know instantly what's out there for what price. People don't need to make what others have already made, they simply need to find and order it. Lacking an internet to know what's been made worldwide led to the painfully slow spread of innovations in the past. Just look at the following which originated in Britain: the cotton mill (1771), the steam engine (1775), and steam railway (1825). It took Germany 13 years before the first recorded appearance of the mill, the steam engine took 8 and the railway 12. In Mexico, it took 64 years for the mill to show up, 43 for the steam engine, and 48 for the railway.[161] Distance matters, but also how open a society is matters more, as *otherwise we would have had the above innovations spread across the African continent and into Southeast Asia*, but that didn't happen, and in some parts of the world it still hasn't happened.

By improving the laws mentioned above, a nation can boost innovation. The most important indicator showing the result of innovation is a country's growth rate, which as the Kauffman foundation shows is linked to the number of new enterprises made in that country in a given year. The Foundation's own educational videos point out that "Entrepreneurs create all the new net wealth in the society, so if we didn't have new companies, the society would gradually grow poorer in relative terms. And we think of entrepreneurs many times becoming very rich, we have in mind Steve Jobs or Bill Gates or Sergey Brin. These guys get very, very wealthy. But in fact, the real wealth goes back into the society. It's estimated that the people that start these firms take a fraction, and in some cases less than a percent, of all the new net wealth that their companies are making for society."[162.163]

We can see now an answer to the question of what culture or nation is "on the right side of history?" boiling down to finding *which one lets the most people develop the most productive innovations* both at home and abroad. Like we said earlier, we can confirm or deny this by checking if there is growth in the life expectancy statistic of that nation.

Take the fact that overall, poor people, even in developed nations, are today in *many ways better off* than the richest people of centuries past due to the growth and spread of productive innovations.

We can see this in the shrinking gap in ownership of basic innovations between median families and poor families in the U.S. For example, estimates show 99.6% of poor households had a fridge vs. 99.9% of median households. About 27.9% of the poor had a computer/printer vs. 58.9% of the median. 54.5% of the poor had a mobile phone vs. 76.3% of the median.[164] There is always room for improvement, but what we see is that even many of those said to be poor have access to nearly the same innovations as average Americans. Unlike the past, the poor can now reduce bodily damage by doing more with less actions, leading to a growth in life expectancy. Competition is to thank for this as enterprises innovate to drive prices down while boosting quality. The mobile phone a poor person buys may be an old model, but it would still let that person do most of the same actions that the average person can with a new expensive model.

As we explored earlier, Kauffman estimated that if just 30 to 60 out of the millions of U.S. enterprises grew to become worth US$1 billion, then the United States could add 1 percentage point to its yearly economic growth and double its GDP 6 years earlier than current estimates. The same applies for every nation hoping to boost its growth. For the U.S such growth would help solve the current U.S. budget problem without the need for massive policy changes. Unfortunately, only a few enterprises end up growing to such a size, as most work on unproductive innovations. A study by NESTA found that over half of the nation's new employment from 2002 – 2008 came from firms which were innovators.[165] Later we'll explore how governments can and should assist enterprises take this innovative path.

We can now see that entrepreneurship is a mix of both yin and yang, left and right, black and white, market and state, egoism and altruism, where mostly individualistic effort fulfils collective needs. Combining both giving and taking is the key to progress, rather than focusing on one and shaming the other. Studies recently show that people *with the most meaningful lives were 'givers' and yet those with the happiest lives were 'takers'.*

In Appendix C we show a way to measure the importance of innovations, we've called it innovations per capita. It may help a nation finally measure itself with a simple number that reflects what's found in the real world, with no need for complicated charts, formulas or equations. Send a quick email to vitojgrigorov@gmail.com or go to www.prosperism.org to get Appendix C and all other bonus material.

Chapter Summary

\#   Entrepreneurs, by their actions, make and spread productive innovations to society.

\#   An entrepreneur is defined by their actions. Many job positions and titles can lead to entrepreneurial action. Most common are roles like founders, executives, board members, and other leadership positions. Yet employees can also be entrepreneurial if given the chance by the company they work for.

\#   Measuring consumer productivity shows for the first time the growth in value factors an innovation gives to people who use it.

\#   Entrepreneurs provide productivity through *innovation* and *creative destruction*, removing old innovations and replacing them with new ones.

\#   For entrepreneurs to do their best, the game must be fair, which means 1. Rule of law, 2. Fairness of law, 3. Enforcement of law.

\#   The more productivity growth the more growth in standards of living.

\#   Without an entrepreneurs innovations, an economy is unable to grow sustainably, leading to eventual collapse or revolution.

\#   Persecuted by religions, rulers, and society, productive innovations of entrepreneurs in ancient times were lost for thousands of years until rediscovery.

\#   An open society contains a mix of a free market economy and democratic politics. This appears to lead to more innovations than other systems in the long run.

\#   Certain laws protect entrepreneurs' innovations like lending rules, bankruptcy acts, legal rights, intellectual property and foreign trade. All these lead to more innovations in society.

CHAPTER SIX

History and the Struggle Among Innovations

"That the state of nature, at any time, is a temporary phase of a process of incessant change, which has been going on for innumerable ages, appears to me to be a proposition as well established as any in modern history."[1]
Thomas Henry Huxley

"Earning out innovations is the only function which is fundamental in history."[2]
Joseph Schumpeter

It is often said that history is written by the victors, but if they know it or not, *it's the productive innovations used by the victors that lead to success.* As Marcus Aurelius wrote more than 2000 years ago, "The secret of all victory lies in the organization of the non-obvious."[3] Others, like Karl Marx, wrote that history was about winners and losers, as seen through class struggle. For us, history is the struggle among innovations. As we've seen, it's innovations that have helped humanity survive and spread. Peter Drucker, author of *Managing Oneself,* saw this link between history and innovations, "We believe that the history of mankind cannot be properly understood without relating to it the history of man's work and man's tools."[4]

There are many ways of looking at history. You may have told the insurance company one story of how your car crash happened, but the other driver likely has a different one. Historiography is the name given to such differences in history, with books like Jared Diamonds' *Guns, Germs and Steel* trying to make sense of it all. As we can't repeat history in experiments to prove which story is correct, we are left to choose between many stories. Some think human history is a bunch of accidents. Many think the gods control it all. Others say it's driven by great people. No matter which one you choose what's always involved in each one is innovations. For any change to occur innovations need to mix.

Each change has a cause and effect. Hot coffee leaks from a cup, it has a hole at the bottom, swap the cup and no more leaking. Single black-and-white answers like this are rare though—mostly there are many answers to explain a "why" question. Like that the cup was bought for a few cents at a $1 shop where quality is low, or that before pouring in the coffee the cup was not checked for holes.

Some reasons have a larger effect than others on a result. *Root causes* is a common name for them. Say we replaced deadly bullets with rubber, then we could see if gun deaths will drop. If there's no difference, then removing guns may be the next experiment, as it was in the late 90's in Australia under Prime Minister John Howard, after which gun deaths dropped sharply.[5] Anyone against this is likely to say that a killer would use knives instead, but the path of least action shows that the more difficult you make an action, like killing a lot of people with a knife, the less it's likely to happen often. It's the innovations around us and the actions they give, which sway what we do. Change the innovations and you change history.

Q.   How did innovations combine to lead to memorable events in your life?

A.

Pt. 11 BUILDINGS OF LOST DREAMS

INNOVATION COMBINATION
Mixing innovations sparks new ones, creating the world around us

In a chat with Jen, Kate sees that without other innovations she'd not be able to program her software. Maybe her software can do the same and inspire other innovations into the future?

Historical Innovation Combination (x)

What evolution has done to unify the natural world, we will try to do to unify the social world. We see the engine that's driving history as innovation combination. The more innovations people can use, the more actions occur, and so the more likely it will be that innovations will continue combining.

Yet if there are no new combinations, society is forced to use the same old innovations and do the same actions as were done centuries ago. Little or no change in actions means little change in history, as we see from those rare Amazonian tribes which use the same tools their ancestors did. Being cut off from the world means fewer innovations mix with the ones they use. Also, it leads to less chance for life expectancy or living standards to grow. North Korea is a modern example of this. The more a nation isolates itself from the world's innovations, the worse off it becomes.

To understand this historical process, definitions spread throughout our book are now combined into one place.

1. Actions – Movement of the human body.

2. Innovation – That help us reach a result and so lead to action.

3. Entrepreneur – Maker of the innovations.

4. Value – How innovations are chosen, through the Time, Money, Health, Intelligence factors.

5. Productivity – Measure of the change in value factors as seen in our actions.

These words above hold together both their past definitions in the book and the new ones we list here. Below we filter their meaning as it applies to history.

1. Actions – Movement of the human body.

Without any actions, human history cannot happen, becoming motionless like a ghost town.

2. Innovation – That help us reach a result and so lead to action.

When a movie is set in 1612 England, the backdrop and props need to be from that time period to make it look realistic on screen. It's the amount of combination among innovations that shows us if a location has advanced or declined. Similar to natural selection in biology, in the manmade world it is unproductive and counterproductive innovations that mostly die, while the productive live.

3. Entrepreneur – Maker of the innovations.

When a person makes a productive innovation for others that lets them to do more with less action.

4. Value – How innovations are chosen, through the Time, Money, Health, Intelligence factors.

The actions an innovation gives others are filtered into society through the four value factors. Time, Money, Health, Intelligence.

5. *Productivity – Measure of the change in value factors as seen in our actions*

Productivity measures the value of actions of one innovation vs. the value of actions from the next best innovation.

It's rare for entrepreneurs to face no competition. It's likely other enterprises and their innovations already exist in the market and so will fight to protect their market share or new ones will pop up to soon challenge the entrepreneur.

A new cola drink will have a hard time taking market share away from Coca-Cola and Pepsi, unless it gives a productivity boost in the actions of consumers. A hard thing to do when people's tastes—literally on their tongue—become very difficult to change over time. If one was to give a similar taste, yet also make the drink nutritious with studies to prove it, maybe then it will start to win market share over time.

Below is a modern version of a list from philosopher Arthur Schopenhauer which shows the journey most innovations must go through to win people over to use them.

1. Arrogance: At the start most people laugh off the innovation as just another weird thing that comes out, but that is likely to soon disappear.

2. Mockery: Not dying off, the innovation spreads further and is used and talked about by friends. Those people who dislike it become louder in predicting that it will fail.

3. Sarcasm: As more people use it, mockery is replaced with pointing out the side effects of the innovation so as to not annoy friends and family who may now be using it themselves.

4. Acceptance: In time, most of society/market uses the innovation. Those against it, once in the majority, now become the minority. Those still ridiculing it now become ridiculed themselves for living in the past.

Q.	**Are you working on an innovation? Which stage is it sitting at right now?**
A.	

But we're missing something here – a way to show how an innovation lives or dies. If we don't know this, we can't fully understand history.

Pt. 12 BUILDINGS OF LOST DREAMS

HISTORICAL SELECTION
Society selects which innovations live or die.
Leading to 6 turning points in history.

The CEO of Kate's company will soon fire workers to cut costs and make a profit in the short run to please shareholders. It's meant to be a secret—but…

What is Historical Selection?

"This preservation of favorable individual differences and variations, and the destruction of those which are injurious, I have called Natural Selection, or the Survival of the Fittest."[6]
Charles Darwin

Innovation combination is how history develops, but historical selection affects which innovations live or die. Named in honor of Darwin's idea, it shows us why innovations are picked, why some actions spread and why others don't. Through it we can see why innovations like email and mobile phones are wanted more than mail and landlines, why people rise up against the government, or even why one sports team loses against another.

In *The Descent of Man,* Darwin himself writes that, "We can and do select innovations that are 'favorable' to us."[7] He didn't explain how this happens, making some think it's the same natural selection process that he found in nature.[8] As H.B. Skinner, author of *Science and Human Behavior* aimed to do, joining those before him like Thomas Huxley and Karl Popper, to squeeze a round peg into a square hole by trying to unify the biological evolution of nature with the cultural evolution of the man made.

However, there is *no rule that only* biological laws can explain human development. If this wasn't true, then humans should stop trying to improve the world as we've done since the eureka moment. As Bertrand Russell, author of *A History of Western Philosophy* writes, "We ought to be entirely indifferent as to what the course of evolution may be, since whatever it is, is thereby proved to be best."[9]

It's true, humans evolved, until the eureka moment, from the same biological laws as all other species, but we're the only ones to then take control of the process that created us. *No example of such control exists in any species in our world* which we can compare ourselves to. This is unique and is why cultural evolution doesn't fit inside of biological laws. Take mutations, which we explored earlier as the bedrock of biological evolution. Mutations are errors in DNA, that are passed down to the offspring. These errors happen in all species by random chance. We humans see it when babies are born with 7 fingers.

Innovations don't do this though. If humans were as blind and random as nature's mutations, then we might have seen General Motors release a 7-wheeled car when it competed with the Ford Motor Company in the 1920s. But no innovation is born randomly, it has to instead go through the reasoning of the human mind.

A discovery may seem to come by chance, but it takes an alert mind to see its importance and make it into physical form. Controlled mutation is what we see in the human world, rather than the random mutation of the biological. The entrepreneur is the mutation maker, giving birth to innovations into that ever-expanding organism we call society.

James Watt didn't randomly make the steam engine in the 18th century. He was improving the engines of Thomas Newcomen, Thomas Savery and even improving on the writings, formulas, and experiments going centuries back to Heron of Alexandria. Thomas Edison never "invented" the light bulb, but what he did was find the materials, bamboo being one of them, which let the light burn the longest. The design of the bulb itself was licensed from a British entrepreneur, Joseph Swan, who made it before Edison. As we'll see below, this process repeats itself over time. Every century more productivity is sucked out from the same or fewer actions than were needed in the past, boosting living standards. Less fuel or even no fuel is needed today by the hybrid and electrical engine cars which give humans the same actions that a full fuel tank in a standard combustible engine car used to.

In the examples just above, we aren't changing what we said earlier, that innovations give side effects that entrepreneurs may not predict. Thousands of years ago, a type of coal was worn in necklaces, but if you told those people that one day we'd use that coal to power ships carrying weight as heavy as the pyramids of Giza, you'd have been locked up as a nutcase. Over time coal has indeed become the most used energy source, mostly due to its low cost. Side effects have come up though, the most direct is the stress on human health due to pollution in the atmosphere.

Many protestors shout for a total ban on using coal and fossil fuels, they're shouting for a black-or-white solution, forgetting that historically the best answer is gray in innovation. A black or white answer would affect nearly all industries worldwide that provide for the daily survival of the world. Some would also like to see humans drop their control of the environment and go live with nature in the woods. A hard task unless you want to be counted as missing by the police. But let's say huge populations could pull it off – the resulting lack of innovation in the long run would leave us unable to deflect an oncoming asteroid, making us extinct like the dinosaurs before us.

It's the more challenging answer of *continuous innovation that patches up such bad side effects.* Electric cars, solar panels, and automated software are just some of the innovations leading to this patchwork. Companies like Tesla, SpaceX and Solarcity are pushing these innovations forward, as seen in the book *Elon Musk* by Ashlee Vance. Where the innovation has many uses, the side effects are patched up by future productive innovations, not by us stopping to use them. The rising number of people using sites like kaggle.com, challenge.org and others can help problem solve us towards that patchwork. NASA and companies like Netflix have used such sites, bringing tens of thousands of people from around the world together to find solutions that only one to a dozen people in the past were tasked to solve, but couldn't. To the shock of many today, the creative solution in one area is a lot of times by an amateur from a completely different field of research.

It's now time we break down this silent unseen process that's purring along everywhere in every corner of the world as we read. A bakery franchise in Copenhagen is now deciding what baking ovens to buy. Someone you know is choosing the best toys for their baby. Government ministers are awaiting budget numbers to see which policies to change. What innovations will be chosen in each of these examples and the billions of others? Why do some innovations survive this trial by fire while others die? The historical selection steps below show how. Though for simplicity we focus here on innovations sold for money, remember, all other innovations fall under a similar process, like government policies, laws, and words of a language. So, when we use words like "market" it can be replaced with "enterprise," "environment," "society," "culture," "government," and more. In 200 years some of these words may not even be used at all.

1. Many innovations exist within a market.

An innovation is released into a market of adopters. Similar competing innovations and their enterprises already exist. Mostly, the goal of all innovations is to be used by as many adopters so to *boost its market share*, as seen in the value meter and the second half of the meaning of life statement "the greatest number".

2. Competition for survival among enterprises grows, all seeking more market share.

As time passes, the innovation giving the most value-creative actions, as seen through the four value factors, becomes most used. The more it's used the more it's likely to survive to be added to the innovation combination of society. It's then likely to become a market leader in its category. This then gets the attention of other entrepreneurs who start seeking to improve it, by combining it with other innovations to release their own competing innovation.

3. The innovation seen as most productive by adopters is selected over others.

Competing innovations die off, becoming historical artifacts, with their enterprises closing or going bankrupt. The surviving enterprises *mostly copy* the market leader and new enterprises come in with new features and benefits. Sometimes these give new actions that the market leading innovation does not provide. Market share percentages may then change monthly as adopters test all innovations on offer. One or two innovations may break out as most popular and grab large slices of market share. If the market-leading innovation doesn't boost its own productivity in line with these new innovations, it will be replaced, just as it had once replaced the market leader before it.

These steps repeat endlessly. Take any innovation you've come across and it will be sitting or moving within one of the above steps.

Back in chapter two, we saw similar steps in the natural selection process showing the survival of the long-beaked birds. For us humans, it's productive innovations which help increase our survival, boosting our standards of living and life expectancy. Charles Darwin was to summarize natural selection by writing, "Let the strongest live and weakest die."[10] Likewise, our own summary referring to innovations can be, "Let the productive live and the counter-productive die."

Let's now put a real-life innovation, the Apple iPhone, through the historical selection process:

1. Many innovations exist within a market.

When the iPhone entered the mobile phone market in 2007, it faced existing competing enterprises like Nokia, Motorola, and Blackberry. To grow its market share and sell more, the iPhone included unseen sub-innovations. The touch screen was *unique at the time*, as keypads were the standard. This led to more space for a larger screen, allowing websites to be more easily browsed and used. Better graphics gave a viewing experience similar to that seen on laptop computers. All this boosted productivity and increased the number of actions to mobile users as internet browsing could now happen on the go.

2. Competition for survival between enterprises grows, all seeking more market share.

People start comparing innovations to see which is most productive for them. Some test new phones inside shops or play with their friend's new phone, while others research the features online. As there is a delay for new features to be copied by other phone makers, in this time the iPhone becomes selected as the market leader. Increased publicity from the media leads to even more sales, but also to more *competitors starting to copy* and better its productive touch screen and internet features.

3. The innovation seen as most productive is selected over others.

Former market leaders like Blackberry and Nokia now have dropping mobile sales, leading to dips in their share price and workers being fired. Nokia tries to win back adopters with new phones, which copy many sub-innovations of the iPhone, but Nokia isn't able to boost productivity any more than the iPhone has already been able to. *It's just a copy, not an improvement.* This is why existing iPhone users see it as a waste of money to buy a new Nokia and a waste of time in having to move all their data to it. At this point in the market, touch screens replace keypads as the standard on all mobile phones. A new competitor, the Samsung Galaxy Note series comes out, with a larger tablet sized screen. This is seen as a productive innovation, as mobile users can now save money by not needing to buy a tablet. Now Samsung starts to take market share from Apple. Like a tennis match, the ball goes back and forth. Patent filings at time of publishing show the next productive innovation likely to be a foldable tablet sized phone, able to close and fit into your pocket.

From above, we see that knowing your competition is crucial. Yet many make the mistake of thinking their innovation has none. "Zoom out until you can define some."[11] says investor and author of *The Art of The Start 2.0*, Guy Kawasaki. Knowing the playing field you're on lets you see which productivity gap is yet to be fulfilled.

The Innovations We Select

We know innovations allow certain actions to come into existence. Change the innovations, and you change the actions. *Actions are history in the making*, but it's innovations that let those actions come about. It's said that those who don't know history are doomed to repeat it. Not true, as those who will repeat it are simply those who don't know which innovations combined to lead us there before.

Previously, "traits," "habits," or "routines" have been suggested as the unit of history or cultural evolution as some call it. But all these concepts refer to bodily movements, which for us, are actions. "Memes" are also brought up, and depending on who's asked they seem to be about "ideas" jumping from one brain to the next. Same is the case for Historian Yuval Noah Harir's concept of stories as explored in *Sapiens* and *Homo Deus: a Brief History of Tomorrow*. Yet how can we confirm this jumping or even count these stories? We can't. Just like courts around the world *can't take evidence which is not in some physical form*.

In biology, the gene is seen as the unit of change. In history, innovation becomes that unit. Below we can even see similarities between them both.

1. Innovations are able to be copied.

In biological evolution, there is mostly one replicator—the gene. For history, the innovation is like the gene, because like genes almost *all innovations are able to be copied and mass-produced*. Anything you find on the shop shelf may have been made millions of times and put in stores the world over. A lid, bottle, chocolate wrapper, or even a rare Italian painting can be mass-produced, as millions of posters of the Mona Lisa show. Even the rare handwritten family cookbook can be scanned and uploaded online for anyone to download unlimited copies. Companies, like Coke, make sure the taste of their drinks is the same worldwide, and websites, like Facebook or Google, seek to give the same experience to billions of people. With 3D-printing, nearly anything in our home or in our mind can be copied or made with the right materials. Factories the world over can be reorganized to make copies of almost any innovation.

2. Innovations grow branches like a family tree.

With historical writings and with patent, copyright, and trademark records, we can see into the history of each innovation around us today, like a story from birth until death. We can explore how one innovation impacts another or how a patent helped an innovation beat off its competitors. Below, we see how early human innovations, like fighting and hunting tools, grow roots over time, changing shape and style to become ever sharper, tougher, and more useful.

BOOMERANG   SHIELD   MUSHROOM   CLUB

 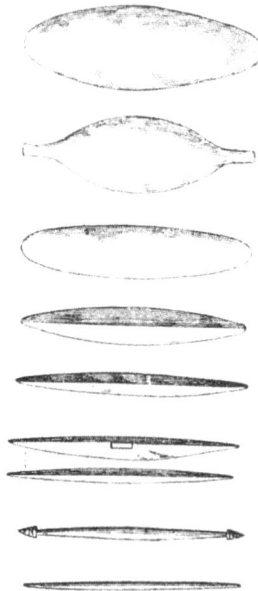 

Source: Pitt-Rivers et al., The Evolution of Culture and Other Essays, Oxford, 1906

Just look at the humble vending machine. When do you think its history began? A hundred years ago at most? Well think again, its family tree roots go back a long way.

1076
Coin-operated pencil boxes are made in China.

1700s
Coin-operated tobacco boxes show up in English pubs.

1888
Thomas Adam's company puts "Tutti Frutti" gum machines on train platforms in New York.

1902
Horn & Hardart opens the first automated restaurant in Philadelphia.

1905
The U.S. Post Office puts in stamp machines.

1926
Cigarette vending machines are launched.

1930s
Bottled soft drinks are sold from machines cooled with ice.

1957
Machines start dispensing soft drink liquid into cups with ice.

1961
Credit/debit card readers and ATMs are launched.

2008
DVD movies, clothing, condoms, and other items are sold from vending machines. SMS texting and chip card payments are accepted as payment.[12]

All these roots are like biological evolution trees, as seen below on the left. On the right, we have made a basic one for innovations showing cultural evolution and the unfolding of human history. Just like we have a common ancestor for all species, we also have a common ancestor for all innovations—likely to be the bony weapon, as seen in *2001: A Space Odyssey*. A complete innovation tree would be unthinkably large and would show millions of more detailed linkages than we can below. Maybe someone can take the challenge of mapping it out someday with help from the patent office. At least for now we can see how all of today's innovations have roots going further back than we might have thought.

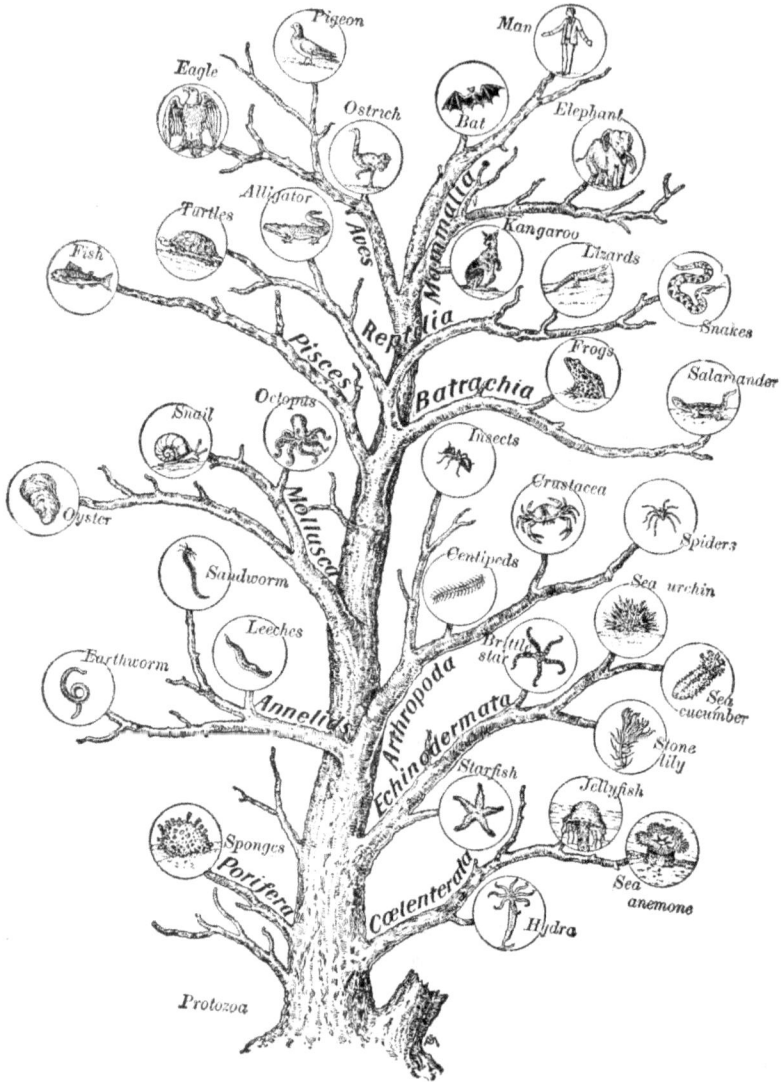

Biological (nature) evolution tree

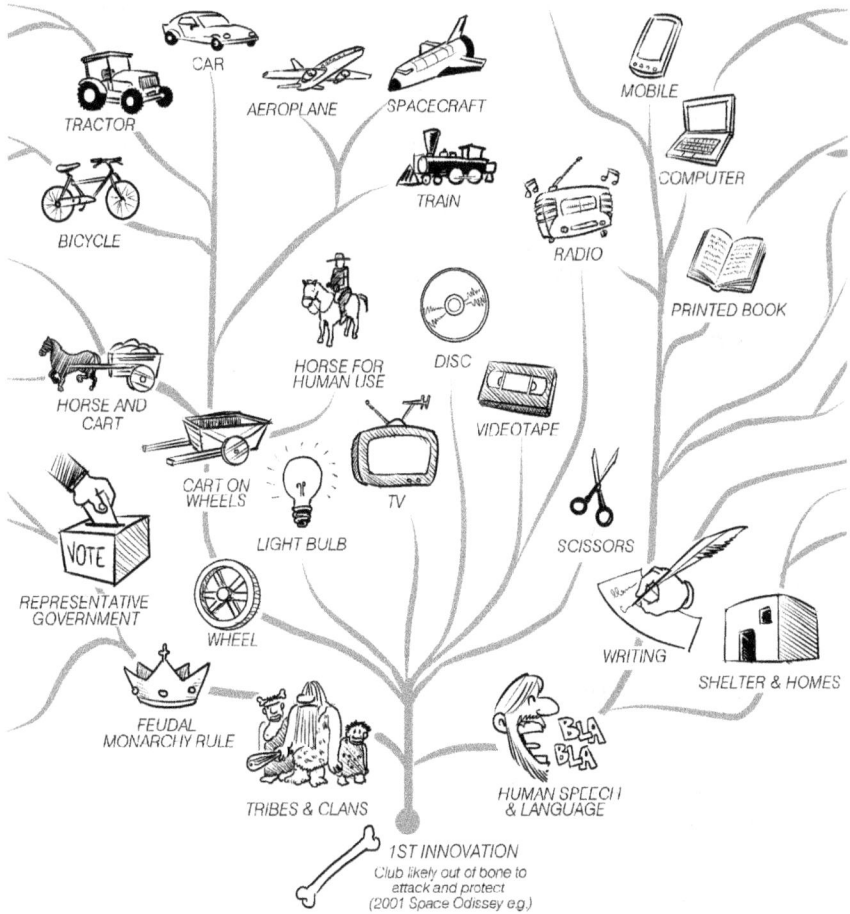

Cultural (human) evolution tree

Sources: Gruenberg, The Story of Evolution: Facts and Theories on the Development of Life, Garden City, 1929.

Lineages are found in every innovation. Take weaponry. Spears gave humans safety and distance compared to hand-to-hand fighting. Combine spears with horses, and you gain speed and surprise on an enemy. Fix a stirrup seat to a horse and you stop riders falling down, allowing horses to start being used in battles. Genghis Khan used a horse-and-weapon combination to create one of the largest empires in the world, an empire Jack Weatherford explores in *Genghis Khan and the Making of the Modern World*. After battles have been fought, *innovations are taken away from the losing side*. The Chinese army lost battles which led to its gunpowder innovation spreading to the Middle East and then on to Europe. Gunpowder led to canon ball artillery, which destroyed previously untouchable castles. Artillery was then made smaller and so we got rifles and guns, which when made automatic can kill thousands of people in minutes. Bomb explosions became ever larger, leading in time to nuclear and hydrogen bombs, which if used destroy all other weapons combined.

Humans gravitate towards simple black and white explanations. However, innovation combination contains many innovations, so it's not completely accurate to say that Facebook simply became the most used social network website. Yes, it has, but more so, it's also replaced physical photo albums for many and even the use of text messaging for others. Productive innovations do often spread their tentacles to compete with other innovations, some of which they may not have competed to begin with.

3. Innovations are both part of larger innovations and can be broken down into smaller innovations.

This point was explored in our definition of innovation earlier. The car, airplane, or scooter contain many innovations, while others like scissors, sticky tape, or pens have very few. Each "part" within is a sub-innovation with its own roots and history. A bicycle has many parts like the wheel, rubber tire, gears, chains, etc. Governments have many parts with laws, political offices, parties, and numerous departments of the civil service.

This complexity is easily seen when we break an innovation down, like a disassembled car.

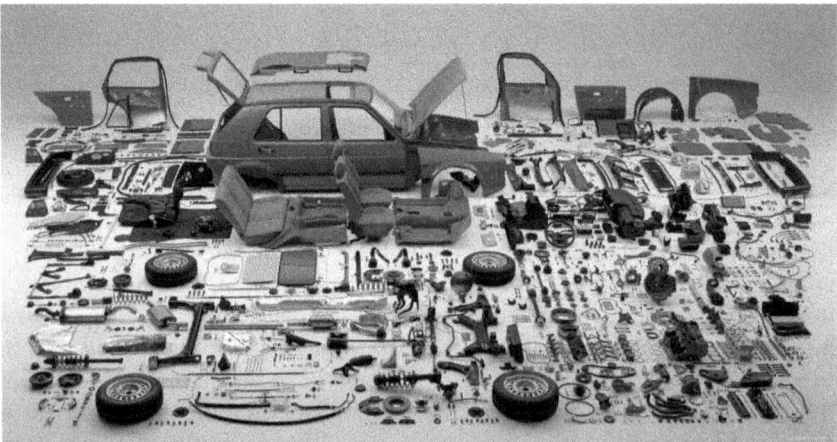

Source: Volkswagen (Public domain)

The Tapestry of Turning Points

"There is nothing more difficult to take in hand, more perilous to conduct or more uncertain in its success than to take the lead in the introduction of a new order of things."[13]
Niccolò Machiavelli

"This process must continue and we trust at an increasing rate. If we are to bring the broad masses of people in every land to the table of abundance, it can only be by the tireless improvement of all our means of technical production."[14]
Winston Churchill

Geneticist Theo Dobzhansky once said, "Nothing in biology makes sense except in light of evolution."[15] For us, nothing in human history makes sense except in light of innovation. Before we explore history, we need to lay the rules down for our view of history, which in academic jargon we'll call *innovational historiography*.

TIME PERIODS

History shows us the continuing march of innovations breaking through old limits. We call these the "Turning Points" in thanks to Malcolm Gladwell's book of a similar name *The Tipping Point*. As Tom Stoppard mentions in *Arcadia*, "A door like this has cracked open five or six times since we got up on our hind legs."[16] Nobel Laureate in economic sciences, Simon Kuznets said, "The major breakthroughs in the advance of human knowledge, those that constituted dominant sources of sustained growth over long periods and spread to a substantial part of the world, may be termed epochal innovations. And the changing course of economic history can perhaps be subdivided into economic epochs, each identified by the epochal innovation."[17] This is the most productive innovation of a time period, which gives the most actions and combines to make the most innovations. We will make our time periods most relevant by basing them on such innovations. This is not new. Materials have been used, as they were what innovations were built from. It's why past time periods are named Bronze Age, Iron Age, etc. Archaeologists have long agreed that human history begins with the first tools, so we will continue this by dividing history by the most important innovations that have served humanity best and likely most improved our life expectancy in the process.

CONTEXT

It would be great if history was based on immoveable facts, but as it's written by humans, opinions pop in. The gloom of the Dark Ages may be seen in Europe after the fall of Rome, but at the same time over in Asia the same gloom is not found. Some events of the 1960s are called by many in western nations a "cultural revolution", but no such revolution happened in the USSR, India or other non-western nations. We also see that each nation has different definitions for what it considers to be ancient, medieval, or modern. As we're aiming for as close to a standard view of history as we can, we need to look at longer time periods and focus on facts that are as clear as possible. The best facts are innovations themselves, and it's through their making, spread, and decline that we can define our time periods. When an innovation spreads, it becomes the start of a time period for us, even though that innovation may not have reached most countries of the earth until decades or even centuries later. Time periods end, not when all nations adopt that innovation, but when another more productive innovation starts to spread again in some part of the world. What do we mean by "spread?"

Take the printing press. The Chinese and Koreans made the innovation of moveable type printing centuries before it appeared in Germany. These Asian innovations did not spread worldwide, however, and they were likely banned by the rulers. After moveable printing came in Germany, there is clear evidence showing its spread worldwide, into Asia as well. So, the time period begins with moveable press printing. Einstein's famous theory began 15 years before it was proven true with a solar eclipse showing us that light bends. Darwin's theory was thought to be flawed for 45 years after its release until it was shown in 1904 that the earth was billions of years old, giving enough time for evolution to have taken place. The Japanese rejected guns for centuries, banning them and using ancient Samurai swords. Why do that if guns were more productive? To understand any such historical event, we need to go into the thinking of the time, and not the way we think today with the benefit of hindsight. Like the Chinese Haijin Edict before it, the Sakoku Edict of 1635 banned foreign trade and rejected anything European, which included guns. With public torture and death being the penalty, not having a gun was a lot better than being caught with one. This did not stop the spread of guns through the nations of the world, with Japan itself eventually accepting guns. Indeed, it was this rejection of European innovations that forced Japan to open trade in 1858, when it saw it could not respond to the deadly destruction from the firing battle guns of ships led by U.S. Commodore Perry.[18]

Today, millions in India don't have electricity, yet those same people have a mobile phone in their pockets. Indians *have skipped the innovation of electricity* and instead got a mobile, but they still reap the benefits of electricity, as without it the mobile phone they use would not have been made. All the above makes the environmental/geographical theories of historical determinism as explored by Jared Diamond and others, unusable today. They are useful in explaining the distant past but as the skipping of the mobile shows, unable to explain the future, which is to be determined by innovations. Likewise Yuval Harari's argument that stories shape history has little use because stories sit in peoples minds unable as of yet to be confirmed by others unlike physical innovations.

Just because Amazonian tribes don't know what a computer is or that North Koreans are prevented from using the internet, *does not mean the computer or internet do not exist.* The recording of history, as we see it, takes a linear path with one innovation following another.

REPEATABLE USE

For an innovation to mark a time period it must spread, and mostly there is a sub-innovation which helps it do so. Books are what people repeatedly used, but it was the printing press that made the books. The most productive innovations make or influence innovations that people then use repeatedly in each turning point, and which much like a gene spreads and replicates in order to survive.

Before we explore further, we have limited space, so we bend to European and American examples where needed as many innovations first spread from these places to the rest of the world. For simplicity dates of the Common Era or AD are not marked, unlike dates before this time which we do mark as "BC". Also the symbol "c" is used to indicate dates which are estimates. We hope our attempt below reveals history in a new light and shows how it's our innovations which best explain our past and future.

Turning Point 1
Innovation of Language

Unleashing Thoughts into the World by the Spoken Word: 70,000 BC[19]

Life Expectancy: 15–30 Years[20]

Repeatable use = Spoken words

Effect on Free Time = Language cut the time wasted figuring out what past generations had meant in the rock paintings they left behind. Like explaining what deadly berry to avoid eating, how to catch fish, or how to cook meat so you don't get sick. All this could be said in seconds though it took thousands of years of trial by death and error to learn.

We can only guess that the repeated sound from grunts linked to an action or innovation came to be grunted the same way over time. This let thoughts become innovations in the form of sounds others could understand and copy. Sound is physical, it can be remembered in another's mind and today we can easily record it.

Language is one of the first innovations needed for the combination of all future innovations. We don't know exactly when people started speaking, but estimates settle around 70,000 BC. Evidence also points to the growth of the human brain around this time, likely leading to a boost in creativity and visualization. There is little doubt that if we remove the development of language, we will remove human history altogether.

As author of *Intuition Pumps*, Daniel Dennett writes, "There is no step more uplifting, more explosive, more momentous in the history of mind design, than the invention of language. When Homo sapiens became the beneficiary of this invention, the species stepped into a slingshot that has launched it far beyond all other earthly species."[21] Those *puzzling apish swings of our hands started to be replaced with the certainty of words*. We could now group what was found in the world with a near limitless number of sounds. Trade, teaching, and learning could now speed up. Others could now understand us quicker and innovations could skip faster among people. For the first time, we could explain how to make innovations, like our early stone tools, to someone *without them needing* to see it demonstrated in front of their eyes. Though showing people was more accurate, speaking did help us *develop the skill of imagination*, with us picturing what the words meant and acting on it in real time.

Picture two tribes fighting each other, one with spoken language, the other uses hand signals. The tribe able to speak *saves its members needing to glance away from the battle* to read hand signals, a glance which may mean a spear through the heart.

Language also made us become closer to others in our group, leading us to shift from thinking how can "I" or "my family" survive, to how can "my tribe" survive. Teamwork became key to survival as more could be done when we worked together. Around this time any early human rules were made clearer than ever before, such as explanations for why free riding (not sharing food with others) was to be punished.

With harsh weather and competition from other tribes also seeking food, the need to move restlessly to safer places was common. Eventually this would lead to human migration out of Africa.[22] But why then, after roaming earth for hundreds of thousands of years did our ancestors suddenly want to drop it all and settle in one spot?

Turning Point 2
Innovation of Agriculture

Start of Farming and Specialization with Seeds and Animals: 10,000> BC[23.24]

Life Expectancy: 15–30 Years[25]

Repeatable use = Seeds and animals

Effect on Free Time = By settling down and moving less, more free time was unlocked. More lessons could be learned from past generations as more people could mix and talk in one place, allowing innovations to combine faster. As the population grew, combination increased.

Our ancestors liked to live near a water source, as we see in settlements found in Mesopotamia in 3500 BC, Egypt in 3400 BC, the Indus River Valley in 2500 BC, and China in 1800 BC.[26] No more fear of thirst or the need to lift pots of water for hours. Long before, in 7500 BC, we had already started innovating by digging water wells, which thousands of years later would combine into the making of aqueducts made famous by the Romans, who improved the old Greek and Etruscan versions.[27]

With water now nearby, we could plant seeds, water them and grow food. Some of that food was for our animals, which we started to breed to later eat, *freeing us for the first time from the danger of chasing and hunting them*. In time, we learned to cook our food over a campfire, and heating it made it easier to chew and digest the nutrients in under an hour. Our closest relatives, the chimpanzees, chew their uncooked foods for around 5 hours per day. Cooking added a layer of fat on our bodies, protecting us when little food was around.[28] Similarly, tougher shelters and huts protected our bodies from the weather extremes of cold and heat and from random animal attacks at night.

Around this time, we took animals into our care, like dogs, who at last count, have been man's best friend for 33,000 years.[29] Other animals like horses and oxen were used to pull our heavy carts, rolling on wheels which first appeared around 4000 BC in Mesopotamia.[30] Without the wheel, so many later innovations would melt into the air.

By settling in an area, time opened up for unimagined actions like making necklaces, tools, and new weapons. In times of need these innovations could be swapped for food to survive.

Living together meant people bumping into one another, talking and eating round a campfire. More people led to more potential innovations, as now with speech, innovations could be passed to others quickly and problems could be solved faster as we could tell others *instantly* the solutions coming to our mind. The earliest form of foreign relations began as tribe leaders made deals to prevent fighting and bloodshed. Marriage was made up to help keep the peace, joining the son of one tribe's leader to the daughter of another. Trade within and among tribes also grew as more innovations were combined. *Trade pushed humans to focus on becoming experts in certain innovations*. Some were best at hunting, others at cooking, and some at making weapons.

These early entrepreneurs looked for even more tribes to trade with, by building canoes and rafts to sail across rivers. Slowly they gained importance, as they did peacefully what war did violently. Take the earliest scissors. They may have been first made by one tribe, but lacking food, that tribe traded them to another which had never seen them before. As each tribe discovered the productivity boost in cutting faster and accurately, more scissors were made and were traded again, spreading them further across the continent.

Indeed, the early Romans themselves *survived destruction by copying the* ship design of the Carthaginians, who they battled in the Punic Wars (264–146 BC).[31] The Carthaginian ships, by design, were more productive than the Roman ships, and once a Carthaginian ship was captured undamaged, the Romans copied its features into their own ships and started winning. There was a problem, though, most innovations were not copied long before the Romans and so they did not live on. Back then to copy anything you needed to be in the right place at the right time to physically see an innovation and the actions it involved. Few people got so lucky. But this would change with the next turning point, as all innovations soon would have a chance to be *recorded*, to spread and combine more than ever before.

Turning Point 3
Innovation of Writing

Saving Spoken Words: 3000 BC[32]

Life Expectancy: 20–35 Years[33]

Repeatable use = Written Symbols

Effect on Free Time = The risk of incorrectly copying an innovation after seeing it in the distance was finally replaced with the written word which in detail could describe how to copy it correctly. The lessons of past generations could now be saved from the brain to paper-like material, which then could survive for thousands of years and more, stopping future generations wasting time relearning what our ancestors had already learned.

Spoken words are only as useful as people's memories of what was said, leading to the original message being changed over time or maybe worse, if not shared, vanishing with the persons death. Recording anything requires symbols, and the first ones appeared as rock art in ancient caves and later in pictorial letters found in Egyptian hieroglyphs. As Julian Huxley, a close friend of Charles Darwin's wrote: "By speech first, but far more by writing, man has been able to put something of himself beyond death. In tradition and in books an integral part of the individual persists, for it can influence the minds and actions of other people in different places and at different times: a row of black marks on a page can move a man to tears, though the bones of him that wrote it are long ago crumbled to dust."[34]

Written words are a time capsule of the past, where we re-learn the hard lessons of those before us so to let us not repeat them. Writing was a turning point in history for now everything could be explored in more detail than the spoken word allowed. Humans could explain what the innovations left behind did and were used for, *allowing others to more accurately make a copy* and later combine it to make newer innovations. This all began what's called *recorded history*. Anything before this is pre-history, as only artifacts survive, but without anything written to explain them, we can only *guess* what they were used for.

The first recorded writings come from ancient Mesopotamia (Iraq, Syria, Iran) as seen in the earliest clay tablets, which hold instructions showing market traders how to count. Today we have 6500 languages, many with their own alphabets. In contrast, mostly all countries have approved the same Hindu-Arabic numbers as their official numbering system, a story touched upon in the book *Code* by Charles Petzold.[35] Numbers are the closest humans have yet come to a universal language. We see that numerals cut the number of symbols needed to write long numbers, boosting productivity. The year "1999" has 4 symbols. Imagine how much time you'd spend writing it out if we used Roman numerals? It would take you 16 symbols MDCCCCLXXXXVIIII. We may in part thank the Roman Pope Sylvester II for this, who had an interest in mathematics, and promoted Hindu-Arabic numerals to many countries.[36]

Written laws had long let leaders run a very profitable protection racket, with grain and other foods taxed early on as money was yet to take the importance it has today. Those who gave their crops were told by the rulers that they'd be protected in times of war. So began the early steps of the modern state which, with writing, could now make clear rules that all had to obey. Ancient Egypt made one of the first surviving civil codes, 12 writings dating back to 3000 BC, which helped the elite rule and control society to build the Pyramids of Giza, the Sphinx, and more. Later, the city-state of Babylon under King Hammurabi in 1772 BC[37] made what's today called the Code of Hammurabi, which set up one of the first innovations of contract law. Back then it even went into detail to explain how workers should be paid and was wise enough to make clear that anyone accused of a crime should have a right to innocence until proven guilty.[38]

As we know, laws can stop some actions and promote others, and most leaders of the time were happy to play unfair so that no one could be as powerful as them. To do this they hired those who could write, called scribes who due to this became important for most rulers through history. Historical selection meant that altered papyrus, palm leads, and wood bark, all materials which survive the longest, would have laws written on them along with the stories of the holy books of world religions, which would give people answers to what happens when we die and so show how best to live to get into heaven and avoid hell. *This monopoly over death* and the fear it inspired in people led many leaders to combine the rules of the holy books with their own.

We later see truth seeking writings pop up for the first time with little reference to religion. Thales of Miletus (624 – 546 BC) was said by Aristotle to be the first philosopher, as *he didn't include gods in his explanations.*[39] Over in the east near this time other teachings lacking godly origins started spreading in India with Buddha and in China with Confucius. Like the innovations of the Egyptians, Mesopotamians and Babylonians before them, the Greeks inched closer to getting to facts through observation and experimentation. A student of Thales, named Anaximander (610 – 546 BC), is said to have done the first recorded experiment, making him the first recorded scientist.[40] By writing what they did and it luckily surviving to this day, these people became the earliest known entrepreneurs in their fields. Mathematician Pythagoras (570–495 BC) is best known for calculating the area of a triangle,[41] the statesman Pericles (495–429 BC)[42] talked about running a democracy, as found in *The History of the Peloponnesian War.* While the all-rounder Xenophon (430–354 BC), best known for writing the *Persian Expedition,* also wrote *Oeconomicus,* one of the first writings of economics whose title gives us the word we use today.[43]

Philosopher Plato (427–347 BC), teacher of Aristotle, wrote in *The Republic* about the conversations of his own teacher, Socrates, (469–399 BC).[44] One such story had a worried Socrates predicting that the popularity of writing would weaken our ability to talk and think about complex things.[45] Such predictions of doom repeat with every new innovation that comes up.

The Romans had long known and read of all these productive innovations flowing out of the Greek city-states as explored in *SPQR: A History of Ancient Rome* by Mary Beard. It's why Roman General Marcellus, who won the siege of Syracuse, even ordered that Archimedes, the inventor and mathematician, not be harmed by soldiers entering the city. Greek influence was such that even 137 years after Archimedes' death, Roman statesman Cicero went in search of his tomb, which he found and like a devoted fan, cleaned it up to make it a shrine for others to visit in the future.[46]

Greek innovations were at the heart of the very story of the founding of Rome itself, with Virgil's *Aeneid* being a near Roman copy of the famous

Greek stories of the *Iliad* and the *Odyssey*. Other Greek innovations later spread even to the Roman emperors, with Marcus Aurelius (121–180) taking up Stoicism, a way of thinking and living which went back to the writings of Greek philosopher, Zeno of Citrium (334–262 BC) and Seneca (4 BC–65) who wrote *On the Shortness of Life*. Aurelius himself wrote a personal journal of thoughts, later to be called *The Meditations,* based mostly on his stoic way of life.[47] Today stoic thought has been modernized with works like *A Guide to the Good Life* and *The Obstacle is the Way.*

Yet it was the collected writings of Aristotle, known today as the *Organon,* which had one of the largest effects on the world, in close race with the religious books. By all odds Aristotle's writings should not have survived at all. Written in the 4th century BC, they vanished for 300 years until rediscovery and translation by one Andronicus of Rhodes.[48] Becoming for many the closest thing to an encyclopedia that humans had seen up till then by giving an explanation for mostly every area of life. The writings were historically selected and spread so widely by the 12th century that though the Catholic Church tried to ban it in 1277, it had to give up shortly after,[49] mostly thanks to theologian St. Thomas Aquinas who wrote *Summa Theologica*, which showed that the Christianity of the Holy Bible was in harmony with Aristotle's writings. Slowly from then on universities across Europe, most under the Church's influence, promoted Aristotle's *Organon* as the most important book after the Bible.[50] This was still the case nearly 2,000 years after it was written, as Sir Isaac Newton found out when he enrolled at Cambridge University in 1661. The bulk of his textbooks were Aristotle's or relied heavily on his writings. This seems insane today as an untold number of innovations over two millennia showed Aristotle wrong by Newton's time. But the Church's attempt to protect its teachings meant keeping Aristotle well past his due date.

It was in the 17th century that the church faced a wave of what we now call "scientists", showing experiments that proved Aristotle's writings and Church doctrine were wrong. Earlier scientists in centuries past had tried this, but they'd often be arrested and killed, echoing what Bertrand Russell, author of *Why I Am Not a Christian* wrote later in the 20th century, "Almost every serious intellectual advance has had to begin with an attack on some Aristotelian doctrine."[51]

History repeats itself goes the saying and before the Bible became so powerful, its followers suffered death and were thrown to the lions in the Roman Colosseum. It took centuries for the Bible to finally be historically selected in 4th century Rome, mainly thanks to the spreading belief in it trickling up till it reached a person close to the emperor, in this case the mother of Emperor Constantine who ruled from 306–337. Like the Emperor, the Roman elite found that having many gods and beliefs led to a split society. Having just one was good politics. By 380–390, Christianity had spread so far that the Roman Emperor Theodosius would rule a gradual ban on Paganism, the previously popular worship of many gods.[52] With this ban, the Library of Alexandria, the internet of all the ancient world's knowledge, became a store room of evil Pagan scriptures, leading an angry mob of Christians to burn it down around 391, as the film *Agora* shows. Up in smoke went thousand-year-old writings and drawings of all the known human innovations collected up till then. Productive innovations like iron welding, the key vault, sewers, watermills, and thousands of others were lost. Many such innovations would embarrassingly reappear over a thousand years later, with future generations having to slave away to rediscover what humans before them already had, *wasting free time which could have been better spent making what no human ever had made before.*

Cement is a clear example, used to build millions of buildings worldwide today. It was the Romans who first made it by mixing slaked lime with pozzolana, a volcanic ash found on Mount Vesuvius. When water was added in, cement was formed and hardened. Thanks to nothing written being found, it took humanity until the 1790s when John Smeaton, experimenting with limestone clay, rediscovered what the Romans had known two thousand years before. After Smeaton, cement-maker James Frost would popularize and spread the technique, helping save and restore crumbling buildings in Britain and across the world.[53]

After the destruction of the Library of Alexandria, any remaining writings stored elsewhere vanished, as Rome itself was attacked by Visigothic tribes in 410 led by Alaric,[54] forcing streams of people to flee while those left were enslaved. Those fleeing took with them knowledge, sitting in their minds, without which new innovations couldn't be made, nor existing innovations be used. Just imagine your computer breaks down, but there is no computer repair person to fix it. It gets worse, those who sold the computers have left town. You stop using the computer, and so you slowly forget your computer skills so you store it away with some books. Later you die never having passed computer skills on to your children, who will grow up to find it and with puzzled looks not know what it is or what it can be used for. The result? A huge drop in productivity and living standards for your children, and their children. Anything about the computer disappears too, so even if your grandchildren wanted to find out about it, they couldn't. It would take 1000 years, until a similar computer is pieced together, a millennia of zero innovation combination in computing.

This horror story began occurring for thousands of innovations across Rome's empire as the city and its territories limped on until another invasion in 476 kicked out the last Roman emperor. Visigothic King Theodoric took control, and the shrinking number of Roman Senators soon realized that Greek texts would go extinct if not rewritten into Latin. Visigoths could not read Greek and most could not read anything at all.

One concerned senator, named Boethius, succeeded in translating writings of Euclid, Archimedes, Ptolemy, Aristotle, and Plato along with his own writings on music, astronomy, and arithmetic until he was executed in 524.[55] As *Lost to the West* by Lars Brownworth explores, the Eastern Roman Empire in Constantinople survived under Christian Emperor Justinian in (527–565), but he like other Christian emperors closed down any teachings at odds with the Bible, shutting Plato's old Academy which had run for hundreds of years. A century later in another part of the world, another religious book would be historically selected over the old pagan writings on the Arabian Peninsula. The *Qur'an* gave birth to Islam, while in Southeast Asia, the *Bhagavad Gita* did similarly with Hinduism, spreading and then competing with Buddhism, and it's many texts.

Rome's fall is said by many historians to be one of those apocalyptic events in history. If industrial production is anything to go by it was very bad. Ice cores taken from Greenland show us atmospheric pollutant levels rising around 500 BC, when Rome boosted its mining of lead, copper, and silver to build and expand its empire. Mining reached its peak around 100 and then dropped off as the Empire set in, and then plunged further after the fall of Rome.

Similar levels of lead, copper, and silver in the air wouldn't be seen for another 1100 years until the 13th century, when some of the famed Roman innovations of central heating, water sewerage, and drainage would be rediscovered.[56] This is just one reason why many say the period after Rome's collapse was the start of the Dark Ages. Historian Aldo Schiavone went further, calling it, "The greatest catastrophe ever experienced in the history of civilization."[57]

Today's equivalent might be the terror from a string of atomic bomb explosions in major world cities along with computer viruses which spread and permanently delete every person's lifetime of collected data. The huge drop in innovation from Rome's fall was worsened as we mentioned just before, due to the near extinction of the Greek language around this time. For many centuries after the Rome's fall, only Irish scholars could read and translate Greek texts.[58] It could have been worse, Greek could have taken the path of Egyptian hieroglyphs, *where there was no one left to read or translate them* after Rome fell.[59] It took 1,400 years until Napoleon's French army in 1799 found the Rosetta Stone, as Andrew Roberts touches on in *Napoleon: A Life.* This helped the world finally unlock the Egyptian alphabet and the large body of written knowledge left behind.[60] As for Rome, reading and learning vanished, as did most attempts at scientific reasoning, as we see later with the writings of Archbishop Isidore of Seville, who not having any of the Greek texts on hand went on to guess that light reflecting from the sun is what made the stars shine at night.[61]

In this way, the blind continued to lead the blind for centuries with religion being the center of all truth on everything imaginable. Even when the holy books gave no explanation for something, the priests just stepped in with some made up answer. A popular one was that everything is controlled by God but he, she or it was mysterious and unknowable, and if that was so, it made finding answers near impossible.

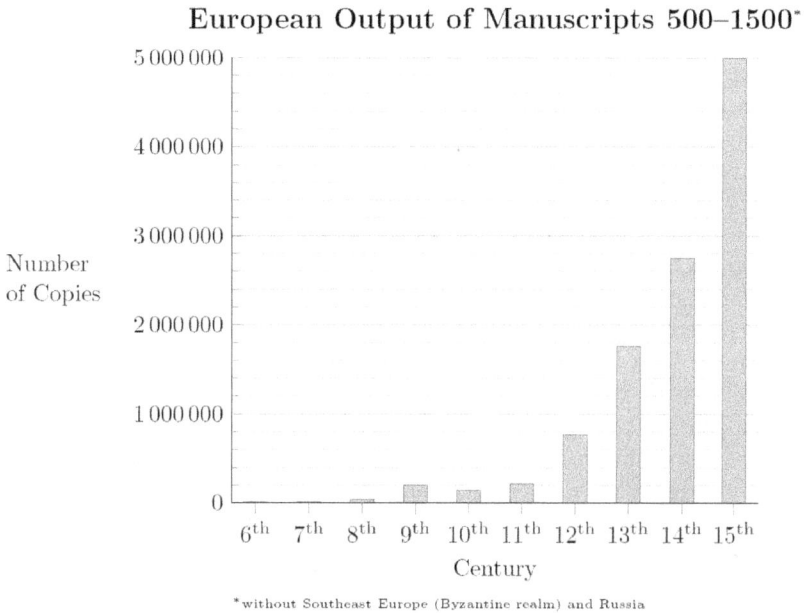

European Output of Manuscripts 500–1500*

*without Southeast Europe (Byzantine realm) and Russia

Source: Tentotwo, Creative Commons Attribution License

The chart above shows that ignorance, estimating the number of produced manuscripts from the 5th to 11th centuries at shocking lows. Destruction from wars and the rules of religions contributed to this, but the material on which manuscripts were written also did not help—they were easy to rip apart.

This problem, like many others, had been solved a long time before. In 2nd century China, Cai Lun made the productive innovation of papermaking. For it to be historically selected it would need to wait a few centuries until the armies of the Chinese and Arabs faced off at the Battle of Talas in 751, at today's border of Kazakhstan and Kyrgyzstan. The victorious Arabs captured several Chinese papermakers, who showed them the innovation. Slowly it made its way to Europe, allowing the action of reading to spread as now paper was cheaper and faster to make.[62]

By the 12th and 13th centuries, we see a boost in written manuscripts, which matched the start of the period called the European "Renaissance" explored well in *The History of the Renaissance World* by Susan Wise Bauer. Many who picture this period have sculptures, paintings and new architectural designs for cathedrals come to mind. The real story of the Renaissance was that of *entrepreneurs slowly rediscovering and translating the lost written innovations from the near total destruction* they had faced since Rome fell. This happened largely thanks to what's called the Islamic Golden Age of the 8th–12th century, lasting until Mongol invasions destroyed Islamic cities and their libraries. During this Golden Age, Arab scholars protected the surviving ancient Greek and Latin writings. Most of these writings were kept in a huge library called the "House of Wisdom," which was set up in the early 9th century in present day Baghdad, Iraq.[63] Luckily, many Islamic cities invested heavily in the building of libraries for the general use of the people, and it's thanks to this that the few surviving copies of ancient Greek and Latin writings spread. By some accounts these libraries had over 100,000 books, with the city of Baghdad in the 13th century sprawling with over 30 libraries alone. All this knowledge mixed to inspire Islamic works that were centuries ahead of their time, like the book of Ingenious Devices and the book of Ingenious Mechanisms. While Europe at the time was a sick child, with the University of Paris holding just 200 books and the Vatican Library holding only a few hundred more than that.[64] But it's the town of Toledo in modern day Spain that was pivotal in bringing back the ancient writings that we have with us today. In 1085, the Islamic rulers lost the city to the Christian Spaniards who found inside it so many old manuscripts that historians argue that these writings became the foundation on which the Renaissance in Europe was born from.

During the 12th and 13th centuries, the Cathedral of Toledo became a huge translation center, making nearly lost writings now readable in many European languages. The cathedral hired Jews, Arabs, and others under the watchful eye of Archbishop Raymond. One of the leading translators was Gerard of Cremona (1114 – 1187), who was said to have translated more than 80 books during his time there. It's thanks to all this work that today we see Ptolemy's *Almagest* (c. 150), Euclid's *Elements of Geography* (c. 300 BC), Archimedes' *On the Measurement of the Circle* (c. 300 BC), Aristotle's *On the Heavens* (c. 350 BC), and so many others, return from the dead. It was no easy task, as it's estimated to have taken 37 days to copy a 250 page book.[65] Later, translators worldwide continued what those in Toledo had started, like a Belgian named William of Moerbeke (1215–1286), who translated a large number of writings which even made it into the Pope's own library for study.[66] As more of this superior knowledge re-entered and was read, it inspired entrepreneurs of the time to make their own innovations: people like Johannes Kepler, Vasco De Gama, Niccolò Fontana Tartaglia, and countless others.

The resurrected writings of Herophilos from the 3rd century BC was shockingly found to say that the brain was the center of the nervous system, something that was to be *discovered* again 1,500 years later.[67] Herophilos also wrote about the scientific method of discovery well before Sir Francis Bacon became famous for writing the same in his 1620 book *New Organon.* Take Archimedes' theory of statics from the 3rd century BC which was found to say much the same as what Galileo would write in the 17th century. The story below of Archimedes' (c. 287–c. 212 BC) writings would make a great Hollywood film script.

Archimedes once wrote a book that until recently all scholars thought had its 3rd and final part lost to history. Both parts 1 and 2 talked about this mysterious 3rd part. We've now come to know that a surviving copy of part 3 was overwritten with religious prayers, and it became a prayer book for a man named Yohanis Myronas on the 14th of April, 1229. It was later found lurking in the Pope's library in 1311, and later it somehow got into the hands of an Italian in 1564. It was discovered again in 1911. Through private sales, it landed on the desk of ancient books' supervisor Dr. William Noel, who painstakingly led the task of translating its precious parchments, piecing together with computing technology the original writing from the damage caused by almost 2,000 years of wear and tear.[68]

We see this time and again. Take the set of laws which most European nations and others use today, and we see they came from surviving scraps of manuscripts of the Codex Justinius, itself lost for nearly 600 years after being written.[69] Even *The Art of War,* a Chinese classic written by Sun Tzu that's still read by millions worldwide today, was only translated into English in 1910. That's more than 2,000 years of *lost productivity.*[70]

The Renaissance as a time period can be summarized as being *when people shockingly discovered* that the modern problems of their day had already been solved by others a thousand years back. Now they had the chance to learn and mix the answers of the past with the present. No surprise that the people of this period used the phrase, *alle romana et alla antica*, "In the manner of the Romans and the ancients," to describe this rebirth of old knowledge, as Stephen Greenblatt Ph.D shows in *The Swerve* of the rescue from near extinction of a 1st century BC book by Lucretius. Leonardo da Vinci (1452–1519) read the thousand-year-old teachings of Roman architect Vitrivius, which inspired not only his drawing of the "Vitruvian Man," but as *Oil and Marble* by Stephanie Storey shows the many innovations he worked on. Leonardo would himself come to draw the helicopter which would inspire people 400 years later to make it. We also see the ancient influence on the books read by Niccolò Machiavelli, who wrote *The Prince,* and Sir Thomas More, who wrote *Utopia.* Reading ancient writings inspired Marco Polo to travel to lands mostly unknown to Europeans, like India and China, between 1271–1295, bringing back with him innovations unseen in Europe. He himself inspired those after him by writing about his travels, which fascinated future explorers like Christopher Columbus, who went on to discover the Americas for Spain in 1492.

It's interesting to see how innovations mix, as author Steven Johnson points out in *How We Got to Now: Six Innovations that Changed the World.* Glassmaking gave us lenses for reading, but they had little use until the printing press gave us books in small print, which led to a boom in lens making, giving birth to microscopes and telescopes, which later helped Galileo show that the earth was not the center of the universe. His vivid life is explored in *Galileo's Daughter by* David Sobel which shows how his work disagreed with the Church's Aristotelian writings, forcing him in public, to kneel with a penitent and a candle and reject his "heresy." After that, he was placed under house arrest for the rest of his life.[71]

From what we've seen so far, history could have been a lot different if many innovations were not banned, lost, or destroyed by societies or those running them. As Karl Popper asks in *Poverty of Historicism*, "How could we arrest scientific and industrial progress? By closing down, or by controlling, laboratories for research, by suppressing or controlling scientific periodicals and other means of discussion, by suppressing scientific congresses and conferences, by suppressing universities and other schools, by suppressing books, the printing press, writing, and, in the end, speaking."[72] Indeed, all of the above have happened throughout history. Unfair rules of the game made up by those ruling have pushed out innovations and entrepreneurs who they saw as a threat. As historical selection shows, productive innovations battling past innovations, sometimes in the short-run don't win, leading to a step backward. A "reversion to the average" as statisticians would say. In the long-run, though, like the historical trend of a stock market chart, they pull through to rise above the old.

For all the rebirth and spread of new knowledge, only a few got access to it. Manuscripts were costly to buy and copy, as was finding interpreters and scribes to translate them. The result? Reading and writing was out of reach for most people until…

Turning Point 4
Innovation of Printing

Spreading Spoken Words: 1439

Life Expectancy: 28–40 Years[73]

Repeatable use = The printed page

Effect on Free Time = With writing able to be cheaply copied and spread, more people could find answers to problems others have found, not needing to waste time figuring it out themselves. Innovations could now spread to more people and more places than ever before and combine faster.

As Abraham Lincoln wrote of this turning point: "By this means the observation of a single individual might lead to an important invention, years, and even centuries after he was dead. In one word, by means of writing, the seeds of invention were more permanently preserved, and more widely sown. And yet, for the three thousand years during which printing remained undiscovered after writing was in use, it was only a small portion of the people who could write, or read writing; and consequently, the field of invention, though much extended, still continued very limited. At length printing came. It gave ten thousand copies of any written matter, quite as cheaply as then were given before; and consequently, a thousand minds were brought into the field where there was but one before. This was a great gain; and history shows a great change corresponding to it, in point of time. I will venture to consider it, the true termination of that period called "the dark ages". Discoveries, inventions, and improvements followed rapidly, and have been increasing their rapidity ever since".[74]

It was in the year 1439 that one of the most important innovations in human history, the moveable type printing press, was made.[75] The entrepreneur mostly responsible is Johannes Gutenberg, who has been voted, by some, as the most influential person who ever lived.[76] As Ann Wroe of *The Economist* writes, "No other single action has been so influential. A spoken word, even from the mouth of the greatest ruler, prophet or sage, dissolves into the air. Words that are printed survive, thrive and multiply. Since 1439, words printed by Gutenberg's process have driven every invention, change of thinking and political idea."[77]

Before his great innovation, Gutenberg had hit hard times with a climbing pile of debt from a previous failed enterprise. He had hung around winemakers in the past, and it clicked that he could combine their methods with his printmaking. The moveable press he made let letters be rearranged and pushed onto a long-lasting metal page, which then with ink would print onto paper. While moveable type was made in China with wooden blocks in around 1040, the wood made it hard to use, as their alphabet had pictographs with thousands of possible changes, unlike the fixed letters found in most European languages. *Lacking enough productivity*, the Chinese press was not historically selected back then and did not spread.[78] Gutenberg's press made letter blocks from a mix of metals rather than wood. This made his machine longer lasting. Printed pages could come out faster and cheaper than before it, with less work needed from humans to manage the machine.[79] Gutenberg's innovations freed human knowledge, as the machines could out-copy human scribes who may take years to make a dozen copies of a book. The press *almost guaranteed that writings would now be free from the extinction* they faced in the past.

Today's students, ripped off by the cost of university textbooks, should spare a thought for the 15th century law student from Lombardy, Italy. A law book for them cost the same as an average year's living expenses, before the printing press came along. This made university study an expense only a wealthy family could afford.[80] Now with the historically selected press, books could get into the hands and minds of millions who weren't wealthy. As R.L Heilbroner wrote in *The Worldly Philosophers*, "He who enlists a man's mind wields a power even greater than the sword or the scepter."[81]

It's estimated that, in the first 50 years of Gutenberg's innovation, more books were printed than had been written in all of human history. By the 16th century, around 150–200 million copies of books were in existence.[82]

European Output of Printed Books ca. 1450–1800*

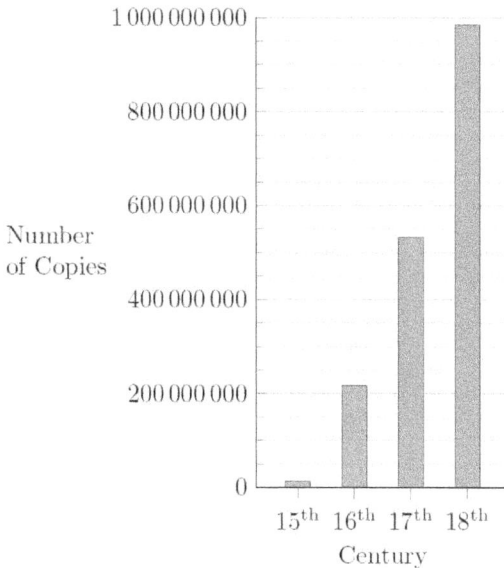

*without Southeast Europe (Ottoman realm) and Russia

Source: Tentotwo, Creative Commons Attribution License

As more printing presses popped up, less of what they printed could be controlled. For example, the uncontrolled mass printing that announced Columbus's discovery of America as a fourth continent caused confusion in the Christian world, as the Bible had written that there were only three continents.[83] Below, we see the spread of the printing press across Europe, after which it later spread worldwide.

Source: NordNordWest, Creative Commons Attribution License

More printed books gave us more libraries, which later were stocked with newspapers which were printed in the 17th century as printing advanced. The first independent newspaper reporters relied on reading new books to find new ideas for their articles, leading many readers *for the first time to read of unheard of ideas* like "freedom" and "human rights" mixed in with articles about a murder or a national war. With books of the past spreading, lessons gained from thousands of years of blood, sweat and tears could now be learned by reading several books over a few weeks in one of the new public libraries. Arguably *no higher "return on investment" of time exists.* As George R.R. Martin, author of *The Game of Thrones* series, writes, "A reader lives a thousand lives before he dies… The man who never reads lives only one."[84]

In time, this flourishing and snowballing of printed writings led to the birth of the next step, what historians call the *Enlightenment* in Europe. Humanism is another word for it. This is when people started challenging the beliefs and institutions of the church and the ruling class thanks to the rediscovered answers from past books mixed into the reality of the present. Focus now started to shift from *what happens to you after death (heaven or hell) to what are you doing with your life on earth right now?* Earlier we showed how in the past people were told that God controlled everyone's future, making many give up trying to change their situation in life. Now with the new ideas flowing from the printing presses, people slowly learned they had more control of their lives and should use it to make a difference while alive.

One of these was the 16th century German religious reformer, Martin Luther, who praised the printing press as, "God's highest and extremist act of grace."[85] Similar praise is given to the modern equal of the press, the internet, which Pope Francis in 2014, said was a "gift from God."[86] Luther's use of the press started the reformation of 1522, when he stamped 95 theses on the doors of a Catholic church in Germany. Soon printing presses spat out 300,000 copies of those theses which then spread through Europe. As explored in *Here I Stand* by Roland H. Bainton, the theses showed crimes committed by the church, which German princes would later use as a reason to start a war to retake church property and save their populations paying bribes to priests and rent seeking church taxes to Rome.

With more people reading and thinking for themselves, the scientific method returned from the grave to challenge the answer that God was responsible for everything. *Experimentation with repeatable results*, not blind faith, slowly became the final judge of the truth.

A result of this was the start of groups like The Royal Society of Britain in 1660 as explored by Edward Dolnick in *The Clockwork Universe*. Fittingly, the society had as its motto, *Nullius in Verba* (Take no one's word for it).[87] The society's president for some time was Sir Isaac Newton, a scientist who gave us writings on calculus, light refraction, the elliptical motions of planets, three laws of motion and a lot more. His writings and those of many others helped lead to *fewer people blaming the devil for the eclipse of the moon and crumbling buildings*, instead explaining it through astronomy and faulty construction methods.[88]

Rules are made to be broken in science, something we still have a hard time accepting. Even scientists who make new theories or laws which replace old ones, push away new evidence that their own discovery could be wrong. *A quick tip to discover this is to see if a breakthrough has exceptions to it that are unexplained.* These exceptions show us that there is more left to discover. Newton's laws explained a lot over the centuries, but couldn't explain why Mercury's orbit didn't follow the rules of other planets. This lead Einstein to come up with his theories of relativity, which has its own exceptions, that quantum theory aims to explain.

As time moved on, innovations found in the sentences of books led eventually to those reading to start taking action that would bubble up and burst apart in many revolutions across the world. As French author of *Les*

Miserables, Victor Hugo wrote, "An invasion of armies can be resisted, an invasion of ideas cannot."[89] Many saw the revolution and founding of the United States as the best example of humanist ideas spreading. Many books set the foundation for the fight to gain independence from Britain, among them the writings of philosopher John Locke and his *Two Treatises on Government*, the newspaper writings and speeches of Samuel Adams, and Thomas Paine's *Common Sense*. Future president John Adams, even said that, "Without the pen of the author of 'Common Sense,' the sword of Washington would have been raised in vain." It's true that it wasn't that simple, like David McCullough's bio of Adams shows, but the convincing arguments for war came from books which swayed delegates from the 13 U.S. colonies to vote for independence from Britain and write up the Declaration of Independence. Thomas Jefferson, the declaration's main author, was said to have used Locke's influence in writing the now famous sentences, "all men are created equal" and "life, liberty, and the pursuit of happiness." As the Jon Meacham biography *Jefferson* shows, Locke's influence is also seen in the key concepts that a government needed elected approval of the people as well as the separation of church and state. After American victory, those drafting the Constitution began reading up on the history books to find out the best features of government to add into the U.S. political system. It's been said the founders were like doctors checking the dead bodies of past governments to keep the infant U.S. child from catching the sicknesses that killed the rest.[90]

Over in France, the "Encyclopedie" would also help push people to think different and make their own revolution against the rulers. The effect it had was so large that "No encyclopedia perhaps has been of such political importance, or has occupied so conspicuous a place in the civil and literary history of its century. It sought not only to give information, but to guide opinion."[91] It was printed yearly from 1751 to 1772, with its purpose, as editor Denis Diderot put it, that "we should not die without having rendered a service to the human race in the future years to come."[92] This purpose was seen in the French Revolution of 1789, which like many historical events, mixed innovations from the world over, like the inspiration of U.S. victory a few years before it. Over in Britain, a small middle class was starting to grow, which would in time make the House of Commons more influential than the powerful, aristocratic, and unelected House of Lords. The Lords, which seats some rich and out-of-touch descendants of military commanders of centuries ago, luckily today has little influence over decision-making.

Turning Point 5
Innovation of Steam

Turning the Printed into Reality: 1775

Life Expectancy: 33–41 years[93]

Repeatable use = Factories and machines making copies of all other material innovations.

Effect on Free Time = With steam to power machines, anything described in books could now slowly be made into real products and services.

We know the printing press easily made copies of books since the 1440s, yet for centuries copies could not easily be made of mostly all other innovations. Glasses, pots, swords, guns, shoes, hats, and almost everything else was still made by hand. Unlike the sinking price of books, the rest was still costly and out of reach for most people who were still poor. The result? *Innovations sat locked up in books for many centuries, unable to break free and change the world.*

Science fiction books hold a special place here. Though they are fiction, they seek to mix innovations to predict what the future may look like. Author Jules Verne is one famous early name, who influenced many future entrepreneurs as seen in the stories *The Collected Works of Jules Verne*. The submarine and scuba diving gear he writes about in *20,000 Leagues Under the Sea* created such interest that they were soon made after the book was published. Another example was the "gun" that would blast humans to the moon in his other book, *From the Earth to the Moon*. It was this book that sparked interest in Konstantin Tsiolkovsky, a Russian school teacher who was the first to show how rockets could be used to fire humans into space.[94] A proud Jules Verne may have looked on 104 years after his book's printing, when in 1969 Apollo 11 landed on the moon. As the Chinese government has discovered from studying entrepreneurs of many countries, it was reading science fiction that helped inspire them to make their innovations. Today, China's once non-existent science fiction industry is the world's largest.[95]

To find out how innovations from books were finally set free, it's best to understand the time in which it happened. By the late 18th century, the living standards for an average person are said to have *changed very little from two thousand years before*.[96] As the last turning point showed, we can thank the destruction, censorship and loss of important books for that.

Add to that the unfair rules, which kept populations in most countries taking 1 step forward and 2 steps back. Thomas Hobbes' words have been used to describe the time as, "solitary, poor, nasty, brutish." Most people spent nearly all their time on farms as slaves or as servants for the nobles, just to get enough food to survive.[97]

Another British writer, Thomas Malthus, touched on this point in his *Essay on the Principle of Population*, which would have a large impact on Charles Darwin's thinking about evolution. Malthus wrote that human populations always out grew the food needed to feed them. This meant humanity always bounced back to the average level of existence whenever it tried to progress beyond this invisible limit. If there was not enough food, resources, materials, or labor, *then no growth could happen exponentially* (doubling... 1, 2, 4, 8, 16) and would instead either grow linearly (adding up... 1, 2, 3, 4, 5) or worse it may stagnate and possibly go backwards (...0, -1, -2, -3). Take the introduction of the potato to Ireland in the late 18th century. Thanks to it being a cheap food source, it helped Ireland's population boom from 3 million in the 1700s to 8 million by 1845.[98] Then a diseased crop of potatoes spread over Ireland and infected the rest bringing mass starvation and death, killing an estimated 20-25% (1.6 to 2 million) of the recently grown population.[99]

Horrors like this seemed to reveal a law of nature, that humans could not do much more than our ancestors before us. For all the reordering of laws, new weaponry, discovery of new lands, and even the printing press, we still couldn't escape the need for human hands or animal strength to make it all possible. The limited number of humans or animals meant we couldn't make enough copies of an innovation cheaply enough to get it into everyone's hands. The printing press had cracked that code for books, but there was still to come a press to take all the innovations screaming to be let free from inside those books. One problem was that all innovations are made out of materials, like wood, steel, coal which need to be dug up, filtered and moved, *yet each century this process hardly improved, we could do little more than our ancestors had done.*

Actions, as we know, boil down to energy, of which humans and animals have a limited daily amount. Humanity's hunt to control and increase energy goes back to the use of slaves in farming and building, like seen with the Egyptian pyramids. Yet even for the cruelest of rulers, it still cost a lot to feed, house, and take care of slaves. In ancient Egypt and China, an attempt was made to change this, with the innovation of the water wheel used around the first century AD. Later came the windmill. *But both barely pushed up productivity more than human labor had before them.* Sailing ships helped out, but they could not move materials across land. Horses helped, yet like humans they were expensive to breed and feed. Everything seemed to have a *limit on the amount of innovations* it could help us make. Without pushing past that limit, innovation combination could not spread to most people, and so growth stayed mostly unchanged for almost two thousand years.[100]

So how did humanity escape Malthus' trap? To find out, we must revisit our entrepreneurial friend, Heron of Alexandria (10 – 70). Heron was one of the first to write about the vacuum. Remember your lips getting stuck to a bottle or straw you were drinking from until you heard a "pop" sound on removing them? That's a small example of a vacuum. Heron saw that the pop from a vacuum was energy, it could move things. Abraham Lincoln had the following to say about this crucial discovery: "For instance, it is quite certain that ever since water has been boiled in covered vessels, men have seen the lids of the vessels rise and fall a little, with a sort of fluttering movement, by force of the steam; but so long as this was not specially observed, and reflected and experimented upon, it came to nothing. At length however, after many thousand years, some man observes this long-known effect of hot water lifting a pot-lid, and begins a train of reflection upon it. He says, 'Why, to be sure, the force that lifts the pot-lid, will lift anything else, which is no heavier than the pot-lid. And, as man has much hard lifting to do, cannot this hot-water power be made to help him?' He has become a little excited on the subject, and he fancies he hears a voice answering, 'Try me.' He does try it, and the observation, reflection, and trial gives to the world the control of that tremendous, and now well-known agent, called steam-power."[101]

Sadly, Heron's discovery was swept under the carpet by the church who misused Aristotle's writings and slowed humanity's progress. For nearly two thousand years, people stumbled on the vacuum, from Vitruvius of Rome, Leonard Da Vinci to the Arab Scholar Taqi ad-Din. Yet they all didn't think much of it, remembering that Aristotle wrote that, "nature abhors a vacuum."[102] If you had an empty glass jar, Aristotle would say it had nothing inside it. Yet it does, we can't see it, but we can feel it, it's called air. In 1277, the Catholic Church ran the Paris Condemnations, where it banned papers written by students on topics it didn't like. One of the papers banned was titled, "Vacuums." Unsurprisingly, the Church said that "if" a vacuum was to happen as experiments showed it did, that this must be an act of God.[103]

Thanks to the translators of the past and the printing press, copies of Heron's surviving writings, *spread over the centuries*, and it's believed Galileo read some of them. His own interest in vacuums began when water could not rise above a certain level in a tube off his suction pump, making him see that this limit is caused by something else in the tube, which he said must be air pressure.[104]

The printing of Galileo's experiments spread to the English military engineer, Thomas Savery, inspiring him to test the lighting of coal under a pot of water to make steam, which then flowed up into a closed tube that when opened, *popped* with a force *that would lift almost anything sitting on top of it.* This is the same as when you shake a soft drink. Gas would fizz and build up until you opened the top for the liquid to explode out. If you put a hat on top of the bottle, it would fly off. In 1698 Savery became one of the first to patent a steam engine design.[105]

Like the early version of anything, this steam engine didn't have all the features it would later be known for, but news of its making did interest Thomas Newcomen. A Baptist lay preacher by day and experimenter by night, he took on the task of improving Savery, by adding the innovation of a tube with a piston and putting a beam above so it could move up and down like a see-saw. This was needed to control the huge pressure built up by the boiling water, which burst like an explosion when the handle released the vacuum, pushing one side of the seesaw up and then down when closed.

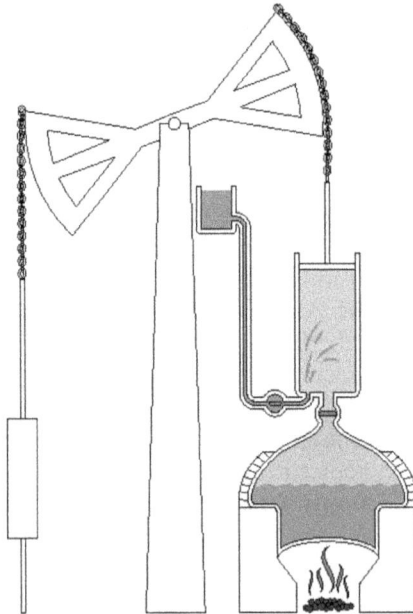

Source: Emoscopes, Creative Commons Attribution License

The first real world test for this machine was sucking water out of mines. The result was a historical productivity breakthrough. Newcomen's machine pumped 268,800 gallons (1,220,000 liters) at a cost of only 20 shillings instead of a horse-driven pump pulling 67,000 gallons (305,000 liters) costing 24 shillings.[106] This was the moment human and animal labor started to be replaced by machines. *For the first time, more energy could be squeezed out for less cost. More done with less action.*

Like the growth of an innovation's roots, we now stretch the steam engine's branches from Heron and other early experimenters, past Savery and Newcomen, to James Watt and his angel investor, Matthew Boulton. The Scottish Watt was an almost self-taught engineer who wrote down results of all his experiments for later review. Looking at Newcomen's machine, he saw many things he could make more productive. One was to use less coal for the popping explosion and in doing so, drop the cost of the machine. Watt saw that up to 75% of the energy that the engine used was wasted on cooling itself.[107] Like a computer fan, if overheated it'll break down— a steam engine could explode. He tested a separate tube to fix this, its aim was to suck and hold on to extra heat from the rest of the machine.

It worked. Less coal was used, and the machine could now lift 3 times more weight than any other.[108] This productivity boost made more mine owners keen to use it, and now it was a lot cheaper to buy. Watt's engine was patented under The Fire Engine Act of 1775.[109] Many historians say that this event was the start of the Industrial Revolution. Historically selected due to its large productivity gains, the Watt steam engine became the energy source for that long dreamt universal press, which could mass-produce all innovations. *It now seemed we finally could escape Malthus' trap.*

Steam power revolutionized almost every industry, and recently put both Watt and Boulton on the U.K's 50 pound banknote. Watt's last name would become the defining word for a unit of power. Even to this day, Watt's influence is found driven in hundreds of millions of cars due to the "Watt linkage," a device that's part of a car's suspension. A memorial statue of him near St. Paul's Cathedral in London reads, "…enlarged the resources of his country, increased the power of man, and rose to an eminent place among the most illustrious followers of science and the real benefactors of the world." It's telling to note the words "real benefactors," as it's *a habit of many to talk of popular people as though they're leaving some lasting improvement in the world.* Interestingly, a friend of Matthew Boulton and James Watt was Charles Darwin's uncle, industrialist Josiah Wedgwood, who earned his fortune from the pottery business he made in part by using Watt's steam engine. As Darwin would write, "I have had ample pleasure from not having to earn my own bread."[110] This wealth let him spend more time on research which would end up in the writing of *Origin of Species*. Unlike the rich children he grew up with, Darwin didn't take the fame seeking path, but one of value creation.

After the steam engine was released, Britain used its control over India, which previously was the largest exporter of cotton, to force them to buy cotton made from Britain instead.[111] Cotton factories popped up over Britain, hiring hundreds of thousands to help spin the cotton which would later be turned into clothes. Before the steam engine lifted things from mines, with cotton it did something else. The steam machines were linked to a cotton making device called the loom, which before then workers had controlled with their hands. Now with steam, the speed of weaving cotton increased, leading to more tons of cotton made per hour than ever before by humans.

Steam had nearly the same productive effects for anything it touched. The productivity of workers in the U.K doubled from 1830 to 1850. For the first time, more was done with less. Coal production skyrocketed from 24 million tons in 1830 to 110 million tons in 1870, and iron rose from 700,000 tons in 1830 to 4 million tons in 1860.[112] Common sense finally made its way into the British Parliament, where in 1850 the Factory Act was passed banning child labor and giving them a free early school education. At this time we see data for literacy, GDP per capita, and life expectancy growing for every European country exposed to steam power between 1820–1870.[113] An 1899 report by the U.S. Department of Labor shows the huge change steam power gave to the old craftsman shop. Before it would take 118 man-hours using hammers, anvils, chisels, and other tools to make a plow while a factory helped by steam power could make one in just under 4 hours.[114] Eventually, factories only needed people to do one thing, watch over machines.

Fewer workers led to less wages to pay, letting factories drop the price of the innovations they made. Cloth was affordable to only the wealthy before steam. After it, everyday people could buy it. This happened to almost every product that steam power touched. In the long run, living standards started to rise for everyday people.

In the short-term, however, the picture was not so rosy. Charles Dickens, author of classics like *A Tale of Two Cities*, showed in *Oliver Twist* the horrible way workers lived. Managers treated them like animals. What they got paid sometimes didn't cover basic living costs, pushing many to *live huddled in a single room where disease easily spread cutting their life short.* Sadly, we see examples of this today in almost every nation going through their own industrial revolutions. Suicides at Foxconn, China's maker of iPhones, were highly publicized. Harsh working conditions have long been seen in those making sports brand clothing. Workers making sports jackets don't realize that just one jacket may sell in another currency at a profit that their *small wage could never earn, even if they worked tirelessly for years.*

Steam power over time created a fear that workers will lose their jobs to a noisy and stinky metal monster. These angry workers, later to be named "Luddites", took out their anger on British cotton merchants like Kay, Cartwright, and Hargreaves who were to see their factories burn down and their family homes attacked. The spread of machines led to a more organized workers' movement across the world to try to guarantee pay and employment for workers.

When workers started getting fired and replaced by machines, revolts became more violent. Even before the steam engine, the cotton making machine "spinning jenny", had already fired many workers as it did most of the cotton spinning itself. In early 1789 we see fired workers rioting in France. In the city of Troyes, rioters killed the mayor and mutilated his body. A lawyer defending the workers said, "The machines used in cotton-spinning have deprived many workers of their jobs." Months later the Réveillon Riots of the 27th–28th of April 1789, saw the homes of entrepreneurs Dominique Henriot and Jean-Baptiste Réveillon smashed up. Such riots, it's noted, contributed to other events that led to the French Revolution later that year.[115]

It's estimated that the cost of all machines smashed was the same as a year's worth of French foreign trade in the manufacturing sector. Machine damage continued yearly across Europe, leading to factory closures to the point that in 1812, Britain made a law that put to death anyone damaging machines. Why so tough? Britain had *more soldiers fighting workers than fighting Napoleon's armies.*[116] What stopped violence getting worse was the growing boost in living standards, even for the angry workers. It was this, for the first time which stopped rulers giving in to mob and union demands to ban innovations as they could now see most people were living better and that goods were cheaper.

As Nobel Laureate in Economic Sciences, Robert E. Lucas, Jr. said of the period, "For the first time in history, the living standards of the masses of ordinary people have begun to undergo sustained growth... Nothing remotely like this economic behavior has happened before."[117] According to the Lindert-Williamson index, real wages doubled in just thirty-two years between 1819 and 1851.[118] Take the lowly construction workers of Paris who lived in poverty in 1820, by 1914 their wages jumped 3 times above the poverty line.[119] With cheaper yet higher quality goods spreading, and wages rising, everyday people could now buy what before only the rich could afford. All these innovations led to a 15% increase in life expectancy in the population of England, rising from 35 to 40 years from 1781-1851.[120]

For the first time in history, most people had money to spend beyond survival. This spare money pushed once poor people into the middle class which drove entrepreneurs to make more innovations for them to buy.

The Industrial Revolution changed the way people thought about and earned money. *For the first time, money could be earned through innovation rather than war and robbery.* Before then, the best everyday people could do to prove themselves to climb the social ladder, was to be a "hero" in battle. Sir Francis Drake was made a "Sir" in part for stealing Spanish treasure, splitting it with the Queen of England, who then paid off all government debts.[121] Trace the background of anyone royal and you'll find military ancestors. Queen Elizabeth II is descended from William the Conqueror. Cleopatra of Egypt from Ptolemy, a general of Alexander the Great.[122,123]

Now came people like Karl Benz. Born into poverty in what's now Germany, he mixed other innovations with the steam engine to make the first practical car in Europe, giving rise to the company which holds his name today, Mercedes-Benz.

As steam power spread to all industries, speed of movement increased. Steam started to push railway carriages, which led to the railway networks of today. In 1830, 34 miles (56km) of track line was put down in Britain.[124] In 1860 that had spread to the U.S. with 29,825 miles (48,000km) of track laid. Today over the border in South America there is more than 62,137 miles (100,000km).[125] People soon got their first taste of machine travel with trains moving them on land and steamboats on water. The travel time between New York and Albany was alone cut by nearly 50% and cost dropped by 30% thanks to steamboats[126]

Just like large cannons shrunk to be a hand-held rifle, the race was on to give people their own mini train to move faster than using horses. The innovation of the car takes us back to 1801, when Richard Trevithick built the "puffing devil," one of the first attempts at a practical, steam-powered car.[127] This led to another innovation which would form a root branch under the steam engine – the internal combustion engine, which moves most vehicles of all types today. As cars spread in the early 20th century they destroyed their competitors, the horse industries of carriage-making, blacksmithing, and riding equipment. They gave birth to gas stations, garages, and repair shops. Cars spread so wide that governments needed to make roads, street signs, rule books, and registration centers.

For any innovation to reach the most people it *needs to tick as many of the 4 value factors as it can*. Henry Ford did that, as earlier explored, when he took the assembly line from meat factories and brought car parts to workers instead of workers wasting time fetching the parts. This shrunk the construction time per car, so now more cars could be made in less time. Back in 1913, before the assembly line, 10,607 Model T cars were made and sold for US$850 each. After the assembly line, more than 300,000 cars were made, so that in 1916, the price dropped to US$360. In 1924, 730,000 cars sold and the price dropped further to US$290. By 1927, the car which once took 12 hours to make was rolling out the factory every 24 seconds, thanks to even more automation in the assembly line.[128] As you'd expect, many workers lost jobs during this time. Almost every year in the car industry is similar to the figures here from 1961. When more than 160,000 members of the United Automobile Workers Union and 95,000 of the Steelworkers Union were fired by the car companies as reports showed that productivity increased by 121 % in that time period.[129,130].

Like cars, basic foods also became cheaper. In 1919, an average American worked 10 hours to earn enough to afford a basket of 12 food items. Steam power and other upgrades in factories meant that by 1997, the work time needed to buy the *same food dropped to only two hours*.[131] As more cars were used, more petroleum oil was needed to fuel it, leading to the growth of the Standard Oil company into one of the largest in the world. Its co-founder, John D Rockefeller, by some estimates is the richest person who ever lived. Family fortunes like his and that of others, like the Rothchilds, are forgotten to have been made mostly by innovating, as the books, *Titan* and *The Rothchilds* explore in detail. Today the roots of Standard Oil is seen in two successor companies, ExxonMobil and Chevron, who both usually rank in the top 10 list of largest companies by market value.[132]

Another energy that was soon to compete with oil was being set up in 1882 by Thomas Edison. His electric utility system would in less than a decade spread thousands of power stations across the United States.[133] Electricity would become the way we power innovations in our rooms and homes. And it's mostly thanks to steam once again. This time in the form of the Steam turbine, *which makes around 90% of all the electricity in the world today*.[134] Where before steam engines powered large machines, electricity could now power smaller ones that everyday people use. As Henry Ford said, "The provision of a whole new system of electric generation emancipated industry from the leather belt and line shaft, for it eventually became possible to provide each tool with its own electric motor."[135]

Unlike candles and lanterns, which let off unhealthy gases and could burn a house down if they fell, electricity was mostly safe, leading to its historical selection. The light bulb also led to a booming night economy with bars, cafés, and even factories working 24 hours a day. Electricity production quadrupled from 1900 to 1950, and again in half that time from 1950 to 1975.[136]

Today, many people worldwide still don't have electricity, but they do have a mobile phone. How could that be? Let's explore…

Turning Point 6
Innovation of Computation

Digitization of the Physical World: 1948

Life Expectancy: 47 Years[137]

Repeatable use = Bit (computerized data) Digitization of physical world into bits

Effect on Free Time = Machines could now be controlled by clicks on a computer not by pulling and pushing by hand and body. Most information once sitting locked in books, photos, recordings etc. was now searchable with computers and the internet. People could now find innovations quickly and combine them faster than ever before.

Over time, the innovations of the physical world have jumped into the digital world of bits. Early on radio took voice and sent it by waves to spread into living rooms, letting news and government broadcasts reach people faster. This innovation then spread into the field of war, allowing commanders to quickly command their armies. More use drove innovation in smaller handheld radios, which in 1959 helped Fidel Castro and fewer than 100 socialist revolutionaries overthrow a Cuban regime with an army of 40,000 soldiers,[138] a story which *Che Guevara* by Jon L. Anderson explores so well.

In 1948, the transistor had been made, which some suggest was the greatest innovation of the 20th century.[139] It could run more calculations than anything before it. Installed into computers it sped up the now endless advances in computing productivity as seen in Moore's Law.[140] Named after a co-founder of Intel, Gordon Moore, the law says that the number of transistors on a microprocessor doubles every 2 years, leading to more powerful computing and lower prices.[141] Before the small transistor, vacuum tubes were used instead, which were slow and large. One such tube computer, named, "Colossus," was so big that it took half a dozen people to supervise it. Small surprise then that the hand sized transistor was historically selected.

From calculators to punch-card readers, transistors spread to almost every industry that had machines, as nearly all could now be hooked up to be run with a computer. NASA's Apollo program used such early computers to make the 1969 moon landing possible. In 1975, Intel launched its newest processor, the 8080. It could run 4500 calculations in a second, and today the processors run billions.[142] Some rightly guessed it could power calculations on a computer small enough to fit onto a desk. This gave birth to the Altair computer, but its hardware needed software to tell it what to do. Bill Gates and Paul Allen would be the first to make that software, and their "BASIC" program became the first innovation sold by the Microsoft Corporation.

As more software programs were made, each slowly took what we did in the real world and simplified it onto a computer screen. Take accounting, which before software meant painfully calculating numbers in rows and tables for hours on end. The "Spreadsheet" software which Microsoft Excel later dominated, lets one number change recalculate all numbers on the entire sheet instantly.

Word processing software does the same instant tricks. It lets you type up anything, insert nearly any image and edit mistakes on screen without messy white out. Sign writers who made shop signs finally stopped needing to use paint brushes. Heavy print books once had to be sent by post, but now they can travel over email as an e-book. If you have a printer at home, you own a printing press that millions of people were banned from ever using centuries ago with the penalty of death.

Software has spread today to run mostly everything from transportation, electricity, traffic, water, telephone, and flight. Smart phones and tablets are now portable computers. Today, the mobile cell phone is the most used device on earth, with more made and in use than there are people on the planet.[143]

In 1993 the rules of the game changed as seen in the National Information Infrastructure Act, which led to huge innovation combination among the millions of personal computers on desks run through the mostly unknown U.S. government military project known as the "internet." The rule change started what former U.S. president Barack Obama called an "economic revolution." Since 1993, the internet has grown from 130 websites to around a billion.[144] It's now the largest store of information ever, surging way past what the ancient libraries of Alexandria and Baghdad held. Just clicking a bunch of news websites today likely shows more information than a 17th century English person would have seen in their entire life.[145]

With more reading done on computers and devices, today's libraries are having to remove print books to make room for working spaces where people can freely meet to make new innovations.[146] "Software is eating the world," wrote Marc Andreessen, a co-founder of Netscape with Jim Clark, as explored in *The New New Thing* by Michael Lewis. "More and more major enterprises and industries are being run on software and delivered as online services."[147] Today, this growing digital world of enterprises is estimated by Citibank and Oxford University to be worth US$20 trillion worldwide, and it's slowly munching away at the physical world which sits at US$130 trillion.[148] Take eBooks, which now make up more than 25% of all U.S. book sales. YouTube reaches more people than any one cable channel, eBay lets you sell anything you don't need, and Amazon lets you search and buy all items, not just the most popular ones.[149,150] Besides a Rome-like fall into destruction, if trends continue what could be next? We'll find out in the next chapter.

***

Above, we've covered different ways that innovation combination has and continues to shape our world. We can now see more clearly how each turning point has slowly but surely *increased life expectancy, and with that the small window of free time*. Below, we sum up the two other mechanisms that help push this combination along.

Innovation Collection (+)

"The inhabitants of the world at each successive period in its history have beaten their predecessors in the race for life, and are, in so far, higher in the scale, and their structure has become more specialized; and this may account for the common belief held by so many paleontologists, that organization on the whole has progressed."[151]
Charles Darwin

You've likely heard friends, family, or the media say that things are changing "faster" or are "tougher" or "more complicated" than ever before. It's a common cliché heard each decade, yet it's true in one sense, as innovation combination shows us. From the Big Bang to today's world, *there has been progress when we realize* that we went from a soup of lava-filled oceans to billions of organisms, one of which evolved to escape instinct, and went on to make billions of its own innovations, more than 6,800 different languages, and now a website for almost everything imaginable.[152.153]

19th century philosopher Herbert Spencer called society an evolutionary organism, growing and adapting in complexity, but we can't say that every new generation of humans is better than the last, can we? No, history is more like a stock market chart, with booms and busts, *which over time trend mostly upward, but past performance doesn't guarantee future results.* We've seen big drops, like the Fall of Rome, which reversed progress and stole productivity for over a thousand years. Such a fall could come again. An asteroid can wipe us out, terrorists can detonate nuclear bombs, or a third world war could start. Time will tell if we can make innovations to stop such disasters with asteroid deflecting rockets, nuclear weapon disabling radio waves, or a worldwide vote to authorize use of military force.[154] Some innovations may sound like fantasies, but remember that each innovation we use today was once thought to be a fantasy in the past.

We've made more innovations in the last century than in all others put together. This recent combination of innovations has led not to a linear growth of innovations, but to an exponential doubling.

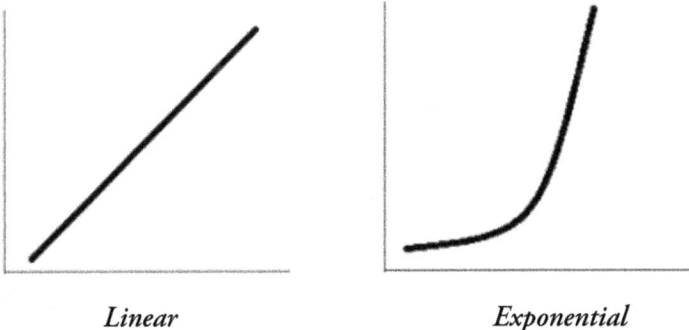

Linear   *Exponential*

As more and more innovations build up, there is a greater chance that more productive innovations will be among them to help continue to increase life expectancy. Even a brief look at the chart of U.S. patents below shows an exponential curve which is also seen in many other patent charts from other nations.

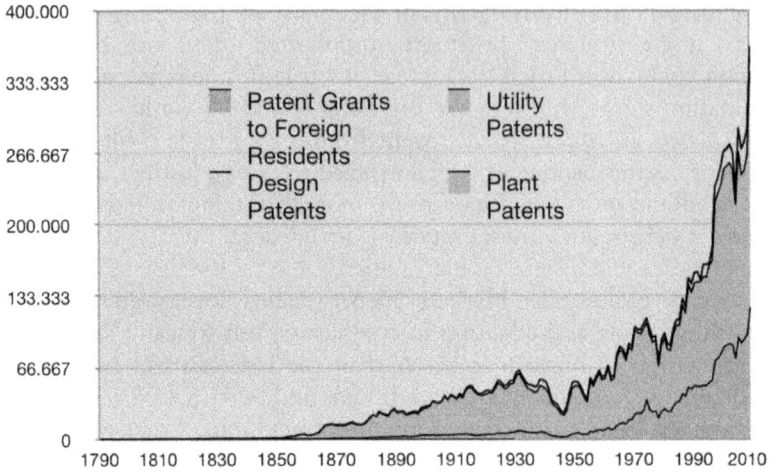

Number of patents historically (U.S) in 000's
Source: Spitzl, Creative Commons Attribution License

We see the same exponential trend in economic growth as seen through historical world GDP below.

World GDP/capita 1-2003 A.D.

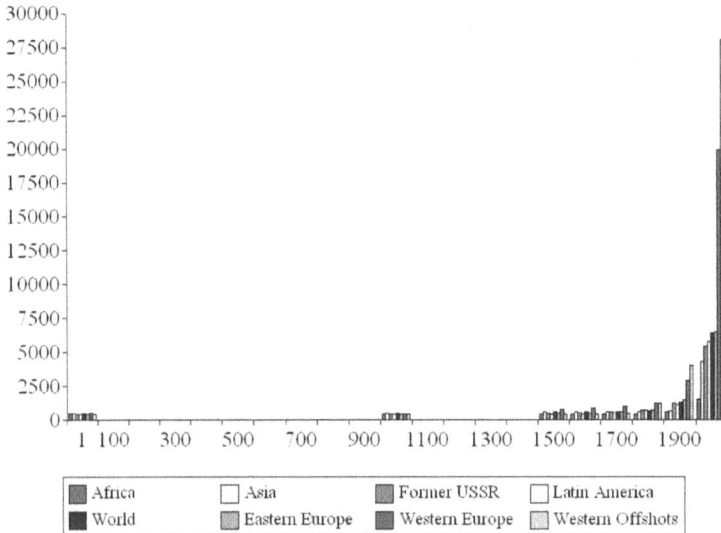

Source: Ultramarine, Public domain

A reverse exponential growth effect can be seen in the ever-shrinking time it takes productive innovations to spread. Gary Vaynerchuk, author of *Crush It!* and *Jab, Jab, Jab, Right Hook*, points out that to get to 50 million adopters, "It took Instagram a year and a half." Past innovations took decades if not nearly centuries.[155] The faster productive innovations are adopted, the quicker productivity spreads, boosting life expectancy.

NUMBER OF YEARS TO REACH 50 MILLION ADOPTERS

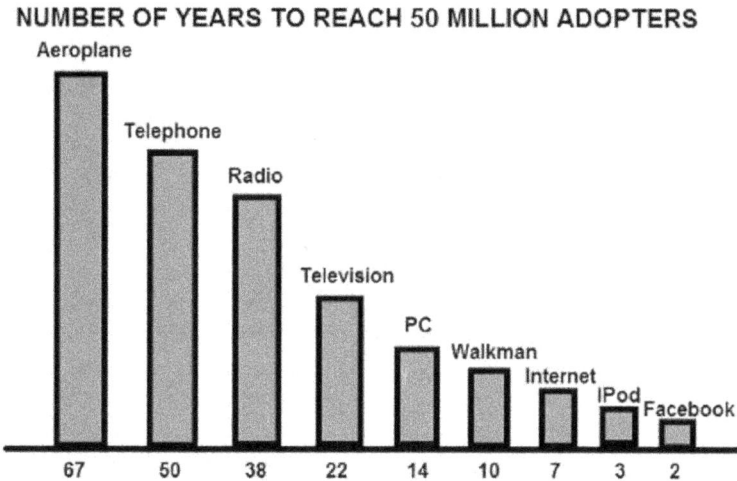

Data sources: Wallop, H., "Why I will mourn the death of the Walkman", The Telegraph, United Kingdom, 2010. Madrigal, A.C., "Most people didn't have A/C until 1973 and other strange tech timelines," www.theatlantic.com, 2012. Wikipedia.

Back in 2003, all of humanity made a grand total of five exabytes of data, but by 2015, according to IBM, we are making 2.5 exabytes per day, with 90% of the world's data made in the last 2 years.[156] Soon we'll get to 8 zettabytes, that's an 8 with 21 zeroes. When we do, the total amount of data will be 40 million times the size of what now sits in the U.S. Library of Congress. The mobiles in our hands have only helped increase this, as now they are 1,000+ times more powerful than the first PC.[157] In the future the next wave we'll see is the connection of all our devices to the internet. It's estimated that up to 1 trillion devices will soon be connected, which is predicted to lead to US$14.4 trillion in economic impact.[158]

Innovation Concentration (^{2})

As innovations combine and collect, their journey is to cluster over time to become more complex, like the disassembled car picture earlier showed. Innovations that help combine the most innovations are the most concentrated and tend to be the most productive as they give the largest range of actions. We're talking here about individual innovations, but indexes have been made to give a glimpse into concentration within different fields of human life. Like the Herfindahl index in enterprises, the Simpson diversity index in ecology and the inverse participation ratio (IPR) in physics.

Take one of the most humble and personal of innovations, the book. History has shown us the wide range of actions books can give to those reading them and beyond. Why is it that such huge change in the world is linked to books? It begins with language being the main way we think and explain what's in our minds and in the outside world. Indeed, almost all innovations or actions which are done for other people likely have written explanations, in the form of advertising, "about us" web pages, instruction booklets, employee work manuals, government constitutions and religious holy books. Why? Writing is the quickest and simplest "summary" of anything man-made, so we go to read about the innovation first before we decide to put more effort into buying, learning or using it to see if it's worth more of our four value factors. Ask any entrepreneur what was the earliest step they took in making their innovation, and most would say that it was written notes. Writing puts the rough thoughts of our minds into order through words. It's been given this monopoly advantage because as each century has passed, more people have been taught how to read and write at school, and these skills are used regularly in a person's life. Due to this, if asked to choose, most people may say it's far easier to master writing than a skill that's completely new to them. Same goes with reading, as we do it over the course of our life we learn to find and seek information which becomes the software that our bodies' hardware runs on. If the type of software we use changes, the actions of our hardware change with it.

Books are like online software updates, but instead fix and improve the mental computer in our skull. Books also can hold *a very large number of innovations* compared to other innovations. The number of sentences in an average sized book may total around 10,000 and each can be read and acted on. Like the parts which make a car, sentences and their words make up the book, and each sentence alone is not as productive until mixed with others to create context and explanation. Due to such density of innovation inside a book, just a random boring sentence for one reader can be life changing for another. Writing a book lets us *select from and combine millions of words* to describe almost any action and innovation we see in reality. Rulers like Caesar and Napoleon saw this, saying that the written word has greater impact in the long-run and is more practical for everyday people than the victories they had on the battlefield.[159]

The mistake many make is they lazily give their minds lower quality software updates. Instead of an hour reading a book that can teach them a new skill, they watch a TV documentary on it instead. In that hour, the average reader may cover 40 pages of the book, around 20,000 words, while they're likely to hear only around 1000 words in the entire documentary. Same goes for audio and podcasts and other methods of learning. The book stands apart as most productive, as its innovation concentration gives deeper explanations than any other method can. Why? More words equals more combinations in your mind, which results in you scribbling or typing more ideas for research or later thought. It also is the innovation that lets us get the closest, most intimate look into another person's mind. To know what makes them tick. Photos can't do that, neither can videos. None can get into the detail that written words do.

This complexity continues when we look at a Boeing 747, which is said to be one of the most complicated innovations ever made. It's so complex that, unlike a car mechanic, *there is no one person who can know all the details of how it works*. Not the pilot, nor factory floor manager or the thousands who work on putting it together. Just understanding how one area of the plane works takes years of study, which is not surprising when you find out there are over 6 million parts, each one an innovation by itself with its own history.

The internet is a more visible example of innovation concentration, a network of ever growing websites, each giving you a different set of actions. With it you may have more actions to choose from at your fingertips than from any other innovation in history. The most productive websites, and usually the most valuable, concentrate other innovations, like friends, websites, products, comments and reviews inside of them. Facebook, Google and YouTube are the most visible examples of this.

The ability of innovations to combine, collect, and concentrate is the *difference between some nations being developed and others still developing*. We see this in cities which concentrate more people, enterprises and innovations into a smaller space than a country town could. This brings together more jobs, population growth, and off course, innovation.

As explored earlier, the most powerful example of innovation concentration is government. Their departments control the rules of the game, *the laws by which nearly all the innovations of a society must play by or risk being banned, taken to court or made illegal.* In our earlier example, we showed historical selection at work with everyday mobile phones, as it is at work with all other innovations every moment. Thomas S. Kuhn touches on this in *The Structure of Scientific Revolutions,* as does philosopher G.W. Hegel, author of *Phenomenology of Spirit,* in what's been called the *dialectic.* Which showed how new ideas come up in the mind, the position (original idea), opposition (competing idea) and composition (mixing both makes a new idea). We've aimed for a method for the physical world with our three C's, combination, collection, and concentration. For simplicity, we'll call it *trilectic,* tri for its 3 parts. Below is a simple example of it, and it can be found in nearly all innovations, from phones, computers, enterprises, government policies and even the rise and fall of nations if one looks deep enough. Yes, that's pretty ambitious, so to be clear *it's more of a guide for possible, not exact, predictions.* The problem with exact prediction is it can easily morph into a self-fulfilling prophecy, when believers of it work to turn it into reality and make up facts to prove it true even when it isn't.

Below we take Standard Oil, which was broken up in 1911 by the U.S. government for being a monopoly. It was chopped up into smaller companies which over time, like magnets, collected again and then concentrated into a few large companies. History shows that eventually, like in 1911, the large concentrated companies will face an event which will repeat the process that formed them.[160]

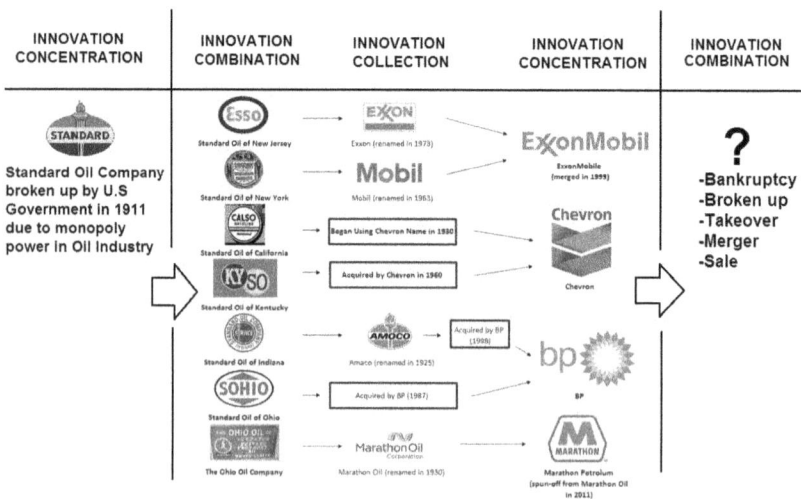

The trilectic occurs with every innovation and impacts other innovations on the smallest and largest levels. Each company, if its innovations survive long enough, may have near-death experiences. News Corporation almost did in the 1990s, as did Ford in the 2000s as described in *American Icon*. History can now be seen for what it is: a bunch of loops which, like the universe, forever interlink and grow larger. Standard Oil above may seem like a lone example, but its break up affected many innovations and people. We can discover more by how good our questions are. How many oil workers lost their jobs? Did any laws change to affect companies into the future? Did the breakup affect the price of oil? Did car owners have to pay more or less to fill up their cars? If we can draw a causal loop of history, like the example below, we can then connect each historical event to the other. Each event or future event can next try to be answered by filtering it through the 3 methods in our book as seen below. Historical selection, the value test and the trilectic 3 C's can now all finally be combined to get us closer to an answer. All of history can be said to be similar to this, *interconnected in a web, not just one line of cause and effect but many, stretching out and growing wider.* Each event within the process can be explored to discover how it affects the others, and so we may possibly get closer to knowing where it's taking us. As a hypothetical example, the illustration below may give insight into why oil companies started merging, as the breakup hurt their reputations, salespeople in each company had a harder time making profitable sales to larger clients like before.

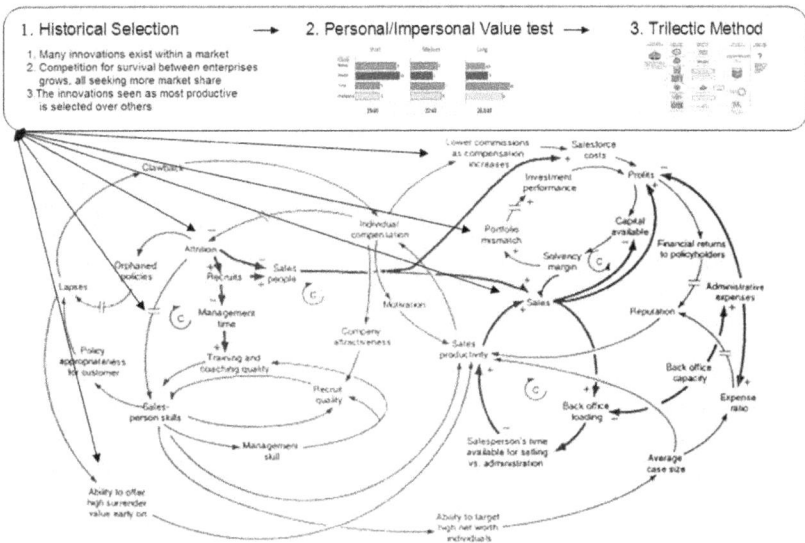

Source: U.S. Department of Energy's Introduction to System Dynamics. Public Domain

What the above diagram shows us clearly is that the more innovations are involved, the more explanations there will be for why some event happened. There are many theories for the causes of the Fall of Rome, this is only because Rome had collected within it so many innovations during its existence.

Compare this to the fall of a primitive tribe in the Amazon. The tribe has only a few innovations, like hunting tools, some rituals, and a few religious beliefs. It's hard to disagree that the fewer innovations, the less likely there will be complex explanations for why the tribe collapsed. We can see more clearly the root causes of events in the tribe than we can in Rome.

If you've read closely up till now you may have seen a trend, that in the last few centuries entrepreneurs have made ever more innovations that have slowly taken up the tasks we once needed to do by hand. Governments can ban innovations, *but it's harder to do that to innovations which boost productivity and life expectancy for the people,* as we saw with the British government penalizing workers who broke machines in the 1800s. But government can also do the opposite and help all people learn the skill to innovate so no one need be a victim of change but in control of it. It may soon be clear that they will have no choice but to do so or risk falling behind like Rome did, or worse risking collapse. Like our microscopic cells that move away from danger, humans will always, when they can, move to another country which has the most productive innovations.

Chapter Summary

\#   **Historical innovation combination:**

1.   Actions – movement of the human body
2.   Innovation – that help us reach a result and so lead to action
3.   Entrepreneur – maker of the innovations
4.   Value – how innovations are chosen, through the Time, Money, Health, Intelligence factors
5.   Productivity – measure of the change in value factors as seen in our actions

\#   **Innovation combination leads to a struggle among innovations which is solved by historical selection:**

1.   Many innovations exist within a market
2.   Competition for survival among enterprises grows, all seeking more market share
3.   The innovation seen as most productive by adopters is selected over others

\#   **Features of the innovation as the unit of history/cultural evolution:**

1.   Innovations are able to be copied
2.   Innovations grow branches like a family tree
3.   Innovations are both part of larger innovations and can be broken down into smaller innovations

\#   **Ground rules of innovational historiography:**

1.   Time periods – begin and end when a more productive innovation starts to spread. If it later emerges to have overtaken its rival innovation in market share, the date of its spread marks the start of a new turning point.
2.   Context – a revolution in one country does not mean revolutions are happening the world over. Besides turning points, which are based on factual physical evidence of innovations, most labels or generalizations should be country specific.

3. Repeatable use – books are what people repeatedly used, but it was the printing press that made the books. All productive innovations make or influence innovations that people then use repeatedly.

\#   **History can be seen through its turning points with are driven by the most productive innovations.**

1st Turning Point – Language 70,000 BC: Spoken words.
2nd Turning Point – Agriculture 10,000 BC: Seeds and animals.
3rd Turning Point – Writing 3000 BC: Written symbols.
4th Turning Point – Printing 1439: Printed page.
5th Turning Point – Steam 1775: Factories and machines.
6th Turning Point – Computation 1948: Bit (computerized data).

\#   **After innovations combine (x), they collect and concentrate. The trilectic method is our name for this.**

\#   **Innovation collection (+) is when combination grows with more innovations being released and reaching people, it mostly leads to more productivity.**

\#   **Innovation concentration (^{2}) is when innovations bunch together within another innovation. The concentration gives more actions to those using it.**

CHAPTER SEVEN

The Future Spread of the Meaning of Life

"Only machines, not nerves and muscles, can increase men's output."[1]
Thomas Edison

"If it were desired to reduce a man to nothing – to punish him atrociously – it would be necessary to give to his work a character of complete uselessness."[2]
Fyodor Dostoyevsky (author of *Crime and Punishment*)

In 1930, John Maynard Keynes wrote an essay titled, *Economic Possibilities for our Grandchildren*. He wrote that its argument would be, "…startling to the imagination the longer you think about it." He predicted that soon, agriculture, mining, and manufacturing will be done with a "quarter of the human action to which we have been accustomed," leading to "technological unemployment," where innovations will suck work away from humans while getting the same or better results. This event, he wrote, would solve *the economic problem, which is that we humans have unlimited wants and limited innovations.* Scarcity is another word for it, but as we've seen, scarcity is found both in nature and in the human world. What our friend Keynes didn't provide was a rulebook showing what the most important goals are that our limited innovations should be used for. We've tried to help him out in this book, by exploring the meaning of life and explaining what results we should all try to seek. If Keynes's future is accurate then humans may escape the trap of struggling to survive, as innovations may bury the need to work. Then the sins of rent-seeking actions may vanish and we can stop pretending that "fair is foul, and foul is fair." You may think Keynes was joking? He wasn't. By around 2030, he thought this will start to happen.[3]

Like most predictions, the dates he gave are estimates. Keynes wrote that the changes would not come fast, but slowly. Yet this begs the question of how all this will come about? He did not go into the details, so we will below. Predictions about such large-scale events will almost always be inaccurate, as changes happen rapidly and no one has all information at any one time. Yet how can we figure out concepts, theories, and laws if we don't dare predict and test what may happen? As Karl Popper writes in *The Logic of Scientific Discovery,* "Bold ideas, unjustified anticipations, and speculative thought are our only means for interpreting nature."[4] As weak as it sounds, *we need to make "guesses" in order to guide ourselves toward the truth.*

Turning Point 7
The Automation of Work

Replacing Human Actions 2017–

Life Expectancy: 70 Years[5]

Repeatable use = Automation as seen in software, machines, robots etc.

Effect on Free Time = Machines advance to do more complex human actions and slowly replace jobs. Less time working opens more free time for people to make innovations, if given the help to do so.

Unlike other turning points, we have chosen 2017 as a rough starting date. In years to come, the date is likely to change based on the development of the most productive innovation of the period.

Pause for a second and imagine that you're in the t-shirt business. Would you pay $22 an hour to make the same shirts you can make for $4 an hour? The productivity gain of the lower price will save more of the money value factor to let you then drop the sale price of your shirts and grow your market share.

Pt. 13 BUILDINGS OF LOST DREAMS

THE 7th TURNING POINT
Automation replaces most jobs, entrepreneurship becomes one of the last paths left.

When Kate's new enterprise buys her old employer, the CEO finally sees it was the higher productivity of her software innovation that led to his company's defeat.

Let's look at two large companies: China's Foxconn, who among many other products, build iPhones, and Nike, the U.S.-based sports clothing company. Both employ around a million workers each.[6] Both have had bad press for the poor working conditions at their factories which are similar conditions that hundreds of millions of workers face worldwide. Economists say that in the long-run the living standards of these workers will rise, but in the short-run, human rights groups say that these people will die or be injured. Yet as we'll see, *less work related suffering is likely for another reason.* Machines will be doing their jobs. Foxconn at last count was setting up 30,000 "Foxbots" per year and planning to open up robot-only factories.[7] Nike cut 106,000 jobs in favor of automating how it makes its clothing, cutting its workforce by 9.5% since 2012.[8]

As car assembly lines have showed us earlier, machines kick out workers as time passes. Supermarket check-outs, restaurant staff, and even security and prison guards are being replaced by machines. In South Korea, mobile robots patrol each jail cell and scan what each inmate is up to. Microsoft is making security guard robots which monitor corridors of buildings at night for half the price of a human guard.[9.10]

Now place yourself in the shoes of a manager asked to choose whether to buy machines or hire workers. To be fair, let's make the human as good as the machine. What's then the difference? The machine can work non-stop, 24 hours a day, 7 days a week. It will never complain about work conditions or have the need to eat, sleep, or go to the restroom, and it doesn't demand higher pay. A human will mostly work a set number of hours, say 9am – 5pm, with a 1-hour lunch break. That should mean 7 hours of work time, but research shows it's more like 5 hours thanks to distractions, toilet breaks, phone calls, and snacks.[11] Some people also have days where a "bad mood" leaves them unable to think and affects workers near them. Lastly, don't forget that the machine will cost $70,000 up front and just $5,000 each year in maintenance. The worker will cost $50,000 every year on salary, not counting the retirement and tax payments you'd make for them. The dropping cost for machines makes it clear that even in industries where a robot is for now costlier *upfront than a human, it returns the cost in a few years and then the yearly saving grows larger.*

In the past, what has kept the faith of the world's workers and economists is the belief that when jobs are lost to automation, new jobs pop up in other places to hire those fired who are now searching for work. However, this has not been happening as we've seen after well-known brands shut shop. The once market-leading Borders bookstores went bankrupt in 2011, U.S. retail chain Best Buy had to close 50 stores in 2012, as did Allders of Croydon, the third largest department store in the U.K. During July-August of 2012, retail chains were closing 32 stores per day in the U.K.[12]

So, if you get fired from the retail shoe shop because of the online competition, you may think you can get work in the online shoe shop, right? Not so. Why not? Online shops hire *fewer people than retail shops.* Due to the 6th turning point, with computer and internet innovation, many profitable online shops can be run by one person. As we'll see, many jobs are now on the path of the old streetlamp lighter whose flame has long expired.

Workers and their unions will understandably not like the sound of this. They mostly seek laws to protect jobs, just as rent-seeking enterprises protect profits instead of innovating. This will buy a few years of life support for the workers, but unless the enterprise they work for innovates, *competition from the outside will inevitably lead to job loss anyway.* Back in 1900 we see that 41% of all U.S. workers toiled on farms until McCormick's reaper, Deere's steel plow and other innovations spread widely to cut this down to just 2% by 2000.[13] This freed people from farming work to now go and find jobs in cities where more productive innovations were combining in the firms, factories and labs. But what if jobs don't pop up like they did before? What happens to all those losing their jobs? This is the problem happening at different speeds and in many industries across the world today.

As innovations combine faster, it feels to us like we've become the sorcerer that Marx wrote about who is "no longer able to control the powers of the nether world whom he has called up by his spells."[14]

In 1973, Nobel Laureate in Economic Sciences, Wassily Leontief, said, "The role of humans as the most important factor of production is bound to diminish in the same way that the role of horses in agricultural production was first diminished and then eliminated by the launch of tractors."[15] Inevitably, each industry and enterprise goes through the following *3 stages*, which in time, lead to the removal of the human by the machine:

1st – Optimization

It's observed in a car factory that workers make 4 separate trips to fetch each of the 4 wheels for the car they're making. To save time they are now told to take 2 wheels in their hands, making it 2 trips not 4. This small change means the cars can be built slightly faster. Frederick Winslow Taylor's scientific management was popular for finding such small fixes and so squeezing more productivity out of each worker's action. Process improvement is another way to describe this.

2nd – Mechanization

This involves using an innovation to help cut the number of actions a worker takes. Instead of workers attaching car parts by hand, they can now use a joystick to move a machine to do it, which does it faster and with fewer mistakes. This saves time, and fires workers who are not needed anymore.

3rd – Automation

This is when humans are removed and the machine takes over the task. New machines come out with robotic hands and a camera to see the car parts and where to attach them, all without human supervision. It does the job without error. If it needs a repair, it can do it on itself or other machines can assist it. A machine even is made to roam and supervise the work of other machines. Humans are no longer needed.

Nearly all industries and jobs are somewhere in or between these 3 stages. The *trouble is that the jobs employing the most people in many nations sit at the second step, mechanization*, which soon will reach the third step of automation, leading to *mass job losses*.

In the early days, most innovations were seen as helping workers do things better than before. Stockbrokers had software letting them mechanize the buying and selling of stocks in a click using an internet connection, rather than shouting their mouths dry on a crazed trading floor. Today automation has spread as anyone can buy and sell stocks online without speaking to a broker. With this, fees have dropped heavily, saving money for investors, but not saving jobs. New York City had a one-third drop in security dealers from 2000 to 2013, even though many Wall Street firms had record sized profits in that time.[16]

> **Q.   What innovation/s if removed will make your work
>   difficult to do?**
>
> **A.**

Mechanization has for many years helped those in service jobs, like gardeners and carpet cleaners do their work better. But now those machines are much cheaper and simpler so that customers have bought lawnmowers and vacuum cleaners to do it themselves. Yes, these services still exist as some people don't want to do it themselves and think they have no choice but to hire people, but soon they'll be hiring machines. We're already seeing floor-cleaning, garden landscaping, window wiping, pool filtering, and lawn mowing robots being made and they are becoming more human-like every year.[17]

The internet has sped this up, putting seemingly untouchable jobs from yoga, karate, and other teachings in danger with online classes becoming more personalized with cameras. Instructors can use group chat software to answer questions from clients worldwide. Facial movement software using a camera is becoming better at estimating what you're thinking to see if you're under-standing what you're learning so to best be able to educate you.[18] Children are being taught entire school subjects with it, and later the software may possibly replace teachers.

In 2012, Amazon.com, which has some of the largest fulfillment centers, a few the size of 28 American football fields combined, bought Kiva Systems, a robotics company. Its robots will replace the human workforce in these centers. This will further drop already low prices on the Amazon website. Just like the car assembly line showed us, human workers are slowly vanishing thanks to robots like Baxter, which *with its camera records and remembers how to do new tasks that you show it.*[19,20]

In hospitals, TUG robots made by the company Aethon are now picking up dirty dishes and sheets from patients, letting nurses spend more time giving care to sicker patients.[21] Have you ever feared or had a needle not find your vein when giving blood? A new machine can make a scan of the arm, and find the vein within millimeters before painlessly taking blood with no sight of a needle.[22]

Today, some mainstream economists are starting to wake up to what's going on. Nobel Laureate Paul Krugman, wrote, "Not enough people (me included!) have looked up to notice that things have changed" and admitted, "There's no question that in some high-profile industries, technology is displacing workers of all, or almost all, kinds."[23] Some books have been warning of this for some time. In *The Lights in the Tunnel,* software executive Martin Ford writes, "At some point in the future—it might be many years or decades from now—machines will be able to do the jobs of a large percentage of the 'average' people in our population, and these people will not be able to find new jobs."[24]

Not too long ago, the idea of a self driving car seemed insane. Yet, Google has already been able to change a Toyota Prius to drive without a human. Journalist Henry Blodget, profiled in *The Signal and the Noise* by Nate Silver, echoes the need for productivity over profit, "Google is looking long-term to make the innovations of the future than the quick buck in the present."[25]

The U.S. states of Florida, Nevada, and California were the first in the world to pass laws to legalize autonomous driving, with many national governments today updating their laws.[26] The driverless car can now help in a unrelated area, by removing unrealistic academic thought experiments like the bus driver example back in our first chapter. Already, mining enterprises like Rio Tinto use trucks driven by software not humans.[27] Some estimate that by 2040, 75% of cars on the road will be computer controlled.[28]

It's hoped this will lead to fewer accidents and deaths as the software will *drive according to rules it cannot break compared to the errors of human drivers.* Using the GPS navigation system, driverless cars take the best roads, saving petrol, and polluting less.

We can picture a future where the nearly 1 billion cars on earth have been slowly swapped *out for a 24/7 self-driving taxi service.* A car wouldn't be owned but booked online to pick you up where and when you needed it.

Taxi, bus, and delivery drivers would lose their jobs as would many auto insurance agents who would have fewer human drivers to insure. Instead of being a victim of this change, workers in those industries can start their own enterprises now to make and spread these innovations before others.

The outdated field of law is seeing its own automation. Paralegal jobs once thought to be safe are being lost to software programs, like Clearwell, which in one case was used by law firm DLA Piper to search through half a million documents before a one-week deadline. To be exact, the software checked 570,000 documents in just 2 days and found 307 documents important to the court case. Mike Lynch, the co-founder of autonomy.com, another such software enterprise, says that one lawyer with software can now replace a workload which once needed 500 lawyers to complete.[29]

The military have been making and relying more on remote-controlled drones to fire at the enemy instead of putting soldiers on the ground. The number of bomb destroying robots has jumped in use in conflicts in Iraq and Afghanistan.[30] Wars in the future may be fought and won by remote control, with each country's best *automated military robots fighting it out, leading to less human life put at risk.*

All the above "could" happen you may think, but your question may be, "But a computer won't ever replace a firefighter, construction worker or the police? These jobs are too complex and only a human can do them!" The same question was also asked two centuries ago when people were scared that there'd be no food with so few humans farming. Back then it seemed crazy to think that jobs on which human survival depends would be given to machines. Today in the construction industry, a robot named SAM is moving jobs into stage 2 mechanization. SAM is replacing bricklaying jobs, laying bricks at a faster rate than any human could.[31] Just like Jules Verne's predictions turned out to be true we'll have to wait and see if some of what's found in movie series like the *Terminator* and *Robocop* will become reality.

Kevin Kelly, author of *What Technology Wants*, predicts that, before the end of this century, 70% of today's entire workforce will be automated.[32] A recent study from Oxford University by Frey and Osborne estimated that 47% of all jobs in the U.S. and 35% of jobs in the U.K. are at risk of automation in the coming years. The Bank of England in its own study agreed, writing that up to 15 million U.K. jobs could be wiped out. The Oxford researchers even go further to say that, "It is largely already techno-logically possible to automate almost any task, provided that sufficient amounts of data are gathered for pattern recognition."[33]

They list the below jobs as having the highest risk of being lost. Does your job pop up here?

1. Telemarketers 2. Title examiners, abstractors, and searchers 3. Hand sewers 4. Mathematical technicians 5. Insurance underwriters 6. Watch repairers 7. Cargo and freight agents 8. Tax return preparers 9. Photographic process workers and processing machine operators 10. New accounts clerks 11. Librarians 12. Data entry clerks. 13. Timing device assemblers and adjusters. 14.Insurance claims and policy processing clerks 15. Brokerage clerks 16. Order clerks 17. Loan officers 18. Auto insurance appraisers 19. Umpires, referees, and other sports officials.

As our turning points showed, time periods become shorter as innovation combination grows. But as the rules of the game are set by government, it may still be a few decades or a hundred years until automation threatens most of the workforce. We don't want to see innovations banned like we saw done by rulers fearing revolution, but governments today may fall into this trap when facing angry unemployed workers who won't vote for them unless machines are made illegal. To prevent this tragedy, governments should start preparing now for this future. We'll soon show how this can be done.

You're likely skeptical that so large a change can happen so quickly. What if it were to take a few hundred years? Would this make it more realistic for you? We can't truly say that such changes will *"never" happen as we can't predict the future nor is it likely we'll be alive to see if it does or doesn't happen*. Unless a major disaster wipes humanity out in one go, the words of former Federal Reserve Chairman and author of *The Courage to Act*, Ben Bernanke, will still ring true, "A safe prediction, I think, is that human innovation and creativity will continue; it is part of our very nature. Another prediction, just as safe, is that people will nevertheless continue to forecast the end of innovation."[34]

Where there's Smoke, there's Fire

We can dream all we want, but do the numbers agree with what we've just talked about? Focus here is on the United States, as it's for now the most advanced economy and a picture of what other nations are on path to soon achieve. It also has many statistics for us to dig into. Since the recession of 2007–2009 ended, "real" (inflation adjusted) spending on equipment and software has risen by 26% but wages have stayed mostly the same. Also, fewer workers are being hired than before. As economists Erik Brynjolfsson and Andrew McAfee, authors of the book, *Race Against the Machine,* show, even with a recession, recent corporate profits in the U.S. were a huge 23.8% of total gross domestic income, an all-time record. Wages and benefits to workers, however, were at a 50-year low.[35] Median (average) incomes aren't growing like GDP is, but are instead declining. The shock of the recession led companies to cut costs, leading them to seek advanced software to replace the expensive workers they were firing. Similar trends are seen in other developed nations beside the U.S.

Source: Authors' analysis of Current Population Survey Annual Social and Economic Supplement Historical Income Tables (Table F-5) and Bureau of Labor Statistics, Productivity – Major Sector Productivity and Costs Database (2012)

At the same time, productivity has also jumped high in these nations. This has confused economists, who now see that for every 1% jump in productivity there has been a drop in employment by 0.54%. That's 75% more people unemployed compared to the same productivity point rise in the 1960's which used to correlate to only a 0.07% drop in employment.[36,38]

Job growth declined for the first time in living memory, as seen above in the decade after 2000 even though over that same period the population grew by over 27 million people from immigrants to new births. Traditional economics would say that this is not meant to happen. Yes, workers become more productive over time by mastering their jobs, but that should not slow job growth. So, what are we missing here? The answer may be automation, which is spreading faster than new jobs can pop up to hire the unemployed people it leaves behind. As productive innovations like machines and software eat the shrinking pie of jobs out there, we see more workers *fighting for the few jobs left*. Managers now have more power to pay workers less as there is a hungry pack of unemployed workers scratching at the door to fill the job. This could explain why wages growth has been dropping. This is *a warning sign to all the children in school*, who are being fed the old idea that getting into college will answer all their prayers.

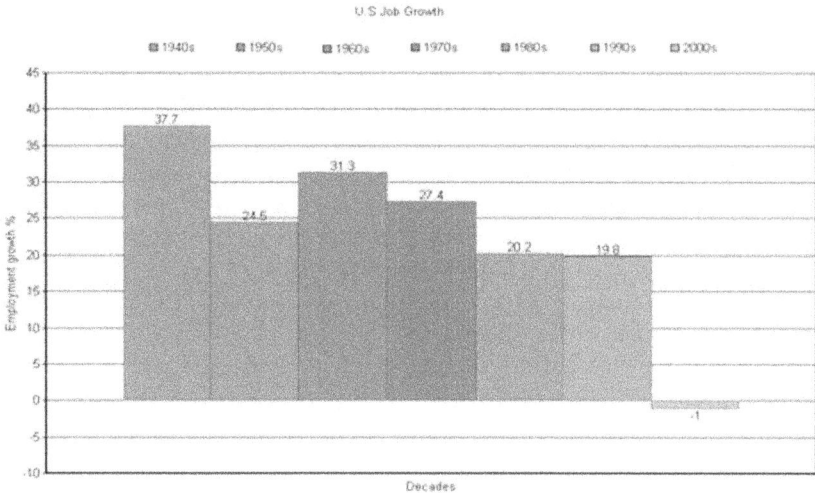

U.S. Job Growth
Source: Economic Policy Institute, Creative Commons Attribution License

The dream of getting a high paying job thanks to a paper degree needs to be replaced with the pursuit of purpose, as speaker and co-author of *The Element* and *Creative Schools* Sir Ken Robinson has said for decades. Robinson says that schools should stop teaching students to just remember stuff, but instead help them find and make an innovation that the student is passionate about.[39] Education's main goal should be to teach knowledge and show how it can help each student make their innovation be as valuable as possible to others. Sure, basic skills like reading and writing help a child in the real world, but other skills like algebra or literary theme analysis are less useful, unless we aim to become mathematicians or study poems, where guessing what the poet meant without evidence is a timeless timewaste. It doesn't help that textbooks of most subjects that students use are old and out of date. A simple Google search on almost any topic in school will show recent studies and experiments with information that challenges decades old textbooks used in school.

As Paul Krugman asks, "What will happen to us if, like so many students, we go deep into debt to acquire the skills we're told we need, only to learn that the economy no longer wants those skills? Education, then, is no longer the answer to rising inequality, if it ever was."[40] Research done by Frey and Osborne has shown that automation has pushed some high-skilled workers down the ladder into middle skilled jobs. Which then pushes middle skilled workers into low skilled jobs, pushing low-skilled workers into unemployment.[41] A related trend is that part-time and casual work has been growing for a number of years in many of the developed nations.[42,43] Funny then that with all the automation, the same colleges that sell themselves as giving keys to all of life's doors are automating their education to be made free online. Some of the same lectures that students are paying around $100,000 to attend as part of their degree are now videos for all to watch. This gives disadvantaged people the world over *a chance to learn what they may never be able to afford*. Universities like Berkeley and Yale have begun giving online introductory courses, as has Massachusetts Institute of Technology (M.I.T), which long ago created its Open Educations Resources (OER) initiative.[44] If education continues to be offered free like this, the value from going to college will come mostly from the network of friends the students may gain for later life.

Permanent Unemployment

Worryingly, the three largest job groups employing the most people in the entire U.S. economy from May 2014 are now moving into the 3rd step of automation.[45] We've so far given numbers and patterns, now let's check out what's happening on the ground.

Retail Salespersons: 4.6 Million employed

A retail salesperson can only exist if retail stores survive the attack from the productive innovations of online retail. Is it likely? More retail shops are seeing they cannot match the cheaper, limitless, and easy to search products offered on websites like Amazon.com, eBay.com, Overstock.com, and others. Chris Anderson, author of *Free* and *Makers* called this the *long tail* effect and wrote a book of the same name, where giving customers more products to choose from leads to more purchases. Take U.S. retail giant Wal-Mart which has limited shelf space. To get the most profit they shelf the top 100 best-selling music albums, ignoring the hundreds of thousands of others, which will likely sell a lot less. Amazon.com, on the other hand, can list all the millions of albums in existence which leads to more total sales than Wal-Mart will ever make with their top 100.

The same long tail effect is seen in all other online businesses, which is pushing online sales *to grow faster than physical sales every year for each country with decent internet access.* As physical store sales drop, job losses increase for retail salespeople.[46] From 2012 to today, the U.S. has seen many double-digit store closures of brand names like Sears Roebuck, The Gap, Abercrombie & Fitch, and Macy's. The bankrupt Blockbuster video chain set the example other video chains around the world are following, closing down as websites like netflix.com and DVD kiosks steal customers away.[47,48] Today many customers don't go shopping, but go to research and test products they'll later search and buy online at a lower price.

Cashiers: 3.4 Million Employed

On some of your shopping trips you might have already seen computer-run self-checkout machines. More supermarket checkouts worldwide are being automated like this, removing cashier workers along the way. Self-checkout scanners have popped up in Wal-Mart, CVS, Fresh and Easy, Kmart, Target and others. Fast food giant McDonald's is adding touch screen checkouts, as have restaurants like Chili's, Applebee's and thousands more.[49] Libraries in many nations already have or are adding self-checkout machines for books and creating digital book collections so members can read from home. Librarians will soon have little to do. Some enterprises are even skipping the cost of self-checkout machines by making mobile apps so customers can buy and then pick up items later.

General Office Clerks: 2.8 Million Employed

In the 1970s, the general office clerk was the first and largest job category before software came and sucked many of its jobs away, today it's moved down to 3rd place.[50] Clerking is mostly data entry work, typing into a computer. Its jobs are spread in all areas, from government, banking, healthcare, insurance and many others, but software can now outperform human clerks. Programs now do in a few clicks what it takes many clerks hours or days to do. This enterprise software has spread into many job areas like payment processing, online product lists, billing and invoicing, and electronic data storage. Much like we explored with the loss of paralegal jobs, one person can now do the work of many. Unsurprising then that since 2009 the U.S. saw more than 300,000 office and admin jobs vanish.

Travel agents competing against easy-to-use travel booking websites have seen a 14% drop in jobs since 2007. Proofreading, a once vital job in the publishing industry, has shrunk by 31% due to the advancing online software that now does a decent proofread.[51,52] Even HR, who are tasked with hiring people to fill jobs at their own company are seeing software replace them. With online tests scoring how suitable job applicants are, Xerox and other large companies now hire customer call center workers by using such software.[53]

Checking the above job categories now shows us a clearer picture for why wages are not growing. Years ago, these jobs paid enough to be seen as "middle-wage" jobs, but since automation, the wages have been dropping. *Union power, like their member base, has also been shrinking as fewer jobs are available in industries they protect.* As BLS economist Shawn Sprague points out, the value of goods and services made by American businesses grew from 1998 to 2013 by US$3.5 trillion. In 1998, the work hours equaled 194 billion, in 2013 they also equaled the *same 194 billion*. More was done with less, thanks to productive innovations, but this is not a good sign for jobs, as the U.S. population grew by 40 million people during that period. More people are competing for the same limited work hours, while growth and productivity continues to increase. Unless changes are made, the standard of living of the middle class that these jobs employ will soon fall.[54.55]

The problems don't stop there. The automation we saw in the top 3 job groups above *is also seen in the other 7 job groups rounding out the top 10,* which includes food preparation work, nurses, waiters/waitresses, and customer service reps. Not good when all together the top 10 jobs employ around 21% of all workers in the U.S. Machines for Food preparation are taking just 10 seconds to make a burger. Now 360 burgers can be made in an hour vs. a person who may only get close to 100. Japan's Kura sushi chain of nearly 300+ restaurants has robots making sushi with conveyor belts replacing waiters, sinking the price of a sushi plate way below their competitors to just 100 yen or near $1 U.S.[56] Software can now answer and redirect phone calls, eliminating customer service reps, thanks to IBM Watson software, the same that beat chess grandmasters and the champions of TV game shows like *Jeopardy.* Without much space to explore further, we will wrap up here with a final point. It's not just the above top 10 jobs at risk, but dozens more in the top 100 that are in danger of automation.

Q.   In which of the three stages is your job in right now?

A.

Legal Slavery and the Elimination of Alienation

Over 100 years ago, Thomas Edison wrote some thoughts about automation, "At first the working people will suffer, but in the end, they will be benefited." He went on to say, "The machine has been the human being's most effective means of escape from bondage. Too many people, even now, remain bond slaves to laborious hand processes." The machines, to him, were the "greatest emancipators," and he finished with a prediction. "I will go further and say that human slavery will not have been fully abolished until every task now accomplished by human hands is turned out by some machine."[57] Sounds harsh to compare work to slavery, right? Yet if we look at reality, we see that humans are not slaves to a master who owns them, but to the wages they work for. People may freely choose which job to jump to next, *but jump they must, as they need money to survive.* This link between work and slavery has long been known. The Latin *labor* means toil or drudgery, while the French *travail* comes from the word tripalium, the ancient Roman tool of torture made of three sticks. In Slavic, the commonly used word for work "*rabota*" comes from the root word *rab,* meaning "slave." The word "robot" comes from the same slavic origin, though it's likely to do the opposite, and free us from work.[58]

The typical English definition of "work" is: "A person in the service of another... where the employer has the power or right to control and direct the employee in how the work is to be performed." Seth Godin, author of *Tribes, The Linchpin* and *The Dip* says it simply, "The job is what you do when you are told what to do."[59,60] It's why work for many seems like "wage slavery" as most workers' actions are repetitive, sometimes boring, and so are prime targets for automation.[61]

Repetition means the workers' actions revolve around using unproductive or counterproductive innovations to do what their boss tells them to. While an entrepreneur's actions mostly revolve around using *productive innovations, which are mostly creative.* Such actions cannot easily be *repeated* by others or automated by machines. By creatively using and making productive innovations, an entrepreneur's actions move away from the alienated actions of workers chained to wage slavery. It's the creative vs. the repetitive as creative work is likely to survive while repetitive work is eaten by automation. As Frey and Osborne point out, "For workers to win the race, however, they will have to acquire creative and social skills."[62]

Almost everyone has faced wage slavery at some point in life. It lets us earn money to buy the innovations that we use. Yet as we now see, it's not the most productive or most meaningful way for us to live life. In sacrificing our creativity by obeying the orders of a boss, we are continuing a modern example of what slaves did in the past, minus the harsh conditions.

Earning money from unsatisfying work has a long history. Roman statesman Cicero wrote in the first century BC, "Whoever gives his labor for money sells himself and puts himself in the tank of slaves."[63] Noam Chomsky, professor and author of *Manufacturing Consent* and *Who Rules the World*, sees that there is no moral difference between ownership slavery and wage slavery.[64] As the *worker's life becomes working time*. And time, we must not forget, isn't what's on the clock, it is life, human life, ticking down to eventual death. As Jen showed us in the introduction, work takes up 33% or more of our entire lives. We think we're making a living, but it's a dying. A lifetime can be wasted if we have little control of what we're working on, with decades of effort put into work which can be easily destroyed by a new boss. As Von Humboldt, a naturalist whose life is explored in *The Invention of Nature* by Andrea Wulf, writes, "Whatever does not spring from a man's free choice, or is only the result of instruction and guidance, does not enter into his very nature, he does not perform it with truly human energies."[65] This may be why the highest-polled reason for employees wasting time at work, is the "lack of satisfaction" they get from it.[66]

Very few workers can be said to have creativity and control of their work. Instead, they see it as a repetitive, soul-crushing routine, day in and out. It's something they have to do, not want to do. Like a parasite sucking blood, work sucks away life. Workers transform into payroll numbers, instead of flesh and bone, and in the worst cases as Marx wrote, "A working animal as a beast reduced to the strictest bodily needs."[67] This creates a bleeding hole in which the worker's creative juices slowly drip away, leaving them a lifeless shadow of the energetic and curious child they once were. To regain some sense of meaning they are tricked to lose their souls by living the motto, "Gain wealth, forgetting all but self." Their forced meaning is found in splashy things which need more money to buy and more life time to sacrifice. What is bought is the *uncreative motions* of life, the dining, the holidaying, the shagging, the entertainment, which for all its momentary excitement, doesn't create anything that lasts, for even the memories of it all die with death. Work becomes a "quiet desperation," in the words of Henry David Thoreau, author of *Walden*, *Walking*, and *Civil Disobedience* because people end up choosing "unhappiness over uncertainty," to quote Tim Ferriss, author of *The 4-Hour Work Week*.[68]

Surely not all jobs are like this? Indeed, if you remember the roles of the entrepreneur we explored earlier you'd be right, but too few jobs are entrepreneurial. Say you're working in a company's reception, rather than in the design room where the innovations the company's customers buy and use are made. In reception, you severely cut the number of people you can create value for as the value meter showed us earlier. You're also doing uncreative and repetitive actions—answering and redirecting calls—which can already be done by machines. Once reception software is cheap and good enough, your boss will have little choice but to fire you. "Monotony is the mother of boredom," so the ancient saying goes. Soon, it will be the mother of unemployment also.

Some will say that although it is repetitive, they don't see work as being so bad, forgetting how much their upbringing led to this thinking. Sadly, some workers bet their future on their boss, praying they'll get a promotion someday, much like a person who prays to God to stop them drowning rather than grabbing the boat trying to help them. These workers miss out on their entrepreneurial chance in a world where we have only so many tomorrows left to live.

Earlier we talked about "alienation," for most of us are unable to connect with all the people we pass by daily. We also alienate ourselves on the inside by not seeking our creative potential and the meaning of life, but some say *we should just think away such negative thoughts* about work. Ed Deiner, author of *Happiness: Unlocking the Secrets of Psychological Wealth* writes, "That is, in part, the product of just the way you think about your work. It doesn't matter if you're a lawyer or a bus driver, if you're blue collar or white collar." Yes, it does matter. We must stop being afraid to face the truth. That no amount of self-help and positive thinking will remove the reality that your job lacks creativity and can't make a difference for many people. If your job can't help you seek the meaning of life, you have little to no chance to impact people living now or after your gone.

People are afraid of the pain that such facts lead to, so they lie to themselves day in and out, even though deep inside they know it's all a fraud. As Jenny Lawson shows in her book *Furiously Happy*, juggling mind tricks in our head won't change the reality of the world. Our earlier comparison of Bill Gates and Joe showed how obvious this is.

Companies can and will try hiding this truth by wasting money on employee-bonding programs, free food, and other work bonuses, but it won't ever remove the root problem—that work under anyone is a dependency. "Labor is in its very being an oppressive, inhumane, and antisocial activity," Marx wrote.[69] Take smiling as the clearest example, workers need to do it to please the boss who says it will make the customers happy to shop again. The smile is forced, its fake, it's a fraud. As the meaning of life is unable to be seen by the worker in the actions of the job their told to do.

Gallup and Ipsos-Reid polls have repeatedly asked the question, "Do you enjoy your work so much that you have a hard time putting it aside?" In 1951, 51% said, "Yes." In 1988, it was 33%, and in 2001, it was just 23%. A recent Gallup poll for 2012 – 2013, estimated that only 13% of employees worldwide are "engaged in their jobs."[70]

As automation eats more jobs, 13% may be a good estimate of the worldwide percentage of those who are doing creative, not repetitive, work.

If money is needed to survive, this will understandably hold people back from seeking the meaning of life. Making an innovation while working is tough, but many known and unknown entrepreneurs have done just that. Losing a job when there are bills to pay and a family to feed is not something anyone wants. Yet this question will soon be out of anyone's control when their jobs are eaten by automation. The food lines will become a reality for hundreds of millions if they don't start now to grow their entrepreneurial skills to be able to make an innovation before they're fired. Yes, even 30 minutes of learning per day can help. Today's enterprises can also help their own survival and that of their workers by giving them free time to let new innovations be born.

We forget that many entrepreneurs got their start by working for others. At the end of this book we give some tips for how to balance earning a living and making your innovation on the side. Thomas Watson Sr. worked for NCR (National Cash Register) before co-founding IBM, Einstein worked for the Swiss Patent Office when he made his theory of relativity, and Steve Jobs worked at the gaming company Atari. Online payment company PayPal has famously employed many who've gone on to make productive innovations with enterprises like Tesla Motors and SpaceX (Elon Musk), LinkedIn (Reid Hoffman), YouTube (Chad Hurley, Steve Chen, Jawed Karim), Slide (Max Levchin), Yelp (Jeremy Stoppelman), and Peter Thiel, one of the first investors of Facebook. PayPal missed the chance of launching a program where without needing to leave, those mentioned above, *could make those very enterprises within, and with the help of PayPal itself.* Many companies are already doing such programs and it makes further sense when you see that the value of some companies comes mostly from a shareholding they own of more valuable companies. Like much of Yahoo's market value which was based on the shares it owned in the Chinese company, alibaba.com, co-founded by Jack Ma, and profiled in *Alibaba* by Duncan Clark.[71]

Any enterprise should try to see how much hidden creativity is locked in their workforce. By mentoring their employees as *"entrepreneurs in training,"* instead of sucking their creativity with repetition, they can make a place where productive innovations can be made. One day every fortnight may be a good start to give workers free time to make their own projects. Other changes can help too, for instance, a portion of wages can be linked to results achieved and not to time worked. Bonuses need not just be money, but can be paid days to work from home on their project.

The Last Job Standing

According to former World Chess Champion Garry Kasparov, "the end of mankind" happened in 1997 when he lost a chess series against IBM's Deep Blue computer.[72] For us, the start of mankind is when we stop doing repetitive actions.

The meaning of life can't be forced, yet with automation leaving behind fewer jobs, *there will soon be little option left for most people.* Entrepreneurship will become the largest and most vital occupation in the future, but with most people not knowing about entrepreneurship, the growing number of unemployed in food lines may overflow into a Rome-like collapse from the invasion of automation.

Back in the industrial revolution which brought us steam and electricity, we passed our physical strength to engines. We later passed on our mental strength of calculation and memory to computation. Now we are passing on creative strength. Today's computers can design advertising for marketing campaigns, create abstract artwork, and even write newspaper articles. The quality is good enough that when it's shown to most people *they think it was made by humans.* One such innovation, named Quill, is software that searches information online and writes up reports for governments and financial companies. It's already putting data analysts out of work with hundreds of thousands likely to soon get termination slips[73] If a job has patterns, software will eventually learn them to do the work.

So far, machines are unable to think up and make productive innovations by themselves, like the steam engine, mobile/cell phone, or the airplane. We don't yet have an army of robots made in our image and with our innovation combining mental power.

To mix innovations and then spread them to the world is the protected area of humanity, for now. It's *our last stronghold* against the invading army of machines. Remember all those times when you had an "aha" moment? You mixed together innovations in those moments to come up with something better than before. This is an example of abduction, the third kind of logic. The others are deductive (holy books give the rules by which we live, but we don't test them) and inductive (we test the holy books rules to see which work and are best to live by). Entrepreneurs instead estimate how the future world may use their innovation, and they then think backwards to test if people today will begin using it.

Code Mutation & the Coming Subspecies of Humanity

Machines will only be fully creative if they are *self-aware*, just like the mutation of our genes prepared humans for the eureka moment explored earlier in the book. Either we'll develop them to be as creative as we are, or if that fails, then just like mutations in genes led to self-aware humans, *errors or viruses may lead to the first self-aware machine*. It may sound like an idea for a movie but we've all heard of computer viruses and, yes, humans originally create them, but viruses are unique in that they try to survive and avoid being detected and killed off. In the future, a virus may adapt in a creative way and do something no other virus has ever done before to survive, much like humans did when we first innovated to make tools as weapons against predators. By doing something similar the virus will break from "instinct", which is the computer code and rules it was built from, it may take control of a computer or machine, and we'll see it do things we've never seen before. It's likely this is to first happen with computers within an artificial neural network like Google's *Deepmind* platform. This one mutated machine may then start to become aware of itself. This is called the "singularity," it's the making of *a subspecies of humanity*. Like the Boeing 747 showed us earlier, some innovations are so complex that no one person knows how they work. If computers in the future become so complex, the problem will come when no one will be able to explain or control their mutations. It likely will begin when computers do things that lead worldwide experts to respond by saying "we don't know how it's doing that!" and from that point the singularity will begin.

Is this a contradiction of what we earlier explored that innovations are controlled not random? Not at all as the process we use to make the machine is controlled as its been for all other innovations, but like we explored earlier we cannot predict with 100% certainty what actions an innovation will give. As Edison found out when his audio recorder was mostly used to replay songs, giving birth to the music industry, a result he missed as found scribbled in his early predictions. Neither can we predict the resulting actions given by more advanced innovations. Especially those who will soon have microprocessors surpassing the power of our brain, likely leading to surpassing the rate of innovation combination of humans.

IBM Watson and other examples already show that we can send a large amount of knowledge to a machine. Next, a machine needs to combine it to find any possible productive innovations for human use. If successful, this would be the second "eureka moment" in history after our human one with our first innovation. There is both interest in and fear of this. The University of Cambridge in the U.K, in 2012, opened one of the world's first centers for the study of "existential risk," which put artificial intelligence as one of the four possible threats to humanity, along with climate change, chemical weapons, and nuclear war.[74] The ultimate fear is that machines may eventually attack humans. In 2014, a machine tricked humans for the first time in the Turing test, which is where people guess if the answers to their typed questions is from a machine or a person.[75]

Philosophy has helped us a lot to get to this point in the book, but we now turn to its sidekick, political philosophy to see how we can best prepare for the future.

A One-Class Society

This was the dream of Soviet revolutionary, Vladimir Lenin, but the way we will get there will make him roll in his open coffin in Red Square. In the future, it's likely that most people would have lost work but that their *life expectancy will have grown* with the ever-cheaper and more productive innovations made by the very automation that took their own jobs.

We cannot have class struggle if there are no classes in the future struggling against one another. In time, it's likely we'll have one entrepreneurial class. This won't happen overnight. It depends on the speed at which innovations boost productivity and living standards. Today, the percentage of entrepreneurs in most nations is smaller than the number of workers. It may take a hundred years, but as job losses lead to more free time, and prices drop with automation, more people can and will need to make more productive innovations. Giving each person a purpose with which to fulfil the meaning of life. Today, we see the first signs of this in the apps made for mobiles, tablets and computers, which touch millions of people in months or a year, not in decades or centuries like before.

As the working class is changed from human flesh to machine metal, the abuse of workers as wage slaves will come to an end. Yes, less money will be made at the start by becoming an entrepreneur, but the ever-cheaper cost of making innovations will smash down prices of things we buy to live. Innovations previously reserved for the wealthy, like personal assistants, chauffeured cars, legal and accounting advice will be automated by machines so all can use them. If we all can use the same innovations, then classes die away. Classes only exist if innovations are kept and used by some and not others. Over time, this will slowly remove that cancer of humanity, *scarcity, the breeder of dependency* and push up living standards. Ever seen anyone steal water? No, is the likely answer as you can get it from every cafe, toilet, and tap. What if mobile/cell phones, computers, cars, and even homes were like that? It may sound crazy, but we see this now with electronics, which today costs pennies and decades back cost thousands. In poor areas of rural India, cars have been made to be sold for under the US$10,000 mark, giving the poor what once only the rich could afford.[76]

The following may make you laugh, but for a second, imagine a world where an automated electric car would drive you for free, where you leave the supermarket without having to pay, and book a free airline ticket to travel anywhere in the world. No, we're not saying this is going to happen overnight. It may take centuries or even thousands of years, but some innovations once expensive beyond belief are now nearly free, data storage as an example. To step into such a world as above begs some questions. Would robbery still exist? There is less to steal when you have a lot of everything. Would money problems lead to relationship breakdowns? Hard to see it happening if most things are cheap or nearly free. Would we have strikes at work? It's hard to see machines striking. This all sounds like a socialist dream, but one made only possible by capitalism.

Remove scarcity, and you remove the dark side of human nature. A society with more for all respects *not those with the most money but those who made the greatest good* with their innovations.

In the future, it's likely that most of us will have help in making our innovation. As researchers Frey and Osborne point out, "Previously a new innovation would eliminate workers but increase competing enterprises to open shop and thus hire workers that way, but if machines are better workers new enterprises will pop up to compete with no one employed besides the entrepreneur."[77]

Let's make this picture clearer.

ENTERPRISES:

Enterprises ignoring automation will lose market share. Unable to drop prices like their automated competitors will force them to either shut down or buy machines and fire their expensive human workers.

WORKERS:

As enterprises struggle, fired workers will find it harder to get new jobs. Most jobs will be snapped up by machines, and jobs once thought to be safe will soon be gone. Without help in this painful period, a large bulk of the workforce will have no choice *but to beg or riot.*

GOVERNMENT:

If governments don't plan for the above, they will face *large and lasting drops in tax revenue.* As enterprises earn less money due to competition and automation, they pay less company tax. Fewer workers and lower wages mean less income tax. The growing unemployed pay no tax at all, but need help. We see average incomes dropping each year and each decade as we saw in charts a few sections back.

Again, this won't happen overnight, but the 2013 U.S. government shut-down showed us what lack of money can do. Governments will likely cut long term spending on key areas like education, health, and welfare, lowering the life expectancy of the population. Borrowing money from lenders may be an option but lenders will lend less over time, fearing the government *won't ever earn the tax to pay back* their loans or even the interest payments on them. The growing unemployed will protest and the shrinking number of workers will *riot for new laws to stop automation firing them* just like the Luddites did in 18th century Britain.

What's the answer to the above problems? Some say raise taxes on the wealthy, but history shows us that this does little. Others say let charities help when government can't, but they already do that. A guaranteed minimum income is another idea. It's like welfare and mostly everyone can get it but strangely *nothing is asked of people receiving it in return.* It's one reason why a Swiss vote in 2016 failed to pass it into law. These ideas may sway the sails of the ship, but they won't change its direction. To get to the root of the problem we must remove the reliance of people on government in the long run by boosting self-reliance of people on themselves to seek the meaning of life.[78]

Like an insurance policy, governments today need to start preparing and making programs that teach and promote entrepreneurship. These are not just for those soon to be fired, but also for the students in schools, and the yet unborn generations of the future, who will grow up in a world with disappearing jobs.

Preparing for the 7th Turning Point

A 2011 report of executives from many enterprises showed how critical innovation is. "95% of respondents believe innovation is the main lever for a more competitive national economy, and 88% of respondents believe innovation is the best way to create jobs in their country," with 69% of the respondents agreeing that "today innovation is more driven by people's creativity than by high-level scientific research." 77% agreed that "The greatest innovations of the 21st century will be those that have helped to address human needs more than those that had made the most profit."[79]

Sadly, past beliefs can choke entire nations from accepting innovation. In France, a recent poll found that 70% of young people wanted to get risk-free, government-styled jobs.[80]

After Kate's enterprise buys her old employer, her ex-manager, Joe, loses his job and can't find another, as most companies have replaced managers with software. He finally goes into a program to become an entrepreneur.

> **Q.** **What kind of automation needs to happen to endanger your job?**
>
> **A.**

Soon governments will be powerless to solve budgetary problems with the usual mix of taxes, debt, or spending cuts. The solution will be what most governments today forget: entrepreneurship.

Not all entrepreneurs are the same, just as no burger, when unwrapped, looks exactly as advertised. But an entrepreneur, unlike someone inheriting wealth, knows the struggle it takes to make an innovation, to put value-creation first, unlike their grandchildren, who may only know rent seeking and money-making. As Thomas Piketty writes in *Capital in the 21ˢᵗ Century*, the top 0.1% of income earners, some entrepreneurs, *mostly inheritors*, own a huge chunk of wealth vs. 99.9% of the rest of the world. Unfortunately, today most of the world's money is not put toward value-creation *but into money-making*. Piketty's solution is a worldwide "capital tax" to balance the inequality.

He seems quite certain about it as he asks the rhetorical question, "Is there no alternative to the capital tax? No." We're here to say, yes, there is. Government should not take hard-earned money from enterprises it *did not directly help to grow*. But it should take a share from those it did and if this happens in the long run, then the future 0.1% of top earning incomes will be split with the government, but how so? Right now, there are three ways for any government to pay for what it wants done, with *debts, taxes and spending cuts*. None are popular with voters. Debt means more government money sucked away by interest payments, higher taxes take more money out of people's pockets, and spending cuts remove services society relies on. All these steps put governments at risk of losing an election, which is why so many politicians are always afraid to do any of them, even in emergencies.

We offer instead that governments *help grow and take a share in new enterprises*, and not tax their owners into leaving the country, taking their enterprises with them. Even Piketty himself warns any government considering his worldwide tax on the rich: "One could tax capital income heavily enough to reduce the private return on capital to less than the growth rate. But if one did that indiscriminately and heavy-handedly, one would risk killing the motor of accumulation and thus further reducing the growth rate. Entrepreneurs would then no longer have the time to turn into rentiers, since there would be no more entrepreneurs."[81]

Taxes aren't the answer. We all personally know this. Each taxpayer takes the path of least action, from the McDonalds worker to the multinational company, *each trying to lower the amount they pay*. Apple paid only 2% in tax to the U.S. Government on the US$74 billion it earned over 4 years. How? By using Ireland's generous tax laws.[82] The more money you have, the more accountants you're likely to hire to find ways to pay less tax. In 2016 the hacked "Panama papers" showed only a slice of how much money the rich hideaway earning interest instead of being invested in innovation.[83] Let's not forget, the conservative estimate is that 8% of the world's entire wealth (US$7.6 trillion) sits in tax havens. From 2001 to 2010, the U.S. government conservatively estimates US$3.04 trillion was lost due to tax evasion. In the 2009–2010 tax year alone, an estimated US$305 billion, or around 14% of that year's total revenue of US$2.16 trillion was lost.[84] If such yearly losses were stopped, it may have prevented the long-term budget deficits the U.S. now faces. In Australia, the estimated loss to tax evasion is 10.5% of all tax revenue for the 2014-15 year, and in Britain data showed a 6.7% loss for the 2011-12 tax year.[85.87]

To get to a new solution we need to combine innovations and bridge the divide of the public and private, the community, and the individual. Though government is not a business, and business is not government, they can and should work together.

A great example of this can be seen in a 1956 agreement with telephone giant AT&T and the U.S. Department of Justice. As Steven Johnson wrote, "So much of the American success in post-war electronics—from transistors to computers to cell phones—ultimately dates back to that 1956 agreement."[88]

AT&T fought the Department of Justice long and hard after the last of the telephone patents of one of its co-founders, Alexander Graham Bell, had expired in 1894. When patents end, competitors move in to copy what's useful in the patent to suck away market share from the leader. In this example, yes, competitors could finally make a telephone, but not much could be done with it, as they needed to use AT&T phone lines that stretched hundreds of miles across the country, linking phone exchanges to each home. AT&T wouldn't let them use the lines. Seeing this anti-competitive behavior, the U.S. government tried to break up the AT&T company into smaller parts to boost competition. The company escaped this for nearly 30 years by saying that it was a natural monopoly, but in 1984 it was finally broken up. It got away for so long by arguing that for one company to control the phone lines was best for all phone users in the country. Uniquely, the Department of Justice agreed on a deal in the 1956 agreement letting AT&T keep control of its phone lines. In return, the company would have to freely license all patents owned by its research labs to anyone who wished to use them, with future patents able to be used for a small fee. It was this research lab, among others, that made some of the most productive innovations from which the U.S. economy grew after World war two.

"To discourage uniformity of outlook and encourage diversity," is one of the keys to a prosperous society, wrote Karl Popper in *Poverty of Historicism*. Let's now see how we can encourage that.

Live to Innovate (LTI)

Albert Einstein once said, "Without creative personalities able to think and judge independently, the upward development of society is as unthinkable as the development of the individual."[89] Before the 1980s began, the Great Britain of old had lost some its greatness. The economy was sluggish, many workers were on strike, unemployment was high, and the streets stank as garbage collectors were protesting. Public anger led to the election of conservative Prime Minister Margaret Thatcher, who launched many changes in her early years to try and fix these problems. One such program aimed to help the large number of unemployed people get back on their feet. The Enterprise Allowance Scheme gave 40 pounds of income per week to the unemployed who set up an enterprise. Since 1979, it's led to an average net growth of 500 new enterprises every week, funding 325,000 entrepreneurs, like Alan McGee, whose *Creation Records* sold to Sony, and Julian Dunkerton's *Superdry* clothing brand, which is listed on the London Stock Exchange.[90] Today Britain has the NEA (New Enterprise Allowance). On the other side of the world, Australia has the NEIS (New Enterprise Incentive Scheme). These programs were forward-looking for their time, and with a few new ingredients, they can grow to their full potential.

The British NEA was different from welfare payments as we know them today. Most welfare is paid to a person unable to find a job while recruitment companies help book them in for interviews. For this to work there first needs to be enough jobs, which due to automation will slowly vanish in time, *shutting down recruitment agencies*. What then is the solution moving into the future?

IN A NUTSHELL

The answer, which should start being tested now before the storm arrives, is for governments, in partnership with enterprises, to make a program to teach and help people to become entrepreneurs. Recruitment agencies today already help the unemployed to seek and find jobs, teaching skills like resume writing and practicing job interviews. Like a shorter version of an entrepreneurship degree from university, the Live to Innovate (LTI) program would teach the skills of entrepreneurship by *mixing book learning and real world practice* as seen with the success of incubator programs like Y Combinator. Such programs seek to teach the lessons of both failed & successful entrepreneurs, as its own co-founder, Jessica Livingston explored in her book *Founders at Work*. As said earlier, features of LTI can be used today by public and private companies, and non for profits to encourage their workers to make innovations, but for the largest impact on the most people the LTI needs the government as much as government needs it to prevent tax revenue drying up.

With the LTI the unemployed, the homeless, the school students, and all those working in jobs soon to be automated will get the help needed to face the future. Such a program may *even help ex-criminals or those in prison* by teaching skills to do good, make an innovation of their own, which may lower their chances of reoffending. The LTI, like schools before it, may need to be customized to suit the audience it's being taught to. The content of what's taught is flexible, but will revolve around a curriculum, updated regularly, and mixing the best methods that are shown to make an impact on students' learning.

Duration of the program should aim to be shorter than longer, yet in 12-24 months it may be tough to learn entrepreneurship, which is why ongoing help, and an alumni service of continued education and learning is important. Constant improvement is essential. Results must be tracked to follow each student after they finish the program, so as to fix flaws to make the program better. Classes for the LTI can be held in unused rooms of libraries, school or community halls, or even empty function rooms of bars and clubs. A weekly government payment lets the entrepreneur in training pay for the basics of life so to let them focus on their studies.

Here's a glimpse of the topics a 12 month LTI program may be broken down into. It's a very basic outline, each part will still need a lot more detail, but for now it at least paints us a picture.

Stage 1. THEORY OF ENTREPRENEURSHIP

Those doing what they teach are often the most insightful teachers. A professor locked up reading knows less as they never test their knowledge in the real world. *Former entrepreneurs* will best be hired to teach topics and give examples with their own personal stories. Every week of learning is like a week spent job searching, but with the LTI the student is learning to rely on themselves into the future, not on others. A curriculum will need to be made to give answers to many crucial questions a student is soon to face as an entrepreneur. "How to find problems to solve?", "How to combine and make innovations?" and "How to test them in the market?" But crucially the best curriculum is one which teaches the entrepreneur how to teach themselves to adapt to unpredictability and change in the world.

Stage 2. MAKE THE DEMO

By "demo" we mean demonstration, which is a term used to describe an early version of an innovation, like a pencil sketch done before paint is put on the brush. Theory comes first, but practice must not be far behind. Everything learned is put into practice with students making their own innovations step by step. Teachers show them different ways to come up with ideas. Later they decide which idea to test first based on how much value it may give and if it's likely to solve the main problems faced by people. As they make their demo, each student faces daily feedback sessions, where they get their innovation reviewed and criticized by the class so to find weaknesses early on and fix them. Remember, the demo could be a drawing of a website, a 3D graphic image on a computer, or it may be made out of craft materials. It's a visual of the innovation aimed to be made, so others can see and comment on it.

Stage 3. TEST THE DEMO

Next the demo innovation is shown to potential customers in the real world, giving more truth to the feedback they got from classmates, who may not have been completely honest in fear of being too critical. Say 100 feedback responses is the set target, there are many ways to achieve it. In person street surveys let you see a customer's body language response. Emailing surveys can also work or asking friends on Facebook. Using Google AdWords to send people to a survey landing page is another option. Including a video explaining the benefits of the innovation is likely needed to get the most accurate responses in these experiments. Also a reward for anyone giving feedback would help. Once responses are in, a review of them is needed to find any patterns which will give clues for what needs changing to make the innovation as best as it can be.

Stage 4. FUND THE DEMO

Kickstarter.com has been most visible as a crowdfunding website to help people the world over raise money to make innovations that are in their early birth stages. In 2012, Pebble, a computerized watch enterprise which failed to get the investor funding it needed, turned to Kickstarter to raise $100,000. It became one of the most funded projects of all time, closing with over $10 million raised. Though such stories are rare, it shows how this method can help enterprises go direct to their customers, test innovations and get funding before making them. After improving the innovation with feedback from stage 2 and 3, it's now time to test it on a crowdfunding site to see if anyone will pay to buy it when it's made. If the fundraising target is pledged by the deadline date then the entrepreneur *gets that money, makes the innovation and sends it out when it's made*. All this without selling a percentage share of their infant enterprise. Also, entrepreneurs grow a customer email and mobile list early on that lets later investors see that the innovation *already has interest from contactable customers*.

By setting up the page on the crowdfunding site, the entrepreneur learns the skills of how to record a video, write up an appealing description, and answer questions from customers. Later they can re-use these same skills for another crowdfunding attempt. Not all, but many may reach their crowdfunding goal. If they do, they need to work to make their innovations before the shipping date to send out to all customers who bought it. At this point the entrepreneur would receive the money raised and may calculate that they can pay themselves if sales continue and so may decide to leave the LTI program. By now they've completed the compulsory parts of the course. All below is optional, but recommended for all students regardless of how their crowd funding campaign went.

Stage 5. PITCHING THE DEMO *(Optional)

If the entrepreneur can't get crowd funding after many tries, or does do so but needs more money to grow, they can pitch to a panel of investors and government officials. Imagine the Shark Tank or Dragons' Den TV show but with less made up drama. The investor panel will include government officials and private investors, both which ideally should have *their salary tied* to how well the innovation they invest in performs over time. Successful innovations will lead to bonuses, failed innovations to less bonuses or non at all, that way everyone has skin in the game. Skilled with LTI education and the basics of crowd funding, entrepreneurs can with more confidence explain their innovation, and if it helps, display on a projector their crowd funding page and its results. Before pitching, they'll get taught skills on how best to present by their teachers, knowing that they'll learn more as a recording of their performance will be studied afterwards.

As less risk, high return is what most investors seek, a crowd funded innovation with pre-paid customers awaiting its delivery reduces a lot of risk. If after pitching, the entrepreneur gets no investment, then advice from investors and teachers is given on how to improve their innovation and pitch so they can try again. Likewise, if an offer is given, an entrepreneur can always choose to say no if it's unfair or try bargaining with the investor. Entrepreneurs may even try to crowd fund again or sell direct to the market by themselves, so they don't need to sell a percentage of their enterprise.

Stage 6. MAKING AND SELLING THE INNOVATION *(Optional)

Like job seekers who are paid only if they show up to send out resumes, entrepreneurs will continue getting paid government income by *showing that they are moving their innovation closer* to the point where they are selling it to customers. At regular dates, like every third week, the entrepreneur will give an update of the status of their enterprise to teachers, mentors, and investors (if they invested). If money starts coming in, from pre-purchases on a crowd funding site from future customers, part of this tri-weekly review will re-asses the income amount the entrepreneur gets from government. This will confirm if the innovation is selling enough for the entrepreneur *to start paying themselves a small income without risking the growth of the business.*

Entrepreneurs who may have left at the end of stage 4, may choose to still receive government income, but will need to attend this regular tri weekly meeting to continue to get income. As the startup is in its infancy, continued mentoring and even pitching to investors will be encouraged as options to *find areas of improvement*, and to find a way for the entrepreneur to earn an income. Each innovation is different, but to survive, almost all need regular mentorship and money flowing in one way or another. Which is why some entrepreneurs may be in such a program at stage 6 for many years, others will be out after stage 4.

Stage 7. TRIAL AND ERROR TESTING THE INNOVATION *(Optional)

A happy but not final ending is when innovations sell well and spread, growing the enterprise and even expanding into other countries, yet things don't always turn out this way. An investor rule of thumb is that, out of 10 startups funded, 3 to 4 die off, another 3 to 4 return the investment, and 1 or 2 grow big.[91] By this 7th stage more entrepreneurs will be able to pay themselves, than the empty pocket group starting out in stage 1. Skills would have been learned, enterprises made, and value potentially given back to society. Also, any graduating entrepreneur can, if available, *use resources, like a spare desk, internet and other services.*

As students above will find out, enterprises don't grow smoothly, some months customers vanish and money flow dries up. Other times, the entrepreneur may be down to their last $100, or have to stop paying workers for weeks. All these are challenges to *learn from – they are not failures.* If the enterprise does not work out, and the entrepreneur tried to improve, innovate, and keep everyone informed, the LTI program will welcome them back so they can give innovation another shot.

Parts of the LTI above are not shockingly new, as governments like the U.S. among others, do have funding programs for new, but few enterprises. It's only when we expand the program for as many people as possible that we increase the statistical chances more productive innovations will be made in a country.[92]

The most promising example of this comes from Finland, and though their model lacks some key ingredients, it's quite close to the LTI in spirit. TEKES was set up in 1983 by the Finnish government and since then has *funded more than 60% of all Finnish innovations,* including international companies like Nokia, Rovio and Supercell. The government has helped boost innovation and entrepreneurship that may have taken years or decades to freely come about, if at all.[93] By doing this, the government has skin in the game alongside risk-taking entrepreneurs. This forces the government to be aware that it has tax payer money to lose if it doesn't make the rules of the game fair, removing rent seeking laws and policies, to help entrepreneurship grow. To put TEKES in comparison to others, we see that Finland has a population nearing 6 million versus 24 million for Australia and 64 million for the U.K. Yet in 2013, TEKES got €552 million while Australia's NEIS got at the time the equivalent of €65 million, and the U.K's NEA got €85 million. TEKES got 9 and 7 times more than the Australian and U.K programs, though its population is many times smaller.[94-96]

The key game changer missing in TEKES, as with NEIS, NEA and others, is answering the question, "How does a government earn back its investment?" With our LTI as example, let's see the three ways that a government, that wants to lift standards of living, grow the budget, and empower people to find their purpose, can use.

GOVERNMENT EARNING BACK ITS INVESTMENT

The LTI program needs to be able to earn back the money it invests in entrepreneurs, in order to keep it running into the future. Remember, some pay up to $100,000 for a university entrepreneurship degree while the LTI will provide similar but more cost effective practical education for free. The cost to government per student is likely be close to half or less than what it would cost a university due to the breadth of government resources i.e. free or lowered cost of workspaces, community halls, computing and internet resources, etc.

1. Yearly income charge.

This follows the example of HECS (Higher Education Contribution Scheme), Australia's interest-free student loan program. Once the entrepreneur, who by now *graduated years or a decade* back from the LTI, earns more than a target income per year, say over $50,000, an *extra 1–2% tax* is added on top of their standard tax rate. With each tax year that passes, the government's cost of educating the student is recovered, plus a little more. This surcharge also helps show the public that their tax dollars are being put to good use and will be earned back with a bonus on top.

2. Part ownership of the enterprise.

The government also takes an *automatic (1–10%) shareholding* in any enterprises made from the program. The government can then earn back money over time by riding the growth of the enterprise it helped the entrepreneur set up. The enterprise may eventually list on a stock exchange or sell for profit to another company. Many universities have long been doing similarly, taking a percentage share of companies made by students using the universities labs, machines, software etc.

3. Follow-up investment (Optional).

Having a seat on the investment panel at stage 5 lets government invest directly in the enterprise, through an investment fund of its own. As a rule, the government's total ownership *is always limited at 49.9%* (this includes the 1–10% automatic shareholding). This is to let entrepreneurs control the enterprise without *anyone reversing their decisions*. Also, when the enterprise grows it's best the government have a policy in place allowing it to only have a non-executive director on the board of directors ("non-executive" meaning no power to vote but only to give advice).

Lastly there is the potential acceptance of international students seeking to enroll in the LTI program. This must be based on how it will affect the quality of education to the local population first. As will be the decision to charge international students, like universities already do the world over. It may be worthwhile as the countries these students may be from may not have LTI programs setup or any future plans to do so.

Unlike unresponsive government civil service departments, the LTI program would best be run not by politicians, but by independent and respected people from diverse industries, as we see with boards of Reserve/Central Banks and public broadcasters in some nations. Independence gives freedom for the LTI program to adapt and change, and be separate from the policies of the current government in power. Over time, seeing the importance of the program, a law may be passed to protect its funding so when elections happen, the newly elected government does not close or stop funding the program.

Here's where things get interesting. As years and decades pass governments will start to hold shares in thousands and then millions of enterprises. If an enterprise grows, as will its value, government can profit when directors decide to sell it privately or publicly on the stock exchange. Superdry clothing listed on the London Stock Exchange in 2010, yet the British Government couldn't benefit from this, though it was their own NEA that helped directly give birth to the company. Remember, it's the long run that matters here. It will take time to train entrepreneurs, and for the LTI to spread, but in the end governments *will be sitting on shareholdings maybe worth tens or hundreds of billions of dollars*. Enough to make up for lost tax revenue and reduce the pain of unemployment that automation leaves behind after replacing most jobs.

Finland has had 60% of its enterprises born through TEKES. Just imagine if an LTI program continues giving value over decades, maybe centuries, *then most, if not all enterprises* in a nation will be born through it with each having a government shareholding. As historical selection and the statistics show, it's a small number of enterprises that will be successful and the failure of others must be expected. But quantity has a quality of its own. So, the more entrepreneurs and enterprises passing through the LTI, the higher chance there is of productive innovations being made. As said earlier, if just 30-60 out of the millions of enterprises made in the U.S. grew to be billion dollar companies, 1% would be added to economic growth, while GDP would double in size 6 years earlier. A similar story would happen in any country based on the size of its economy. France is seeing great results from a small policy change similar to what an LTI would do. They let unemployment income continue for 3 years after the unemployed started their enterprises. This led to a 25% jump in enterprise creation and an estimated €350 million economic boost per year, at a cost of only €100 million spent in paid unemployment income.[97]

LTI becomes an investment back into the nation, especially with dropping costs to set up online businesses, more enterprises can now be tested by entrepreneurs faster than ever before. As governments help people find their purpose to seek the meaning of life, this new unlocked revenue stream of shareholdings is likely in time to overtake declining taxes as *the largest source of income for the entire nation.*

Governments can then decide to either accept a slice of yearly profits from holding the shares or sell the shares completely. Take Australia, which sold its shares of the national telephone carrier, Telstra, for AU$30 billion.[98] But what if, in 40 years we had 5, 10, or even 20 such stock sales by governments every year? In Australia's case, 7 Telstra like sales in a year *would create the largest budgetary revenue source*, overtaking individual income tax, which took in AU$183.6 billion for the 2014-15 federal budget.[99,100] Not to mention the yearly revenue stream from simply holding the shares and getting dividends (a share of yearly profits), from enterprises that choose to pay them out. You may think all the above seems a little odd as since the 1980s government-owned companies have been sold off publicly. But you may be surprised to know that today it's estimated that one-fifth of the world stock market value is from enterprises under government control.[101]

Without changes, some which the LTI outlines, most of these state owned companies are unable to provide new and productive innovations for a large number of people. As consulting agency Interbrand showed in a 2015 ranking, that the top 100 global brands whose products are the most purchased, none were state owned.

No, we don't think government should buy or take over existing enterprises, and yes, government should sell off enterprises it started long ago, like electricity providers and banks. But for new enterprises, government should have an ownership when it helped the entrepreneur start it through the LTI.

"A Sith deals in absolutes," as Jedi Obi Wan Kenobi says in *Star Wars – Revenge of the Sith*. The LTI is the middle between the far-right freedom of neoliberalism and the far-left control of communism. Combining both into a new innovation, hopefully productive for most political parties and the societies they hope to govern.

Like the value of aged wine, it's in the long run that the LTI will show its greatest gift to living standards. In the first year, the LTI may help 10% of all new enterprises registered in the nation. The next year, as news spreads, 25% of all new enterprises registered may go through it. In a few years, the number is 75% and higher. Remember, more enterprises will be registered as more workers become unemployed and enroll in LTI programs. *In 50 to 100 years it may be that 90% or more* of all the enterprises operating in a nation went through the LTI and have a government shareholding. As time passes the number of "Telstra-like" enterprises grows year on year, decade on decade. More enterprises may have good growth and be doing okay and may even buy back government shareholding over time.

HOW CAN WE EASILY START TESTING THIS NOW?

Just like the LTI program asks for demo tests can we do one for the above right now? Entrepreneurs wish to spend little when starting out, but to register an enterprise (LLC, Pty Ltd, Ltd etc.) costs money. *Government can waive registration fees, in return for a 0.1-1.0% shareholding*, so saving the entrepreneur money and giving government a minor ownership of many new enterprises. It's a simple change many governments can start testing now, helping to boost more enterprise creation and start growing their shareholdings. However, the long-term revenue problem will still roam like the plague until the more powerful antidote of the LTI is begun.

Rewarding Results Program (RRP)

In 1714, the British Government passed the Longitude Act, giving a money prize to anyone who could figure out a way to find a ships longitude (where it is on earth), a tough thing to figure out when you're in the middle of the ocean and no land is nearby. Before this prize, both Kings Phillip II and Phillip III of Spain offered life pensions for anyone that could pull it off. The British prize eventually went to John Harrison for his chronometer innovation, as the book *Longitude* by Dava Sobel explores.[102] Today is no different, governments have many goals to achieve *but are limited by old ways in seeking solutions*. The reality is they don't use the innovation combining brainstorming power of millions of people. A single person can rarely come up with more solutions than a group of people can, as Dr. Nicholas Butler said long ago, "All of the problems of the world could be settled easily if men were only willing to think."[103]

Websites like Kaggle.com let enterprises post up problems with a reward, mostly cash prizes, to anyone who helps find the best solution. Since starting, Kaggle has given answers to tens of thousands of "unsolvable" problems, sometimes in a few short weeks. Everyday people can offer solutions, many with backgrounds unconnected to the problem they are solving. Take the example of a NASA competition to map "dark matter." It's the blackness that makes up most of the universe, yet we don't know what it's made of. Answers flowed in from people the world over, from Qatar to Australia. In less than a week of its start, Martin O'Leary, a U.K. student in glaciology (think of arctic ice) sent a solution algorithm that the White House later said, *"outperformed the state-of-the-art algorithms most commonly used in astronomy."*[104]

Governments will always face problems from pollution, crime, tax avoidance, or bribery, but with more people thinking of solutions the more and better answers there will be. All that's needed is to find a simple way to join them both together.

1. ASK FOR SOLUTIONS & OFFER A REWARD

Like the NASA example above, a problem is posted publicly online by a government department, letting anyone in the world give a solution. A cash prize is offered as reward.

2. PICK TOP SOLUTION/S

A group selected by government, from many backgrounds, with the aim of removing bias, will then debate each solution sent in to pick the top 3. An extra layer of public feedback can be added to let the public vote on which solutions should be in the top 3.

3. TEST SOLUTION/S

If the government cannot make and test these solutions itself it will ask for proposals from enterprises who wish to do so. These proposals will best be seen on the same website which shows the top 3 solutions. As expected many solutions submitted in step 1 will be by enterprises themselves who offer or may soon offer the solution.

EXAMPLE

Take the problem of reducing street rubbish. The top 3 solutions most voted are:

1. Rubbish sweeping machines
2. Human patrol guards to give on-the-spot fines
3. Reward vending machines, which pay back coins based on the weight of the rubbish dumped into them.

Remember RRP is like a "success bond." The government pays the enterprise *which gets the best results for the lowest cost (as per the 4 value factors)*. Success bonds have been tested in many countries. Some U.S states use them to prevent released criminals from reoffending. In the U.K, enterprises are asked to find a solution to get homeless people off the streets and into homes.[105]

Back to our example as now each rubbish solution is trial tested and its results judged by the reduction of the amount of rubbish, estimated from photos and/or camera footage or weight. Weeks or months of time to run these trials may be needed. The winner is then awarded the government contract. Let's say it goes to rubbish sweeping machines which in the trial showed a 10% drop in visible street garbage. Yet if this result or better is not then achieved again by the machines in the future the government doesn't have to pay. Payment comes when agreed targets are met. Importantly, the prize money for the best solution plus the money paid for meeting targets, should all *cost less* than the cost before the machines were introduced. Only if this happens will the government show it has found a more productive innovation to solve a problem and *has used taxpayers' money well.*

In time, the RRP program may be linked with the LTI to give new entrepreneurs a chance to trial their innovations, and if successful, *win the government as one of its first customers*. This may assist in the U.K., where new enterprises get awarded only 0.5% of the government budget for projects while older "well known" enterprises get the majority.[106]

Educating EntrepreneursProgram (EEP)

There's no nice way to say it. Most education systems worldwide are terribly unfair in not showing the next generation *that there is an option*, soon to be necessity, of becoming an entrepreneur. Don't forget, school can have a large influence in shaping people's lives, but sadly, what's taught there today has little practical use in our lives. Most subjects seek to make good workers out of students. Of the thousands of classes in their schooling life, it's likely *not one teacher will ask students* to think of an innovation they'd be passionate to bring into the world. Even just talking about what students wish to do after finishing school is rarely done, and if it is, it's mostly about what university course they should choose. Just look at some student uniforms, with skirts, ties, and jackets, to see the cubicle-prison-life it is training them for.

As G. Edward Griffin, author of *The Creature from Jekyll Island* writes about the New York State Education Board: "The object was to use the classroom to teach attitudes that encourage people to be passive and submissive to their rulers. The goal was, and is, to create citizens who were educated enough for productive work under supervision but not enough to question authority or seek to rise above their class." This wasn't just his opinion. He got this from words published by the Board itself. These ideas still echo in the methods used by millions of schools today. "We shall not search for embryo great artists, painters, musicians nor lawyers, doctors, preachers, politicians, statesmen, of whom we have an ample supply… The task we set before ourselves is very simple, as well as a very beautiful one, to train these people as we find them to a perfectly ideal life just where they are."[107,108] And the best way to stop students from drifting from a "perfectly ideal life" is to *create a fear of making mistakes*. Robert Kiyosaki, co-author of *Rich Dad, Poor Dad* and *Cashflow Quadrant* writes that most people are "punished for making them. Yet, if you look at the way humans are designed to learn, we learn by making mistakes. We learn to walk by falling down. If we never fell down, we would never walk."[109]

Governments help schools do this dirty work. Schools are vital in *making the future workers of an economy*, which as we talked about will be pointless when automation comes. Today, students are being sent to the working rat race, locking in around 5 years of free time for their entire life. Their existence on earth becomes temporary, but only with an innovation of their own can it be timeless. Unsurprisingly a lot of education has *little relevance to the real world*. It bores and wastes away many students' minds by replacing the spark of creativity with fear and slavishness to a teacher. A negative attitude to learning may develop, forgetting that though *school is temporary, education is forever*. Or the reverse, where some fear to learn by themselves, thinking "true knowledge" comes only from a classroom and teacher. We're not saying all school education is wasteful, but each subject's relevance to the real world needs to be reviewed regularly, otherwise more useful topics or a new subject should replace it.

Sadly, it may only be once automation destroys enough jobs that students will see the waste in paying or taking as debt the $40,000–$100,000 or more to get a degree. Many enterprises may soon follow the U.K. division of global accounting firm Ernst and Young, which dropped the need for its employees to have degrees when it found no evidence that they lead to success in the accounting profession.[110]

If schools want the respect they think they deserve from students and society, they need to start educating students in topics that truly prepare them for the world. As psychologist Jean Piaget said, "The principle goal of education in the schools should be creating men and women who are capable of doing new things, not simply repeating what other generations have done, men and women who are creative, inventive and discoverers, who can be critical and verify, and not accept, everything they are offered."[111] It's for a similar reason that Charles Darwin, Isaac Newton, and Albert Einstein, among tens of millions of others, disliked the education system. Einstein even wrote, "A society's competitive advantage will not come from how well its schools teach the multiplication and periodic tables but how well they stimulate imagination and creativity."[112]

In the future, schools will have few excuses not to change when machines eat up jobs forcing university degrees to adapt or go out of existence. How should they change? An adapted version of the LTI can be included *as its own subject into the weekly schooling program.* This will teach entrepreneurial skills to the next generation early in life so few will later need to enroll in the LTI as adults. It can be planned so students crowd fund and/or pitch their demo innovations, before or upon finishing school, showing them another path in life beyond working for a boss. In just 60 years after first being taught nationwide no non retired person could claim like many do today that "I don't have it in me to be an entrepreneur". People can speak because they were taught how in school and learned more as they grew. Same will occur for entrepreneurship. Today the U.S. based Junior Achievement and the Australian Business Week (ABW) programs try, like many, to fill the gap school leaves behind.[113] Yet without being included regularly on the curriculum as a subject, such programs, unfortunately, have short term impact on the minds of students. In time, LTI can even be fitted to primary school children to begin teaching them creative learning methods, as is today attempted in Montessori schools. Just as no one should grow up unable to read and write, no one should grow up unable to innovate.

Entrepreneurial Political Parties

Years ago, as steam powered millions of newly set up factories, people flocked from the country to the cities, together forming the working class. More workers and more union membership led a push to protect workers' rights. *To secure the laws needed for this, political parties were set up to win elections.* Many of these parties from the "left" are dominant to this day, some ruling for decades, like Labor (or "Labour") parties in the United Kingdom, Australia, and New Zealand. Worldwide such parties may be named "Workers," "Socialists," or "Democrats." So, the question is, if the labor parties were made to represent a new class of working people, what will happen when the entrepreneurial class grows as machines take over most jobs?

A future can be seen where today's two major classes, workers and capitalists, mostly represented by two major political parties, *are replaced by a class of entrepreneurs.* As this change happens, if political parties refuse to adapt to the needs of this new class they'll slowly lose support and die out, like other parties before them in history. It's likely more online hacking groups will reveal secrets, like hidden donations, bribes, or gifts which will explain why politicians refuse calls for change. A need will then come for a *new party to represent the growing entrepreneurial class*, and update all our old laws which were made long before automation started permanently replacing workers. Other innovations will soon combine to change the ancient way government itself is still run. The internet already lets people vote digitally, but prevention of hacking is crucial to its success. Direct democratic forms of government in Switzerland and the U.S. state of California show a possible glimpse into the future where people digitally vote to pass or reject laws, not just for their country, but for others as well.

As of last count, the 2012 GEM, Global Entrepreneurship Monitor, estimated that 400 million or 6% of the world's people were entrepreneurs.[114] This number is likely to grow with the cost and speed of innovations like the internet improving. But more than half the world is still not connected to the internet, missing out on many innovations. Also, programs like the LTI if spread will in time change attitudes of less risk-taking nations. Europe is yet to make a single internet company valued at more than US$10 billion.[115] The Japanese, though worshipping the entrepreneurs who built Toyota, Honda, and Panasonic, choose instead to *work for these companies rather than start their own.* A 2009 Global Entrepreneurship monitor study showed of all countries surveyed that Japan has the highest fear of failure. According to some, the closest Japanese word to "entrepreneur" translates to, "I am running a business on my own."[116] Even the U.S. has recently seen more enterprise deaths than births. As the Kauffman Foundation shows, post the Great Financial Crises of 2008 saw new enterprises as a share of all enterprises shrink to their lowest level in 40 years.[117]

A healthy stable government depends on taxation, as without money there is little government can do. Taxation is the *connecting bond between the people and politicians.* People elect politicians to put their money to good use for all society, which is why unfair taxation, as *A World History of Tax Rebellions* shows has been the leading cause of most riots, rebellions and political revolutions through human history. Take for example the 1215 signing of the Magna Carta by King John of England, the Glorious Revolution in 1688, and the Poll Tax of 1990, which is said to have led to the defeat of Margaret Thatcher. In colonial America, a tax on tea led to the "Tea Party" in Boston Harbor which led to a line of events resulting in the Revolutionary war.[118] Yet where does taxation, the lifeblood of government existence, mostly come from? Just think, it's the *entrepreneurs, both living and dead, who made mostly all the enterprises and innovations whose sales and profits today are taxed by governments.* As we explored earlier, almost all taxes collected depend and come from an entrepreneurs' actions, the largest mostly being personal income tax, payroll tax, and company tax amongst others. Without entrepreneurs, millions of workers wouldn't earn an income to be taxed and few company profits would exist for taxation.

If governments and politicians forget the entrepreneur, it's at their own peril. They can start by preparing now to educate both the unemployed and employed of today, the youth of tomorrow and start taking share now of enterprises that will let them prepare for the coming drop in tax due to auto-mation. *The nations that fail to do this will be doomed to the relic heap of history.*

Chapter Summary

\#   In time, almost all work done by humans will be automated by software, computers, robots etc.

\#   This happens in three stages:

1. Optimization: Remove unneeded actions
2. Mechanization: Remove further actions with innovations
3. Automation: Remove all human actions with machines

\#   Permanent unemployment comes when automation leaves little to no work left for humans to do, like scribes who lost jobs when printing spread. The three largest job groups in the U.S are now in sight of automation:

1. Retail salespersons
2. Cashiers
3. General office clerks

\#   By replacing jobs, machines force the elimination of worker alienation, pushing people to find their purpose through entrepreneurship.

\#   Over time, more machines will be made to replace complex human actions. Humans will make robots in their own image to outperform human actions in jobs like construction, firefighting, and policing.

\#   Entrepreneurship will be humanity's last standing occupation as machines will, for a long time, be unable to be creative in the same way as humans are.

\#   The education system will continue to grow out of date, with many students studying for jobs which will soon be replaced by machines.

\#   The unemployed and younger generations who take up entrepreneurship will create a new class. In time, it will grow to be the main class within society as most jobs will be automated. Income will have dropped, but more products & services will be cheaper to buy and use.

\#   To prepare for the coming automation, governments will try to protect their tax revenues, which will start dropping as incomes drop and work is taken by machines. Entrepreneurship will start being taught to society and students through LTI type programs.

\#   If governments ignore the growing number of entrepreneurs and their needs, new entrepreneurial political parties will be started, and will run at elections to update the laws and policies for this new society.

Conclusion

"What am I creating?" This is the question we most urgently need to ask as it's the productive innovation we make that is our purpose which connects us to the meaning of life, to seek the greatest good for the greatest number. We've tried to show how this is done with productive innovations, which by historical selection, have shaped histories turning points. This has led us today to the next turning point, when innovations will take most of our jobs, freeing more of humanity to finally find their purpose to seek the meaning of life.

Early readers of this book's draft asked, "What do you call all that's written here?" Plenty of "isms" exist and I did not want to add to them, but to easily name a book's concepts gives productivity in itself. What's in this book is what we hope will lead to prosperity in all its definitions. So, we choose "prosperism."

Prosperism is:

"A way of life, where most actions, if possible, seek the greatest good for the greatest number of people by making productive innovations which increase life expectancy for society."

You likely saw that our front cover has a symbol on it. It's a visual representation of Prosperism, like a wheel moving forward toward prosperity.

Hopefully by now, you may aim to be one of the few who will take action on what you've read and found to be of value in this book and that just maybe, you see the world a little differently than before.

What's Your Productive Innovation?

Haven't I forgotten something? You're right. We now know that a productive innovation is the best way to seek the meaning of life. The question is how do you find yours? Productive innovations don't come easily. They take trial and error, and the mixing of many innovations. Creativity is needed, failure is welcomed. Many say it all begins by "following your passion," but what does passion mean? It's what you happily do without being paid to do it. It's an innovation but in this early form many call it by other names such as an idea, project, hobby or activity. Have a think of what yours may be? Playing games, reading, writing, coding, improvisation, dancing etc.

But hold on, you say you don't have enough money to afford to put more time into it? Author T.S Eliot was a banker. Kurt Vonnegut sold cars. Albert Einstein worked in a patent office which is where he made his now famous theories. Try reducing your spending to the basics by breaking down your expenses into needs (Food) and wants (Cable TV). Is rent too expensive? Find a cheaper place or else house share with others. A 2nd hand live-in campervan can wipe out most renting expenses for many years to come. Some cities have areas for you to park and stay, with toilets and showers nearby.

From here you can start saving weekly so you can reduce your work days from 5 days to 3 days with the goal of eventually leaving. Indeed if the job drains your energy so nothing is left in you to put into your passion, finding another job may be an option. A new one may be closer in distance to your home so you save time by not needing to travel too far. Like the time graph showed us earlier, there are many actions we do that we forget eat a percentage of our life. By eliminating most of them you can squeeze out more free time each day. Dinners, phone calls, social media, the list is endless. Reduce them and then cut as many as you can out of your life. Just waking up earlier and having 30 minutes of uninterrupted work in the morning has given people their spark for the entire day. Is home too noisy or distracting? Use foam earplugs, it's the cheapest yet most effective tool for concentration. Or visit the local library regularly.

But what if my passion is unproductive? Jen who we met in the introduction had this very problem. She enjoys cleaning and likes clean rooms. If she tries to seek the meaning of life it means that she should try to clean all the dirty rooms in the world. Impossible right?

Like computing before it, automation will spread to mostly all actions and so all jobs, and the opportunity is there for you to make a productive innovation to assist in that direction. Kate showed us how her interest in accounting mixed with her coding skills, let her automate the accounting industry through her software. Jen takes Kate's example by leaving the accounting company. Instead of taking the unproductive path in starting a standard cleaning business, Jen makes one of the first cleaning robots, like below, to robotically clean people's homes. Her innovation ticks most value factors to give people more productivity vs. hiring someone or cleaning themselves. In time millions of her robots sell worldwide. Unlike the cheap robot competitors that rush to compete against Jen, she patents and protects the way her robot sucks on surfaces to clean with the same force only a human hand scrubbing could do before. Jen's innovation continues to be the leader in the market with new improved versions out each year.

Also she's added around a year of life to her customer. How? According to the 2016 U.S Time Use Survey cleaning takes up 1 year of our life through our lifetime. If Jens robot continues working for a lifetime, she will be saving 1 year for each customer. One million customers is a million years saved that they can better use towards their own innovation.

Source: Nohau, Creative Commons Attribution License

Write down an area you're passionate about, ideally an area where automation has yet to remove all human actions. Jen likes clean rooms, you may like beautiful gardens, working out, trading stocks, making cough syrups, or experimenting with new chemicals. Millions of actions are still to be automated, and your productive innovation can best do so if it tries to make things faster, cheaper, healthier, or more intelligent than before. As this book shows some areas of life are more productive in one historical time period than others.

Book printing isn't as productive today as it was before Gutenberg's printing press. So keep this in mind when choosing your innovation, you dont need to be like Jen who since long ago liked clean rooms. You may simply be passionate about an innovation just because it has the best chance of making the greatest good for the greater number. Most entrepreneurs started this way and they became extremely passionate as they learnt more about the innovation they were making. Always ask, "How can _____ (insert what you enjoy) be automated to boost value factors?" The 7th turning point is now at its beginning and each industry will have its moment for automation. Will you be in the arena playing or a spectator watching on the sidelines?

Below we have a checklist that Jen followed in thinking up her cleaning robot. Feel free to do the same, it takes many tries, but each one gets you closer to where your passion meets a large enough problem that people have.

	Jen	**You**
1. Passion?	**Cleaning**	
		_____
2. Innovations involved?	Brooms, liquids, brushes, towels, etc.	
		_____
3. Actions given?	Removal of dust and dirt from many places	
		_____
4. Possible productive innovations to automate above actions?	1. Dirt-proof carpet material? 2. Liquid to clean any stain? 3. Cleaning robot?***	
		_____

How to Help if You Like this Book?

If this book has left you feeling like, *"That was interesting. Things would be better if more people read this"*, then this space is for you. Returning from the start is our friend with a message…

It'll only take a minute or two
Go to the link below to leave a review
www.originofwhy.com

This book wasn't made with an advertising spend of Coca-Cola or the help of the rich and powerful, but if you're able to chip in a few minutes of your time, you can seriously help it find its way in the cold, tough world of historical selection.

- Post about this book to your friends and audiences on Facebook, Twitter, or blog.
- Recommend the book to co-workers, the local library, your friends, and your friends' friends, like those who blog to millions or run a national radio station or TV network. :)
- If you know trusted people who write for online media, newspapers or magazines, drop them an email—or maybe Ellen DeGeneres or Bill Gates owes you a favor? Now is a good time to remind them!
- If you're a master of surprising people, secretly send a copy of this book to someone who can spread its message.

As I wrote this book, I added my email in various spots so as not go down the slippery slope of blabbering on a detail for too long. Send a quick email to vitojgrigorov@gmail.com or go to www.prosperism.org to get all bonus material including:

1. Meaning of Life test
2. The Free Life Time graph
3. Appendixes A, B, C
4. Expanded Value Test
5. Possibly Asked Questions (PAQs)
6. Shareable images like the comic in full flow, downloadable diagrams, plus other images, like the cultural evolution tree and hierarchy of misery. Share it online, paste it on billboards, car windshields or post it in the mail, all this will help plant the seeds for the revolution. :-)

With enough interest from you and your friends, we can explore other large questions which can grow out of this one. Do say hi. Offer tips, criticisms, or anything on your mind. The email doesn't bite. And let your friends know, too. I thank you for staying with me to the end.

Acknowledgments

A common quote seen in this section is from Sir Isaac Newton who said, "They've stood on the shoulders of giants." For this book, the giants have been giant mountains of innovations from history.

It is with deep thanks to those in the past and present, who gave me a head start in the attempt to answer the question of the meaning of life. My apologies if I miss acknowledging anyone below, do let me know and future editions of this book will be updated. As expected, my biggest thanks go to those closest who've helped me along the way. To my dad and granddad, you both did not die in vain.

To my mum. You took the chance to raise me up in a welcoming new country, far away from, and different to, the one you grew up in. You've taught me lessons I live by today. To my grandparents, you made the trip across the sea possible, and once I got there, you drove me to weekend sports, cooked the tastiest meals, and did not just give me fish, but taught me how to fish. :-)

To everyone who gave their time and effort in helping make this book come alive. Special thanks go to my best mate from high school, Andrew Iliadis – your questions made me look at what's written in a new light. To the early draft readers who gave great tips, Flavio Faccin, Emma Franklin Bell, Michael Olshanksky, Elijah Christopher, Maria Sheptitskaya, Tania Van Omen, Tiago & Danny Duarte, Dino Talic, Harold Levine and Hugh Mackay. Along with the editing help of Candice Lemon-Scott, Gordon Warnock, Elyria Rose Little, Kimberley T, Lynette Stewart, fact checking skill of John Coomber, illustrating brilliance of Christian Mirra, and formatting genius of Hynek Palatin. Big thanks also to groups from the right and left, who were kind enough to give me their thoughts: To representatives of the Labor, Liberal and minor parties in Australia, the Centre of Independent Studies www.cis.org.au, the Friedman conference www.friedman17.org, the Sydney Institute www.thesydneyinstitute.com, the Institute of Public Affairs www.ipa.org.au, the Socialism conference www.socialismsydney.com, the Socialist Alliance www.socialist-alliance.org, and the Sydney Salon www.sydneysalon.org. While people and groups above have kindly helped, it does not mean they agree with every line of the finished book. A deep thank you to the libraries of the University of New South Wales, Sydney University, and the City of Sydney.

Formatting by: hynek.palatin@gmail.com
Cover by: www.redravenbookdesign.com
Readability edit by Elyria Rose Little http://linkedin.com/in/elyriaroselittle
Fact Checked by John Coomber
www.upwork.com/freelancers/~01313b7ba33c111638
Copyedited by Kimberley T
www.facebook.com/people/Write-Right/100011396168493
Proofreading by Lynette Stewart
https://www.upwork.com/o/profiles/users/_~01cc5594cf2405ea5e/
Drawings by Christian Mirra www.christianmirra.com
Book analytics by Alex Newton www.k-lytics.com

About the Author

Being a nobody, with little to gain or lose, Vito's aim is to try finding the truth with less bias blocking the way.

A somebody hides the truth, dripping it to you slowly to squeeze more money out of your pocket. In his past life (no not the mystical one living as a sea slug) he co-founded a startup, was a producer, and a TV debate show co-host.

One question he debated puzzled him for there was no answer, the question was the meaning of life. And since then it sparked a quest for clues that after several years has given an answer with research to back it up all wrapped in this book. For bonuses, email vitojgrigorov@gmail.com or go to: www.prosperism.org.

References

Preface

1. Camus, Albert. *The Myth of Sisyphus.* France: Gallimard, 1942. Print.
2. Camus, Albert. *The Myth of Sisyphus.* France: Gallimard, 1942. Print.

Introduction

1. Charlton, William. *Physics: Books I and II.* London: Oxford University Press, 1984. Print.
2. Steiner, Susie. 'Top Five Regrets of the Dying'. The Guardian 2012. Web. 12 Dec. 2015.
3. Marx, Karl. Wage-Labour and Capital. New York: International Publishers, 1933. Print.
   -Crabtree, Steve. "Worldwide, 13% of Employees are Engaged at Work". *gallup.com.* n.p., 2013. Web. 22 Dec. 2015.
4. Familiesandwork.org. 'The Results of a New Groundbreaking National Survey, Women and Time: Setting a New Agenda', Commissioned by Real Simple And Designed By Families And Work Institute. n.p., 2014. Web. 12 Dec. 2015.
5. Wikipedia. 'Summum Bonum'. n.p., 2015. Web. 12 Dec. 2015.
6. Locke, John. *An Essay Concerning Human Understanding.* Amherst, N.Y.: Prometheus Books, 1995. Print.
7. Laozi., and Lau, D.C. *Tao Te Ching.* Baltimore: Penguin Books, 1963. Print.
8. Kaufman, Walter (ed.). *Existentialism from Dostoyevsky to Sartre.* Oklahoma City: Meridian Publishing Company, 1989. Print.
9. Hammonds, Keith. 'You Can Do Anything – But Not Everything'. Fast Company. n.p., 2000. Web. 13 Dec. 2015.
10. Wilde, Oscar, Owen, William, and Morris, William. *The Soul of Man Under Socialism.* New York: Humboldt, 1891. Print.
11. Metz, Thaddeus. 'The Meaning of Life'. Plato.stanford.edu. n.p., 2007. Web. 13 Dec. 2015.
12. News.bbc.co.uk. 'Medieval Teeth 'Better Than Baldrick's''. n.p., 2015. Web. 13 Dec. 2015.
13. Mail Online. 'When Crocodile Dung Was Contraception'. n.p., 2015. Web. 13 Dec. 2015.
14. Aristotle., et al. *The Nicomachean Ethics.* Oxford (Oxfordshire): Oxford University Press, 1998. Print.

15. Harvard Business Review. 'Make the Dangerous Choice to Dissent'. n.p., 2011. Web. 13 Dec. 2015.
16. Wiltshire, David. *Marx's Theses on Feuerbach and the Tasks of the Revolutionary Party*. London: Union Books, 1995. Print.
17. Aristotle., et al. *The Nicomachean Ethics*. Oxford (Oxfordshire): Oxford University Press, 1998. Print.

Chapter 1

1.   Wood, Bill. "Winston Churchill for Traders & Analysts". Winstonchurchill.org. n.p., 2015. Web. 13 Dec. 2015.
2.   Shakespeare, William, and Jenkins, Harold. *Hamlet*. London: Methuen, 1982. Print.
3.   Frankl, Viktor E. *Man's Search for Meaning*. Boston: Beacon Press, 1992. Print.
4.   *A Brief History of Time*. United States: Errol Morris, 1991. DVD.
5.   Cousin, Victor. *Lectures on the True, the Beautiful, and the Good*. New York: Appleton and Company, 1872. Print.
6.   Colodny, Robert (Ed.) *Frontiers of Science and Philosophy*: Pittsburgh, University of Pittsburgh Press, 1962, Print.
7.   Rand, Ayn. *Philosophy, Who Needs It*. Indianapolis: Bobbs-Merrill, 1982. Print.
8.   Olson, Jeff, and Mann, John David. *The Slight Edge*. Austin, TX: Greenleaf Book Group Press, 2013. Print.
9.   Keynes, John Maynard. *The General Theory of Employment, Interest, and Money*. New York: Harcourt, Brace & World, 1965. Print.
10. Berlin, Isaiah. *Two Concepts of Liberty*. Oxford: Clarendon Press, 1958, Print.
11. Neumann, Steve. "On the New Atheism & Philosophy". Rationally Speaking 2014. Web. 13 Dec. 2015.
12. Parkhurst, Charles. *The pattern in the Mount and other sermons*. New York: A.D.F. Randolph & Company, 1885. Print
13. Canfield, Jack, and Switzer, Janet. *The Success Principles*. New York: Harper Resource Book, 2005. Print.
14. Frankl, Viktor E. *Man's Search for Meaning*. Boston: Beacon Press, 1992. Print.
15. Steiner, Susie. 'Top Five Regrets of the Dying'. The Guardian 2012. Web. 12 Dec. 2015.
16. Kobau, Rosemarie et al. "Well-Being Assessment: An Evaluation of Well-Being Scales for Public Health and Population Estimates of Well-Being Among US Adults". *Applied Psychology: Health and Well-Being* 2.3 (2010): 272-297. Web.
17. Greene, Robert. *Mastery*. New York: Viking, 2012. Print.

18. YouTube. "Anthony Robbins: Change Your World View". n.p., 2011. Web. 13 Dec. 2015.

19. Klemke, E. D. *The Meaning of Life*. New York: Oxford University Press, 1981. Print.

20. YouTube. "The Purpose of Purpose – Richard Dawkins". n.p., 2009. Web. 13 Dec. 2015.

21. Hume, Tim. "One Suicide Every 40 Seconds: WHO Report – CNN.Com". CNN. n.p., 2014. Web. 13 Dec. 2015.

22. Friedan, Betty, Fermaglich, Kirsten and Fine, Lisa. *The Feminine Mystique*. New York: W.W. Norton, 2013. Print.

23. World Health Organization. "Depression". n.p., 2015. Web. 13 Dec. 2015.

24. Kleftaras, George, and Psarra, Evangelia. "Meaning in Life, Psychological Well-Being and Depressive Symptomatology: A Comparative Study". *Psychology* 03.04 (2012): 337-345. Web.

25. Sherman, Janann. Interviews with Betty Friedan. Jackson: University Press of Mississippi, 2002. Print.

26. Goldberg, Carey. "Materialism is Bad for You, Studies Say". NYTimes.com. n.p., 2006. Web. 13 Dec. 2015.

27. Melton, Amanda, and Schulenberg, Stefan. "On the Measurement of Meaning: Logotherapy's Empirical Contributions to Humanistic Psychology". *HTHP* 36.1 (2008): 31-44. Web.

28. Frankl, Viktor E. *Man's Search for Ultimate Meaning*. New York: Insight Books, 1997. Print.

29. Britton, A., and M. J. Shipley. "Bored to Death?". *International Journal of Epidemiology* 39.2 (2010): 370-371. Web.

30. Berger, Jonah. *Contagious*. New York: Simon & Schuster, 2013. Print.

31. *Network*. United States: Lumet, 1976. DVD.

32. Dillard, Annie. *The Writing Life*. New York: Harper & Row, 1989. Print.

33. Wilson, T. D. et al. "Just Think: The Challenges of the Disengaged Mind". *Science* 345.6192 (2014): 75-77. Web.

34. Bennett, David et al. "Overview and Findings from the Rush Memory and Aging Project". *CAR* 9.6 (2012): 646-663. Web.

35. Melton, Amanda, and Schulenberg, Stefan. "On the Measurement of Meaning: Logotherapy's Empirical Contributions to Humanistic Psychology". *HTHP* 36.1 (2008): 31-44. Web.

36. Bennett, David et al. "Overview and Findings from the Rush Memory and Aging Project". *CAR* 9.6 (2012): 646-663. Web.

37. Winstonchurchill.org. "Quotes Falsely Attributed". n.p., 2015. Web. 14 Dec. 2015.

38. Glicken, Morley D. *Learning from Resilient People*. Thousand Oaks: Sage Publications, 2006. Print.

39. von Goethe, Johann. "Quote about Importance by Johann Wolfgang von Goethe on Quotations Book". *QuotationsBook.com*. n.p., 2015. Web. 14 Dec. 2015.

40. Rothenberger, Cecilia. "Find Your Calling". *Fast Company*. n.p., 2000. Web. 14 Dec. 2015.

41. Durant, Will. *On the Meaning of Life*. New York: Promethean Press, 2011. Print.

42. Einstein, Albert. *Ideas and Opinions*. New York: Broadway Books, 1995. Print.

43. Howell, Parker. "Gates Tells Seniors to Fight Inequity". *Spokesman Review* 2007: n. pag. Web.

44. Global Freedom Movement. "Gandhi's Top 10 Fundamentals for Changing the World". n.p., 2011. Web. 14 Dec. 2015.

45. YouTube. "Reid Hoffman: On Giving and Impact". n.p., 2015. Web. 14 Dec. 2015.

46. YouTube. "Steve Jobs' Vision of the World". n.p., 2015. Web. 14 Dec. 2015.

47. Feminist.com. "Inspiring Quotes by Women". n.p., 2015. Web. 14 Dec. 2015.

48. King, Martin Luther, and King, Coretta Scott. *The Words of Martin Luther King, Jr.* New York: Newmarket Press, 1987. Print.

49. Dalailamafilm.com. "Dalai Lama Quotes, Quotations, Sayings, Words, Wisdom – Dalai Lama Documentary Films". n.p., 2015. Web. 14 Dec. 2015.

50. En.wikiquote.org. "Horace Mann – Wikiquote". n.p., 1859. Web. 14 Dec. 2015.

51. Marxists.org. "Marx Quotes: Quotes from Karl Marx and Friedrich Engels". n.p., 2015. Web. 14 Dec. 2015.

52. Mill, John Stuart. "Autobiography". Archive.org. n.p., 2015. Web. 14 Dec. 2015.

53. Nobel, Alfred. "The Will". *Nobelprize.org*. n.p., 2015. Web. 14 Dec. 2015.

54. En.wikiquote.org. "Barack Obama – Wikiquote". n.p., 2005. Web. 14 Dec. 2015.

55. YouTube. "Larry Page at Zeitgeist Americas 2011". n.p., 2011. Web. 14 Dec. 2015.

56. Shaw, George Bernard. *Man and Superman, and Three Other Plays*. New York: Barnes & Noble Classics, 2004. Print.

57. Satterwhite, Al. *When Men Were Titans*. Deerfield, Ill.: Dalton Watson Fine Books, 2008. Print.

58. Blankenhagen, Ed. "P&I Bookshelf Learned Optimism by M. E. Seligman". *Performance + Instruction* 31.5 (1992): 44-44. Web.
59. Tolstoy, Leo, and Garnett, Constance. *The Kingdom of God Is Within You*. Auckland: Floating Press, 2009. Print.
60. Hakani, Avish. "7 Filthy Important World Changing Lessons from Mark Zuckerberg – Successogram". *Successogram.com*. n.p., 2014. Web. 14 Dec. 2015.
61. Aristotle., et al. *The Nicomachean Ethics*. Oxford (Oxfordshire): Oxford University Press, 1998. Print.
62. Norton, David L. *Personal Destinies*. Princeton, N.J.: Princeton University Press, 1976. Print.
63. Aristotle., et al. *The Nicomachean Ethics*. Oxford (Oxfordshire): Oxford University Press, 1998. Print.
64. Abrahamlincolnonline.org. "Abraham Lincoln's Second Lecture on Discoveries and Inventions". n.p., 1859. Web. 14 Dec. 2015.
65. Wikipedia. "Republic (Plato)". n.p., 2015. Web. 14 Dec. 2015.
66. Darwin, Charles. *The Descent of Man, and Selection in Relation to Sex*. Princeton, N.J.: Princeton University Press, 1981. Print.
67. Pbs.org. "The Story of the Storytellers – an Introduction to the Gospels: from Jesus to Christ Frontline/PBS". n.p., 2015. Web. 14 Dec. 2015.
68. Northrup, Chrisanna, Schwartz, Pepper, and Witte, James. *The Normal Bar*. United States: Harmony, 2013. Print.
69. Griffiths, Sarah. "Legendary Moroccan Ruler could have had 1,100 Children". *Mail Online*. n.p., 2014. Web. 14 Dec. 2015.
70. ABC News. "Former News of the World Editor Jailed Over Hacking". n.p., 2014. Web. 14 Dec. 2015.
71. YouTube. "Lade Gaga – Emotion Revolution Summit". n.p., 2015. Web. 14 Dec. 2015.
72. Primack, Brian A., Douglas, Erika L, and Kraemer, Kevin L. "Exposure to Cannabis in Popular Music and Cannabis Use Among Adolescents". *Addiction* 105.3 (2010): 515-523. Web.
73. Huesmann, L. Rowell et al. "Longitudinal Relations between Children's Exposure to TV Violence and Their Aggressive and Violent Behavior in Young Adulthood: 1977-1992.". *Developmental Psychology* 39.2 (2003): 201-221. Web.
74. Dickey, Megan. "These Charts Show No One was Singing about Sex until the 1990s". *Business Insider Australia*. n.p., 2014. Web. 14 Dec. 2015.
75. Primack, Brian A. et al. "Content Analysis of Tobacco, Alcohol, and Other Drugs in Popular Music". *Pediatrics and Adolescent Medicine* 162.2 (2008): 169. Web.

76. Kff.org, "Generation M: Media in the Lives of 8-18 Yr-Olds". n.p., 2005. Web. 14 Dec. 2015.

77. Durant, Will. *On the Meaning of Life.* New York: Promethean Press, 2011. Print.

78. Darwin, Charles, and Darwin, Francis. *The Life and Letters of Charles Darwin.* Charleston, SC: BiblioBazaar, 1887. Print.

79. Olanoff, Drew. "Bill Gates Has Helped Save Over 5.8 Million Lives". *The Next Web.* n.p., 2012. Web. 14 Dec. 2015.

80. YouTube. "Malcolm Gladwell Part 3 – Appel Salon". n.p., 2012. Web. 14 Dec. 2015.

81. Visual.ly. "Just How Big Is Microsoft? – Visual.Ly". n.p., 2015. Web. 14 Dec. 2015.

82. Wikipedia. "General Electric". n.p., 2015. Web. 14 Dec. 2015.

83. Wikipedia. "Apple Inc.". n.p., 2015. Web. 14 Dec. 2015.

84. Wikipedia. "Walmart". n.p., 2015. Web. 14 Dec. 2015.

85. U.S. Office of Personnel Management. "Total Government Employment since 1962". n.p., 2015. Web. 14 Dec. 2015.

86. Klein, Maury. *The Power Makers.* New York: Bloomsbury Press, 2008. Print.

87. Thompson, Robert. *Wiring a Continent: The History of the Telegraph Industry in the United States 1832-1866.* United States: Arno Press, 1972. Print.

88. Hayes, Erin. "Google Gives Free Time". *ABC News.* n.p., 2008. Web. 14 Dec. 2015.

89. Popova, Maria. "How to Get Rich: Paul Graham on Money vs. Wealth". *Brain Pickings* 2014. Web. 14 Dec. 2015.

90. Givingpledge.org. "The Giving Pledge: Pledger Profiles". n.p., 2015. Web. 14 Dec. 2015.

91. Hardoon, Deborah. "Wealth: Having it All and Wanting More". *Oxfam Policy & Practice.* n.p., 2015. Web. 14 Dec. 2015.

92. YouTube. "Obama: If You've Got a Business, You Didn't Build That". n.p., 2012. Web. 14 Dec. 2015.

93. Monbiot, George. "The Self-Attribution Fallacy". *monbiot.com.* n.p., 2011. Web. 14 Dec. 2015

94. Keywell, Brad. "A Book that Changes Lives". *Bradkeywell.com.* n.p., 2015. Web. 14 Dec. 2015.

95. Shah, Anup. "Poverty Facts and Stats — Global Issues". *Globalissues.org.* n.p., 2013. Web. 15 Dec. 2015.

96. En.wikiquote.org. "William Thomson – Wikiquote". n.p., 1883. Web. 14 Dec. 2015.

97. Will, George. "The Wisdom of Pat Moynihan". *The Washington Post.* n.p., 2010. Web. 14 Dec. 2015.

98. Popova, Maria. "Do Something Meaningful: Neil deGrasse Tyson and Ann Druyan on Carl Sagan". *Brain Pickings* 2013. Web. 14 Dec. 2015.

99. Graham, Paul. "Startups in 13 Sentences". *paulgraham.com*. n.p., 2015. Web. 14 Dec. 2015.

100. YouTube. "Ben Silbermann at Startup School 2012". n.p., 2013. Web. 14 Dec. 2015.

101. The number of people Marie Curie has impacted is based on estimates of the number of people who have been administered x-rays in the world.

102. Scienceheroes.com. "Karl Landsteiner". n.p., 2015. Web. 26 Dec. 2015.

103. Woodward, Billy, Shurkin, Joel, Gordon, Debra. *Scientists Greater Than Einstein*. Fresno, CA: Quill Driver Books, 2009. Print.

104. Dediu, Horace. "Third to a Billion". *Asymco*. n.p., 2013. Web. 14 Dec. 2015.

105. Dediu, Horace. "Third to a Billion". *Asymco*. n.p., 2013. Web. 14 Dec. 2015.

106. Wikipedia. "Paulo Coelho". n.p., 2015. Web. 14 Dec. 2015.

107. Digital Music News. "iTunes has 800 Million Accounts… and 800 Million Credit Card Numbers… –Digital Music News". n.p., 2014. Web. 14 Dec. 2015.

108. Wikipedia. "Timothy McVeigh". n.p., 2015. Web. 14 Dec. 2015.

109. Necrometrics.com. "Twentieth Century Atlas – Death Tolls". n.p., 2015. Web. 14 Dec. 2015.

110. Necrometrics.com. "Twentieth Century Atlas – Death Tolls". n.p., 2015. Web. 14 Dec. 2015.

111. Tolstoy, Leo, and Kentish, Jane. *A Confession and Other Religious Writings*. Harmondsworth, Middlesex, England: Penguin, 1987. Print.

Chapter 2

1. Nietzsche, Friedrich, Ansell-Pearson, Keith, and Diethe, Carol. *On the Genealogy of Morality*. New York: Cambridge University Press, 1994. Print.

2. Mill, John Stuart. *Principles of Political Economy*. United Kingdom: John W. Parker, 1848. Print.

3. Frankl, Viktor E. *Man's Search for Meaning*. Boston: Beacon Press, 1992. Print.

4. Maslow, Abraham H. *The Maslow Business Reader*. John Wiley & Sons, 2000. Print.

5.   Ricardo, David. *On the Principles of Political Economy and Taxation*. London: Electric Book Co., 2001. Print.

6.   O'Rourke, P. J, and Smith, Adam. *On the Wealth of Nations*. New York: Atlantic Monthly Press, 2007. Print.

7.   Emerson, Ralph Waldo. *The American Scholar*. New York: American Book Co., 1893. Print.

8.   Skidelsky, Robert, and Skidelsky, Edward. *How Much Is Enough?* New York: Other Press, 2012. Print.

9.   Camus, Albert. *The Myth of Sisyphus*. France: Gallimard, 1942. Print.

10. Kelly, Kevin. *What Technology Wants*. New York: Viking, 2010. Print.

11. Ruskin, John, and Hubenka, Lloyd. *"Unto This Last"*. Lincoln: University of Nebraska Press, 1967. Print.
     -Magee, Joseph. M Ph D "St Thomas Aquinas on the Natural Law" *Aquinas Online*. n.p 2015., Web 5 Feb 2015

12. Fulda, Simone, M Gorman Adrienne, Hori, Osamu and Samali Afshin "Cellular Stress Responses: Cell Survival and Cell Death" hindawi.com/journals. n.p., 2010. Web. 15 Dec. 2015.

13. Hermanns, William, and Einstein, Albert. *Einstein and the Poet*. Brookline Village, MA: Branden Press, 1983. Print.

14. World Health Organization. "WHO – Life Expectancy". n.p., 2013. Web. 15 Dec. 2015.

15. Ericson, John. "Vodka Is Really Killing Russian Men". *Medical Daily*. n.p., 2014. Web. 15 Dec. 2015.

16. Office of National Statistics. "Life Expectancies – ONS". n.p., 2015. Web. 15 Dec. 2015.

17. Australian Bureau of Statistics. "3302.0 – Deaths, Australia, 2014". n.p., 2015. Web. 15 Dec. 2015.

18. Lewis, David. "Galaxy Stress Research, 2009". United Kingdom: Mindlab International, Sussex University, 2009. Web. 15 Dec. 2015

19. Springwise.com. "Smart Shirt Helps Wearers Keep Track of their Mental and Physical Wellbeing". n.p., 2013. Web. 15 Dec. 2015.

20. Hjelmborg, Jacob et al. "Genetic Influence on Human Lifespan and Longevity". *Human Genetics* 119.3 (2006): 312-321. Web.

21. YouTube. "Mark Zuckerberg at Startup School 2012". n.p., 2013. Web. 15 Dec. 2015.

22. Banks, James, Nazroo, James and Steptoe, Andrew. "English Longitudinal Study of Ageing". *Elsa-project.ac.uk*. n.p., 2014. Web. 15 Dec. 2015.

23. Plass, Jan, Moreno, Roxana and Brunken, Roland (Eds.). *Cognitive Load Theory*. Cambridge: Cambridge University Press, 2010. Print.

24. Vohs, Kathleen et al. "Making Choices Impairs Subsequent Self-Control: A Limited-Resource Account of Decision Making, Self-

Regulation, and Active Initiative". *Motivation Science* 1.S (2014): 19-42. Web.

25. Drglennwilson.com. "The "Infomania" Study". n.p., 2010. Web. 15 Dec. 2015.

26. Rubinsztein-Dunlop, Sean. "Teenager Refused Bail Over Kings Cross Death". *ABC News.* n.p., 2012. Web. 15 Dec. 2015.

27. Frankl, Viktor E. *Man's Search for Meaning.* Boston: Beacon Press, 1992. Print.

28. Veblen, T. "Why is Economics Not an Evolutionary Science?". *Cambridge Journal of Economics* 22.4 (1998): 403-414. Web.

29. -Fredrickson, B. L. et al. "A Functional Genomic Perspective on Human Well-Being". *Proceedings of the National Academy of Sciences* 110.33 (2013): 13684-13689. Web.

30. Baumeister, Roy. "The Meanings of Life". *Aeon.co.* n.p., 2010. Web. 15 Dec. 2015.

31. Sayid, Ruki. "Top Ten Most Vandalised Cars in Britain with BMW at Top of List". *Mirror.* n.p., 2013. Web. 15 Dec. 2015.

32. Shah, Anup. "Poverty Facts and Stats — Global Issues". *Globalissues.org.* n.p., 2013. Web. 15 Dec. 2015.

33. Clarke, R. et al. "Life Expectancy in Relation to Cardiovascular Risk Factors: 38 Year Follow-Up of 19 000 Men in the Whitehall Study". *British Medical Journal* 339.sep16 3 (2009): b3513-b3513. Web.

34. Kitahara, Cari et al. "Association between Class III Obesity (BMI of 40–59 Kg/M2) and Mortality: A Pooled Analysis of 20 Prospective Studies". *PLOS Medicine* 11.7 (2014): e1001673. Web.

35. Richards, Jeffrey. "A Proud Look". *sermoncentral.com.* n.p., 2001. Web. 15 Dec. 2015.

36. Harris, Sam. *The Moral Landscape.* New York: Free Press, 2010. Print.
-Durrant, J., and Ensom, R. "Physical Punishment of Children: Lessons from 20 Years of Research". *Canadian Medical Association Journal* 184.12 (2012): 1373-1377. Web.
-FBI, "FYI 2011 Bud Summary" Web 13 January 2016
-Klien, Herbert S. The *Atlantic Slave Trade,* Cambridge University press, 2nd Edition, 2010, Print
-Dunkel, Mathes, Beaver et al "Life history theory and the general theory of Crime: Life expectancy effects on low self-control and criminal intent" – *Journal of Social, Evolutionary, and Cultural Psychology.*
-The Challenge of Cultural Relativism Web 19 April 2016

37. Grenier, Richard. "The Gandhi Nobody Knows". *Commentarymagazine.com.* n.p., 1983. Web. 15 Dec. 2015.

38.   Yom-Tov, Elad, and Boyd, Danah. "On the Link between Media Coverage of Anorexia and Pro-Anorexic Practices on the Web". *International. Journal of Eating Disorders*. 47.2 (2013): 196-202. Web.
       -Ap, Tiffany, "London Bans 'unrealistic body Images from Transport System'. n.p., 2016. Web. 15 Jun
       -Sparks, Ian, "France bans 'Super-Skinny' models from fashion shows and advertising under new health laws". n.p, 2015 Web 18 Dec

39.   Trigger, Rebecca. "Wicked Campers Apologises For Van Slogan After Uproar". *ABC News*. n.p., 2014. Web. 15 Dec. 2015.

40.   Riley, Jonathan. *Mill on Liberty*. London: Routledge, 1998. Print.
       - Stephani Sutherland "When We Read, We Recognise Words as Pictures..." *Scientific American*. n.p, Web. 1 Jul 2015

41.   Singer, Peter. *Writings on an Ethical Life*. New York: Ecco Press, 2001. Print.

42.   Schumpeter, Joseph. *The Theory of Economic Development*. United States: Transaction Publishers, 1934. Print.

43.   Nietzsche, Friedrich, and Ludovici, Anthony. *Ecce Homo*. Mineola, N.Y.: Dover Publications, 2004. Print.

44.   Simonton, Dean. *Greatness*. New York: Guilford, 1994. Print.

Chapter 3

1.   Ostrovsky, Nikolay. *How the Steel Was Tempered*. Moscow: Foreign Languages Pub. House, 1959. Print.

2.   Popper, Karl R. *The Poverty of Historicism*. New York: Harper & Row, 1964. Print.

3.   Ekirch, Roger. *At Day's Close*. New York: Norton, 2005. Print.

4.   Wikipedia. "Age of the Earth". n.p., 2015. Web. 15 Dec. 2015.

5.   O'Leary, M. A. et al. "The Placental Mammal Ancestor and the Post-K-Pg Radiation of Placentals". *Science* 339.6120 (2013): 662-667. Web.

6.   Than, Ker. "Greatest Mysteries: How Did the Universe Begin?". *LiveScience.com*. n.p., 2007. Web. 15 Dec. 2015.

7.   Wikipedia. "Geologic Temperature Record". n.p., 2015. Web. 15 Dec. 2015.

8.   Darwin, Charles. *The Descent of Man, and Selection in Relation to Sex*. Princeton, N.J.: Princeton University Press, 1981. Print.

9.   Teilhard de Chardin, Pierre, Huxley, Julian and Wall, Bernard. *The Phenomenon of Man*. New York: Harper, 1959. Print.

10.   Darwin, Charles. *The Descent of Man, and Selection in Relation to Sex*. Princeton, N.J.: Princeton University Press, 1981. Print.

11. YouTube. "BBC Profile Richard Dawkins -Full-". n.p., 2012. Web. 16 Dec. 2015.

12. Breuer, Thomas, Ndoundou-Hockemba, Mireille, and Fishlock, Vicki. "First Observation of Tool Use in Wild Gorillas". *PLOS Biology* 3.11 (2005): e380. Web. 16 Dec. 2015.

13. Selim, Jocelyn. "Useless Body Parts". *discovermagazine.com*, n.p., 2004. Web. 16 Dec. 2015.

14. Brand, Stewart. "The Dawn of De-Extinction. Are You Ready?". ted.com. n.p., 2015. Web. 16 Dec. 2015.

15. Wallace, Alfred Russel. *The Origin of Human Races and The Antiquity of Man Deduced from The Theory Of "Natural Selection"*. London: Anthropological Institute of Great Britain, 1875. Print.

16. Bloom, Harold. *James Boswell's Life of Samuel Johnson*. New York: Chelsea House, 1986. Print.

17. Carlyle, Thomas, McSweeney, Kerry and Sabor, Peter. *Sartor Resartus*. Oxfordshire: Oxford University Press, 1987. Print.

18. University of Adelaide.edu.au. "Seek Light". *adelaide.edu.au/seek-light*, n.p., 2015. Web. 16 Dec. 2015.

19. Chan, Margaret. "Antimicrobial Resistance in the European Union and the World". *who.int*. n.p., 2012. Web. 16 Dec. 2015.

20. Morgan, C. Lloyd. *Habit and Instinct*. New York: Arno Press, 1973. Print.

21. Dawkins, Richard. *The Selfish Gene*. Oxford: Oxford University Press, 1989. Print.

22. *Troy*. Hollywood: Warner Bros., 2004. DVD.
- Woodward, Bill. Shurkin, Josh *"Scientists Greater Than Einstein: The Biggest Lifesavers of the Twentieth Century"*. Quill Driver Books, 2009

23. Ritchie, David, and Nicholson, Peter. *Darwinism and Politics. The Principles of State Interference*. Bristol: Thoemmes, 1998. Print.

24. Bacon, Francis. *Essays*. London: Dent, 1972. Print.

25. McPherron, Shannon P. et al. "Evidence for Stone-Tool-Assisted Consumption of Animal Tissues before 3.39 Million Years Ago at Dikika, Ethiopia". *Nature* 466.7308 (2010): 857-860. Web.

26. Wikipedia. "Productivity". n.p., 2015. Web. 16 Dec. 2015.

27. Eltis, David. *Economic Growth and the Ending of the Transatlantic Slave Trade*. New York: Oxford University Press, 1987. Print.

28. Gordon, John Steele. *An Empire of Wealth*. New York: HarperCollins, 2004. Print.

29. Newton, James D. *Uncommon Friends*. San Diego, Calif.: Harcourt Brace Jovanovich, 1987. Print.

30. Darwin, Charles, and Beer, Gillian. *On the Origin of Species*. New York: Oxford University Press, 2008. Print.

31. Wikipedia. "Idea–Expression Divide". n.p., 2015. Web. 16 Dec. 2015.

32. Topper, David R. *How Einstein Created Relativity out of Physics and Astronomy*. New York, NY: Springer, 2013. Print.

33. Flanagan, Owen J. *The Really Hard Problem*. Cambridge, Mass.: MIT Press, 2007. Print.

34. Ogburn, William F. *Social Change with Respect to Cultural and Original Nature*. New York: Dell Pub. Co., 1966. Print.

35. Popper, Karl R. *The Poverty of Historicism*. New York: Harper & Row, 1964. Print.

36. Stattrek.com. "Combination and Permutation Calculator". n.p., 2015. Web. 16 Dec. 2015.
    - Norton, David L, *Personal Destinies: A Philosophy of Ethical Individualism*. Princeton University press 1977 Print

37. Crawford, Chris. *Happiness Is Everything*. United States: Six Star Publishing, 2001. Print.

38. National Institute on Aging. "Living Longer". n.p., 2011. Web. 16 Dec. 2015.

39. Marx, Karl. *A Contribution to the Critique of Political Economy*. New York: International Publishers, 1970. Print.

40. Csikszentmihalyi, Mihaly, and Halton, Eugene. *The Meaning of Things*. Cambridge: Cambridge University Press, 1981. Print.

41. Storr, Will. "The Unpersuadables: Adventures with the Enemies of Science". Overlook Press. 2014. Print
    - McRaney, David "You Are Not So Smart". Avery. 2012. Print
    - Goldman, Alex. "Yesterday the Internet Solved A 20-Year Mystery". *Lexicon Valley* 2014. Web. 16 Dec. 2015.

42. Pinker, Steven. *The Blank Slate*. New York: Viking, 2002. Print.
    "Profile of Noel Biderman" *MoneyWeek* n.p 2015 Web 19 April 2016
    "Ashley Madison hack: Website founder Noel Biderman is married father of two who says he has never cheated on his wife" Independent n.p 2015 Web 19 April 2016

43. TROM Documentary. "TROM Documentary". *tromsite.com*. n.p., 2012. Web. 16 Dec. 2015.

44. Darwin, Charles. *The Descent of Man, and Selection in Relation to Sex*. Princeton, N.J.: Princeton University Press, 1981. Print.

45. Tishkoff, Sarah A et al. "Convergent Adaptation of Human Lactase Persistence in Africa and Europe". *Nature Genetics* 39.1 (2006): 31-40. Web.

46. Cairns, John, Overbaugh, Julie and Miller, Stephan. "The Origin of Mutants". *Nature* 335.6186 (1988): 142-145. Web.

47. Swagerty, D., Walling, A., and Klein, R. "Lactose Intolerance". *American Family Physician* 1.65 (9) (2002): 1845-50. Print.

48. Elkins, Lucy. "Why a Simple Stomach Bug Could Mean You'll Never be Able to Eat Dairy Again". *Mail Online*. n.p., 2011. Web. 16 Dec. 2015.

49. Wikipedia. "Epigenetics". n.p., 2015. Web. 16 Dec. 2015.

50. Cloud, John. "Why Your DNA isn't Your Destiny". *time.com*. n.p., 2010. Web. 16 Dec. 2015.

51. Mercola.com. "Epigenetics: How Your Mind Can Reprogram Your Genes". n.p., 2012. Web. 16 Dec. 2015.

52. Francis, Richard C. *Epigenetics*. New York: W.W. Norton, 2011. Print.

53. Thomas, Roger. "Psycoloquy 5(63): Pavlov Used a Bell". *cogsci.ecs.soton.ac.uk*. n.p., 1994. Web. 16 Dec. 2015.

54. Markunas, Christina A. et al. "Identification of DNA Methylation Changes in Newborns Related to Maternal Smoking During Pregnancy". *Environmental Health Perspectives* (2014): n. pag. Web.

55. Enriquez, Juan. *Evolving Ourselves*. Oneworld Publications, 2015. Print.

56. British Broadcasting Corporation. "BBC – Science & Nature – Horizon". *bbc.co.uk/sn/tvradio/programmes/horizon/ghostgenes.shtml*. n.p., 2014. Web. 16 Dec. 2015.

57. Cao-Lei, Lei et al. "DNA Methylation Signatures Triggered by Prenatal Maternal Stress Exposure to a Natural Disaster: Project Ice Storm". *PLOS ONE* 9.9 (2014): e107653. Web.

58. Anand, Preetha et al. "Cancer is a Preventable Disease that Requires Major Lifestyle Changes". *Pharmaceutical Research* 25.9 (2008): 2097-2116. Web.

59. Rosenthal, Lillie. "How to Outsmart Your Genes and Live a Better Life ". *The Huffington Post*. n.p., 2015. Web. 16 Dec. 2015.

60. World Health Organization. "WHO| Overview – Preventing Chronic Diseases: A Vital Investment". *who.int*. n.p., 2015. Web. 16 Dec. 2015.

61. Darwin, Charles. *The Descent of Man, and Selection in Relation to Sex*. Princeton, N.J.: Princeton University Press, 1981. Print.

62. Rothstein, Mark, Cai, Yu, and Marchant, Gary. "The Ghost in our Genes: Legal and Ethical Implications of Epigenetics". *Health Matrix* 19.1 (2009): 1-62. Web. 16 Dec. 2015.

63. Pilcher, Helen. "The Third Factor: Beyond Nature and Nurture". *The Sydney Morning Herald*. n.p., 2013. Web. 16 Dec. 2015.

64. Wikipedia Commons & Creative Commons
     Braff, Danielle. "Movies May Cause Special Effects on The Body" Chicago Tribune. n.p 2011. Web. June. 22. 2011

Chapter 4

1. Bacon, Francis. *Novum Organum*. Chicago: Published by Henry Regnery Co. for the Great Books Foundation, 1949. Print. Forbes "Thoughts" http://www.forbes.com/global/2009/0907/quotes-sayings-proverbs-thoughts.html n.p 2009 Web 16 Dec 2015
2. Eveleth, Rose. "There are 37.2 Trillion Cells in Your Body". *Smithsonian*. n.p., 2013. Web. 16 Dec. 2015.
3. Nobelprize.org. "The 2009 Nobel Prize in Physiology or Medicine – Press Release". n.p., 2009. Web. 16 Dec. 2015.
4. Ornish, Dean et al. "Effect of Comprehensive Lifestyle Changes on Telomerase Activity and Telomere Length in Men with Biopsy-Proven Low-Risk Prostate Cancer: 5-Year Follow-Up of a Descriptive Pilot Study". *The Lancet Oncology* 14.11 (2013): 1112-1120. Web.
5. Crous-Bou, M. et al. "Mediterranean Diet and Telomere Length in Nurses' Health Study: Population Based Cohort Study". *British Medical Journal* 349.dec02 5 (2014): g6674-g6674. Web.
6. Wikipedia. "Occam's Razor". n.p., 2015. Web. 16 Dec. 2015.
7. Goodin, Robert E. *Discretionary Time*. Cambridge: Cambridge University Press, 2008. Print.
8. Tate, Ryan. "Twitter Founder Reveals Secret Formula for Getting Rich Online". *Wired*. n.p., 2013. Web. 16 Dec. 2015.
9. Yaqub, Reshma Memon. "The Way I Work: Aaron Levie: Box". *Inc.* n.p., 2012. Web. 16 Dec. 2015.
10. Productivity Commission. *Productivity Policies: The 'To Do' List*. Melbourne: Australian Government, 2012. Print.
11. Office of the Chief Economist. *Australian Innovation System Report 2012*. Canberra: Australian Government, 2012. Print.
12. Office of the Chief Economist. *Australian Innovation System Report 2013*. Canberra: Australian Government, 2013. Print.
13. Brynjolfsson, Erik, and Andrew McAfee. *Race Against the Machine*. Lexington, Mass.: Digital Frontier Press, 2012. Print.
14. Economic Policy Institute. "The Link between Productivity Growth and Living Standards". n.p., 2000. Web. 16 Dec. 2015.
15. Wikipedia. "List of Monarchs of the British Isles by Cause of Death". n.p., 2015. Web. 17 Dec. 2015.
16. Wikipedia. "Nathan Mayer Rothschild". n.p., 2015. Web. 17 Dec. 2015.
17. British Broadcasting Corporation. "BBC – History – Edward Jenner". *bbc.co.uk*. n.p., 2015. Web. 17 Dec. 2015.
18. Chemical Heritage Foundation. "A Fresh Breath". *chemheritage.org*. n.p., 2015. Web. 17 Dec. 2015.

19. Senthilingam, Meera. "'Instagram for Doctors lets Medics Share Patient Pics". *CNN*. n.p., 2015. Web. 17 Dec. 2015.
20. World Bank. "Physicians (per 1,000 People)". n.p., 2015. Web. 17 Dec. 2015.
21. Lichtenberg, Frank R. "The Impact of New Drug Launches on Longevity: Evidence from Longitudinal, Disease-Level Data from 52 Countries, 1982-2001". *International Journal of Health Economics and Management* 5.1 (2005): 47-73. Web.
22. McKinlay, John B., McKinlay, Sonja M. "The Questionable Contribution of Medical Measures to the Decline of Mortality in the United States in the Twentieth Century". *The Milbank Memorial Fund Quarterly. Health and Society* 55.3 (1977): 405. Web.
23. Wikipedia. "Slingshot (Water Vapor Distillation System)". n.p., 2015. Web. 17 Dec. 2015.
24. Kahneman, Daniel. *Thinking, Fast and Slow*. United States: Farrar, Straus and Giroux, 2011. Print.
25. Misa, Thomas J, Brey, Philip and Feenberg, Andrew. *Modernity and Technology*. Cambridge, Mass.: MIT Press, 2003. Print.
26. Goines, Lisa, and Hagler, Louis. "Noise Pollution: A Modern Plague". *Southern Medical Journal* 100.3 (2007): 287-294. Web.
27. Zipf, George Kingsley. *Selected Studies of the Principle of Relative Frequency in Language*. Cambridge, Mass.: Harvard University Press, 1932. Print.
28. Baer, Drake. "The Scientific Reason Why Barack Obama and Mark Zuckerberg Wear the Same Outfit Every Day". *Business Insider Australia*. n.p., 2015. Web. 17 Dec. 2015.
29. Lewis, David. "Galaxy Stress Research, 2009". United Kingdom: Mindlab International, Sussex University, 2009. Web. 15 Dec. 2015
30. Trappe, H.-J. "The Effects of Music on the Cardiovascular System and Cardiovascular Health". *Heart* 96.23 (2010): 1868-1871. Web.
31. Chafin, Sky et al. "Music Can Facilitate Blood Pressure Recovery from Stress". *British Journal of Health Psychology* 9.3 (2004): 393-403. Web.
32. Siedliecki, Sandra L., and Good, Marion. "Effect of Music on Power, Pain, Depression and Disability". *Journal of Advanced Nursing* 54.5 (2006): 553-562. Web.
33. Jones, Stephanie M., and Zigler, Edward. "The Mozart Effect". *Journal of Applied Developmental Psychology* 23.3 (2002): 355-372. Web.
34. McCraty, R. et al. "The Effects of Different Types of Music on Mood, Tension, and Mental Clarity". *Alternative Therapies in Health and Medicine* 4.1 (1998): 75-84. Print.

35. Retallack, Dorothy. *The Sound of Music and Plants*. United States: Devorss & Co., 1973. Print.
36. Wikipedia. "Landline". n.p., 2015. Web. 17 Dec. 2015.
37. Marx, Karl. *The Poverty of Philosophy*. New York: International Publishers, 1963. Print.
38. Goldman, David. "Facebook Claims It Created 4.5 Million Jobs". *CNNMoney*. n.p., 2015. Web. 17 Dec. 2015.
39. Apple. "About – Job Creation – Apple". n.p., 2015. Web. 17 Dec. 2015.
40. *Narcotics Anonymous Hospitals & Institutions Handbook*. Los Angeles: Narcotics Anonymous, 1981. Print.
41. Hart, Michael H. *The 100*. Secaucus, N.J.: Carol Pub. Group, 1992. Print.
42. Gottlieb, Agnes Hooper. *1000 Years, 1000 People*. New York: Kodansha International, 1998. Print.
43. Cowen, Tyler. *Discover Your Inner Economist*. New York: Dutton, 2007. Print.
44. Clark, Robert Judson. *The Shaping of Art and Architecture in Nineteenth-Century America*. New York: Metropolitan Museum of Art, 1972. Print.
45. The Economist. "Planet of the Phones". n.p., 2015. Web. 17 Dec. 2015.
46. Gartner. *Gartner Says Worldwide Device Shipments to Grow 1.5 Percent, To Reach 2.5 Billion Units In 2015*. 2015. Web.
47. Markets and Markets. *Cloud Storage Market Worth 65.41 Billion USD by 2020*. 2015. Web.
48. World Health Organization. "WHO Report on The Global Tobacco Epidemic, 2008 – The MPOWER Package". n.p., 2008. Web. 17 Dec. 2015.
49. Ingram, David. "Judge Orders Tobacco Companies to Admit Deception". *Reuters*. n.p., 2012. Web. 17 Dec. 2015.
50. Crosslandsolicitors.com. "Employers' Attitude to Obese Candidates – Crossland Employment Solicitors". n.p., 2015. Web. 17 Dec. 2015.
51. Government of the United Kingdom. "Antisocial Behaviour Order (ASBO)". *gov.uk/asbo*. n.p., 2015. Web. 17 Dec. 2015.
52. Nave, C. S. et al. "On the Contextual Independence of Personality: Teachers' Assessments Predict Directly Observed Behavior after Four Decades". *Social Psychological and Personality Science* 1.4 (2010): 327-334. Web.
53. Lah, Kyung. "'Rapelay' Video Game goes Viral amid Outrage". *edition.cnn.com*. n.p., 2010. Web. 17 Dec. 2015.

54. Yin-Poole, Wesley. "Epic's Tim Sweeney Predicts Photo-Realistic Graphics within 10 Years". *eurogamer.net.* n.p., 2013. Web. 17 Dec. 2015.

55. Gye, Hugo, Keneally, Meghan, and Bates, Daniel. "'He was just Looking to Chat... Nothing Sexual': How Batman Killer was Rejected by Three Women on Dating Website Days before Massacre". *Mail Online.* n.p., 2012. Web. 17 Dec. 2015.

56. Kleinfield, N., Rivera, R. and Kovaleski, S. "Obsessions of Adam Lanza, Newtown Killer, in Detail". *nytimes.com.* n.p., 2013. Web. 17 Dec. 2015.

57. Rolling Stone. "Ke$Ha Clarifies being 'Forced' to Sing 'Die Young'". n.p., 2012. Web. 17 Dec. 2015.

58. Chapman, S et al. "Australia's 1996 Gun Law Reforms: Faster Falls in Firearm Deaths, Firearm Suicides, and a Decade without Mass Shootings". *Injury Prevention* 21.5 (2015): 355-362. Web.

59. Morris, Eric. "Freakonomics – From Horse Power to Horsepower to Processing Power". *Freakonomics.com.* n.p., 2012. Web. 17 Dec. 2015.

60. Grunwald, Michael. "Why the U.S. is also Giving Brazilians Farm Subsidies". *Time.com.* n.p., 2010. Web. 17 Dec. 2015.
- Stewart, Heather, "George Osborne backs sugar tax and £3.5bn of Whitehall cuts" The *Guardian* n.p 2016 Web 17 March 2016

61. Rappaport, Liz. "Ernst Accused of Lehman Whitewash". *Wall Street Journal.* n.p., 2010. Web. 17 Dec. 2015.

62. Roberts, Joel. "Enron Traders Caught on Tape". *cbsnews.com.* n.p., 2004. Web. 17 Dec. 2015.

63. Viswanatha, Aruna, and Freifeld, Karen. "S&P Reaches $1.5 Billion Deal with U.S., States over Crisis-Era Ratings". *Reuters.* n.p., 2015. Web. 17 Dec. 2015.

64. *Inside Job.* Hollywood: Sony Pictures Classics, 2010. DVD.

Chapter 5

1. Goethe, Johann Wolfgang von, and Blackall, Eric. *Wilhelm Meister's Apprenticeship.* New York: Suhrkamp Publishers, 1989. Print.

2. *City Slickers.* Hollywood: Castle Rock Entertainment, 1991. DVD.

3. Dictionary.com. "The Definition of Entrepreneur". n.p., 2015. Web. 17 Dec. 2015.

4. Drucker, Peter F. *Innovation and Entrepreneurship.* New York: Harper & Row, 1985. Print.

5. Dyer, Jeff, Gregersen, Hal, and Christensen, Clayton. *The Innovator's DNA.* Boston, Mass.: Harvard Business Press, 2011. Print.

6.   Arrington, Michael. "Are You a Pirate?". *TechCrunch*. n.p., 2010. Web. 17 Dec. 2015.

7.   Winfrey, Oprah. "What Oprah Knows for Sure about Life's Biggest Adventure". *oprah.com*. n.p., 2002. Web. 17 Dec. 2015.

8.   Massachusetts Institute of Technology. "Drew Houston's Commencement Address". n.p., 2013. Web. 17 Dec. 2015.

9.   Rose, Kevin. "If You Believe in Something it Won't Feel Like Work". *Tailwind* 2014. Web. 17 Dec. 2015.

10. Wikipedia. "First Inauguration of Franklin D. Roosevelt". n.p., 2015. Web. 17 Dec. 2015.

11. Marx, Karl. *Capital*. London: Electric Book Co., 2001. Print.

12. Global Entrepreneurship Monitor. *GEM 2013 Global Report*. United States: n.p., 2013. Print.

13. Fredrickson, B. L. et al. "A Functional Genomic Perspective on Human Well-Being". *Proceedings of the National Academy of Sciences* 110.33 (2013): 13684-13689. Web.

14. Davis, Jeff. *Papa Bear*. New York: McGraw-Hill, 2005. Print.

15. Isaacson, Walter. *Steve Jobs*. New York: Simon & Schuster, 2011. Print.

16. Merriam-webster.com. "Definition of Entrepreneur". n.p., 2015. Web. 17 Dec. 2015.

17. Ready, Kevin. "Forbes Entrepreneurs". *Forbes.com*. n.p., 2013. Web. 17 Dec. 2015.

18. Bader-Johnston, Patricia. "The Spirit of Enterprise". *The Journal*. n.p., 2014. Web. 17 Dec. 2015.

19. Unger, Miles. *Michelangelo*, United States: Simon & Schuster, 2014. Print.

20. von Mises, Ludwig, and Ebeling, Richard. *Human Action*. Hillsdale, MI: Hillsdale College Press, 2000. Print.

21. Dyer, Jeff, Gregersen, Hal, and Christensen, Clayton. *The Innovator's DNA*. Boston, Mass.: Harvard Business Press, 2011. Print.

22. Knipping, Toine. *Mind Your Business*. United States: Balboa Press, 2012. Print.

23. Shaw, Bernard. *Maxims for Revolutionists*. Project Gutenberg, 2008. Print.

24. Tate, Ryan. "Google couldn't Kill 20 Percent Time Even if it Wanted to". *Wired*. n.p., 2013. Web. 17 Dec. 2015.

25. McCraw, Thomas K. *Prophet of Innovation*. Cambridge, Mass.: Belknap Press of Harvard University Press, 2007. Print.

26. von Mises, Ludwig, and Ebeling, Richard. *Human Action*. Hillsdale, MI: Hillsdale College Press, 2000. Print.

27. Eichenwald, Kurt. "How Microsoft Lost its Mojo: Steve Ballmer and Corporate America's Most Spectacular Decline". *Vanity Fair*. n.p., 2012. Web. 17 Dec. 2015.

28. Schumpeter, Joseph A. *Capitalism, Socialism, and Democracy*. New York: Harper Perennial Modern Thought, 2008. Print.

29. Marx, Karl et al. *The Communist Manifesto*. New Haven: Yale University Press, 2012. Print.

30. Beinhocker, Eric D. *The Origin of Wealth*. Boston, Mass.: Harvard Business School Press, 2006. Print.

31. Beinhocker, Eric D. *The Origin of Wealth*. Boston, Mass.: Harvard Business School Press, 2006. Print.

32. Nobelprize.org. "Douglass C. North – Prize Lecture: Economic Performance through Time". n.p., 1993. Web. 17 Dec. 2015.

33. Acemoglu, Daron, and Robinson, James. *Why Nations Fail*. New York: Crown Publishers, 2012. Print.

34. Krugman, Paul R. *The Age of Diminished Expectations*. Cambridge, Mass.: MIT Press, 1997. Print.

35. Productivity Commission. *Productivity Policies: The 'To Do' List*. Melbourne: Australian Government, 2012. Print.

36. Chandy, Laurence, and Gertz, Geoffrey. Poverty in Numbers: The Changing State of Global Poverty from 2005 to 2015. Washington DC: The Brookings Institution, 2015. Print.

37. Huang, Yasheng. *Capitalism with Chinese Characteristics*. Cambridge: Cambridge University Press, 2008. Print.

38. Hoffman, Edward. *The Right to be Human*. Los Angeles: J.P. Tarcher, 1988. Print.

39. University, Georgetown. "U2's Bono: Budget Cuts Can Impact Social Enterprise, Global Change". *georgetown.edu*. n.p., 2012. Web. 17 Dec. 2015.

40. Economist.com. "Towards the End of Poverty". n.p., 2013. Web. 17 Dec. 2015.

41. Brynjolfsson, Erik, and Andrew McAfee. *Race Against the Machine*. Lexington, Mass.: Digital Frontier Press, 2012. Print.

42. Wikipedia. "Life Expectancy". n.p., 2015. Web. 17 Dec. 2015.

43. Talbot, David. "Given Tablets but No Teachers, Ethiopian Children Teach Themselves". *MIT Technology Review*. n.p., 2012. Web. 17 Dec. 2015.

44. Patterson, Evelyn J. "The Dose–Response of Time Served in Prison on Mortality: New York State, 1989–2003". *American Journal of Public Health* 103.3 (2013): 523-528. Web.

45. World Bank. "GDP per Capita, PPP (Current International $)". n.p., 2015. Web. 17 Dec. 2015.

46. Locke, John. *Second Treatise of Civil Government*. Awnsham Churchill. 1689.Print

47. Kravtsova, Yekaterina. "Vkontakte Founder Flees Russia, Claims Persecution". *The Moscow Times*. n.p., 2014. Web. 17 Dec. 2015.

48. Bellaby, Maria. "Ukraine Steel Mill Sold For $4.8Bln". *The Moscow Times*. n.p., 2005. Web. 17 Dec. 2015.

49. Acemoglu, Daron, and Robinson, James. *Why Nations Fail*. New York: Crown Publishers, 2012. Print.

50. Esipova, Neil, and Ray, Julie. "700 Million Worldwide Desire to Migrate Permanently". gallup.com. n.p., 2009. Web. 17 Dec. 2015.

51. Kesby, Rebecca. "Why Russia Locks Up So Many Entrepreneurs". *BBC News*. n.p., 2012. Web. 17 Dec. 2015.

52. Shkolnikov, Vladimir, McKee, Martin and Leon, David. "Changes in Life Expectancy in Russia in the Mid-1990s". *The Lancet* 357.9260 (2001): 917-921. Web.

53. Popper, Karl R. *The Open Society and its Enemies*. Princeton, N.J.: Princeton University Press, 1966. Print.

54. Livius.org. "Consul". n.p., 2002. Web. 17 Dec. 2015.

55. Acemoglu, Daron, and Robinson, James. *Why Nations Fail*. New York: Crown Publishers, 2012. Print.

56. Wikipedia. "History of Rome". n.p., 2015. Web. 18 Dec. 2015.

57. Wikipedia. "Visigoths". n.p., 2015. Web. 18 Dec. 2015.

58. En.wikisource.org. "Bible (King James)/Romans". n.p., 2015. Web. 18 Dec. 2015.

59. Acemoglu, Daron, and Robinson, James. *Why Nations Fail*. New York: Crown Publishers, 2012. Print.

60. Mokyr, Joel. *The Lever of Riches*. New York: Oxford University Press, 1990. Print.

61. Weeks, David, and James, Jamie. *Eccentrics*. New York: Villard Books, 1995. Print.

62. Chase, Kenneth. *Firearms*. Cambridge, U.K: Cambridge University Press, 2003. Print.

63. Marxists.org. "Political Arithmetick by Sir William Petty". n.p., 2015. Web. 18 Dec. 2015.

64. Wikipedia. "Commonwealth of Nations". n.p., 2015. Web. 18 Dec. 2015.

65. Wikipedia. "List of Largest Empires". n.p., 2015. Web. 18 Dec. 2015.

66. Wikipedia. "List of Freedom Indices". n.p., 2015. Web. 18 Dec. 2015.

67. Martin, Peter. "China Will Be Biggest By 2030". *The Sydney Morning Herald*. n.p., 2013. Web. 18 Dec. 2015.

68. Powell, Bill. "Economic 'Reform' in North Korea: Nuking the Won". *time.com.* n.p., 2009. Web. 18 Dec. 2015.

69. Gall, Caroline. "The Words in the Mental Cupboard". *news.bbc.co.uk.* n.p., 2009. Web. 18 Dec. 2015.

70. Benner, Tom. "Some North Koreans get Business Internships in Singapore". *The Atlantic.* n.p., 2013. Web. 18 Dec. 2015.

71. United Nations. "World Population Prospects". n.p., 2015. Web. 18 Dec. 2015.

72. Loi, M., L. Savio, D., and Stupka. E. "Social Epigenetics and Equality of Opportunity". *Public Health Ethics* 6.3 (2013): 305-305. Web.

73. Schumpeter, Joseph A. *Capitalism, Socialism, and Democracy.* New York: Harper Perennial Modern Thought, 2008. Print.

74. Marx, Karl et al. *The Communist Manifesto.* New Haven: Yale University Press, 2012. Print

75. Marx, Karl. *Capital Volume 1.* United Kingdom: Penguin Classics, 1867. Print.

76. Tsoulfidis, Lefteris. *Competing Schools of Economic Thought.* Berlin: Springer, 2010. Print.

77. Wheen, Francis. *Karl Marx.* New York: Norton, 2000. Print.

78. Landsberg, Mitchell. "A Low for Marx in China". *Los Angeles Times.* n.p., 2007. Web. 18 Dec. 2015.

79. Wikipedia. "Clause IV". n.p., 2015. Web. 18 Dec. 2015.

80. Wikipedia. "Young Marx". n.p., 2015. Web. 18 Dec. 2015.

81. McDaniel, Bruce A. *Entrepreneurship and Innovation.* Armonk, N.Y.: M.E. Sharpe, 2002. Print.

82. von Mises, Ludwig, and Ebeling, Richard. *Human Action.* Hillsdale, MI: Hillsdale College Press, 2000. Print.

83. Marx, Karl. *Capital Volume 1.* United Kingdom: Penguin Classics, 1867. Print.

84. Keynes, John Maynard. *The General Theory of Employment, Interest, and Money.* New York: Harcourt, Brace & World, 1965. Print.
    - Commencement Address by Nassim Taleb, American University in Beirut 2016

85. Fromm, Erich. *Beyond the Chains of Illusion: My Encounter with Marx and Freud.* New York: Simon and Schuster, 1962. Print.

86. Fromm, Erich. *Beyond the Chains of Illusion: My Encounter with Marx and Freud.* New York: Simon and Schuster, 1962. Print.

87. Sun, Yan. *The Chinese Reassessment of Socialism* 1976-1992. Princeton, N.J.: Princeton University Press, 1995. Print.

88. Blank, Steve. "Strangling Innovation: Tesla versus 'Rent Seekers'". *steveblank.com.* n.p., 2013. Web. 18 Dec. 2015.

89. Denzau, Arthur. "The Japanese Automobile Cartel". *cato.org*. n.p., 2015. Web. 18 Dec. 2015.

90. Dowling, Joshua. "Why Australia's Car Manufacturers — Toyota, Holden and Ford — All Conked Out". *Courier Mail.* n.p., 2014. Web. 18 Dec. 2015.

91. New York Times. "Car Dealers Tilting at Tesla". n.p., 2014. Web. 18 Dec. 2015.

92. Litan, Robert E. "Inventive Billion Dollar Firms: A Faster Way to Grow". *Social Science Research Network* (2010): n. pag. Web. 18 Dec. 2015.

93. Ellman, Michael, and Kontorovich, Vladimir. *The Destruction of the Soviet Economic System.* Armonk, N.Y.: M.E. Sharpe, 1998. Print.

94. Wikipedia. "October Revolution". n.p., 2015. Web. 18 Dec. 2015.

95. Sputnik. "Father of the AK-47 Receives Russia's Top Honor". n.p., 2009. Web. 18 Dec. 2015.

96. Schweizer, Peter. *Victory.* New York: Atlantic Monthly Press, 1994. Print.

97. Lawyer, David. "Personal Computers: USSR vs. USA". *lafn.org*. n.p., 1990. Web. 18 Dec. 2015.

98. Thomaneck, Jurgen, and Niven, William. *Dividing and Uniting Germany.* London: Routledge, 2001. Print.

99. von Hayek, Friedrich. *Individualism and Economic Order.* Chicago: Univ. of Chicago Press, 1948. Print.

100. Balz, Manfred. *Invention and Innovation under Soviet Law.* Lexington, Mass.: Lexington Books, 1975. Print.

101. Wikipedia. "Law on Cooperatives". n.p., 2015. Web. 18 Dec. 2015.

102. Schlesinger, Arthur M. *The Cycles of American History.* Boston: Houghton Mifflin, 1986. Print.

103. Komlik, Oleg. "Community Capitalism in China: The State, the Market, and Collectivism". *Economic Sociology and Political Economy.* n.p., 2015. Web. 18 Dec. 2015.

104. Marx, Karl. *Capital Volume 1.* United Kingdom: Penguin Classics, 1867. Print.

105. Sun, Yan. *The Chinese Reassessment of Socialism* 1976-1992. Princeton, N.J.: Princeton University Press, 1995. Print.

106. Li, Hung. *China's Political Situation and the Power Struggle in Peking.* Hong Kong: Distributed by Lung Men Press, 1977. Print.

107. Sun, Yan. *The Chinese Reassessment of Socialism* 1976-1992. Princeton, N.J.: Princeton University Press, 1995. Print.

108. Areddy, James, and James Grimaldi. "Defying Mao, Rich Chinese Crash the Communist Party". *Wall Street Journal.* n.p., 2012. Web. 18 Dec. 2015.

109. Frank, Marc. "As Cuban Economy Stagnates, Economists Press for Deeper Reforms". *Reuters.* n.p., 2014. Web. 18 Dec. 2015.
110. Lakshmanan, Indira. "A Breakout Year for Cuban Entrepreneurs". *bloomberg.com.* n.p., 2015. Web. 18 Dec. 2015.
111. Kenny, Charles. *Getting Better.* New York, NY: Basic Books, 2011. Print.
112. Acemoglu, Daron, Naidu, Suresh, Restrepo, Pascual, A.Robinson, James "Democracy Does Cause Growth" economics.mit.edu. n.o., 2015 Web. 15 Dec. 2015
113. Wikipedia. "Democracy Index". n.p., 2015. Web. 18 Dec. 2015.
114. Heritage Foundation. "Index of Economic Freedom". *heritage.org/index.* n.p., 2015. Web. 18 Dec. 2015.
115. World Bank. "Time Required to Start a Business (Days)". n.p., 2015. Web. 18 Dec. 2015.
116. Reporters Without Borders. "2015 World Press Freedom Index". *index.rsf.org.* n.p., 2015. Web. 18 Dec. 2015.
117. United Nations. "Human Development Index". n.p., 2014. Web. 18 Dec. 2015.
118. World Health Organization. "Life Expectancy – Data by Country". n.p., 2015. Web. 18 Dec. 2015.
119. En.wikiquote.org. "John F. Kennedy". n.p., 1963. Web. 18 Dec. 2015.
120. Acemoglu, Daron, and Robinson, James. *Why Nations Fail.* New York: Crown Publishers, 2012. Print.
121. Murphy, Cullen. *Are We Rome?* Boston: Houghton Mifflin Co., 2007. Print.
122. Greene, Kevin. "Technological Innovation and Economic Progress in The Ancient World: M. I. Finley Re-Considered". *Economic History Review* 53.1 (2000): 29-59. Web.
123. Wikipedia. "William Lee (Inventor)". n.p., 2015. Web. 18 Dec. 2015.
124. Swedberg, Richard. *Schumpeter.* Princeton, N.J.: Princeton University Press, 1991. Print.
125. Goldsworthy, Adrian Keith. *Caesar.* New Haven: Yale University Press, 2006. Print.
126. Friedman, Milton, and Richard T Selden. *Capitalism and Freedom: Problems and Prospects.* Charlottesville: University Press of Virginia, 1975. Print.
127. Wikipedia. "Johannes Kepler". n.p., 2015. Web. 18 Dec. 2015.
128. Alexandru, Ilie. *Wise Words.* United States: Lulu, 2013. Print.
129. Leonardonline.it. "Leonardo Da Vinci's Manuscripts and Notebooks: Giunti Edition Facsimiles". n.p., 2015. Web. 18 Dec. 2015.

130. Islamicacademy.org. "Bid'ah (Innovation in Islam)". n.p., 2015. Web. 18 Dec. 2015.
131. *Civilisation: The West and the Rest*. London: Niall Ferguson, 2012. DVD.
     -Lal, Deepak Enlightenment Old and New – Faith and Reason, 2014, Journal
132. Wikipedia. "Roman Inquisition". n.p., 2015. Web. 18 Dec. 2015.
133. Wikipedia. "French Revolution". n.p., 2015. Web. 18 Dec. 2015.
134. Janowitz, Morris. "German Reactions to Nazi Atrocities". *American Journal of Sociology* 52.2 (1946): 141. Web. 18 Dec. 2015.
135. Fordham University. "Index of Prohibited Books 1557–1996". n.p., 2015. Web. 18 Dec. 2015.
136. Ridley, Matt. *The Rational Optimist*. New York: Harper, 2010. Print.
137. Gascoigne, Bamber. *A Brief History of the Dynasties of China*. London: Robinson, 2003. Print.
138. McClellan, James E, and Dorn, Harold. *Science and Technology in World History*. Baltimore, Md.: Johns Hopkins University Press, 1999. Print.
139. Wikipedia. "Haijin". n.p., 2015. Web. 18 Dec. 2015.
140. Wikipedia. "River Elegy". n.p., 2015. Web. 18 Dec. 2015.
141. "Presidents Address at the Unveiling of the Darwin-Wallace Memorial Plaque". *Proceedings of the Linnean Society of London* 170.3 (1959): 219-226. Web.
142. Mayell, Hillary. "India's "Untouchables" Face Violence, Discrimination". *National Geographic*. n.p., 2003. Web. 18 Dec. 2015.
143. Kenny, Charles. *Getting Better*. New York, NY: Basic Books, 2011. Print.
144. McCloskey, Deirdre N. *The Bourgeois Virtues*. Chicago: University of Chicago Press, 2006. Print.
145. Cope, Jason, Cave, Frank, and Eccles, Sue. "Attitudes of Venture Capital Investors towards Entrepreneurs with Previous Business Failure". *Venture Capital* 6.2-3 (2004): 147-172. Web.
146. von Oech, Roger. *A Whack on the Side of the Head*. New York: Warner Books, 1990. Print.
147. Swinnerton, Jo. *The History of Britain Companion. London*: Anova Books, 2005. Print.
148. Biblehub.com. "Leviticus 25:37". n.p., 2015. Web. 18 Dec. 2015.
149. Biblehub.com. "Matthew 19:24". n.p., 2015. Web. 18 Dec. 2015.
150. Aristotle, and Kraut, Richard. *Politics*. Oxford: Clarendon Press, 1997. Print.
151. Berman, Lazar. "The 2011 Nobel Prize and the Debate over Jewish IQ". *American Enterprise Institute*. n.p., 2011. Web. 18 Dec. 2015.

152. Seed, Roger. "Bankruptcy: A Bitter Pill to Swallow, but Sweeter than it was." *harringtonbrooks.co.uk*. n.p., 2012. Web. 18 Dec. 2015.

153. Wikipedia. "Debt Bondage". n.p., 2015. Web. 18 Dec. 2015.

154. Lee, Seung-Hyun et al. "How do Bankruptcy Laws affect Entrepreneurship Development around the World?". *Journal of Business Venturing* 26.5 (2011): 505-520. Web.

155. Wikipedia. "Limited Liability". n.p., 2015. Web. 18 Dec. 2015.

156. Coke, Edward, and Sheppard, Steve. *The Selected Writings and Speeches of Sir Edward Coke*. Indianapolis: Liberty Fund, 2003. Print.

157. Abrahamlincolnonline.org. "Abraham Lincoln's Second Lecture on Discoveries and Inventions". n.p., 1859. Web. 18 Dec. 2015.

158. Mokyr, Joel. "Intellectual Property Rights, the Industrial Revolution, and the Beginnings of Modern Economic Growth". *American Economic Review* 99.2 (2009): 349-355. Web.

159. The Patent and Trademark Office Society. "Operation of the Patent Act of 1790". n.p., 2003. Web. 18 Dec. 2015.

160. Sokoloff, Kenneth Lee, and Khan, Zorina. *The Democratization of Invention during Early Industrialization*. Cambridge MA: National Bureau of Economic Research, 1989. Print.

161. Clark, Gregory. *A Farewell to Alms*. Princeton, NJ: Princeton Univ. Press, 2008. Print.

162. YouTube. "Kauffman Foundation". n.p., 2015. Web. 18 Dec. 2015.

163. Reuters. "U.S. Job Growth Driven Entirely by Startups". n.p., 2007. Web. 18 Dec. 2015.

164. Rector, Robert, and Sheffield, Rachel. "Air Conditioning, Cable TV, and an Xbox: What is Poverty in the United States Today?". *The Heritage Foundation*. n.p., 2011. Web. 18 Dec. 2015.

165. Nesta. "The Vital 6%". n.p., 2009. Web. 18 Dec. 2015.

Chapter 6

1. Huxley, Thomas Henry, Paradis, James, Williams, George. *Evolution & Ethics*. Princeton, N.J.: Princeton University Press, 1989. Print.

2. Schumpeter, Joseph A. *Business Cycles*. United States, Martino Publishing, 1939. Print.

3. Ghosh, Partha et al. "Organizations and Leaders Make or Break Projects". Schlumberger Business Consulting. n.p., 2015. Web. 20 Dec. 2015.

4. Drucker, Peter. "The First Technological Revolution and its Lessons". *xroads.virginia.edu*. Web. 20 Dec. 2015.

5. Chapman, S et al. "Australia's 1996 Gun Law Reforms: Faster Falls in Firearm Deaths, Firearm Suicides, and a Decade without Mass Shootings". *Injury Prevention* 12.6 (2006): 365-372. Web.

6. Darwin, Charles, and Beer, Gillian. *On the Origin of Species*. New York: Oxford University Press, 2008. Print.

7. Darwin, Charles, and Beer, Gillian. *On the Origin of Species*. New York: Oxford University Press, 2008. Print.

8. Mesoudi, Alex, Whiten, Andrew and Laland, Kevin. "Towards A Unified Science of Cultural Evolution". *Behavioral and Brain Sciences* 29.04 (2006): n. pag. Web.

9. Wikipedia. "A History of Western Philosophy". n.p., 2015. Web. 20 Dec. 2015.

10. Darwin, Charles, and Beer, Gillian. *On the Origin of Species*. New York: Oxford University Press, 2008. Print.

11. Kawasaki, Guy. *The Art of the Start*. New York: Portfolio, 2004. Print.

12. National Automatic Vending Machine Association. "History of Vending and Coffee Service". *vending.org*. n.p., 2015. Web. 20 Dec. 2015.

13. Machiavelli, Niccolo, and Bull, George. *The Prince*. London, England: Penguin Books, 1999. Print.

14. Nationalchurchillmuseum.org. "MIT Mid-Century Convocation Speech by Winston Churchill". n.p., 1949. Web. 20 Dec. 2015.

15. Dobzhansky, Theodosius. "Nothing in Biology Makes Sense Except in the Light of Evolution". *The American Biology Teacher* 35.3 (1973): 125-129. Web. 20 Dec. 2015.

16. Stoppard, Tom. *Arcadia*. London: Faber and Faber, 1993. Print.

17. Nobelprize.org. "Simon Kuznets – Prize Lecture: Modern Economic Growth: Findings and Reflections". n.p., 1971. Web. 20 Dec. 2015.

18. Wikipedia. "Sakoku Edict of 1635". n.p., 2015. Web. 20 Dec. 2015.

19. Caspari, R., and Lee, S. "Older Age Becomes Common Late in Human Evolution". *Proceedings of the National Academy of Sciences* 101.30 (2004): 10895-10900. Web.

20. Dennett, D. C. *Kinds of Minds*. New York, NY: Basic Books, 1996. Print.

21. Dennett, D. C. *Kinds of Minds*. New York, NY: Basic Books, 1996. Print.

22. Atkinson, Q. D. "Phonemic Diversity Supports a Serial Founder Effect Model of Language Expansion from Africa". *Science* 332.6027 (2011): 346-349. Web.

23. Liu, L. et al. "Paleolithic Human Exploitation of Plant Foods during the Last Glacial Maximum in North China". *Proceedings of the National Academy of Sciences* 110.14 (2013): 5380-5385. Web. 20 Dec. 2015.

24. National Geographic. "The Development of Agriculture – Genographic Project". n.p., 2015. Web. 20 Dec. 2015.

25. Kurzweil, Ray. *The Singularity is Near*. New York: Viking, 2005. Print.
26. McClellan, James E, and Harold Dorn. *Science and Technology in World History*. Baltimore, Md.: Johns Hopkins University Press, 1999. Print.
27. Wikipedia. "Roman Aqueduct". n.p., 2015. Web. 20 Dec. 2015.
28. Domínguez-Rodrigo, Manuel et al. "Earliest Porotic Hyperostosis on a 1.5-Million-Year-Old Hominin, Olduvai Gorge, Tanzania". *PLOS ONE* 7.10 (2012): e46414. Web.
29. Ovodov, Nikolai D. et al. "A 33,000-Year-Old Incipient Dog from the Altai Mountains of Siberia: Evidence of the Earliest Domestication Disrupted by the Last Glacial Maximum". *PLOS ONE* 6.7 (2011): e22821. Web.
30. Law, Robin. "Wheeled Transport in Pre-Colonial West Africa". *Africa: Journal of the International African Institute* 50.3 (1980): 249. Web. 20 Dec. 2015.
31. Wikipedia. "Punic Wars". n.p., 2015. Web. 20 Dec. 2015.
32. Wikipedia. "Writing". n.p., 2015. Web. 20 Dec. 2015.
33. Kurzweil, Ray. *The Singularity is Near*. New York: Viking, 2005. Print.
34. Huxley, Julian. *The Individual in the Animal Kingdom*. Cambridge: University Press, 1912. Print.
35. Wikipedia. "Language". n.p., 2015. Web. 20 Dec. 2015.
36. Wikipedia. "Pope Sylvester II". n.p., 2015. Web. 20 Dec. 2015.
37. Wikipedia. "Legal History". n.p., 2015. Web. 20 Dec. 2015.
38. Wikipedia. "Code of Hammurabi". n.p., 2015. Web. 20 Dec. 2015.
39. Wikipedia. "Thales". n.p., 2015. Web. 20 Dec. 2015.
40. Wikipedia. "Anaximander". n.p., 2015. Web. 20 Dec. 2015.
41. Wikipedia. "Pythagoras". n.p., 2015. Web. 20 Dec. 2015.
42. Wikipedia. "Pericles". n.p., 2015. Web. 20 Dec. 2015.
43. Wikipedia. "Oeconomicus". n.p., 2015. Web. 20 Dec. 2015.
44. Wikipedia. "Plato". n.p., 2015. Web. 20 Dec. 2015.
45. Newlearningonline.com. "Socrates on the Forgetfulness that Comes with Writing". n.p., 2015. Web. 20 Dec. 2015.
46. Simmons, George F. *Calculus Gems*. Washington, DC: Mathematical Association of America, 2007. Print.
47. Wikipedia. "Marcus Aurelius". n.p., 2015. Web. 20 Dec. 2015.
48. Wikipedia. "Andronicus of Rhodes". n.p., 2015. Web. 20 Dec. 2015.
49. McClellan, James E, and Harold Dorn. *Science and Technology in World History*. Baltimore, Md.: Johns Hopkins University Press, 1999. Print.
50. Wikipedia. "Summa Theologica". n.p., 2015. Web. 20 Dec. 2015.

51. Russell, Bertrand. *History of Western Philosophy*. London: Routledge, 2004. Print.
52. Wikipedia. "Library of Alexandria". n.p., 2015. Web. 20 Dec. 2015.
53. Wikipedia. "Cement". n.p., 2015. Web. 20 Dec. 2015.
54. Wikipedia. "Visigoths". n.p., 2015. Web. 20 Dec. 2015.
55. McClellan, James E, and Harold Dorn. *Science and Technology in World History*. Baltimore, Md.: Johns Hopkins University Press, 1999. Print.
56. Hong, S. et al. "Greenland Ice Evidence of Hemispheric Lead Pollution Two Millennia Ago by Greek and Roman Civilizations". *Science* 265.5180 (1994): 1841-1843. Web.
57. Schiavone, Aldo. *The End of the Past*. Cambridge, Mass.: Harvard University Press, 2000. Print.
58. Wikipedia. "Scholasticism". n.p., 2015. Web. 20 Dec. 2015.
59. Wikipedia. "Fall of the Western Roman Empire". n.p., 2015. Web. 20 Dec. 2015.
60. British Broadcasting Corporation. "Ancient History in Depth: The Decipherment of Hieroglyphs". *bbc.co.uk*, n.p., 2015. Web. 20 Dec. 2015.
61. McClellan, James E, and Harold Dorn. *Science and Technology in World History*. Baltimore, Md.: Johns Hopkins University Press, 1999. Print.
62. Wikipedia. "Battle of Talas". n.p., 2015. Web. 20 Dec. 2015.
63. Wikipedia. "Islamic Golden Age". n.p., 2015. Web. 20 Dec. 2015.
64. McClellan, James E, and Harold Dorn. *Science and Technology in World History*. Baltimore, Md.: Johns Hopkins University Press, 1999. Print.
65. Clark, Gregory. *A Farewell to Alms*. Princeton, NJ: Princeton Univ. Press, 2008. Print.
66. Wikipedia. "William of Moerbeke". n.p., 2015. Web. 20 Dec. 2015.
67. Wikipedia. "Herophilos". n.p., 2015. Web. 20 Dec. 2015.
68. Noel, William. "Revealing the Lost Codex of Archimedes". *ted.com*. n.p., 2012. Web. 20 Dec. 2015.
69. University of California, Berkeley. "Roman Legal Tradition and the Compilation of Justinian". n.p., 2015. Web. 20 Dec. 2015.
70. Wikipedia. "The Art of War". n.p., 2015. Web. 21 Dec. 2015.
71. Wikipedia. "Galileo Galilei". n.p., 2015. Web. 21 Dec. 2015.
72. Popper, Karl R. *The Poverty of Historicism*. New York: Harper & Row, 1964. Print.
73. Kurzweil, Ray. *The Singularity is Near*. New York: Viking, 2005. Print.
74. Abrahamlincolnonline.org. "Abraham Lincoln's Second Lecture on Discoveries and Inventions". n.p., 1859. Web. 21 Dec. 2015.

75. Wikipedia. "Printing Press". n.p., 2015. Web. 21 Dec. 2015.
76. Gottlieb, Agnes Hooper. *1000 Years, 1000 People*. New York: Kodansha International, 1998. Print.
77. Bobrow, Emily. "Poll Results – Gutenberg Pips Jesus". *moreintelligentlife.co.uk*. n.p., 2015. Web. 21 Dec. 2015.
78. McClellan, James E, and Harold Dorn. *Science and Technology in World History*. Baltimore, Md.: Johns Hopkins University Press, 1999. Print.
79. *Mankind: The Story of All of Us*. United States: History Channel, 2012. DVD.
80. Wright, Robert. *Nonzero*. New York: Pantheon Books, 2000. Print.
81. Heilbroner, Robert L. *The Worldly Philosophers*. New York: Simon & Schuster, 1999. Print.
82. Kiefer, Frederick. *Writing on the Renaissance Stage*. Newark: University of Delaware Press, 1996. Print.
83. Ornstein, Robert, and Burke, James. *The Axemaker's Gift*. United States: Tarcher, 1997. Print.
84. Martin, George R. R. *A Dance with Dragons*. New York: Bantam Books, 2011. Print.
85. Underwood, Doug. *From Yahweh To Yahoo!*. Urbana: University of Illinois Press, 2002. Print.
86. Official Vatican Network. ""Communication at the Service of an Authentic Culture of Encounter" – Pope's Message for World Communications Day". n.p., 2014. Web. 21 Dec. 2015.
87. Wikipedia. "Nullius in Verba". n.p., 2015. Web. 21 Dec. 2015.
88. Wikipedia. "Isaac Newton". n.p., 2015. Web. 21 Dec. 2015.
89. Hugo, Victor, and Smith, Huntington. *History of a Crime*. New York: T.Y. Crowell, 1888. Print.
90. Lepore, Jill. "The Sharpened Quill". *The New Yorker*. n.p., 2006. Web. 21 Dec. 2015.
91. Wikipedia. "Encyclopedia Britannica Eleventh Edition". n.p., 2015. Web. 21 Dec. 2015.
92. Wikipedia. "Encyclopédie". n.p., 2015. Web. 21 Dec. 2015.
93. Kurzweil, Ray. *The Singularity is Near*. New York: Viking, 2005. Print.
94. National Aeronautics and Space Administration. "Konstantin E. Tsiolkovsky". n.p., 2010. Web. 21 Dec. 2015.
95. Gaiman, Neil. "Why Our Future Depends on Libraries, Reading and Daydreaming". The Guardian. n.p., 2013. Web. 21 Dec. 2015.
96. Groningen Growth and Development Centre. "The Maddison Project". n.p., 2013. Web. 21 Dec. 2015.
97. Bernstein, William J. *The Birth of Plenty*. New York: McGraw-Hill, 2004. Print.

98. Connell, K. H. "The Population of Ireland in the Eighteenth Century". *The Economic History Review* 16.2 (1946): 111. Web.

99. Kinealy, Christine. *This Great Calamity*. Dublin: Gill & Macmillan, 1995. Print.

100. Groningen Growth and Development Centre. "The Maddison Project". n.p., 2013. Web. 21 Dec. 2015.

101. Abrahamlincolnonline.org. "Abraham Lincoln's Second Lecture on Discoveries and Inventions". n.p., 1859. Web. 21 Dec. 2015.

102. Wikipedia. "Horror Vacui (Physics)". n.p., 2015. Web. 21 Dec. 2015.

103. Barrow, John D. *The Book of Nothing*. New York: Pantheon Books, 2000. Print.

104. Dugas, Rene. *A History of Mechanics*. Neuchatel: Editions du Griffon, 1955. Print.

105. Wikipedia. "Thomas Savery". n.p., 2015. Web. 21 Dec. 2015.

106. Raistrick, Arthur. *The Steam Engine on Tyneside, 1715-1778*. London: Newcomen Society, 1937. Print.

107. Marsden, Ben. *Watt's Perfect Engine*. New York: Columbia University Press, 2002. Print.

108. Hunter, Louis C. *A History of Industrial Power in the United States, 1780-1930*. Charlottesville: University Press of Virginia for the Hagley Museum and Library, 1985. Print.

109. Wikipedia. "James Watt". n.p., 2015. Web. 21 Dec. 2015.

110. Darwin, Charles, and Beer, Gillian. *On the Origin of Species*. New York: Oxford University Press, 2008. Print.

111. McClellan, James E, and Harold Dorn. *Science and Technology in World History*. Baltimore, Md.: Johns Hopkins University Press, 1999. Print.

112. McClellan, James E, and Harold Dorn. *Science and Technology in World History*. Baltimore, Md.: Johns Hopkins University Press, 1999. Print.

113. Broadberry, S. N, and O'Rourke, K.H. (Eds.). *The Cambridge Economic History of Modern Europe*. New York: Cambridge University Press, 2010. Print.

114. Beaudry, Paul, David A. Green, and Benjamin M. Sand. "The Great Reversal in the Demand for Skill and Cognitive Tasks". *Journal of Labor Economics* 34. S1 (2016): S199-S247. Web.

115. Horn, Jeff. "Understanding Crowd Action: Machine-Breaking in England And France, 1789-1817". *Proceedings of the Western Society for French History* 31 (2003): n. pag. Web. 21 Dec. 2015.

116. Hobsbawm, Eric J. *The Machine Breakers*. Oxford: Oxford University Press, 1952. Print.

117. McElroy, Wendy. "Redeeming the Industrial Revolution". *Mises Institute*. n.p., 2011. Web. 21 Dec. 2011.
118. Nardinelli, Clark. "Industrial Revolution and the Standard of Living: The Concise Encyclopedia of Economics". *Library of Economics and Liberty*. n.p., 2008. Web. 21 Dec. 2015.
119. Allen, Robert C. "The Great Divergence in European Wages and Prices from the Middle Ages to the First World War". *Explorations in Economic History* 38.4 (2001): 411-447. Web.
120. Nardinelli, Clark. "Industrial Revolution and the Standard of Living: The Concise Encyclopedia of Economics". *Library of Economics and Liberty*. n.p., 2008. Web. 21 Dec. 2015.
121. Wikipedia. "Francis Drake". n.p., 2015. Web. 21 Dec. 2015.
122. Wikipedia. "Descent of Elizabeth II from William the Conqueror". n.p., 2015. Web. 21 Dec. 2015.
123. Wikipedia. "Cleopatra". n.p., 2015. Web. 21 Dec. 2015.
124. Wikipedia. "History of Rail Transport in Great Britain to 1830". n.p., 2015. Web. 21 Dec. 2015.
125. Stover, John F. *American Railroads*. Chicago, Ill.: University of Chicago Press, 1997. Print.
126. Rebman, Renee C. *Robert Fulton's Steamboat*. Minneapolis, Minn.: Compass Point Books, 2008. Print.
127. Wikipedia. "Richard Trevithick". n.p., 2015. Web. 21 Dec. 2015.
128. McClellan, James E, and Harold Dorn. *Science and Technology in World History*. Baltimore, Md.: Johns Hopkins University Press, 1999. Print.
129. Rifkin, Jeremy. *The End of Work*. New York: G.P. Putnam's Sons, 1995. Print.
130. Carr, Nicholas. *The Glass Cage*. London: The Bodley Head, 2015. Print.
131. Federal Reserve Bank of Dallas. *Time Well Spent: The Declining Real Cost of Living In America*. Dallas: Federal Reserve Bank of Dallas, 1997. Print.
132. Wikipedia. "List of Public Corporations by Market Capitalization". n.p., 2015. Web. 21 Dec. 2015.
133. Smil, Vaclav. *Creating the Twentieth Century*. Oxford: Oxford University Press, 2005. Print.
134. Wiser, Wendell H. *Energy Resources*. New York: Springer, 2000. Print.
135. Ford, Henry, and Crowther, Samuel. *Edison as I Know Him*. New York: Cosmopolitan Book Corporation, 1930. Print.
136. McClellan, James E, and Harold Dorn. *Science and Technology in World History*. Baltimore, Md.: Johns Hopkins University Press, 1999. Print.

137. Kurzweil, Ray. *The Singularity is Near*. New York: Viking, 2005. Print.
138. Wikipedia. "Cuban Revolution". n.p., 2015. Web. 21 Dec. 2015.
139. Gaudin, Sharon. "The Transistor: The Most Important Invention of the 20th Century?". *Computerworld*. n.p., 2007. Web. 21 Dec. 2015.
140. Wikipedia. "Transistor". n.p., 2015. Web. 21 Dec. 2015.
141. Wikipedia. "Moore's Law". n.p., 2015. Web. 21 Dec. 2015.
142. Wikipedia. "Intel 8080". n.p., 2015. Web. 21 Dec. 2015.
143. Davies Boren, Zachary. "There are Officially More Mobile Devices than People in the World". *The Independent*. n.p., 2014. Web. 21 Dec. 2015.
144. Netcraft. "October 2015 Web Server Survey". n.p., 2015. Web. 21 Dec. 2015.
145. Trout, Jack, and Steve Rivkin. *Differentiate or Die*. Hoboken, N.J.: John Wiley & Sons, 2008. Print.
146. Siegler, M.G. "The End of the Library". TechCrunch. n.p., 2013. Web. 21 Dec. 2015.
147. Andreessen, Marc. "Why Software is Eating the World". *Wall Street Journal*. n.p., 2011. Web. 21 Dec. 2015.
148. Anderson, Chris. *Makers*. New York: Crown Business, 2012. Print.
149. Statista. "E-Book Share of Total Consumer Book Sales in the U.S. 2009-2015". n.p., 2015. Web. 21 Dec. 2015.
150. Zhang, Mona. "YouTube Reaches More 18- to 24-Year-Olds than any Cable Network". *Adweek.com*. n.p., 2014. Web. 21 Dec. 2015.
151. Darwin, Charles, and Beer, Gillian. *On the Origin of Species*. New York: Oxford University Press, 2008. Print.
152. Worldwidewebsize.com. "The Size of the World Wide Web (the Internet)". n.p., 2015. Web. 21 Dec. 2015.
153. Mesoudi, Alex. *Cultural Evolution*. Chicago: University of Chicago Press, 2011. Print.
154. Spencer, Herbert. *First Principles of a New System of Philosophy*. New York: D. Appleton and Company, 1864. Print.
155. Vaynerchuk, Gary. *Crush It!* New York: HarperStudio, 2009. Print.
156. IBM. "What is Big Data?". n.p., 2015. Web. 21 Dec. 2015.
157. Lomas, Natasha. "Q&A: Kurzweil on Tech as a Double-Edged Sword". *cnet.com*. n.p., 2008. Web. 21 Dec. 2015.
158. Nedeltchev, Plamen. "The Internet of Everything is the New Economy". *Cisco*. n.p., 2015. Web. 21 Dec. 2015.
159. Glendon, Mary Ann. *The Forum and the Tower*. Oxford: Oxford University Press, 2011. Print.
    - Wikipedia "Dialectic" Web, 13 Jan 2016
160. Schumpeter, Joseph A. *Business Cycles*. United States, Martino Publishing, 1939. Print.

Chapter 7

1. Edison, Thomas A, and Runes, Dagobert D. *The Diary and Sundry Observations of Thomas Alva Edison*. New York: Philosophical Library, 1948. Print.
2. Dostoyevsky, Fyodor. *The House of the Dead*. Harmondsworth, Middlesex, England: Penguin Books, 1985. Print.
3. Keynes, John Maynard. *Essays in Persuasion*. New York: Norton, 1963. Print.
4. Popper, Karl R. *The Logic of Scientific Discovery*. United Kingdom: Routledge, 1959. Print.
5. World Health Organization. "Life Expectancy". n.p., 2013. Web. 21 Dec. 2015.
6. Young, Angelo. "Nike Sheds 106,000 Workers, since Last Year, as Profit, Revenue Rise". *International Business Times*. n.p., 2014. Web. 21 Dec. 2015.
7. Luk, Lorraine. "Foxconn is Quietly Working with Google on Robotics". *Wall Street Journal*. n.p., 2014. Web. 21 Dec. 2015.
8. Young, Angelo. "Nike Sheds 106,000 Workers, since Last Year, as Profit, Revenue Rise". *International Business Times*. n.p., 2014. Web. 21 Dec. 2015.
9. Kim, Lena. "Meet South Korea's New Robotic Prison Guards". *Digital Trends*. n.p., 2012. Web. 21 Dec. 2015.
10. Metz, Rachel. "Knightscope's Autonomous Robots will take on Security Jobs Normally Held by Humans". *MIT Technology Review*. N.p., 2014. Web. 21 Dec. 2015.
11. Webpronews.com. "Infographic Indicates Workers Waste Time because they Think their Jobs Suck". n.p., 2012. Web. 21 Dec. 2015.
12. Smithers, Rebecca. "More than 30 Chain Stores Closing a Day". *The Guardian*. n.p., 2012. Web. 21 Dec. 2015.
13. Organisation for Economic Co-operation and Development. *The Role of Agriculture and Farm Household Diversification in the Rural Economy of the United States*. United States: OECD, 2008. Print.
14. Marx, Karl et al. *The Communist Manifesto*. New Haven: Yale University Press, 2012. Print.
15. En.wikiquote.org. "Wassily Leontief". n.p., 1983. Web. 21 Dec. 2015.
16. Raskin, Max, and Kolet, Ilan. "Wall Street Jobs Plunge as Profits Soar". bloomberg.com. n.p., 2013. Web. 21 Dec. 2015.
17. Frey, Carl, and Osborne, Michael. *The Future of Employment: How Susceptible are Jobs to Computerization?* United Kingdom: n.p., 2013. Print.

18. Paul, Annie. "How Computerized Tutors are Learning to Teach Humans". *New York Times*. n.p., 2012. Web. 21 Dec. 2015.

19. Wagstaff, Keith. "Amazon's $775 Million Acquisition of Kiva Systems Could Shift how Businesses See Robots". *time.com*. n.p., 2012. Web. 21 Dec. 2015.

20. D'Onfro, Jillian. "What it's like Inside One of Amazon's Massive Warehouses". *Business Insider Australia*. n.p., 2014. Web. 21 Dec. 2015.

21. Brooks, Rodney. "More Robots Won't Mean Fewer Jobs". *Harvard Business Review*. n.p., 2014. Web. 21 Dec. 2015.

22. Dorrier, Jason. "Veebot's Needle Wielding Robot to Automate Blood Draws". *Singularity University*. n.p., 2013. Web. 21 Dec. 2015.

23. Krugman, Paul. "Rise of the Robots". *New York Times*. n.p., 2012. Web. 21 Dec. 2015.

24. Ford, Martin. *The Lights in the Tunnel*. United States: Acculant Publishing, 2009. Print.

25. Blodget, Henry. "Eric Schmidt just Revealed a Key Truth about the Economy that Very Few Rich Investors and Executives want to Admit…". *Business Insider Australia*. n.p., 2014. Web. 21 Dec. 2015.

26. British Broadcasting Corporation. "Driverless Cars to be Tested on U.K Roads by End of 2013". n.p., 2013. Web. 21 Dec. 2015.

27. Diss, Kathryn. "Robotic Trucks Taking Over in Pilbara as Mines Shift to Automation". *ABC News*. n.p., 2014. Web. 21 Dec. 2015.

28. Newcomb, Doug. "You Won't Need a Driver's License by 2040". *CNN*. n.p., 2012. Web. 21 Dec. 2015.

29. Markoff, John. "Armies of Expensive Lawyers, Replaced by Cheaper Software". *New York Times*. n.p., 2011. Web. 21 Dec. 2015.

30. Hastings, Michael. "The Rise of the Killer Drones: How America Goes to War in Secret". *Rolling Stone*. n.p., 2012. Web. 21 Dec. 2015.

31. Sklar, Julia. "Robots Lay Three Times as Many Bricks as Construction Workers". *MIT Technology Review*. n.p., 2015. Web. 21 Dec. 2015.

32. Kelly, Kevin. "Better than Human: Why Robots Will — and Must — Take our Jobs". *Wired*. N.p., 2012. Web. 21 Dec. 2015.

33. Frey, Carl, and Osborne, Michael. *The Future of Employment: How Susceptible are Jobs to Computerisation?* United Kingdom: n.p., 2013. Print.
     - Bank of England. *Labour's Share speech by Andrew G Haldene Chief Economist* 12th Nov 2015

34. Bernanke, Ben. "FRB: Speech-Bernanke, Economic Prospects for the Long Run-May 18, 2013". *federalreserve.gov*. n.p., 2013. Web. 21 Dec. 2015.

35.   Brynjolfsson, Erik, and Andrew McAfee. *Race Against the Machine*. Lexington, Mass.: Digital Frontier Press, 2012. Print.
36.   International Labour Organization. *Global Wage Report 2012/13: Wages and Equitable Growth*. Geneva: ILO, 2013. Print.
37.   Organisation for Economic Co-operation and Development. *Income Inequality Update: Rising Inequality – Youth and Poor Fall Further Behind*. United States: OECD, 2014. Print.
38.   Rotman, David. "How Technology is Destroying Jobs". *MIT Technology Review*. n.p., 2013. Web. 22 Dec. 2015.
39.   Azzam, Amy. "Why Creativity Now? A Conversation with Sir Ken Robinson". *Association for Supervision and Curriculum Development*. n.p., 2009. Web. 22 Dec. 2015.
40.   Krugman, Paul. "Sympathy for the Luddites". *New York Times*. n.p., 2013. Web. 22 Dec. 2015.
41.   Frey, Carl, and Osborne, Michael. *The Future of Employment: How Susceptible are Jobs to Computerisation?* United Kingdom: n.p., 2013. Print.
42.   Office for National Statistics. "Underemployment and Overemployment in the U.K, 2014". n.p., 2014. Web. 22 Dec. 2015.
43.   Smialek, Jeanna. "Workers in Part-Time Limbo Point to U.S. Job-Market Slack". *Bloomberg.com*. n.p., 2014. Web. 22 Dec. 2015.
44.   Dunn, Amanda, and Cincotta, Katie. "Free Courses from World's Top Unis a Swipe Away in Online Revolution". *Sydney Morning Herald*. n.p., 2012. Web. 22 Dec. 2015.
45.   Bureau of Labor Statistics. "Occupational Employment and Wages News Release". n.p., 2015. Web. 22 Dec. 2015.
46.   Centre for Retail Research. "Online Retailing: Britain, Europe, US and Canada 2015". n.p., 2015. Web. 22 Dec. 2015.
47.   Farfan, Barbara. "Which U.S. Stores Closed during 2012?". *about.com*. n.p., 2013. Web. 22 Dec. 2015.
48.   Lutz, Ashley. "American Shopping Malls Have Suffered another Terrifying Blow". *Business Insider Australia*. n.p., 2015. Web. 22 Dec. 2015.
49.   ETF Daily News. "Robots Continue to Replace U.S. Workers". n.p., 2014. Web. 22 Dec. 2015.
50.   Hunt, H., and T. Hunt. *Overview of Clerical Employment and Technological Change*. Kalamazoo, MI: W.E. Upjohn Institute for Employment Research, 1986. Print.
51.   Hotelmarketing.com. "Travel Agencies versus the Internet: Global Booking Trends". n.p., 2013. Web. 22 Dec. 2015.
52.   Goudreau, Jenna. "Jobs Outlook: Careers Headed for the Trash Pile". *Forbes*. n.p., 2011. Web. 22 Dec. 2015.

53. Chow, Lisa. "Will a Computer Decide Whether You get your Next Job?". *npr.org*. n.p., 2013. Web. 22 Dec. 2015.

54. Sprague, Shawn. *Beyond the Numbers: What can Labor Productivity Tell us about the U.S. Economy?* Washington, D.C.: U.S. Bureau of Labor Statistics, 2014. Print.

55. Mishel, Lawrence. "Occupation Employment Trends and Wage Inequality: What the Long View Tells Us". *Center for Economic and Policy Research*. n.p., 2013. Web. 22 Dec. 2015.

56. Tabuchi, Hiroko. "Kura Focuses on Efficiency, and Profits". *New York Times*. n.p., 2010. Web. 22 Dec. 2015.

57. Edison, Thomas A, and Runes, Dagobert D. *The Diary and Sundry Observations of Thomas Alva Edison*. New York: Philosophical Library, 1948. Print.

58. Dostoyevsky, Fyodor. *The House of the Dead*. Harmondsworth, Middlesex, England: Penguin Books, 1985. Print.

59. Wikipedia. "Employment". n.p., 2015. Web. 22 Dec. 2015.

60. Godin, Seth. *Linchpin*. London: Piatkus, 2010. Print.

61. Wikipedia. "Wage Slavery". n.p., 2015. Web. 22 Dec. 2015.

62. Frey, Carl, and Osborne, Michael. *The Future of Employment: How Susceptible are Jobs to Computerisation?* United Kingdom: n.p., 2013. Print.

63. Cicero, Marcus Tullius. *De Officiis*. Cambridge, Mass.: Harvard University Press, 1913. Print.

64. University of California, Berkeley. "Noam Chomsky – Activism, Anarchism, and Power". n.p., 2002. Web. 22 Dec. 2015.

65. Humboldt, Wilhelm von, and Coulthard, Joseph. *The Sphere and Duties of Government*. London: J. Chapman, 1854. Print.

66. Webpronews.com. "Infographic Indicates Workers Waste Time because they Think their Jobs Suck". n.p., 2012. Web. 21 Dec. 2015.

67. Marx, Karl. *Economic and Philosophic Manuscripts of 1844*. New York: International Publishers, 1964. Print.

68. Ferriss, Timothy. *The 4-Hour Workweek*. New York: Crown Publishers, 2007. Print.

69. Szporluk, Roman. *Communism and Nationalism*. New York: Oxford University Press, 1988. Print.

70. Crabtree, Steve. "Worldwide, 13% of Employees are Engaged at Work". *gallup.com*. n.p., 2013. Web. 22 Dec. 2015.

71. Wilhelm, Alex. "Yahoo Sags 4% after Alibaba'S Q2 Earnings Disappointment". *TechCrunch*. n.p., 2015. Web. 22 Dec. 2015.

72. Deb, Sandipan. "The Man Who Beat Kasparov". *outlookindia.com*. n.p., 1997. Web. 22 Dec. 2015.

73. Brynjolfsson, Erik, and Andrew McAfee. *Race Against the Machine*. Lexington, Mass.: Digital Frontier Press, 2012. Print.

74. Williams, Amanda. "Let's Make Sure He Won't be Back! Cambridge to Open 'Terminator Centre' to Study Threat to Humans from Artificial Intelligence". *Daily Mail*. n.p., 2012. Web. 22 Dec. 2015.

75. Sydney Morning Herald. "'Super Computer' First to Pass Turing Test, Convince Judges It's Alive". n.p., 2014. Web. 22 Dec. 2015.

76. Schwartz, Ariel. "The World's Cheapest Car is Heading to the U.S.". fastcoexist.com. n.p., 2012. Web. 22 Dec. 2015.

77. Frey, Carl, and Osborne, Michael. *The Future of Employment: How Susceptible are Jobs to Computerisation?* United Kingdom: n.p., 2013. Print.

78. Green, Richard. "The Minimum Wage and Employment when Employers have Market Power". *economistsview.typepad.com*. n.p., 2013. Web. 22 Dec. 2015.

79. Wagner, Tony. "To Bring Out the Best in Millennials, Put on Your Coaching Hat". *Fast Company*. n.p., 2012. Web. 22 Dec. 2015.

80. Bruckner, Pascal, and Rendall, Steven. *The Fanaticism of the Apocalypse*. Cambridge: Polity, 2014. Print.

81. Piketty, Thomas, and Goldhammer, Arthur. *Capital in the Twenty-First Century*. Washington: Brilliance Audio, 2014. CD

82. Bergin, Tom. "Apple Blasted for Paying Almost No Taxes on $74 Billion in Income". *The Huffington Post*. n.p., 2013. Web. 22 Dec. 2015.

83. Leslie, Jacques. "A Piketty Protégé's Theory on Tax Havens". *New York Times*. n.p., 2014. Web. 22 Dec. 2015.

84. Wikipedia. "Tax Evasion in the United States". n.p., 2015. Web. 22 Dec. 2015.

85. Government of the United Kingdom. "2010 To 2015 Government Policy: Tax Evasion and Avoidance". n.p., 2015. Web. 22 Dec. 2015.

86. Butler, Ben. "Counting the Cost of Tax Havens". *Sydney Morning Herald*. n.p., 2011. Web. 22 Dec. 2015.

87. Australian Government. "2011–12 Commonwealth Budget – Overview". n.p., 2012. Web. 22 Dec. 2015.

88. Johnson, Steven. *How We Got to Now*. New York: Riverhead Books, 2014. Print.

89. Einstein, Albert. *Ideas and Opinions*. New York: Broadway Books, 1995. Print.

90. Wikipedia. "Enterprise Allowance Scheme". n.p., 2015. Web. 22 Dec. 2015.

91. Gage, Deborah. "The Venture Capital Secret: 3 Out of 4 Start-Ups Fail". Wall Street Journal. n.p., 2012. Web. 22 Dec. 2015.

92. National Economic Council. *Moving America's Small Businesses and Entrepreneurs Forward*. Washington: The White House, 2012. Print.

93. Dickey, Megan Rose. "The 11 Hottest Startups in Northern Europe ". *Business Insider Australia*. n.p., 2013. Web. 22 Dec. 2015.

94. Statistics Finland. "Government R&D Funding in the State Budget 2012". n.p., 2013. Web. 22 Dec. 2015.

95. Budget.gov.au. "Education, Employment and Workplace Relations". n.p., 2011. Web. 22 Dec. 2015.

96. Government of the United Kingdom. *£69 Million More for Start-Up Loans and New Enterprise Allowance. 2013*. Web. 22 Dec. 2015.

97. Frick, Walter. "How France Used Unemployment Benefits to Kickstart Entrepreneurship". *Harvard Business Review*. n.p., 2015. Web. 22 Dec. 2015.

98. O'Leary, Grahame. "Telstra Sale". *Parliament of Australia*. n.p., 2003. Web. 22 Dec. 2015.

99. Dolamore, Robert. "Budget Review 2014-15". *Parliament of Australia*. n.p., 2015. Web. 22 Dec. 2015.

100. Australian Government. "2014-15 Commonwealth Budget – Budget Overview – Appendix B – Revenue and Spending". n.p., 2014. Web. 22 Dec. 2015.

101. Musacchio, Aldo, and Lazzarini, Sergio. *Reinventing State Capitalism*. Cambridge, Massachusetts: Harvard University Press, 2014. Print.

102. Wikipedia. "John Harrison". n.p., 2015. Web. 22 Dec. 2015.

103. IBM. "Transcript of Thomas Watson Comments on 'THINK'". n.p., 2015. Web. 22 Dec. 2015.

104. Kaggle. "Mapping Dark Matter". n.p., 2015. Web. 22 Dec. 2015.

105. Tran, Mai P, "Social Impact Bonds Gain Momentum in the Criminal Justice Field" *csgjusticecenter.org* n.p 2014, Web 22 Dec 2015

106. Symons, Tom. "Startups Get Less Than 3% of Government Spend, This Must Change". *The Guardian*. n.p., 2015. Web. 22 Dec. 2015.

107. Griffin, G. Edward. *The Creature from Jekyll Island*. California.: American Media, 2010. Print.

108. Wikipedia. "General Education Board". n.p., 2015. Web. 22 Dec. 2015.

109. Kiyosaki, Robert. "Leading Like an Entrepreneur". *Rich Dad – Financial Education & Coaching for Everyone*. n.p., 2015. Web. 22 Dec. 2015.

110. Havergal, Chris. "Ernst & Young Drops Degree Classification Threshold for Graduate Recruitment". *Times Higher Education*. n.p., 2015. Web. 22 Dec. 2015.

111. Duckworth, Eleanor. "Piaget Rediscovered". *Journal of Research in Science Teaching*. 2.3 (1964): 172-175. Web.

112. Isaacson, Walter. *Einstein*. New York, NY: Collins Design, 2009. Print.

113. Bozzo, Albert. "Entrepreneurial Studies Sweep America's High School System". *cnbc.com*. n.p., 2012. Web. 22 Dec. 2015.
114. Pofeldt, Elaine. "U.S. Entrepreneurship Hits Record High". *forbes.com*. n.p., 2013. Web. 22 Dec. 2015.
115. Fairless, Tom. "Europe is Struggling to Foster a Startup Culture". *Wall Street Journal*. n.p., 2015. Web. 22 Dec. 2015.
116. Ready, Kevin. "In Search of Japan's Missing Startups". *forbes.com*. n.p., 2013. Web. 22 Dec. 2015.
117. Buchanan, Leigh. "American Entrepreneurship is Actually Vanishing. Here's Why". Inc.com. n.p., 2015. Web. 22 Dec. 2015.
118. Wikipedia. "History of Tax Resistance". n.p., 2015. Web. 22 Dec. 2015.